What they're saying about *World Vegan Feast*

Bryanna Clark Grogan is a master of the art and craft of cooking, and this collection of international recipes is her crowning achievement. *World Vegan Feast* is rich with helpful tips, generous instructions, and well-researched food facts. With many low-fat recipes and special icons to indicate gluten-free and soy-free recipes, this is an essential book for anyone who wants to eat a healthy plant-based diet and still enjoy the flavors of traditional international dishes.

> — Neal Barnard, M.D., president of Physicians Committee for Responsible Medicine and author of *21-Day Weight Loss Kickstart* and *The Get Healthy, Go Vegan Cookbook*

Bryanna's highly anticipated eighth cookbook is inspiring, unique, beautifully written, and sure to become a classic. Browsing through these exceptional recipes was so exciting, I felt compelled to start cooking my way around the world. You'll find fascinating details on ingredient basics, an abundance of helpful sidebars and tips, menus, and much more. Whether you are a pro or a beginner, a vegan, vegetarian, or just thinking about trying something new, you'll want this book. It's like having Byranna in your kitchen cooking with you.

> — Fran Costigan, author of *More Great Good Dairy-Free Desserts Naturally*

If globetrotting isn't in the cards, you can still send your tastebuds around the world. Bryanna Clark Grogan's *World Vegan Feast* offers plant-based pleasures from Eastern Europe, South America, North Africa, the Middle East, and more from the comfort of your own kitchen with deliciously do-able, fun, and festive recipes.

> —Nava Atlas, author of *Vegan Express*

World Vegan Feast is destined to become a classic, with flavorful, inspired and satisfying meals from around the globe. It's an extraordinary collection of delicious homestyle recipes, perfect for everyday meals to special occasions. This is the cookbook that you will reach for again and again!

> — Julie Hasson, author of *Vegan Diner*

Bryanna Clark Grogan has written books on the cuisines of single countries, but now she takes on the world. As always, she prepares authentic and delicious recipes, which I've had the opportunity to sample. As a bonus, Bryanna includes sidebars about cooking and the art and science of the world of food.

> — Ken Bergeron, Vegan Certified Executive Chef

Every now and then a book comes along that fills a huge void. This book does just that by offering fresh approaches and intriguing recipes all while escorting the reader on a trip around the world. One can smell the dishes and taste the flavors while only just reading. I am starting immediately on my trip through this book, beginning with the New Vegan Tiramisu!

> — Linda Long, author and photographer of *Great Chefs Cook Vegan*

World Vegan Feast is a culinary trip around the word that will introduce you to exciting dishes you never heard of and offer new twists on old favorites. From Creole Grits and Grillades to Peruvian Caramel-Filled Pastries, you'll find enticing recipes with clear instructions and tips that will help even novice cooks create gourmet vegan meals.

> — Susan Voisin, publisher of FatFreeVegan.com

Other books by
Bryanna Clark Grogan

The Almost No-Fat Cookbook

The Almost No-Fat Holiday Cookbook

20 Minutes to Dinner

Nonna's Italian Kitchen

Soyfoods Cooking for a Positive Menopause

Authentic Chinese Cooking for the Contemporary Kitchen

The Fiber for Life Cookbook

World Vegan Feast

200 Fabulous Recipes from Over 50 Countries

Bryanna Clark Grogan

VEGAN HERITAGE PRESS
Woodstock • Virginia

World Vegan Feast: 200 Fabulous Recipes from Over 50 Countries by Bryanna Clark Grogan. (Copyright © 2011 by Bryanna Clark Grogan)

First Edition, September 2011

ISBN 13: 978-0-9800131-4-6
ISBN 10: 0-9800131-4-3

Vegan Heritage Press books are available at quantity discounts. For information, please visit our website at www.veganheritagepress.com or write the publisher at Vegan Heritage Press, P.O. Box 628, Woodstock, VA 22664-0628.

Cover: Food photos by Bryanna Clark Grogan (clockwise from top left): Smoky Spicy Hominy Soup *(Posole)*, page 69; Pasta ala Pescarese, page 90; Almond-Mango Trifle with Indian Spices, page 199. Author photo by Scott Hurlbert. Color insert photos by Bryanna Clark Grogan.

Library of Congress Cataloging-in-Publication Data

Grogan, Bryanna Clark, 1948-
 World vegan feast : 200 fabulous recipes from over 50 countries / Bryanna Clark Grogan.
   p. cm.
 Includes bibliographical references and index.
 ISBN 978-0-9800131-4-6
 1. Vegan cooking. 2. International cooking. 3. Cookbooks. I. Title.
 TX837.G6767 2011
 641.5'636--dc23

                                                        2011020580

Printed in the United States of America

Publisher's Note: The information in this book is correct and complete to the best of our knowledge. Website addresses and contact information were correct at the time of publication. The publisher is not responsible for specific health or allergy needs that may require medical supervision, nor adverse reactions to recipes contained in this book. The author and publisher disclaim all liability in connection with the use of the book.

Dedication

I dedicate this book to my late father, Alejandro Jaime Urbina (Alejo), who forgave me for cutting recipes out of his *Gourmet* magazine collection when I was eleven years old. He had impeccable taste and always supported our decisions, even when he probably had to bite his tongue. I'm also dedicating the book to my late mother, Marie-Evelyn Tonge Urbina (variously and affectionately called "Petie," "Eve," or "Gramma Eve"), who made everything fun, who fed us delicious, healthful meals, and who gave me the freedom to experiment in the kitchen from a very young age. I'm thankful to both of them for opening our minds to the wonderful, colorful, varied world in which we live, and all of its people. They were, simply, the best parents anyone could want.

Contents

Acknowledgments

I have to thank Jon Robertson, my publisher, for his kindness and confidence in me. I also thank Julie Hasson, Fran Costigan, Chef Kevin Dunn, and David Lee for making me feel part of the cooking fraternity, even when I'm on my little island, and for being so fun to be with when we manage to get together. Thanks to my *Vegan Feast* newsletter subscribers for trying out my recipes and giving me feedback (especially Brenda Wiley and Debbie Knight). Thanks to my friends (you know who you are!), including our Denman Island vegan dinner group, for their kindness and inspiration. And thanks to my family, all of you, for keeping me down to earth, especially Brian for putting up with me!

I also want to express a special thank-you to my baking mentors. The no-knead bread method is sweeping the baking world, and I have been swept away as well! I've experimented with many recipes and read several books on the subject, as well as combed numerous websites and blog posts. Eventually, I developed the recipe for the crusty Italian-style artisan loaf in this book with the method and techniques that produced the results my family loved. But I had help from several professionals – my particular recipe is a direct result of their work (books, articles, blogs, and workshops) – and I'd like to thank them.

Thanks to Jim Lahey of Sullivan Street Bakery in N.Y.C. (author of *My Bread*, W. W. Norton & Company, 2009) for the method of baking in a heavy covered pot. Bread baked this way stays crunchy after it cools because the pot acts as a "brick oven," creating the conditions of a professional oven in miniature. And thanks also to Jim for convincing me (through his writing) to use a well-hydrated dough (about 80 percent hydration), which results in more big, irregular holes in the crumb. Thanks to Mark Bittman for bringing Jim's recipes and methods to the public in his *New York Times* food column "The Minimalist." Thanks to Jeff Hertzberg and Zoë François (authors of *Artisan Bread in Five Minutes a Day* and *Healthy Bread in Five Minutes a Day*, Thomas Dunne Books, 2007 and 2009), for the "5-minute" method of mixing and refrigerating the dough, which makes it practical to bake bread fresh every day, reduces the work, and provides spontaneity in the baking process. The cold rise improves the flavor and makes the Lahey-style wet dough much easier to handle, too. Special thanks to Master Baker Peter Reinhart (author of *The Bread Baker's Apprentice*, Ten Speed Press, 2001, and several other books) for writing the most readable and inspiring bread books ever and for being so approachable, both in his books and in his workshops.

World Vegan Feast: An Introduction

This book is for all cooks. Seriously. Yes, it's a book of international and fusion recipes, and while it's not written for the complete kitchen novice, that doesn't necessarily mean difficult recipes or hard-to-find ingredients. After all, there are busy working parents, commuters, and otherwise time-stretched folks in all countries and societies, and everyone wants to eat well, even on the busiest of days.

I'm one of those folks myself – I'm employed outside the home as well as at home with my cookbook writing, recipe development, workshops, etc. I also have four grown children, two stepsons, and nine grandchildren, all nearby, and try to cram in a little socializing and exercise in between. I have a tiny kitchen in a small house and I live on a small island, so I can't run to the store whenever I feel like it.

In this book, I have tried to provide a balance between easy, exciting, everyday recipes made with things you're likely to have in your pantry, and more complex dishes that you might serve at celebrations, company dinners, or at family gatherings, requiring perhaps more planning and shopping as well. It's a personal and eclectic mix, by no means representative of all world cuisines (that would take several large volumes), although many countries and regions of the world are represented.

Take, for instance, the chapter, "Brunch Around the World." Having an impromptu brunch for friends? Not much time to prepare ahead of time? The Yeasted Oven Pancake with Apples is made from a simple batter that can be mixed before you go to bed the night before. Leave it to rise in the refrigerator and pop it into the oven just before your guests arrive. By the time everyone is settled with their coffee or tea, the pancake will be ready to flip over onto a platter and serve with a flourish and warm maple syrup. Other easy last-minute brunch dishes with great flavor and spark include spicy Korean Potato Pancakes *(Kamjajon)*, Coconut Semolina Crepes *(Rava Dosa)*, and Chickpea Flour Omelets *(Gujarati Chilla)*.

If you prefer make-ahead recipes, when you have half an hour, make some Easy Vegan Crespelle and freeze them. With these crepes on hand, and some vegan white cheese in the freezer or refrigerator, you can invite friends at the last minute for an elegant stress-free brunch featuring Roasted Asparagus Crespelle with Besciamella Sauce. Asparagus spears are quickly oven-roasted while you blend and cook the creamy sauce (which can be quickly made in the microwave). Your guests will think you slaved over a hot stove for hours! Another make-ahead recipe is the Bell Pepper and Mushroom Quiche, which is actually improved by an overnight chill in the refrigerator.

In subsequent chapters, I hope I have achieved a similar balance between simple and complex (without skimping on flavor). Quick, tasty stir-fry and noodle dishes, such as Fresh Pineapple-Noodle Stir-Fry, Peruvian Stir-Fry *(Lomo Saltado)*, and Pasta ala Pescarese are tucked in between recipes for an elegant Seitan Wellington with Madeira Gravy and a satisfying French cassoulette.

Simple curries and stews, such as Lentil and Rapini Stew with Spicy Vegan Sausage, Indonesian Green Curry on Roasted Sweet Potatoes, and "Finnan Haddie" with Smoked Tofu, rub shoulders, so to speak, with Deep, Dark Stew a la Sicilia, Greek Nugget Potato and Kalamata Olive Stew, and Jamaican Curry.

For those very special times when you want to impress, consider making the Moroccan Savory Celebration Pie *(Bisteeya)* or Pastry-Wrapped Russian Loaf *(Coulibiac)*, which features mushrooms, dill, and soy "salmon" in a phyllo crust. They may be impressive, but they are not beyond anyone's capabilities, providing that you read the recipe through ahead of time, use the ingredients called for, plan well, and follow the recipe instructions (at least the first time).

I haven't forgotten a carefully chosen array of appetizers, soups, salads, and sides, many of which can serve as everyday main dishes, or the desserts and homemade breads. Ridiculously easy family desserts such as Blueberry-Maple "Poor Man's Pudding" *(Pudding au Chômeur)*, Italian Baked Fruit-Stuffed Peaches, and Ginger Treacle Tart, share space with Almond-Mango Trifle with Indian Spices, Almond Café Latte Cake, and Rose-Scented Baklava. My version of "no-knead" crusty artisanal bread is so easy and convenient that you may never go back to the old-fashioned way of baking. But then, the beautiful Giant Hungarian Poppy Seed Spiral Bread might win you back to the "old way."

One of my goals in writing this book is that I want all of us to have fun in the kitchen. This is one reason why I feel it's important to explain the reasoning behind why I do things the way I do, and what various dishes are supposed to look like. If you have this information, and you get into the habit of organizing your cooking as I describe herein, I guarantee that trying new recipes will be more successful and enjoyable and will inspire more confidence in your own cooking abilities.

Recipe Icons Used in This Book

GF = Gluten-Free
GFO = Gluten-Free Option
SF = Soy-Free
SFO = Soy-Free Option
<30 = Recipe can be made in 30 minutes or less

See page 24 for detailed explanations.

World Vegan Kitchen Essentials

Whether you are a longtime vegan or new to vegan cooking, I think it's helpful to have a basic understanding of the ingredients used in this book. I also want to share a little background about how I plan and cook my meals.

This chapter includes eleven foundational recipes, such as seitan, mushroom stock, vegan mayonnaise, and a homemade vegetable base powder, that can be used in other recipes. At the end of the chapter, you'll also find a dozen special seasonal and holiday menus that take full advantage of the variety of recipes in this book.

Meal Planning and Cooking Tips

To help you make up your own menus, I have arranged the chapters in terms of meals or types of dishes. I've also broken down the main dish recipes into three separate chapters according to ingredients. Desserts are divided into two separate chapters according to cooking method.

My practice (and I recommend this to everyone) is to make as many of the components for a more complex dish ahead of time, and I tell you in the recipes when this is possible or even preferable. I also plan for the whole meal well ahead to make efficient use of my time. Additionally, I make sure oven-baked dishes can fit into the oven at the right time and at the right temperature. This gives me more time with my family or guests and prevents last-minute panic attacks!

Say, for instance, I'm going to make a Seitan Wellington for a busy family gathering. I'll make the "Beefy Seitan" days or even weeks before the date – seitan freezes well. It needs to be thinly sliced before being encased in puff pastry, and this can be done a day ahead or hours before.

I might also choose to make the "Who Needs Fois Gras?" Herbed Mushroom Pâté days or weeks before, because it also freezes well. The mushrooms for the filling, the duxelles, can be made at least a day ahead. The Madeira Gravy can be made a day ahead or hours before serving. With this organization, I can assemble the Wellington in under half an hour, refrigerate it for an hour or two before baking, and place it in a hot oven 30 minutes before the meal is to be served.

Ingredient Basics

This section provides information regarding some ingredients and concepts that might be new to you. The section is by no means exhaustive. For example, I am assuming that you have some basic knowledge of nondairy milks, grains, beans, legumes, and other vegan staples. Unless specified otherwise, the ingredients used in the recipes are "medium-sized."

There are so many new vegan products on the market that a comprehensive list would be outdated before this book hit the shelves, so I have provided website addresses in the Resources section that provide up-to-date information. Those of you, like myself, who don't live in an area where commercial vegan products are readily available, will find there a list of international online and retail sources for vegan products.

At the end of this chapter, I've also included a section on an important component of cooking: *umami*, the Japanese concept of the "fifth flavor" that can help you get the most flavor from your vegan dishes.

Important: Before making any recipe, be sure that you thoroughly wash, scrub, or clean any fresh produce before using.

Now, let's look at some ingredients, beginning with broths.

Vegan Broths and Bouillon

The product you use should contribute full flavor, not just saltiness. Unfortunately, many vegetarian broth powders do not deliver in the taste department. And, sadly, I find that the major organic brands are inadequate – too salty and not enough flavor.

An excellent homemade alternative is my own broth powder mix. It's easy and cheap to make and has excellent flavor – but you must use 2 teaspoons for each cup of water.

Vegan "Chicken-Style" Broth Powder

Makes 1 1/4 cups   SF, GF, <30

I invented this broth powder when I was having trouble finding a natural broth powder here in Canada that actually tastes good. You need to use 2 teaspoons for each cup of water. This recipe makes enough for 30 cups of broth.

1 1/3 CUPS NUTRITIONAL YEAST FLAKES

3 TABLESPOONS ONION POWDER

2 1/2 TABLESPOONS SEA SALT

1 TABLESPOON SOY PROTEIN POWDER (OR RICE PROTEIN POWDER)

1 TABLESPOON SUGAR

2 1/2 TEASPOONS GARLIC POWDER

1 TEASPOON DRIED THYME

1 TEASPOON FINELY CRUMBLED DRIED SAGE (NOT GROUND OR POWDERED)

1 TEASPOON PAPRIKA

1/2 TEASPOON TURMERIC

Blend all the ingredients in a dry blender until powdery. Store in a dry, airtight container. Use 2 level teaspoons per cup of boiling water.

Recommended Brands of Broth Powder or Paste

If you don't want to make your own broth powder, there are a number of brands of instant vegetarian broth or bouillon powders, pastes, and cubes available. The brands vary from region to region, even within North America. Fortunately, we can now order specific brands online if we can't convince our local store to carry them. Here are some brands I like, beginning with my favorite:

◈ **Seitenbacher Vegetarian Vegetable Broth and Seasoning Powder,** a German brand that is widely distributed in the U.S.A., Europe, and online. Seitenbacher is not organic, but it's vegan, MSG-free, and all natural. It contains no oil and is fat-free and gluten-free with no artificial flavor-enhancer.

◈ **Superior Touch "Better Than Bouillon®" No-Chicken Vegan Base** is delicious and rich-tasting. It's a paste, not a powder, and is a bit pricey, so I use it when I want a really rich broth. This brand also has a "No Beef Vegan Base," which is good, and a "Vegetable Base" that also comes in an organic variety. (Unfortunately, their mushroom base contains dairy products.)

◈ For everyday cooking, I like **McCormick® Gourmet All-Vegetable Bouillon Cubes,** but they may only be available in Canada. It is actually the same product as an Australian kosher brand, **Massel Ultracubes.** Both brands label their product "Chicken," "Beef," or "Vegetable," but they are all vegan. Massel also makes an excellent broth powder, and both products are now available in the U.S. from VeganEssentials.com. Both Massel and McCormick broth products contain no trans-fats, no MSG, and have good flavor without too much salt.

To make 1 cup of broth, combine 1 cup water with:

1 TEASPOON SEITENBACHER OR MASSEL VEGETARIAN BROTH POWDER; OR
1 TEASPOON "BETTER THAN BOUILLON" VEGAN NO-CHICKEN OR NO-BEEF BASE; OR
1/2 CUBE MASSEL ULTRACUBES OR MCCORMICK ALL-VEGETABLE BOUILLON CUBES

If you cannot locate any of the above products, I recommend that you order a container of Seitenbacher powder or one of the other above-mentioned brands (perhaps online), so you can taste what you are looking for in one of your local brands. Make a cup of hot broth using the product you purchased and do the same with the brand you have been using, and other brands that are available to you. Conduct a taste-test. If you find one that is very similar to one of my recommended brands, then go ahead and use it. If none of them measure up, then I recommend that you order a supply of one of the recommended brands and take samples to your local grocer and/or natural food store, and ask them to carry it.

Mushroom Broth and Bouillon

I use mushroom broth in recipes that call for a rich "meaty" broth. You can make your own (see below), but it's handy to have some good mushroom bouillon cubes in the cupboard. But watch out – one tasty commercial broth, the "Better Than Bouillon" Mushroom Base, unfortunately contains cultured whey. You have to also look out for beef fat in some "vegetarian" bouillons. My favorite is the Italian "Star" brand, but they may be hard to find outside of a large city.

I use a porcini mushroom powder from Oregon-based Pistol River Mushrooms (www.PistolRiverMushrooms.com). It is available online at a very reasonable price. You can make a rich-tasting broth using 1 cup of your favorite vegan broth mixed with 1/2 tablespoon of the porcini powder (more or less, according to taste).

Rich Mushroom Stock

Makes 11 cups   SF, GF, <30

Here's an easy recipe for mushroom stock, if you'd like to make your own.

1 TABLESPOON VEGAN MARGARINE OR OLIVE OIL
1 MEDIUM ONION, CHOPPED
4 LARGE CLOVES GARLIC, CHOPPED
12 CUPS GOOD VEGETARIAN BROTH OR BOUILLON
2 OUNCES (2 1/2 CUPS) DRIED MUSHROOMS, PREFERABLY PORCINI, OR A WILD MUSHROOM MIX

1. Heat the margarine in a large pot over medium-high heat. Add the onions and garlic and cook until they start to brown. Add the broth and dried mushrooms and bring to a boil. Reduce the heat to low, cover, and simmer for 30 minutes. Remove the pot from the

heat and let the broth cool. Strain off the solids through a sieve.

2. You can freeze the mushrooms for use in other dishes, if you wish. The broth can be frozen in 1 or 2 cup freezer containers, or in ice cube trays (2 tablespoons per cube). The cubes can then be popped out of the trays and stored in zip-top bags.

Seitan or "Wheat Meat"

Seitan is a common term for wheat protein (wheat gluten) that has been simmered in a tasty broth, and it can be purchased ready-made at health food stores. White Wave Seitan is one popular brand. Modern cooks and food producers use vital wheat gluten (pure gluten powder, page 6), sometimes with other flours, grains, and beans, and experiment with various cooking techniques. This book includes two recipes for home-made seitan, the Light Seitan Cutlets, below, and the Beefy Seitan on page 133.

Light Seitan Cutlets

Makes 16 cutlets   SFO

These tasty, tender cutlets are easy to make and very versatile. Use them for scaloppini-type dishes, or slice or cut them for stews or stir-fries. For stews, make the cutlets a bit thicker than the directions instruct. The combination of tofu (or beans) and soy (or chickpea) flour with vital wheat gluten results in seitan that is tender and not a bit rubbery. **Note:** *These cutlets, like most seitan products, definitely improve if made ahead and chilled thoroughly to firm them up before using. If you're in a hurry, transfer them to a platter or baking sheet in the freezer until they cool completely.*

Wet Mix:
12 OUNCES FIRM TOFU (NOT SILKEN TOFU)
(SOY-FREE OPTION: OMIT THE TOFU AND USE 1 1/2 CUPS PACKED, RINSED AND WELL-DRAINED, UNSEASONED
     CANNED OR COOKED CANNELLINI, WHITE KIDNEY, OR GREAT NORTHERN BEANS)
1 CUP PLUS 1 TABLESPOON COLD WATER
3 TABLESPOONS SOY SAUCE (OR SOY-FREE SAUCE, PAGE 12)
1 TABLESPOON OLIVE OIL
Dry Mix:
2 CUPS PURE GLUTEN POWDER (VITAL WHEAT GLUTEN)
1/2 CUP SOY FLOUR OR CHICKPEA FLOUR (BESAN)
1/2 CUP NUTRITIONAL YEAST FLAKES
2 TEASPOONS ONION POWDER
1 TEASPOON GARLIC POWDER
Cooking Broth:
3 CUPS HOT WATER
1/2 CUP HOMEMADE VEGAN "CHICKEN-STYLE" BROTH POWDER (PAGE 2)
2 TABLESPOONS OLIVE OIL
4 CLOVES GARLIC, CRUSHED

1. **Wet Mix:** Blend all the ingredients in a blender or a food processor until smooth.

2. **Dry Mix:** combine all of the ingredients in a medium bowl. Either pour the blended wet mix into the bowl with the dry mix, or add the dry mix ingredients to the wet mix in a food processor.

3. If mixing by hand, stir until it's too difficult to stir anymore, and then knead the mixture briefly on a clean surface until it is smooth (wet your hands if necessary).

4. If mixing in the food processor, run it until the dough forms a ball on the top of the blade, then keeping running for 30 more seconds.

5. Preheat the oven to 300°F. Divide the dough into 16 approximately equal pieces. Flatten them out on a clean, damp surface with your hands. Make the cutlets a little thinner than you want the end result to be, because they will expand as they cook. Place them in two oiled 9 x 13-inch baking pans. The cutlets can overlap a bit.

6. In a large bowl, combine the cooking broth ingredients. Pour half of the broth over the cutlets in each pan. Cover the pans with foil and bake 30 minutes. Turn the cutlets over and cook covered 15 to 30 minutes longer. You want the cutlets to absorb all the broth, but not to brown, so keep an eye on them. Separate them carefully. Cool the cutlets before cooking with them (place them on a platter and cool them quickly in the freezer, if you wish). You can bread or flour them and fry the cutlets like "schnitzel" in a little oil, or use in recipes that call for seitan.

Pure Gluten Powder (Vital Wheat Gluten)

This product is the dried insoluble gluten protein of wheat flour or semolina from which starch and soluble components have been removed by washing with water (no chemicals). It is then turned into a cream-colored powder by drying and grinding. Most brands now state the gluten's country of origin on the package or bag.

Is Vital Wheat Gluten the Same as "Gluten Flour"?

Good question! Unfortunately, sometimes it is, and sometimes it isn't. I had an instructive kitchen disaster one day. I was making seitan, as I had made many times before. But this time, it seemed so soft that I added 2 cups more of what I thought was pure gluten powder. After I cooked it, it seemed "squishy." After cooling, it just fell apart instead of being firm and easy to slice.

I concluded that I had been sold the wrong product – gluten flour, instead of pure gluten powder (vital wheat gluten). There is a big difference between the two, and if you get the wrong product, your seitan will be a failure. Unfortunately, labeling is not standardized. I was aware of this inconsistency, but it had never happened to me before. I have purchased my pure gluten powder in bulk from the same natural food store for many years. However, the last batch I bought before making this batch of seitan was a different product altogether. (I contacted the store and they corrected the issue right away.)

Gluten flour is very pale in color and feels silky when rubbed between your fingers. Pure gluten powder (vital wheat gluten) is more creamy-beige in color and almost clumps up when you rub it between your fingers. I did a little test with new gluten and the old gluten that I had in my canister and found that I was right. I mixed 1 tablespoon of the new batch (the gluten flour) with 1 tablespoon of water, and did the same with the old batch (the pure gluten powder). I could immediately see and feel the difference. The gluten flour mixture was more yellow in color and sticky; easy to squash into a thin shape. The pure gluten powder (vital wheat gluten) mixture was grayer in color and rubbery with a texture that would not easily flatten out – this is what you want! If you have a chance to check the package (if bought in bulk, ask to see the bag it was shipped in), 1/4 cup of pure gluten powder (vital wheat gluten) will contain 23g of protein. Gluten flour (or "high-gluten flour," as it is sometimes called), will contain only 12g or 14g protein per 1/4 cup. You can't go by name alone. See Resources for reliable sources of pure gluten powder (vital wheat gluten).

Soy Foods

Tofu

Tofu is best described as a soft "cheese" made from soymilk that is curded with mineral salts, drained, and then pressed into different textures. It is used widely in Asian and vegetarian cooking. This protein, iron, and antioxidant-rich soy food is extremely versatile, taking on flavors easily. It can be used to substitute for dairy products, meat, poultry, seafood, and eggs.

Most supermarkets and natural food stores will carry several different types of tofu, including soft tofu, used mainly for drinks and desserts; medium-firm; firm; and extra-firm, sometimes called "pressed" tofu, which is excellent for marinating, stir-frying, and making kebabs. Tofu that is removed from its package should be kept in the refrigerator in a sealed container completely covered by water that is changed daily.

If you freeze tofu (anything from medium-firm to extra-firm) for 48 hours or more, and

Is Your Tofu Too Soft?

A few people tell me that their tofu slices fall apart after a couple of days in a marinade. To remedy this, make sure that you are slicing the tofu evenly and not too thinly – 3/8-inch thick is about right. Also, different brands of tofu vary in what is termed "extra-firm." I use a Canadian brand that is extremely firm, so I never have that problem (and I've left the tofu in a marinade for up to two weeks). If your extra-firm tofu isn't firm enough, experiment with other brands (but don't use silken tofu!) and/or consider getting a tofu press, available from tofuxpress.com.

then thaw it out, it has a very chewy texture after you squeeze out the water. This makes a great hamburger replacement in chili, spaghetti sauces, sloppy Joes, and casseroles.

There are many varieties of prepared tofu available – smoked, baked, and marinated. These can replace meats, poultry, and even smoked fish in stir-fries, sautés, casseroles, salads, and sandwiches.

In addition, you can purchase silken tofu, which is sold in aseptic packages and keeps for about a year unopened. Silken tofu comes in soft, firm, and extra-firm varieties – regular and low-fat. It is wonderful for blended, creamy mixtures, such as puddings, sauces, soups, and pie fillings. I buy it by the case from my food co-op and always have it in my pantry.

The following recipe for Crispy Marinated Tofu Slices is called for in a variety of tofu recipes in this book.

Crispy Marinated Tofu Slices

Makes about 32 slices   GFO, <30

I always have some extra-firm tofu (not silken) slices and/or cubes marinating for up to two weeks in this marinade in the refrigerator so it's always ready for a quick and delicious meal. The marinated tofu can be pan-fried plain in a nonstick skillet or coated with Seasoned Flour (page 9) and fried in a little oil to make a crispy coating that is delectable hot or cold. Serve the slices "as is," in stir-fries, salads, and sandwiches or with any sauce that you would have used on chicken in pre-vegan days. The marinated tofu chunks are great for vegan kebabs.

1 1/2 CUPS WATER

1/4 CUP SOY SAUCE

3 TABLESPOONS NUTRITIONAL YEAST FLAKES

2 TABLESPOONS FRESH CHOPPED SAGE LEAVES OR 2 TEASPOONS DRIED, CRUMBLED

1/2 TABLESPOON FRESH CHOPPED ROSEMARY OR 1/2 TEASPOON DRIED

1/2 TABLESPOON FRESH CHOPPED THYME OR 1/2 TEASPOON DRIED

1/2 TEASPOON ONION POWDER

1 1/2 TO 2 POUNDS EXTRA-FIRM TOFU (NOT SILKEN), DRAINED

SEASONED FLOUR (PAGE 9)

2 TABLESPOONS OLIVE OIL, OR MORE

1. In a 5-cup container with a tight lid, combine the water, soy sauce, nutritional yeast, sage, rosemary, thyme, and onion powder. Mix well.

2. Cut the tofu into 3 x 2-inch slices about 3/8-inch thick and transfer the slices to the marinade so that the tofu is fairly tightly-packed and covered with liquid. Cover and refrigerate for up to two weeks, shaking the container daily.

3. When ready to cook, coat the tofu slices with the seasoned flour. Heat about 1 tablespoon of olive oil in a 10 to 12-inch skillet (cast iron or a nonstick pan work best) over medium heat (no hotter). When the oil is hot, add the coated slices and cook, watching carefully, until golden brown and crispy on the bottom. Turn the slices over and cook until

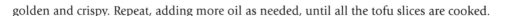

golden and crispy. Repeat, adding more oil as needed, until all the tofu slices are cooked.

To Oven-Fry: arrange the coated slices in single layers on 2 oiled 10 x 15 inch dark baking sheets (foods brown better on dark pans), not touching. Spray the slices with oil from a pump sprayer and bake at 500°F for about 10 minutes per side. Cool on racks if not eating immediately.

Tip: If you are on a low salt diet, use a low-sodium soy sauce.

Seasoned Flour

GFO, SF, <30

2 CUPS WHOLE-WHEAT FLOUR OR OTHER WHOLE GRAIN FLOUR (SUCH AS SPELT, KAMUT, BROWN RICE, ETC.)
1/4 CUP NUTRITIONAL YEAST FLAKES
1 TEASPOON SALT
1 TEASPOON ONION POWDER OR 1/2 TEASPOON GARLIC POWDER, OPTIONAL
FRESHLY GROUND BLACK PEPPER, OPTIONAL

In a container with a tight-fitting lid, combine the flour, yeast, salt, and onion powder and pepper, if using. Mix well, then cover tightly and refrigerate until needed.

Textured Soy Protein and Other Soy Products

Textured soy protein (TSP), also known as the brand TVP®, is a low-fat, inexpensive dry product that's used as a meat substitute. It is not the same thing as "hydrolized plant protein" or "soy isolate," and contains no MSG or other additives. It is made from soy flour, cooked under pressure, then extruded to make different sizes and shapes.

Textured soy protein chunks and cutlets have such a meaty texture that, when cooked in a flavorful mixture, anxious vegetarians have asked me if I'm sure their food includes no meat! Textured soy protein will keep for a long time, has no cholesterol, almost no fat and sodium, and is an excellent source of protein and fiber. It is easily rehydrated for use in soups, stews, casseroles, and sauces (in fact, if your mixture is very brothy, you can just add the textured soy protein in its dry state, and it will absorb the flavorful broth).

The most easily available types are the granules and the chunks or strips. The granules can be used for vegan burgers, sausage, meatballs, meatloaf, and in spaghetti sauces and stuffings for vegetables. The chunks and strips make wonderful stews and stir-fries and can be used in breaded and fried dishes or kebabs.

The general rule for reconstituting textured soy protein granules is 7/8 cup boiling hot liquid to each cup of TSP. This yields about 1 1/3 cups. When I'm substituting for ground meat in a recipe, I figure that 1 pound of meat is equal to about 2 cups of re-constituted granules (1 1/2 cups dry textured soy protein granules soaked in 1 3/4 cups boiling hot liquid for about 10 minutes).

Reconstitute the TSP chunks or strips by cooking 1 1/2 cups in 3 cups flavorful broth or water mixed with 3 tablespoons soy sauce, 3 tablespoons ketchup, and 1 tablespoon nutritional yeast flakes for 15 to 30 minutes, depending upon how tender you like them. This yields a little over 2 cups, which can be substituted for 1 pound boneless meat. Cool and store them in the cooking broth. I usually make 4 or more times this amount and freeze it in 2-cup portions. Drain the cooked TSP before using it, and pat dry before coating with flour, frying, or marinating. See Resources for sources for TSP, including organic and solvent-free.

Butler Soy Curls

I am enthusiastic about a product called Butler Soy Curls®, which is similar to textured soy protein but superior in texture and less processed. It is made from whole non-GMO soybeans, so it contains all of the fiber but no additives or preservatives (and is solvent-free). It is very tender when reconstituted and great for stir-fries. Since it contains the natural oil, I keep this dried product in the freezer. I use the crumbs on the bottom of the box in the same way as TSP granules. When reconstituted by soaking in hot broth for about 5 minutes, the strips resemble tender chicken (though you can flavor them as you like). I usually reconstitute more than I need for a recipe and freeze the remainder for quick meals. Most online vegan stores carry Soy Curls. Many Seventh-Day Adventist ABC stores sell them in bulk, which saves money, so check the Butler Foods company website, ButlerFoods.com, for where to buy.

Alternatives to Seitan and Soy Curls

For quick meals, or times when you have no seitan or Soy Curls in the house, you might want to try various brands of "meaty" vegan strips (sometimes called "tips" or "tenders"), which are excellent in stir-fries and can be used in stews as well. These products are generally made from a combination of soy and wheat proteins. Common brands are Gardein, Yves, Lightlife, Morningstar Farms, White Wave, and PC Blue Menu (Canada). Field Roast products are soy-free. Many of these products are available in natural food stores and large supermarkets, either refrigerated or frozen. Some online vegan vendors (see Resources) will ship them with cold packs.

Tempeh

Tempeh is a cultured soybean product (it sometimes contains other beans and grains as well) that originated in Indonesia. It has a slightly nutty taste and firm texture that many people like as a meat or poultry substitute, especially in stir-fry dishes. It can be marinated, baked, grilled, and deep-fried. It is a good source of protein, fiber, and antioxidants, and is easy to digest. It is usually available frozen in 8-ounce packages (about 4 servings). It should be kept frozen after purchasing and should be cooked first, if it is to be added to a dish for which no other cooking is required.

Miso Paste

Miso is a Japanese fermented soybean and grain paste (usually made with rice or barley) which is used as a soup base and flavoring. It is salty, but highly nutritious and valued for its digestive properties. In vegan dishes, umami-rich (see page 25) miso lends a fermented flavor to "cheesy" mixtures and can be used as a substitute for anchovy paste in dressings and many Italian dishes.

Unpasteurized miso contains beneficial bacteria similar to that in yogurt, so it should be added to cooked foods at the last minute and not brought to the boiling point. Natural food stores carry several varieties: dark, light, yellow, sweet, and so on.

The texture of miso can range from smooth to chunky, and the color from a light yellow-brown to reddish brown to dark chocolate brown. The flavor can range from mildly salty and sweet to strong and very salty. The color of miso is a good indicator of the strength of its flavor and saltiness. Generally, the lighter in color, the sweeter the miso. Among the varieties of miso are:

Fear of Soy

You can eat a perfectly fine vegan diet without soy. If you are soy-allergic, you can find non-soy meat and dairy substitutes, or make them yourself. But it is unfortunate that people with an anti-vegetarian agenda spread nonsense about a food that has sustained humans for thousands of years, distorting history, distorting scientific studies, and spreading hysteria. If you do a search on the Internet, it's hard to find anything but this hysteria – no wonder people are confused! I don't care whether you eat soy or not – I just think we should make decisions from an informed place. (For more information, go to this link on my website: http://www.bryannaclark-grogan.com/page/page/3476771.htm.)

◈ **Shiromiso or 'White' Miso:** is the generic term for golden-yellow to medium brown miso. It is mild, with a slight sweetness, and the most versatile one for cooking.

◈ **Akamiso or 'Red' Miso:** is the generic term for miso that is a dark reddish-brown in color. It is usually more salty and strong in taste than shiromiso.

◈ **Soy-Free Miso:** A non-soy variety made with chickpeas is made by South River Miso and Miso Master, both organic. South River also makes a miso with adzuki beans. Both non-soy miso varieties are gluten-free.

◈ **Gluten-Free Miso:** Choose a miso variety made with rice rather than barley.

The longer a miso is aged, the deeper its flavor. Commercial miso is usually aged from six months to two years. It's difficult to find miso that's aged for one to two years, but it's worth trying because the flavor is definitely superior.

Ideally, you should consume miso within a year of purchase. But, according to our friend Yoshi Yoshihara, master miso maker here on Denman Island, B.C., you can keep unopened miso at room temperature indefinitely. It will simply get stronger in flavor. After opening, it should be refrigerated. I generally use light brown rice or barley miso (shinmeido) made the old-fashioned way by Yoshi and his wife Susan-Marie.

Organic "Bacon" Bits

Soy "bacon" bits are a tasty addition to many dishes, but if you've despaired over finding an organic variety, worry not! Frontier Bac'uns Vegetarian Bits, Certified Organic, are widely available from the vegan stores listed in Resources and online. It's even available in 1-pound foil bags and a 25-pound box!

Soy-Free Seasoning Sauces

If you want to have some great sauces on hand without the soy, make some Soy-Free Sauce and two variations, Teriyaki Marinade and Vegan Worcestershire Sauce (the last two can be made with regular soy sauce instead). **Important:** To replace some of the complex qualities that a good fermented soy sauce or tamari supplies, try adding wine, broth, and/or mushroom broth or concentrate to your dish, in addition to using the soy sauce substitute that follows.

Soy-Free Sauce

Makes 1 3/4 cups   SF, GF, <30

An excellent gluten-free, soy-free alternative to soy sauce or tamari.

> 2 TABLESPOONS MARMITE OR OTHER YEAST EXTRACT (PAGE 21)
> 2 TABLESPOONS SALT
> 1 CUP PLUS 1/2 CUP HOT WATER, VEGAN BROTH, OR MUSHROOM SOAKING WATER, DIVIDED
> 2 TABLESPOONS SOY-FREE GRAVY BROWNER (SUCH AS KITCHEN BOUQUET)

Dissolve the Marmite and salt in the first 1 cup of hot liquid. Mix in the remaining ingredients and store the mixture in a covered jar in the refrigerator. It will keep for several weeks.

Low-Salt Version: Just reduce or leave out the salt – but this doesn't keep very long. (Salt is a preservative.)

Teriyaki Marinade

Makes 1 2/3 cups   SFO,GF, <30

> 1/2 CUP SOY-FREE SAUCE (OR SOY SAUCE OR TAMARI)
> 1/2 CUP WATER
> 1/4 CUP DRY SHERRY, CHINESE RICE WINE, WHITE VERMOUTH, OR DRY WHITE WINE (OR APPLE, PINE-
>   APPLE, OR WHITE GRAPE JUICE TO MAKE THE DISH ALCOHOL-FREE)

1/3 CUP MAPLE SYRUP, AGAVE NECTAR, OR SUGAR

1 TEASPOON GRATED FRESH GINGER (OR 1/4 TEASPOON POWDERED GINGER)

1 CLOVE GARLIC, CRUSHED

Mix together the marinade ingredients in a small pot and simmer for a few minutes over high heat.

Vegan Worcestershire Sauce

Makes about 2 cups SFO, GF, <30

1 CUP CIDER VINEGAR

1/3 CUP DARK MOLASSES

1/4 CUP SOY-FREE SAUCE (OR SOY SAUCE OR TAMARI)

1/4 CUP WATER

3 TABLESPOONS LEMON JUICE

1 1/2 TABLESPOONS SALT

1/2 TABLESPOON DRY MUSTARD POWDER

1 TEASPOON ONION POWDER

3/4 TEASPOON GROUND GINGER

1/2 TEASPOON BLACK PEPPER

1/4 TEASPOON GARLIC POWDER

1/4 TEASPOON CAYENNE PEPPER

1/4 TEASPOON GROUND CINNAMON

1/8 TEASPOON GROUND CLOVES OR ALLSPICE

1/8 TEASPOON GROUND CARDAMOM

Combine all of the ingredients in a blender and blend well. Pour the mixture into a medium saucepan and bring it to a boil. Remove from the heat and pour it into a sterilized pint jar with a tight lid. Store in the refrigerator.

Vegan Alternatives to Eggs and Dairy

Numerous plant-based products are now available to replace eggs and dairy in cooking. Foremost among them are the wide variety of nondairy milks, now stocked in most supermarkets. Nondairy milk choices include soy, almond, rice, oat, and hemp milk. For the recipes in this book, if a particular type is required, it will be specified. Otherwise, feel free to use your own particular favorite.

Vegan Cheese

Vegan cheeses have vastly improved in the last few years (many of them now available in Canada), and I'll wager that quite a few vegetarians have recently taken the next logical step – to being vegan – because of that.

I don't buy these often, but my current favorite all-purpose vegan cheese brand is Daiya, which is made near Vancouver, B.C., not far from where I live. You can buy it in bulk at a big savings and keep it in the freezer. We like the mozzarella type and find it has excellent flavor and melts nicely. We use it sparingly since we got used to doing without cheese over the last more than twenty years, when commercial vegan cheeses were either unavailable or pretty terrible. But my husband is ecstatic to have pizza cheese again. (And a plus for people who are soy-allergic – Daiya is soy-free!)

Tip: All vegan cheeses seem to dry out if they are baked or broiled uncovered for any length of time. To ensure a nice melty, gooey cheese on pizza, layer the cheese under the vegetables and other toppings and spray or drizzle the finished topping with a little olive oil. When using vegan cheese on top of casseroles or lasagne, bake the casserole covered and remove the cover for a few minutes before serving. Or, use the cheese inside the lasagne or casserole and top it with a layer of creamy Besciamella Sauce (page 37).

There is a plethora of new vegan cheese products on the market and the number grows all the time. As of this writing, vegan cheese brands (in addition to Daiya) that I enjoy are Sheese, Vegan Gourmet, and Galaxy Vegan. My favorite commercial brand of parmesan substitute is Galaxy Vegan Grated Topping. Check out your natural food store and vegan online stores regularly (see Resources) for what's new and available. (Dr. Cow brand nut-based cheeses are soy-free.)

Homemade Vegan Cheeses

Before good vegan cheeses were easily available, or even being produced, I devised vegan cheeses of my own. I've included several of them in this book. Here's a list:

Walnut Parm, page 15
Citrus Almond Ricotta, page 40
Creamy Vegan White Cheese Sauce, page 44
Vegan Boursin-Style Spread, page 55
Quick "Feta" Crumble, page 92
Vegan Gruyere, page 97
Tofu Cheese Curds, page 100
Tofu Feta, page 101
Suisse Melty Cheese, page 105
Vegan Mascarpone, page 202
Soy-Free Cream Cheese-Mascarpone, page 202

Walnut Parm

Makes about 1 1/2 cups   SF, GF, <30

If you have a soy allergy or you have a hard time locating a good commercial vegan parmesan substitute, this is an easy and tasty alternative, either as a topping or as an ingredient. This is just about the right amount to fit into two little shaker bottles, but you can easily double, triple, or quadruple the recipe and keep it refrigerated or frozen. Use a food processor or mini-chopper or clean, dry coffee/spice mill for this recipe, rather than a blender.

> 1 CUP CHOPPED RAW WALNUTS
> 1/4 CUP NUTRITIONAL YEAST FLAKES
> 2 TEASPOONS LIGHT MISO PASTE
> 1/2 TEASPOON SALT

Process the ingredients until as fine as possible. Stir to get rid of any lumps. Transfer to a covered container or shaker and keep refrigerated.

NOTE: If you prefer a commercial brand, Galaxy Vegan and Parma! are good choices – Parma! is soy-free (walnut-based). Both are available from the vegan stores and online vendors in Resources.

Egg Replacers

There are mainly three vegan egg replacers or substitutes that one can use in cooking, but there is no hard-and-fast rule about using them.

◆ **Ener-G® Egg Replacer** is widely available in natural food stores in North America, and also online from their own website and from websites that sell allergy supplies and vegan foods.

◆ **Orgran® "No Egg"** is an Australian product and is widely available in Europe, too. I can find it in my local natural food store in Western Canada, and it is available from the Orgran website and from websites that sell allergy supplies and vegan foods.

◆ **Flax Seed Mixture** is not an all-purpose egg replacer, but good in many instances.

When blended with water, high-fiber flax seeds make a viscous mixture similar to egg white, so this makes a good egg substitute in some baked goods when only an egg or two is called for.

To make it, simply blend 1 tablespoon raw brown or golden flax seed with 1/4 cup water for each egg (you can use warm water if the seeds are frozen), and blend it until it is viscous, foamy, and slightly thickened, with little flecks of seed-coat. Use it immediately in your recipe. Blending can be done in an ordinary blender or with an immersion/stick blender. A food processor doesn't work particularly well for this mixture.

If you have no golden flax seeds, but you don't want flecks of brown seed-coat to show, you can strain the mixture through a fine sieve or cheesecloth.

Note: I find that this flax mixture can be a bit drying to some baked goods (flax seeds suck up liquid), so I use it judiciously, not for everything.

Sometimes a certain replacer works fabulously in one recipe, but not in another. It's really a matter of experience, judgment, and experimentation. For instance, I tried my brownie recipe with the flax seed mixture, and then with Ener-G Egg Replacer powder. It was just okay with either one, but not great. Then I tried them mixed together and it was perfect.

Sometimes you don't need a substitute, just more liquid. For muffins, most yeast breads and coffeecakes, and cakes that call for no more than 2 eggs, I usually just use 1/4 cup of soy milk per egg. (Remember that no egg replacer will work in a recipe that depends solely on eggs for structure and leavening.)

News Flash: You can whip Ener-G Egg Replacer or Orgran "No Egg" to a consistency of almost-stiff egg whites! Use 1 to 2 tablespoons powder with 1/4 cup water for 2 egg whites and beat in a stand mixer for about 10 minutes, or until peaks will stay up (they won't be really stiff peaks, though). Fold into your batter as for egg whites. You need a special recipe to use this for baked meringues – check out the recipe on the Orgran website.

> **Note:** You may want to experiment with adding about 1/2 tablespoon of Ener-G Egg Replacer or Orgran "No Egg" per 1/4 cup of flax seed mixture in some recipes, to compensate for the leavening power of the egg, as well. (See sidebar on page 17 for more information.)

Vegan Mayonnaise

I love mayonnaise. Whenever I use it, I want to really slather it on! But, I want it vegan, of course, and I don't want all the fat and calories. So, I devised the following recipe some years ago, loosely based on an old-fashioned "cooked salad dressing" recipe (only I don't like it sweet). The recipe for Vegan Mayo is a revised and refined version of that recipe, which appeared in several of my earlier cookbooks. It contains a small amount of oil – just enough for good flavor and mouth feel. It's smooth and creamy, and a little tangy. Quite a few Hellman's and Best Foods mayo fans have been pleasantly surprised when they tasted it. I've also included a second mayonnaise recipe that is a bit quicker to make than the first. It's made with silken tofu and is appropriately titled Tofu Mayonnaise.

> **Tip:** If you prefer to buy a commercial vegan mayonnaise, I suggest Reduced-Fat Vegenaise or Spectrum Naturals Eggless Vegan Light Canola Mayo.

Functions of Egg Replacers

Before you decide on which egg replacer to use, it's helpful to know just what the function of the egg was for in a particular recipe. Professional bakers cite eight functions of eggs – and by extension, egg replacers – in baked goods:

- **Structure** is provided by the protein in the egg whites. Blended tofu can often provide the needed protein, and it can be blended with a little egg replacer powder for extra "oomph". Starches will gelatinize when mixed with liquid and heated, and can hold air pockets in place, so adding starch to the recipe is another option. Egg replacer powder can do this, but a mix of tapioca flour and potato flour can be used instead, or tapioca flour alone.

- **Emulsifying** of fats and liquids is provided by egg yolk, which contributes to volume and texture and also retards staling. Blended tofu contains soy lecithin, which can go some way to replace the egg lecithin in the yolks. Using a bit of soy flour in the dry mix can also help – soy flour is often thought of as a "dough conditioner," especially in yeast breads.

- **Leavening** is provided by beaten (whole) eggs incorporating tiny air bubbles into a batter, which expands when heated and gives a leavening boost. Beaten egg replacer and flax seed mixture (page 15) can both aerate batters (and you can use them together for a result that is often better than the sum of its parts), in a more limited way. Blended bananas and mangoes can also aerate batters somewhat, if the flavor fits. If you are tempted to use more baking powder or other leavening agent, don't overdo it because it can affect the flavor.

- **Shortening:** The fat in egg yolks acts as a shortening – a large egg yolk contains 5.64g fat. So, you might want to add a bit more oil or other fat.

- **Moisture:** Eggs are 73 percent water, so you must adjust the liquid in your recipe if you are omitting the eggs. Mashed potatoes or a little potato flour can help egg-free dough because the potato starch attracts moisture and keeps the bread moist and soft. The moisture in mixed egg replacer, blended tofu or flaxseed mixture should be enough to make up for the egg in simple batters.

- **Flavor:** Egg yolks add flavor, too, and I have noted that egg-free (veganized) recipes often taste a little "flat." I usually add a little more salt to the recipe to bring out the other flavors. You can also use more seasoning or spices, or add a bit of liqueur to boost the flavor.

- **Nutrition:** Eggs add nutritional value, but I don't think this is a big issue. There are so many ways to get vegan protein and vitamin A, which are what most people worry about when not eating eggs. Tofu and soy flour (and other bean flours) are very nutritious, as is flax seed.

- **Color:** Eggs give a yellow hue to recipes and help crusts brown nicely (soy or nut milk glaze will do the same). Bird's custard powder, Spanish saffron, or a pinch of turmeric will add yellow color to a recipe, as will some fruits and juices.

Vegan Mayo

Makes 2 cups   GF, SF, <30

For those who are allergic to soy, are not crazy about tofu mayonnaise, or don't have access to Vegenaise, this is a delicious and inexpensive replacement. By omitting the agar in the recipe, this mayo makes a good base for cold savory sauces. I recommend using organic cornstarch, available in natural food stores and online. **Note:** *If you prefer Miracle Whip-type dressing to mayonnaise, increase the amount of mustard powder to 1 teaspoon and add 1 more tablespoon vinegar or lemon juice and 1 tablespoon sugar or agave nectar, or more to taste.*

Mix A:

1 CUP ANY NON-DAIRY MILK (CAN BE LOW-FAT)

2 TABLESPOONS APPLE CIDER VINEGAR (OR RICE VINEGAR, WHITE WINE VINEGAR, OR LEMON JUICE)

1 1/2 TEASPOONS SALT

3/4 TEASPOONS MUSTARD POWDER

1/4 CUP EXTRA-VIRGIN OLIVE OIL (OR FLAX OR HEMP SEED OIL; OR HALF OLIVE OIL AND HALF FLAX OR HEMP SEED OIL)

Mix B:

1/2 CUP PLUS 2 TABLESPOONS COLD WATER

1/2 TEASPOON AGAR POWDER

3 1/2 TABLESPOONS CORNSTARCH

1. Combine the Mix A ingredients in a blender and set aside. (Or, if you use an immersion blender, transfer the Mix A ingredients to a narrow 1-quart bowl or pitcher.)

2. In a small saucepan, combine the water and agar from Mix B, and let stand for a few minutes. Add the cornstarch and whisk it in well. Stir the mixture constantly over high heat until thick and translucent, not opaque white. Scrape the bottom of the saucepan, so that no cornstarch gets left at the bottom.

Microwave Option: In a 2-cup microwave-proof bowl, mix together the water and agar from Mix B, and let the mixture stand for a few minutes. Add the cornstarch and whisk it in well. Microwave the mixture on 100% power (default setting) for 30 seconds. Whisk the mixture. Scrape the bottom of the bowl, so that no cornstarch gets left at the bottom. Repeat this procedure about three times, or until the mixture is thick and translucent, not opaque white. (The microwave works well with cornstarch mixtures.) If not cooked thoroughly, using either cooking method ("translucent" is the key word), the mayo won't thicken properly.

3. Add the cooked Mix B to Mix A and blend until the mixture is white and frothy and emulsified (which means that you can't see any oil globules). **Important:** This mayo doesn't thicken up as you blend it, like regular or soy mayonnaise made with lots of oil, so don't over blend it, thinking it will thicken as it blends – it won't! It will thicken in a few hours in the refrigerator.

4. Pour the mayonnaise into a clean pint jar, cover tightly and refrigerate for several hours, until it is set. It should be firm enough to stand a knife in.

Note on Texture: I use the mayo "as is," and it spreads nicely, even though it looks firmer than regular mayonnaise. But if you want it to look "creamier," here's an optional step: As soon as it is set, whisk the mayo right in the jar with a slim whisk until it is creamy. (Do NOT use a hand/immersion blender this time. It will break down the mixture – use a wire whisk instead.) Refrigerate the mayo again. It will set again, but remain creamy. This mayonnaise will keep refrigerated for about 2 weeks.

The Wonder of Agar

Agar (also known as agar-agar and kanten) is a sea-vegetable-derived vegan gelatin, available in natural food stores. The powder form is quick and convenient to use and sets at room temperature. Generally, 1 teaspoon of agar powder is enough to jell 2 cups of liquid. Agar makes a very firm gel, but mixing it with a little cornstarch can improve the mouth feel. Note: If you use agar flakes instead of powder, use 6 times more flakes (by volume, not weight) than powder.

Tofu Mayonnaise

Makes 1 1/2 cups GF, <30

Silken tofu makes a smooth, thick, rich-tasting vegan mayonnaise that doesn't separate. You have the option of adding a little extra-virgin olive oil, flax oil or hemp seed oil for richer flavor, if you like.

1 (12.3-OUNCE) BOX EXTRA-FIRM SILKEN TOFU
2 TABLESPOONS APPLE CIDER VINEGAR (OR RICE VINEGAR, WHITE WINE VINEGAR, OR LEMON JUICE)
1 1/8 TEASPOONS SALT
1/2 TEASPOON MUSTARD POWDER
OPTIONAL: 1 TO 3 TABLESPOONS EXTRA-VIRGIN OLIVE OIL (OR FLAX OR HEMP SEED OIL; OR HALF
    OLIVE OIL AND HALF FLAX OR HEMP SEED OIL)

Combine all of the ingredients in a food processor or blender and blend until very smooth. Scrape the mixture into a clean pint jar, cover tightly, and refrigerate. This will keep refrigerated for about 2 weeks.

Vegan Whipped Dessert Toppings and Frozen Desserts

Making your own whipped dessert topping is easy and economical. I've provided a recipe for Almond Cream Whipped Topping on page 207. However, if you prefer not to make your own, my favorite commercial product is Soyatoo!® Whippable Soy Topping Cream. (I prefer this version to the "Soy Whip" in the pressurized squirt-can.) It's not something I use often, because I have to mail-order it, but it's great for special desserts. You can use it like a classic whipped cream (you whip it yourself), and it has a delicious flavor. It holds nicely in the refrigerator, too. Some natural food stores carry it and you can order it from VeganEssentials.com and other vegan stores (see Resources).

Soyatoo also makes a soy-free Rice Whip (in a pressurized squirt-can), which is light and tasty, but harder to find. However, Whole Foods markets, and VeganEssentials.com carry it.

Another product is MimicCreme™ Healthy Top. It has a big following, and it's soy-free, but I find it overly sweet for my taste. However, if you need a soy-free option, it's available from most of the vegan stores and online vendors in Resources, and from online.

Your local natural food store and even some supermarkets will have a dazzling display of creamy vegan "ice creams," both soy and soy-free. I'm fond of So Delicious and Turtle Mountain's Purely Decadent, both of which come in almost twenty flavors. Turtle Mountain also makes a delicious coconut milk version in 8 flavors (5 are soy-free). There are more brands, too numerous to name, so have fun taste-testing!

Nondairy Yogurt, Sour Cream, and Cream Cheese (Soy-Based and Soy-Free)

You will find a variety of excellent soy yogurts in supermarkets as well as health food stores. Many of them are quite sweet. The plain variety is the most versatile, as it can be used in cooking and you can flavor it yourself with fresh fruit or low-sugar jams. Soy yogurt is not as tart as dairy yogurt, but it's pleasantly creamy and slightly tangy. Try the various brands and see which one you prefer. Nancy's Cultured Soy, Whole Soy, and So Delicious are three excellent brands made with organic soy and live cultures.

Tofu sour cream, or "Sour Supreme" by Tofutti, is also available in many grocery and health food stores and can be used just like the dairy variety.

Soy-free? If you cannot eat soy, look for the "coconut yogurt" (Cultured Coconut Milk) made by Turtle Mountain. I have also included a delicious homemade recipe for Cashew Sour Cream or Yogurt on page 33.

Several of the desserts (see those recipes designated SFO: soy-free option) can be made soy-free simply by using soy-free versions of: whipped toppings, vegan "ice cream," yogurt, sour cream, or the soy-free Dr. Cow brand Cashew Nut Cream Cheese. This product can also stand in for mascarpone, or you can make the Soy-Free Cream Cheese-Mascarpone on page 202.

Vegan Margarine (including soy-free)

I use oil whenever I can, but sometimes you need a butter substitute. The most reliable and tasty vegan margarine in North America is Earth Balance Natural Buttery Spread. It's non-hydrogenated (uses a small amount of palm oil to make a firm spread) and non-GMO. Their varieties are: Original; Soy Garden; Olive Oil; Whipped Organic (not for baking; lower in fat); and Soy-Free. Becel now has a vegan margarine (Becel Vegan), as well. In the U.K., there is a brand called Pure Dairy Free, which makes three non-hydrogenated and non-GMO varieties – the Olive and the Sunflower are also soy-free. It is available in all the major markets. Another is Vitalite, which is non-hydrogenated.

Other Ingredients

Salt

Salt is an essential ingredient in cooking. Used in moderate quantities, salt enhances and brings out flavors (even sweetness). It also affects the way foods smell and brightens colors. For instance, if you sniff two identical glasses of wine, but one is salted, the one with salt will have a stronger aroma. Salt is also an essential ingredient in breads, where it strengthens the gluten and regulates the growth of the yeast.

Cookbook author Marcella Hazan refers to salt as a "magnet," drawing fragrance and flavor from food, and she writes, "To shrink from an adequate use of salt is to leave unmined the deep-lying flavors of food." *(Marcella's Italian Kitchen*, 1986.) Food essayist Robert Farrar Capon calls salt "the indispensable baseline over which all other tastes and smells form their harmonies."

If you follow a vegan diet, you'll have no problem doing away with the salt in cheese and common processed foods, and you won't be ingesting the natural sodium in meat and dairy products. You can use low-salt products, such as soy sauce and canned tomatoes, and restrict your intake of vegan processed foods and salty foods like pretzels, chips, olives, sauerkraut, salted nuts, and seeds. Moderately salt your homemade foods to enhance their flavors, aromas, and colors – and remove that salt-shaker from your table!

Yeast Extract Paste (Marmite)

I'm not one of those folks who eats Marmite on toast, but yeast extracts like Marmite are useful for adding a rich "beefy" flavor to soups, stews and spreads. Yeast extract is a nutritious sticky, dark brown paste with a distinctive, powerful flavor, quite salty and savory, with excellent umami qualities (see page 25).

Nutritional yeast extract is called for in only a few recipes in the book, and there are several brands. I like Marmite the best. In my opinion, the Australian brand, Vegemite, is saltier. Marmite is easy to find in the U.K., Canada, and anywhere else in the British Commonwealth. In the U.S., you may have to go to a gourmet grocery store to find it. online carries it. It's not cheap, but you will use it in small quantities.

Liquid Smoke

Nervous about using liquid smoke? *Cook's Illustrated* magazine did some research and experimenting and found out that it is not a synthetic or creosote-laden liquid! According to the Colgin Company (which has been bottling liquid smoke since the nineteenth century), liquid smoke is made by channeling smoke from smoldering wood chips through a condenser, which quickly cools the vapors and causes them to liquefy. The water-soluble flavor compounds in the smoke are trapped within this liquid, while the non-soluble, carcinogenic tars and resins are removed by a series of filters, resulting in a clean, smoke-flavored liquid to flavor your beans and tofu "bacon."

The *Cooks' Illustrated* staff tried condensing and bottling their own liquid smoke. A whole day and $50 of equipment later, they ended up with three tablespoons of excellent liquid smoke. But they planned to purchase it next time. There are many brands of liquid smoke, so try them out to see which you like best.

Alcoholic and Non-Alcoholic Beverages for Vegans

I call for wine and beer in several recipes. Not only do they add distinctive flavors of their own, but alcohol is a flavor carrier. It has umami compounds (see page 25), so it is a real flavor booster! I'm not familiar with non-alcoholic beer, but I understand that there are quite a few that are very good now, and some are available in food stores as well as liquor stores. To read reviews of the various brands, do a search online (http://barnivore.com). Ariel Vineyards has some prize-winning non-alcoholic wines that can be used in cooking. They are widely available in wine shops, liquor stores, and grocery stores.

What can make alcoholic beverages non-vegan? Usually the offender is the "fining" agent (the substance that is used for refining any particulate matter out of the liquid), but it can sometimes be an ingredient (such as the cochineal, which used to color the aperitif Campari – the company switched to artificial color a few years ago). Anti-foaming agents used in alcohol may also not be vegan-friendly – namely, pepsin, an enzyme from the stomachs of pigs, and glycerine, which can be made from either vegetable or animal fat.

Fining agents that are not vegan-friendly are isinglass (from the swim bladders of fish), gelatine, casein, egg whites or albumen, ox blood (rarely used these days), bone charcoal, or chitin (from lobster and/or crab shells). Vegan fining agents can be hydrolyzed wheat gluten isolate and pea protein isolate, or natural bentonite clay. Fining agents precipitate, or sink, to the bottom of the tank or barrel, and then are removed from the wine before bottling.

There are many vegan-friendly alcohols on the market, all over the world. Legal purity law requirements mean alcohol produced in Germany and Belgium are vegan. Most U.S.-produced beers are also vegan. The best resource for finding vegan wines, beers, and other alcoholic beverages is http://barnivore.com.

Cookware

I recommend that you get the best cookware you can afford, even if that means building up your battery of cookware gradually. Cookware should have a little heft, but not be so heavy that it requires a weight-lifter! Cheap, very light cookware has a tendency to warp and not heat evenly, and may burn foods easily. I prefer not to buy cookware sets. I like to buy each pan according to what use it will be put to and what material, depth, and shape will do those jobs most efficiently. The following are the materials that I prefer, and I have some pans made from each of them:

Anodized Aluminum: To make "anodized aluminum" an electrochemical process renders the aluminum nonreactive and resistant to scratches. It also gives the cooking surface nonstick properties and seals in the aluminum so that it is less likely to corrode into food. It's also attractive and conducts heat well.

Cast-Iron: Cast-iron pans are heavy, thick, durable pans; slow to heat but excellent at retaining and distributing heat. Regular cast iron (you can buy pre-seasoned ones if you prefer) or enamel-coated cast iron pans are excellent for deep, shallow or pan frying, and for dishes that require long cooking periods, such as braises or stews.

Stainless Steel: Stainless steel is durable, non-porous, nonreactive, and resistant to rust, corrosion, and pitting. Because stainless steel is not very conductive, be sure that your stainless steel pans are clad with other metals, such as copper or aluminum, or have an aluminum bottom.

Spun Steel: I have several spun steel Chinese woks and stir-fry pans which I use all the time. They are sturdy, long-lasting, and inexpensive, but need to be cared for like cast iron (seasoned, dried thoroughly before storing).

Nonstick: Manufacturers are now producing safe non-stick cookware that is PTFE/PFOA-free. Besides safety, slickness of the nonstick surface, good size and heft but comfortable maneuverability, and performance holding up under daily kitchen abuse are the other criteria for judging new non-stick cookware. Every year improvements are made so that this type of cookware performs better and lasts longer than the first generation of "green nonstick" pots and pans. GreenPan™ is one well-reviewed brand that has improved over the last few years, but read up-to-date reviews and articles from magazines such as *Cooks' Illustrated* and *Consumer Reports* to keep up with improvements and new trends from other manufacturers.

Steaming Apparatus

You can use collapsible metal steamers, Chinese aluminum or bamboo steaming baskets. If using Chinese baskets, line them with baking parchment. Alternatively, place the food on dinner plates lined with baking parchment. The plate(s) can be balanced on two chopsticks placed across the inside of a wok or stir-fry pan (or 4 chopsticks, "tic-tac-toe" style). (You'll have to steam one plate at a time, unless you have multiple woks.) Cover with the domed wok lid or a large skillet lid while steaming.

You can also improvise a steamer using a large pot with a tight lid. An electric skillet with a domed lid also makes a good steamer. The lid should be 1 to 2 inches above the food so that the steam can circulate around the food. To hold the food above the water in a pot or electric skillet, use large canning jar rings, small cans with the ends removed, or scrunched-up aluminum foil. The food should be supported at least 1 inch above the simmering water.

Recipe Icons

As an added help to people that may be sensitive to gluten or soy, the recipes include icons indicating when a recipes is free of ingredients containing soy or gluten. I've also included an icon to indicate when a recipes takes less than 30 minutes to make so that you can quickly assess recipes suitable for a quick meal when there's little time to cook. In the interest of making these recipes accessible to as many people as possible, you will find that most of the recipes include one or more of the following icons. Here's the key for their meanings:

> **GF = Gluten-Free**
> **GFO = Gluten-Free Option**
> **SF = Soy-Free**
> **SFO = Soy-Free Option**
> **<30 = Recipe can be made in 30 minutes or less**

Some recipes can be made SF simply by using my Soy-Free Sauce (page 12) instead of soy sauce, or using SF yogurt or sour cream (page 20). Such recipes have the icon SFO, for "soy-free option."

Some recipes can be made gluten-free by using GF bread, pasta, matzoh meal, or bread crumbs. (GF bread, pasta, matzoh meal, and breadcrumbs are easily available commercially.) Such recipes have the icon GFO, for "gluten-free option."

Other recipes contain both a soy-free or gluten-free option from which to choose (in a few recipes it will only be possible to be one or the other!). Recipes that fit into these categories will have an icon to indicate that it is SFO and/or GFO.

How Low Is Low-Fat?

Low-fat icons are not included for the recipes in this book for the simple reason that there are varying opinions on what constitutes a "low-fat" recipe. Most diet experts consider 30 percent of calories as fat in the daily diet ideal, so I consider any recipe containing under 30 percent fat to be "low-fat," but others would not agree that a recipe with 29 percent calories from fat is "low-fat." But it's more complicated than that, and I think it's more helpful to think in terms of fat grams per serving than percentages.

For instance, tofu is often cited as a high-fat food because 50 percent of its calories are from fat. But the total amount of calories in tofu is very low, much lower than equivalent amounts of avocado or nuts, for instance. A serving of tofu is about 80 calories – that would be about 6 ounces silken tofu, 4 ounces medium-firm tofu, 3 ounces firm tofu, or 2 ounces extra-firm tofu. When I use 8 ounces of medium-firm tofu in place of oil and eggs in a muffin recipe for 12 muffins, each muffin contains only 1 gram of fat. A traditional "low-fat" recipe with 1 large egg and 1/4 cup oil (not counting any nuts) would result in muffins containing about 5 grams of fat per muffin.

You will notice in my recipes that I talk quite a bit about the amount of fat used or not used in the recipes, and why and how I make decisions about the amount I use. I don't subscribe to a drastically low-fat vegan lifestyle, but I also do not believe that vegan recipes should just be vegan versions or variations of traditional high-fat recipes, with the same amount of of oil, or vegan margarine substituted for the butter. I want the same pleasure quotient from a vegan recipe as a non-vegan one, but I will rework it as much as I can to cut the fat down, to use healthier fats, to use healthier flours, and so on. I can't always achieve this, but it's my goal.

Umami: The (Vegan) Cook's Secret Weapon

Only recently has the West learned about *umami*, the "fifth flavor," which is known in China as *xian*. While we are well familiar with the first four flavors (sweet, salty, sour, and bitter), our tongues can also detect this mysterious fifth flavor through special receptors in our taste buds. With the help of our sense of smell, we sense these flavors in combination with each other. Moreover, we have more than 300 receptor genes that collectively detect every possible flavor known to humankind.

The term umami was first brought to public attention outside of Japan by the scientist Kikunae Ikeda of the Tokyo Imperial University in 1908. In fact, Dr Ikeda coined the term by combining two distinct words: *umai*, which means "delicious" and *mi* which means "essence." He meant it to be a temporary name, but it stuck. The Chinese term xian, on the other hand, goes back to a 3,000-year-old Chinese book called *The Yellow Emperor's Book of Internal Medicine* – thus it is sometimes also called the "forgotten flavor." Although physiologists have long known the chemical compounds that provide its taste, only recently (in this decade) have they discovered the human tongue's receptors for umami. Particular amino acids (the umami "triggers") and nucleotides (the umami "intensifiers"), produced in foods when enzymes, through cooking or fermentation, break down their proteins and stimulate these receptors, which then message our brain to register the deliciously savory taste of

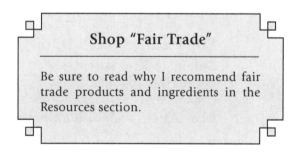

Shop "Fair Trade"

Be sure to read why I recommend fair trade products and ingredients in the Resources section.

umami. In his article "Umami: Taste Receptor, Tactile Sensation and Flavor Intensifier," Matthew Citriglia writes, "Umami is a taste that is stimulated by amino acids and nucleotides. It is a savory, mouth-filling, brothy, flavor intensifier that you experience regularly but may have never identified. This is why I think of it as a three-dimensional taste."

There are now exciting studies showing that umami-tasting compounds have magnifying effects on one another and that combining two umami compounds produces eight times more flavor than you would get from a single umami compound alone! A flavor ex-

(Continued on page 28)

Special Menus

Here are several special menus for a variety of occasions made up from recipes in this book. From a casual summer picnic to a Thanksgiving dinner, let these menus serve as a jumping off point to create your own special menus for all occasions.

A Spring Brunch

Spinach-Filled Soufflé Roulade, *page 43*
Hot German Potato Salad, *page 81*
Fresh Fruit
Hamantaschen, *page 231*

Elegant Spring Celebration Dinner

Pastry-Wrapped Russian Loaf, *page 130*
Hasselback Potatoes, *page 160*
Roasted Asparagus, *page 35*
Lemon-Strawberry Tiramísu, *page 203*

Mother's Day Brunch

Roasted Asparagus Crespelle with Besciamella, *page 35*
Apulian Focaccia, *page 218*
Italian Chocolate-Hazelnut Spread, *page 65*
Italian Baked Fruit-Stuffed Peaches, *page 207*

Father's Day "Steak Dinner"

Seitan Steak au Poivre, *page 137*
Oven-Fries, *page 100*
Green Salad
Chocolate-Hazelnut Praline Lava Cakes, *page 184*

Summer Picnic

Potato Fougasse, *page 220*
Vegan Boursin-Style Spread, *page 55*
Bell Pepper and Mushroom Quiche, *page 47*
Balinese-Inspired Spicy Green Bean Salad, *page 83*
ANZAC Biscuits, *page 167*
Chocolate-Orange Sorbetto, *page 207*

Latin-American-Style Barbecue

Vegan Peruvian Kebabs, *page 138,* with Sweet Potato and Corn
Peruvian Tri-Color Potato Salad Terrine, *page 79*
"Drunken Beans," *page 111*
South American "Three Milks" Cake, *page 179*

A Thanksgiving Dinner to Remember

Moroccan Savory Celebration Pie, *page 127*
Sicilian Winter Squash with Mint and Garlic, *page 162*
Green Salad
Pecan Pie, *page 172*

Christmas Morning Brunch

Creole Grits and Grillades, *page 50*
Clementines
South American-Style Hot Chocolate, *page 234*
Lemon-Ginger Pistachio Biscotti, *page 166*

Vegan Christmas Dinner

Velvety Brussels Sprout Crema, *page 73*
Seitan Wellington, page 132, with Madeira Gravy, *page 135*
Sicilian-Style Mashed Potatoes with Orange, *page 157*
Cranberry Sauce
Roasted Root Vegetables
Scottish Sherry Trifle, *page 198*

Kwaanza Celebration Dinner

Curried Vegan Meatloaf, *page 126*
South African Yellow Rice, *page 156*
South African Mielie Bread, *page 215*
Roasted Sweet Potatoes with Moroccan Spices, *page 152*
North African Potato and Zucchini Salad, *page 82*
Ginger Treacle Tart, *page 175*

In addition to the information in this section, I hope that you will also take advantage of the many tips, additional recipes, variations, options, and intriguing food facts that you will find throughout the book.

plosion, as the Chinese say or, more scientifically, "synergizing umami."

Although difficult to describe in words, umami has variously been described as: savoriness, deliciousness, meatiness, tastiness, mouth satisfaction, the good taste of food, or broth-like. I particularly like the definition "essence of deliciousness."

"Umami can be described as intensity, what helps us determine whether we like something or not and carries a whole constellation of physical reactions," says Master Sommelier and Master of Wine Doug Frost. As *Seattle Post-Intelligencer* food writer Hsiao-Ching Chou wrote: "Explaining umami can get a bit convoluted. But, your taste buds understand, and that's what matters."

Which plant-based foods contain umami compounds? Fermented foods such as soy sauce, miso, balsamic vinegar, and wine (which, along with other alcoholic beverages, also has its own special flavor-enhancing qualities – but that's another story!); dried shiitake or matsutake mushrooms, sea vegetables, green tea, vegan bouillon, tomato juice, and other tomato products. Browning foods by sautéing, grilling, and caramelizing also produces umami compounds.

Mushrooms and fungi are a great source of synergizing umami. Yeasts, both active (including sourdough, a natural yeast) and non-active (nutritional yeast, yeast extract), being a sort of fungi, also contain umami compounds. They also act as synergizers. For instance, in a live yeast or sourdough starter, the enzymic action develops the umami in the gluten of wheat flour to "ripen" the dough and develop its flavor. This process is what turns a simple dough of only flour, water, yeast, and salt, when fermented properly, into a crusty delicacy such as artisanal French bread.

Umami elements can add a powerhouse of flavors in meatless dishes, where it supplies the robust element that meat or poultry often give non-vegan dishes. Try it yourself by using, for instance, deeply browned or caramelized onions in a vegan soup or stew. Or experience umani in Chinese dishes that employ mushrooms, soy sauce, and wine to lend an explosion of savoriness to staples, such as tofu, that are considered bland. Umami can help you take good meat-free cooking to the level of sublime. (For source references, see Resources.)

Recipe Nutritional Data

Those interested in the nutritional analysis data for the recipes in *World Vegan Feast* can find it on my blog listed in chapter order at this link: http://veganfeastkitchen.blogspot.com/p/world-vegan-feast-recipe-nutritional.html (or look for the tab "World Vegan Feast Recipe Nutritional Analysis.")

Brunch Around the World

Brunch is a compatible marriage of breakfast and lunch, usually eaten between 11 a.m. and 3 p.m. and generally on the weekend. In fact, Sunday brunch constitutes one of the busiest times of the week for many restaurants (the absolute busiest on Mother's Day, I am told).

Brunch evolved from a light Sunday midday meal for upper-class British carousers in the 1890s, to a fashionable weekend party or hotel meal for the wealthy and famous in the 1930s, into the egalitarian meal that we know and love today – a little break from the weekday routine or a fun way to socialize or celebrate during the day instead of late into the night.

Unfortunately, many brunch favorites are heavy on the meat, fat, and dairy (never mind the ubiquitous eggs). But there is absolutely no reason why brunch cannot be delicious and healthful and animal-free, as I hope these recipes (some of which I've developed from old favorites from my pre-vegan days) will prove. As a bonus, most of these recipes have components that can be made well ahead of time (as is indicated in the recipes), making the morning much easier for the cook.

For casual brunches, even last-minute ones, you can treat your guests to quick-and-easy, and anything-but-mundane, Korean Potato Pancakes *(Kamjajon)*, the South Indian Coconut Semolina Crepes *(Rava Dosas)*, or Spanish Potato Omelet with Romesco Sauce – meals they won't soon forget. And, on more formal occasions, no one wants to be chained to the stove while the guests are downing mimosas (or layered juice shots) outside in the sunshine!

With a little forethought, recipes such as Sweet Potato and Yukon Gold Latkes with Maple-Pecan Grilled Pears; Creole French Toast with Bananas, Pecans, and Hot Brown Sugar Sauce; and Chai-Spiced Crepes with Citrus Almond Ricotta Filling and Grilled Mangoes (to name only a few) will make a brunch party into a fuss-free celebration that you can enjoy as much as your guests.

The Brunch Recipes

Yeasted Oven Pancake with Apples

FINLAND

Serves 4   SFO

This is a "veganized" version of an old Finnish recipe, Pannu-Kakku. It's nicely golden and puffy and very rich-tasting, despite the absence of the traditional eggs and butter. I often double this recipe and make it in two pans at once. You can use cake pans or cast-iron skillets. It makes a special breakfast or brunch dish, but it can also be served as a dessert. Note: The egg replacers listed are the only ones that whip up sufficiently for this recipe.

- 3 TABLESPOONS WATER
- 3/4 TABLESPOON ENER-G EGG REPLACER POWDER OR OR-GRAN "NO EGG" (SEE PAGE 15)
- 2 TABLESPOONS WARM WATER
- 3/4 TEASPOON DRY ACTIVE BAKING YEAST (OR 1/2 TEASPOON INSTANT YEAST)
- 3/4 CUP WARM NONDAIRY MILK
- 1 TABLESPOON SUGAR
- 1/2 TEASPOON SALT
- 1 CUP UNBLEACHED WHITE FLOUR
- 1 TABLESPOON SUGAR
- 1/4 TEASPOON GROUND CINNAMON
- 1 TABLESPOON VEGAN MARGARINE
- 1 LARGE SWEET APPLE, SUCH AS BRAEBURN OR CORTLAND, CORED AND THINLY SLICED
- TOPPINGS: MAPLE SYRUP, CONFECTIONERS' SUGAR, AND/OR NONDAIRY WHIPPED TOPPING

1. Beat or whisk together in a bowl the 3 tablespoons water and egg replacer powder until very fluffy, using an immersion/stick blender, hand-held mix, or whisk.

2. In a bowl, combine the yeast and warm water, and set aside for a few minutes to dissolve. Add the nondairy milk, along with beaten egg replacer, sugar, and salt. Stir this mixture into the flour in a large bowl. Whisk until smooth. Cover and let rise in a warm spot for about 1 hour. Optionally, you can mix this batter the night be-fore and leave it overnight coverted tightly in the refrigerator. Take it out of the refrigerator 1 hour before baking.

3. When ready to bake, preheat the oven to 375°F. Oil an 8 or 9-inch round cake pan or cast iron skillet well, especially at the edges, or line the bottom of the pan with baking parchment cut to fit. Combine the 1 tablespoon sugar and the cinnamon and sprinkle onto the bottom of the pan or the parchment.

4. Arrange the apple slices in a decorative pat-tern over the cinnamon sugar in the pan. Dot the apples with the margarine. Pour the batter evenly over the apples (don't stir the batter down first). Bake the pancake for 35 minutes. Loosen the edges and the bottom carefully, then cover the pan with a serving plate and flip it over so that the apples are on top. Cut into four wedges and serve hot with your choice of toppings.

VARIATIONS

Depending on the season, you can substitute sliced peaches, pears, nectarines, or plums for the apples, or you can bake the pancake without the cinnamon sugar and fruit on the bottom and serve it with lemon juice and sugar, fruit com-pote, or fresh berries.

Korean Potato Pancakes

Kamjajon

KOREA

Serves 4   <30, SFO, GFO

If you like savory breakfast items, you'll love these spicy treats, called kamjajon in Korea. Chock-full of tasty vegetables and served with a spicy vinegar/sesame sauce, they make a great supper dish, as well.

Sauce:
- 1/4 CUP FINELY CHOPPED GREEN ONIONS
- 2 TABLESPOONS SOY SAUCE

2 TABLESPOONS DRY SHERRY OR CHINESE RICE WINE

2 TABLESPOONS RICE VINEGAR OR APPLE CIDER VINEGAR

1 TABLESPOON SUGAR

1 TABLESPOON DARK SESAME OIL

1 TABLESPOON TOASTED SESAME SEEDS

1 TEASPOON FINELY GRATED FRESH GINGER

1 PINCH CAYENNE PEPPER

Pancakes:

1/3 CUP CORNSTARCH

2 TABLESPOONS WATER

1 TABLESPOON NUTRITIONAL YEAST FLAKES

1/2 TEASPOON SALT

1/2 TEASPOON BAKING POWDER

2 OUNCES SMOKED, MARINATED OR BAKED TOFU OR SEITAN, CHOPPED

1 SMALL RED BELL PEPPER, FINELY CHOPPED

1 TABLESPOON MINCED FRESH OR PICKLED JALAPEÑO CHILES

4 LARGE FRESH SHIITAKE MUSHROOMS (STEMMED) OR CREMINI MUSHROOMS, FINELY CHOPPED

2 GREEN ONIONS, FINELY CHOPPED

2 CLOVES GARLIC, CRUSHED

1 POUND RUSSET POTATOES, SCRUBBED

1/2 TEASPOON FRESHLY GROUND BLACK PEPPER

2 TABLESPOONS VEGETABLE OIL

1. **Sauce:** Whisk together the sauce ingredients and set aside.

2. **Pancakes:** Whisk the cornstarch and water together in a medium bowl. Add the nutritional yeast, salt, baking powder, tofu, bell pepper, chiles, mushrooms, green onions, and garlic. Mix together well. Grate the potatoes right into the bowl, peel and all. Mix quickly, adding the pepper.

3. In a large nonstick skillet, heat 1/2 tablespoon of the oil over medium heat. Using 1/4 of the batter (about 1 cup, not packed), make 1 large pancake, smoothing it out into a round shape with the bottom of the measuring cup or the back of a large spoon. Cover and cook for 3 to 4 minutes, then flip the pancake over and cook 3 or 4 more minutes, uncovered or until crispy and golden brown. Remove from pan and repeat with the remaining batter and oil. Serve hot with the sauce on the side.

Sweet Potato and Yukon Gold Latkes with Grilled Pears

EUROPEAN JEWISH FUSION

Serves 4   GFO, SFO

These potato pancakes are a luscious combination of fall vegetables and fruits. This beautiful dish can be the centerpiece for an elegant brunch any time, but would be particularly good during Hanukkah. This recipe can be easily multiplied as needed. The pears can be cooked ahead of time and the pancakes can be shaped earlier, transferred to baking sheets (any size), covered with plastic wrap and refrigerated until just before cooking and serving.

Pears:

4 RIPE, FIRM PEARS, PEELED, CORED AND THINLY SLICED

4 TEASPOONS VEGAN MARGARINE, MELTED

2 TABLESPOONS PLUS 2 TEASPOONS MAPLE SYRUP

1/4 CUP LIGHTLY TOASTED CHOPPED PECANS

Latkes:

2 2/3 CUPS SHREDDED PEELED SWEET POTATO

2 2/3 CUPS SHREDDED SCRUBBED YUKON GOLD POTATO

1 ONION, SHREDDED

1/2 CUP WHOLE-WHEAT FLOUR (OR GLUTEN-FREE FLOUR MIX)

2 TEASPOONS BAKING POWDER

1 TEASPOON SALT

1/3 TEASPOON FRESHLY GRATED NUTMEG

FRESHLY GROUND BLACK PEPPER

3 TABLESPOONS VEGETABLE OIL, FOR FRYING

To Serve:

TOFU SOUR CREAM (COMMERCIAL OR PAGE 33) OR CASHEW SOUR CREAM (PAGE 33)

1. **Pears:** Preheat the broiler and place the rack on the top setting. You want the pears to be about 3 to 4 inches below the heat source. Transfer the sliced pears to a baking sheet (any size) and toss them with the melted margarine. Broil the pears until they start to brown around the edges. Stir gently and broil further, but don't burn them or make them too soggy.

2. Remove from the oven when they look appe-

tizingly "grilled" but still hold their shape, and transfer them gently to a shallow bowl. Drizzle with the maple syrup and add the pecans, folding gently. Set aside.

3. **Latkes:** Combine both the shredded sweet potatoes and potatoes in a large square of cheesecloth or cotton cloth, gather in the corners, and squeeze and twist them to remove as much of the liquid you can. (This is important!) Transfer the squeezed, shredded potatoes (both kinds) and the shredded onion to a large bowl.

4. In a smaller bowl, whisk together the flour, baking powder, salt, nutmeg, and pepper. Add this mixture to the potatoes and mix well. (This mixture is more solid than the traditional egg-y latke batter.)

5. Divide the potato mixture into 12 equal "balls." Press the balls down on a sheet of baking parchment on a work surface or on a 12 x 17-inch baking sheet, to make pancake shapes.

6. Heat the oil in a large skillet and carefully transfer the latkes to the skillet using a thin non-metal spatula-turner. Pan-fry the latkes in the hot oil over medium-high heat until golden and crispy on both sides.

7. Serve the latkes hot, topped with the pears, with sour cream on the side.

Cashew Sour Cream (or "Yogurt")

Makes 1 1/2 cups   GF, SF, <30

1/2 CUP RAW CASHEW PIECES
1 CUP WATER
1/4 TEASPOON SALT
1/4 CUP RICE, HEMP, OAT, OR ALMOND MILK
2 TO 3 TABLESPOONS FRESH LEMON JUICE

1. Blend the cashews, water, and salt in a blender for several minutes or until extremely smooth. Pour the mixture into a heavy saucepan and stir over medium-high heat until the mixture thickens considerably. Do not allow to burn.

Microwave Option Pour the mixture into a medium microwave-safe bowl and cook on 100% power (default setting) for 2 minutes or until quite thick.

2. Whisk in the lemon juice (2 tablespoons at first, then add the last tablespoon if you prefer more acidity) and the milk of your choice until smooth. Transfer the mixture to a covered container and chill. If it's too thick after chilling, whisk in a little water or more nondairy milk.

"Yogurt" Variation: Reduce the salt to a pinch and use water to thin the mixture to the consistency you want. Add a little more lemon juice if you want more acidity.

Tofu Sour Cream (or "Yogurt")

Makes 1 1/2 cups   GF, <30

1 (12.3-OUNCE) BOX EXTRA-FIRM SILKEN TOFU, DRAINED
    AND CRUMBLED
3 TABLESPOONS FRESH LEMON JUICE
1/2 TEASPOON SUGAR
1/4 TEASPOON SALT
1 TO 2 TABLESPOONS VEGETABLE OIL, OPTIONAL

Process all of the ingredients in a food processor or blender until extremely smooth. Keep in a covered container in the refrigerator for up to a week.

"YOGURT" VARIATION

1. Use 1/4 cup of lemon juice. If it seems too thick, thin with some water to make it the consistency you prefer.

2. For a rich-tasting version that I call "Bulgarian-Style," add 1 tablespoon tahini to the tofu "yogurt" (do not use oil in this case).

Creole French Toast with Hot Brown Sugar Sauce

NEW ORLEANS

Serves 4   SFO, GFO

Puffy, orange-scented, battered French bread topped with a hot brown sugar sauce, sautéed bananas, and pecans make a very special breakfast. Pain Perdu means "lost bread" in French and is a traditional Creole brunch dish from New Orleans. The egg-less batter in this recipe, after a good mixing in a blender, puffs up quite nicely, but also soaks into the thick bread so that the interior remains moist. I have added the intriguing option of orange flower water and citrus zest, as suggested in an old recipe from the 1901 Picayune's Creole Cook Book.

Pain Perdu is usually served with just a sifting of confectioners' sugar, but I have seen recipes suggesting a topping of fruit or cane syrup. It's hard to come by up my way, so I make a brown sugar sauce instead. For this special recipe, I have used bananas and pecans, but you could use other ingredients such as grilled fresh pineapple and toasted large flake coconut. For the nondairy milk, I like to use half soy and half almond in this recipe.

1 1/3 CUPS NONDAIRY MILK

2/3 CUP PLUS 4 TEASPOONS ORANGE JUICE, DIVIDED

3 TABLESPOONS ENER-G EGG REPLACER POWDER OR OR-GRAN "NO EGG" (SEE PAGE 15)

3 TABLESPOONS ORANGE FLOWER WATER, OPTIONAL

4 TEASPOONS GOLDEN FLAX SEEDS

4 TEASPOONS SUGAR

GRATED ZEST OF 1 LARGE OR 2 SMALL ORGANIC ORANGES

2/3 TEASPOON PURE VANILLA EXTRACT

1/3 TEASPOON SALT

2 TO 3 GRINDS FRESHLY GRATED NUTMEG

2 PINCHES TURMERIC

1 BAGUETTE, CUT DIAGONALLY INTO 12 TO 16 (1 1/4-INCH-THICK) SLICES

2/3 CUP BROWN SUGAR

1/3 CUP PLUS 2 TABLESPOONS WATER, DIVIDED

3 RIPE, FIRM BANANAS

4 TEASPOONS ORANGE JUICE

6 TEASPOONS VEGAN MARGARINE, DIVIDED

1/2 CUP PECAN HALVES

2 TEASPOONS RUM, BOURBON, OR BRANDY, OPTIONAL

The Difference Between Yams and Sweet Potatoes

Contrary to the signs in many grocery stores, yams and sweet potatoes are unrelated vegetables, though in both cases you're eating the root of a tropical vine. Sweet potatoes, Ipomoea batatas ("batata" is the original Taino name that morphed into our word "potato"), are the fruit of an American plant of the morning glory family. According to Fun Science Facts from the Library of Congress: "The skin color can range from white to yellow, red, purple, or brown. The flesh also ranges in color from white to yellow orange or orange-red. Sweet potato varieties are classified as either 'firm' or 'soft'. When cooked, those in the 'firm' category remain firm, while 'soft' varieties become soft and moist. It is the 'soft' varieties that are often labeled as yams in the United States."

Yams are of the genus *Dioscorea* and are rarely seen in North America. They are a staple in tropical regions and can grow up to seven feet in length. The name is thought to derive from the West African word nyami, "to eat." There are over 600 varieties of yams and 95 percent of these crops are grown in Africa. Compared to sweet potatoes, yams are starchier and drier.

Today the U.S. Department of Agriculture requires labels with the term "yam" to be accompanied by the term "sweet potato." Unless you specifically search for yams, which are usually found in an international market, you are probably eating sweet potatoes.

2 TEASPOONS CORNSTARCH

CONFECTIONERS' SUGAR, FOR GARNISH

1. In a blender, combine the nondairy milk, the 2/3 cup orange juice, egg replacement powder, flax seeds, sugar, orange zest, vanilla, salt, nutmeg, and turmeric. Blend until smooth and frothy, about 1 minute in a Vitamix or a bit longer in a regular blender. Pour the batter into a 9 x 13-inch baking pan, or use two 8- to 10-inch square baking pans or any shallow receptacle that will accommodate all the bread slices side-by-side and close together. Add the bread slices and soak for about 30 minutes, turning a couple of times and making sure that all surfaces come into contact with the batter.

2. While the bread soaks, combine the brown sugar and water in a medium saucepan. Bring to a boil, then reduce heat to medium and cook for 5 minutes, uncovered. In a small bowl, combine the 2 tablespoons water, the rum, if using, and the cornstarch, and blend well; whisk into the sugar mixture. Stir and cook until slightly thickened. Remove from the heat and set aside.

3. Peel and slice the bananas into 1/4-inch-thick rounds and place in a bowl. Add the orange juice and toss to coat to prevent browning. Set aside.

4. Melt 2 teaspoons of the margarine in a medium skillet. Add the pecans and stir-fry just until slightly toasted. Remove the pecans to a bowl, leaving some of the margarine in the pan. Add the bananas and gently sauté until they have softened a bit. Set aside.

5. Preheat the oven to 300°F. Heat a large non-stick skillet over high heat, along with 2 teaspoons of the margarine. Tilt the pan to spread the melted margarine over the bottom of the pan. Add half of the soaked bread and lower the heat to medium-high. Cover the pan while they cook. When the bottoms of the slices are golden brown, carefully loosen them from the pan using a thin non-metal spatula-turner and turn them over.

6. Cook, uncovered, until the second side is golden brown. Loosen the slices again, carefully. Repeat with the last batch of soaked bread and the remaining margarine. Keep the first batch warm in the oven while you cook the second batch.

7. Divide the toast among 4 heated plates. Sift a little confectioners' sugar over them. Drizzle with some of the brown sugar sauce and top each serving with some of the bananas and a few pecans. Serve immediately.

Tips: All stoves heat differently. You'll have to adjust yours so that the toast doesn't brown too quickly. You want it well-heated in the center, not just seared on the outside.

If you're using the orange flower water option, it can be found in Middle Eastern, Indian, and Greek grocery stores; in some gourmet stores; as well as online.

Roasted Asparagus Crespelle with Besciamella Sauce

ITALY

Serves 5 to 6   SFO, <30

These delicate vegan Italian crepes are rolled around sweet roasted asparagus spears and melty vegan cheese, bathed in a rich vegan sauce – comfort food, indeed! These delicious Italian-style vegan crepes make an easy, but elegant brunch or supper dish. My mother always appreciated them for a Mother's Day brunch. This is a great make-ahead dish for company. You need a knife and fork to eat these crepes, as the asparagus is not cut into pieces. You can make the crepes and the sauce a day or two ahead of time and quickly cook the asparagus just before rolling the crepes. You can assemble the crepes well before the meal, and they can be popped into the oven for 10 to 20 minutes before serving.

2 POUNDS FRESH ASPARAGUS, TOUGH ENDS REMOVED

2 TABLESPOONS OLIVE OIL

COARSE SEA SALT OR KOSHER SALT
15 TO 16 EASY VEGAN CRESPELLE, COOKED (PAGE 36)
2 CUPS SHREDDED VEGAN WHITE CHEESE
SALT AND FRESHLY GROUND BLACK PEPPER
BESCIAMELLA SAUCE (PAGE 37)

1. Preheat the oven to 425°F. Toss the asparagus gently with the olive oil, using your hands, so that they are evenly coated. Distribute the asparagus spears in one layer in a 12 x 17-inch baking sheet or in two 9 x 13-inch baking sheets. Sprinkle the asparagus lightly with salt. Roast for about 15 minutes or until tender-crisp and starting to brown a little. Remove from the oven. Leave the oven temperature at 425°F.

2. To assemble the crepes, divide the roasted asparagus evenly to fill 15 crepes. Place one portion of asparagus almost in the middle of each crepe and sprinkle with about 2 tablespoons of the vegan cheese. Roll the crepe up neatly but not tightly around the asparagus. Carefully transfer the filled crepes to an 8 x 12-inch baking pan, oiled or lined with baking parchment, in one layer, seam-side-down. Use an attractive ceramic or glass 8 x 12-inch baking dish if you plan to serve the dish at the table. Pour the sauce over the crepes, covering evenly.

3. Bake for 10 minutes (15 to 20 minutes if the filled crepes have been refrigerated), uncovered. The sauce should be bubbly and starting to turn a little golden on top. Serve immediately.

Tip: Bend each stalk and the asparagus will naturally snap at the point where it becomes tough.

Variation: I think asparagus is most elegant in this recipe and needs little seasoning, but you can use other vegetables, such as cooked broccoli, if you prefer. Another option would be to spread some sautéed fresh mushrooms over the asparagus.

Easy Vegan Crespelle

Makes 16 crepes   <30

These vegan crepes have that flexible "egg-y" texture of traditional crepes, which makes them easy to handle. You can make them ahead and refrigerate them for several days or freeze them for several weeks.

2 1/4 CUPS NONDAIRY MILK
1 1/2 CUPS UNBLEACHED WHITE FLOUR OR WHOLE WHEAT
    PASTRY FLOUR
3/4 CUP (6 OUNCES) FIRM REGULAR TOFU OR EXTRA-FIRM
    SILKEN TOFU, DRAINED AND CRUMBLED
1/3 CUP SOY FLOUR OR CHICKPEA FLOUR (BESAN)
1 1/2 TABLESPOONS SUGAR
3/4 TEASPOON SALT
3/4 TEASPOON BAKING POWDER
1/8 TEASPOON NUTMEG
1 LARGE PINCH TURMERIC

1. Process all ingredients in a blender until very smooth. You do not need to "rest" the batter before cooking, as you do with egg crepe batter.

2. Heat an 8-inch skillet over medium-high heat and wipe it lightly with oil before making each crepe. Use 3 tablespoons of batter per crepe (stirring the batter before you make each crepe), rolling and tilting the pan until it evenly covers the bottom. Cook for a few seconds or until the top looks dry. Carefully loosen the crepe with a thin non-metal spatula-turner and flip it over. After a few seconds the other side should be dry. Serve immediately with your favorite topping or filling.

3. For filling later, fold each crepe, as it comes from the pan, into quarters or roll like a jelly roll or leave them flat (depending upon how you are going to fill and/or roll or stack them) and transfer them to a large platter or baking sheet. Cover them with a clean kitchen towel.

4. To store for future use, transfer the cooled crepes to a zip-top bag or rigid container (with cut-to-fit pieces of baking parchment in between each crepe) and refrigerate for up to 3 days or

freeze them for use in up to three weeks. Frozen crepes should be thawed thoroughly before filling.

VARIATIONS

Masa Crepes: Instead of 1 1/2 cups white unbleached flour or whole-wheat pastry flour, use 3/4 cup unbleached white flour and 3/4 cup masa harina (corn flour for tortillas). These crepes are more fragile than the original recipe, due to the low gluten content of the masa, so it is advisable to use the unbleached white flour instead of whole-wheat pastry flour. If, however, you prefer to use whole-wheat pastry flour, remember that it is difficult to flip these crepes, so when cooking them, cover the pan and cook for a few seconds or until the top looks dry. Do not turn the crepe over. Carefully loosen the crepe with a very thin non-metal spatula-turner and remove from the pan. Stack the cooked crepes on a plate and cover them with a clean napkin.

Chai-Spiced Crepes: If you like, use a commercial coconut milk beverage (such as So Delicious by Turtle Mountain) for the milk. Add to the batter:

1 TEASPOON GROUND GINGER
3/4 TEASPOON GROUND CARDAMOM
1/2 TEASPOON FRESHLY GROUND BLACK PEPPER
1/2 TEASPOON GROUND ANISE
1/2 TEASPOON GROUND CINNAMON
1/4 TEASPOON GROUND CLOVES

Besciamella Sauce

(Bechamél or White Sauce)

Makes 2 cups   GFO, SFO, <30

This rich-tasting sauce is actually quite low in fat. It can be used as an all-purpose white sauce in all of your cooking, as a topping for many Greek dishes, such as vegan moussaka, and even as a substitute for melted cheese on many casseroles. In Italy, this type of sauce is used on lasagne rather than the heavy melted cheeses in American-style lasagne. The tofu

(or cashews) and vegetable broth powder add rich flavor without much fat.

1 CUP NONDAIRY MILK
1/2 CUP (4 OUNCES) EXTRA-FIRM SILKEN TOFU, DRAINED
    AND CRUMBLED
1/2 CUP WATER
1 TEASPOON VEGETABLE BROTH POWDER OR PASTE (SEE
    PAGE 2)
1/2 TEASPOON SALT
2 TABLESPOONS VEGAN MARGARINE OR OLIVE OIL
1 1/2 TABLESPOONS TO 1/4 CUP UNBLEACHED WHITE FLOUR
    (DEPENDING ON THICKNESS DESIRED)
1 LARGE PINCH NUTMEG
FRESHLY GROUND BLACK PEPPER

1. In a blender, combine the nondairy milk, tofu, water, vegetable broth powder, and salt, and blend until very smooth. Set aside, still in the blender jar.

2. Melt the margarine in a medium, heavy saucepan and whisk in the flour. Whisk it over medium-high heat for a few minutes, but remove from heat before it starts to change color (you want a white roux). Scrape this into the blended mixture and blend for a few seconds, then pour the mixture back into the same pot. Stir or whisk over medium-high heat until it thickens and boils, then simmer on low heat for a few minutes, until thickened to your liking. Whisk in the nutmeg and pepper, to taste. This sauce can be refrigerated for several days in a covered container and gently reheated.

MICROWAVE OPTION

Melt the margarine in a large microwave-safe bowl or 1-quart Pyrex® measuring pitcher on 100% (default setting) power for about 45 seconds. Whisk in the flour and microwave as before for 2 minutes. Scrape this roux into the blended mixture in the blender container. Whiz briefly and pour it back into the bowl or pitcher. (Alternatively, pour the blended mixture into the bowl or pitcher in which the roux was cooked and mix with an immersion/stick blender until smooth.) Microwave the final mixture on 100% power for 2 minutes. Whisk the mixture briefly. Repeat twice. Whisk in the nutmeg and pepper.

VARIATIONS

Low-Fat: Omit the margarine or oil and simply blend the flour with the blended ingredients before cooking as directed. You can use reduced-fat tofu and reduced-fat soy milk, if you wish.

Soy-Free Option: Omit the tofu and use instead 1/4 cup more soy-free nondairy milk (use 1 1/4 in total). Add 1/4 cup raw cashew pieces. Since the cashews have a thickening effect, you'll need less flour, so use 1 to 2 1/2 tablespoons of flour, depending on the thickness you want. Use soy-free vegan margarine or olive oil.

Wheat-Free Option: Omit the first cooking step and add the melted margarine or olive oil (if using) directly to the blended mixture, along with 1 tablespoon to 1/4 cup white rice flour (or mochiko flour) instead of wheat flour. Tip: 1/4 cup of rice flour makes a very thick sauce.

Tip: Sauces made with mochiko flour (sweet/glutinous white rice flour) are excellent for freezing because the sauce will not separate when thawed.

Masa Crepes with Greens and Black Bean and Corn Salsa

SOUTHWEST AMERICAN FUSION

Serves 5

Delicate corn crepes stuffed with spiced-up, cheesy garden greens and topped with luscious low-fat "guacamole" and black bean-and-corn salsa makes a mighty fine brunch for a special occasion! I developed this south of the border-style fusion brunch entree to use up some garden greens, but I had no tortillas in the house and not enough masa harina to make them. The masa crepes made an elegant

---

> ### French or Italian?
>
> Crespelles and besciamella are well-loved in Italian cuisine – in fact Catherine de Medici's retinue of Italian cooks taught their French counterparts to move beyond heavy medieval spicing to the lighter Italian cooking, including delicate sauces, of which besciamella was no doubt one. We simply recognize these foods by their French names, crepes and bechamél, rather than by their Italian names.

substitute for the tortillas I had in mind. You can use regular guacamole, if you prefer.

Have ready:
10 MASA CREPES, COOKED (VARIATION OF EASY VEGAN CRESPELLE, PAGE 36)
1 RECIPE LOW-FAT VEGGIE "GUACAMOLE" (PAGE 39)
1 1/4 CUPS SHREDDED VEGAN CHEDDAR-STYLE CHEESE
Greens for Filling:
1 TABLESPOON OLIVE OIL
4 CLOVES GARLIC, CHOPPED
1/2 TEASPOON RED PEPPER FLAKES
8 CUPS THINLY SLICED CHARD, KALE, OR OTHER FRESH GREENS, TOUGH STEMS REMOVED
SALT AND FRESHLY GROUND BLACK PEPPER
Salsa:
1 1/2 CUPS COOKED OR CANNED BLACK BEANS, RINSED AND DRAINED
1 CUP CANNED OR THAWED, FROZEN SWEET CORN KERNELS, RINSED AND DRAINED
1/2 CUP CHUNKY NO-SUGAR HOT TOMATO SALSA
1/4 CUP CHOPPED CILANTRO OR FLAT-LEAF PARSLEY

1. In a large skillet, heat the oil along with the garlic and red pepper flakes. When the garlic starts to turn golden, add several handfuls of the greens, salt them lightly and stir over high heat until they wilt. Repeat this procedure until all of the greens are just cooked through. Add

pepper to taste. Set aside.

2. Preheat the oven to 400°F. Spoon about 1/4 cup of the cooked greens down the center of each crepe. Top the greens with about 2 tablespoons of the vegan "cheddar" and roll up the crepe. Carefully transfer the filled crepes to an 8 x 12-inch baking pan, oiled or lined with baking parchment, in one layer, seam-side-down. Cover with foil and bake for 20 minutes or just until hot and slightly puffy.

3. While the crepes bake, combine the ingredients for the salsa in a bowl and adjust for taste, if needed.

4. To serve, top each serving of two crepes with some of the salsa and a dollop of the guacamole. Garnish with a sprinkle of cilantro and serve immediately.

Low-Fat Veggie "Guacamole"

MEXICO FUSION

Makes 2 cups   GF, SF, <30

I have played with this recipe for years, and this particular combination of vegetables, silken tofu, avocado, and salsa, is one we just can't get enough of. You'll need a food processor for this recipe.

5 OUNCES YOUNG GREEN BEANS, TRIMMED (OR FROZEN SMALL WHOLE GREEN BEANS, THAWED)

5 OUNCES FROZEN SHELLED BABY LIMA BEANS (DO NOT USE COOKED, DRIED LIMA BEANS)

1 SMALL RIPE HASS AVOCADO, PITTED, PEELED AND CUT INTO 1/2-INCH SLICES

1/2 CUP (4 OUNCES) EXTRA-FIRM SILKEN TOFU, DRAINED AND CRUMBLED

2 TO 3 TABLESPOONS FRESH LEMON OR LIME JUICE

2 CLOVES GARLIC, CRUSHED

1 TEASPOON SALT

1/2 TEASPOON GROUND CUMIN

1/4 CUP CHUNKY NO-SUGAR HOT TOMATO SALSA

1. Cook both types of beans in a medium saucepan in enough water to cover for about 5 minutes or until completely tender but not mushy.

2. Drain the beans well and transfer them to a food processor (not a blender), along with the avocado, tofu, lemon juice, garlic, salt, and cumin. Process the mixture until smooth, stopping the machine a couple of times to scrape the sides and bottom of the bowl.

3. Add the salsa and pulse the mixture just until it is all mixed in. Taste for seasoning (add more citrus juice or salsa to your taste, if you like). Transfer to a covered bowl and refrigerate.

What Is Masa Harina?

Masa harina is the special corn flour used to make tortillas. It is available in most supermarkets, in Latin American grocery stores, or online. Plain corn flour is not the same as masa corn flour. Masa has a different and very distinctive taste. Masa harina ("harina" means flour) is made from corn that is processed with lime (the mineral), which gives it a particular flavor and texture. It is used to make corn tortillas. Hominy corn is made in much the same way as masa harina, but the kernels are left whole or dried and cracked for hominy grits.

Chai-Spiced Crepes with Citrus-Almond Ricotta and Grilled Mangoes

NORTH AMERICA/INDIA FUSION

Serves 4   SFO

These delicate Indian-spiced crepes are well worth waiting for. This has been one of my most successful summer brunch dishes, but it also makes an excellent not-too-sweet dessert (in smaller portions). The crepes and the filling can be made several days ahead and refrigerated.

CITRUS ALMOND RICOTTA FILLING (FOLLOWS)
8 CHAI-SPICED CREPES, COOKED (PAGE 36)
2 RIPE MANGOES, PITTED, PEELED AND THINLY SLICED
1 TABLESPOON VEGAN MARGARINE, MELTED
2 TABLESPOONS MAPLE SYRUP OR 1 1/2 TABLESPOONS
    AGAVE NECTAR
1/2 TABLESPOON FRESH LEMON JUICE
TOASTED SHREDDED COCONUT OR SLIVERED ALMONDS

1. Preheat the oven to 400°F. Spoon 3 tablespoons of ricotta filling down the center of each crepe and roll up, not too tightly. Carefully transfer the filled crepes to an 8 x 12-inch baking pan, oiled or lined with baking parchment, in one layer, seam-side-down. Cover with foil and bake for 10 to15 minutes or just until hot and slightly puffy. Remove the crepes from the oven, leaving them covered and immediately switch the oven from Bake to Broil.

2. Toss the mangoes in a bowl with the melted margarine and transfer to a 12 x 17-inch baking sheet. Set the oven rack so that the mangoes are 3 to 4 inches below the broiler's heat source. Broil the mangoes until they are soft and slightly charred. Toss the mangoes, right on the baking sheet, with the maple syrup and lemon juice.

3. Top each serving of crepes with some of the mangoes and sprinkle with coconut or almonds. Serve immediately.

Citrus Almond Ricotta Filling

Makes 1 1/4 cups   GF, SF

1/2 CUP HOT WATER
1/4 CUP WHOLE BLANCHED RAW ALMONDS
1/2 CUP COLD WATER
2 TEASPOONS FRESH LEMON JUICE
2 TABLESPOONS CORNSTARCH
1/2 TABLESPOON VEGETABLE OIL
1/4 TEASPOON SALT
2 TABLESPOONS SUGAR
1 TABLESPOON LIME JUICE
GRATED ZEST OF 1 SMALL ORGANIC ORANGE OR BLOOD
    ORANGE
CHOPPED FRUIT OF THE ORANGE OR BLOOD ORANGE
GRATED ZEST OF 1 SMALL ORGANIC LEMON

1. Blend the hot water and almonds in a blender until very smooth and creamy. Be patient – it cannot be grainy. Add the cold water, the 2 teaspoons lemon juice, cornstarch, oil, and salt and blend again until very well mixed.

2. Pour the mixture into a medium heavy saucepan and stir constantly over medium-high heat until it thickens and comes to a boil. Turn the heat down to medium and cook 1 minute more, stirring. **Microwave Option:** Pour the blended mixture into a large microwave-safe bowl or pitcher. Microwave the mixture for 1 minute on 100% power (default setting). Whisk the mixture. Microwave as before for 1 minute more or until thickened.

3. Scrape the mixture into a container. Cover and chill. When it is chilled and firm, mash and then stir it with a fork. Mix in the sugar, lime juice, orange zest and fruit, and lemon zest. Refrigerate until you fill the crepes.

Coconut Semolina Crepes

Rava Dosa

SOUTH INDIA

Serves 4   SFO, <30

South Asian dosa are addictive Indian "crepes" usually made from a naturally fermented batter of ground, soaked legumes and grains. However, a semolina batter is also frequently used for quick or "instant" snacks. (Semolina is made from high-protein wheat, the type used for making pasta.) Some rava dosa are made very thin, with a lacy pattern; others are thick and spongy. My version is sort of midway between the two! They make a great addition to a South Asian-style brunch or by themselves as a quick breakfast or snack. Serve with savory and/or sweet chutneys. If semolina flour (rava) is unavailable, use dry Cream of Wheat as a substitute.

- 2 CUPS NONDAIRY MILK
- 1 CUP WATER
- 2 CUPS SEMOLINA FLOUR (RAVA)
- 1/2 CUP UNSWEETENED SHREDDED COCONUT
- 2 TEASPOONS FRESH LEMON JUICE
- 1 TEASPOON SALT
- 2 TABLESPOONS MINCED FRESH GREEN SEEDED HOT CHILES OR PICKLED JALAPEÑOS (OR TO TASTE), OPTIONAL

1. In a blender, combine all of the ingredients, except the optional chiles, and blend on high speed for 2 minutes. The batter should be similar to a regular crepe batter. If you want spicy dosas, stir the optional chiles into the batter.

2. Heat a large skillet or flat griddle, sprayed with oil from a pump sprayer, over high heat. (Traditionally, a cut onion is rubbed over the bottom of the oiled griddle, both to make the surface more nonstick and to flavor the dosa. This is an optional step.)

3. To form the dosa, pour about 1/3 cup of batter into the center of the hot skillet or griddle and spread the batter outwards in concentric cir-cles, with the bottom of the (metal or silicone) measuring cup or the bottom of a flat-bottomed spoon, until it makes a large, thin, round crepe. Make the dosa as thin as you can without making holes (a few little ones are fine).

4. Cook each dosa for a couple of minutes, then flip it over and cook for a few more seconds. The dosa should be slightly browned on the first side and lighter on the second side. Fold in half and serve hot.

Vegan Soufflé Omelet

FRANCE

Serves 6   GF

This is a fluffier vegan omelet than any other I have tried, and it's well-suited to a special breakfast or brunch get-together. Your guests will be impressed. I'm formatting this for six people because this is the size needed for the Soufflé Roulade recipe that comes next, but it can easily be made for four or two (see Variations). You can serve six people in a short time once the batter is ready, even with only one or two skillets, but extra skillets do help. The recipe onl seems long because I have been very specific about instructions so that it comes out the way it should.

Note: the egg replacers listed are the only brands that will whip up properly for this recipe. Among the filling choices for the omelet are: sautéed onions, sautéed mushrooms, your favorite cooked vegetables, shredded vegan cheese, and slivered vegan bacon or ham.

Important: Try to make the "egg whites" first as it takes at least 6 minutes to get it to the right fluffy consistency. Therefore, for economy of time, you should have it beating while you make the batter and assemble the filling.

Beaten "Egg Whites":
- 3/4 CUP WATER
- 3 TABLESPOONS ENER-G EGG REPLACER OR ORGRAN "NO EGG" NATURAL EGG REPLACER (SEE PAGE 15)

Batter:

**12 OUNCES (1 1/2 CUPS) MEDIUM FIRM TOFU OR 1
(12.3-OUNCE) BOX EXTRA-FIRM SILKEN TOFU, DRAINED
AND CRUMBLED**

3/4 CUP NONDAIRY MILK

3/4 CUP CORN FLOUR

1/2 CUP PLUS 1 TABLESPOON NUTRITIONAL YEAST FLAKES

**3 TABLESPOONS GOLDEN FLAX SEEDS, FINELY GROUND IN A
CLEAN, DRY COFFEE/SPICE MILL**

1 1/8 TEASPOONS SALT

1 1/8 TEASPOONS BAKING POWDER

1/8 TEASPOON TURMERIC

For cooking:

VEGAN MARGARINE

Filling of choice:

**SAUTÉED ONIONS, SAUTÉED MUSHROOMS, OTHER COOKED
VEGETABLES, SHREDDED VEGAN CHEESE, SLIVERED
VEGAN BACON OR HAM, ETC.**

1. **"Egg Whites":** Beat the water and egg replacer until a soft peak forms and stays, 6 to 10 minutes. Use a stand mixer, if possible. If using a hand-held electric mixer, beat the "egg whites" first, set them aside, make the batter and then add the "egg whites" to it. (I would not advise using an immersion/stick blender – this didn't work for me, even with the whipping attachment.)

2. **Batter:** Combine all of the batter ingredients in a food processor (first choice) or blender and blend until smooth. Scrape the batter into a large bowl.

3. Scoop the beaten "egg whites" over the batter and fold it in with a non-metal spatula-bowl scraper (using an over-and-under motion rather than a stirring motion), mixing just until you can't discern one mixture from another and the batter looks foamy. The batter will then start to foam up a bit.

4. Heat the skillet(s) over high heat and add 1/2 tablespoon vegan margarine for each omelet. When the margarine starts to sizzle a bit, swirl it around to coat the bottom, spread about one-sixth of the batter (3/4 cup) into the hot skillet.

Smooth it out with the back of a spoon to fit the pan.

5. Immediately turn the heat down to medium-low and cover the pan(s). Cook for about 2 1/2 minutes – the bottom should be getting crispy and golden. (If it is browning too fast, turn down the heat.) Carefully loosen the omelet with a thin non-metal spatula-turner and flip it over. Let the underside firm up for a minute, then flip it back over carefully. With the spatula-turner, cut the omelet in half down the center, but only partway through to facilitate folding it in half.

6. **Filling:** Add some filling to one half of the omelet (and freshly ground pepper, if desired – no salt will be needed), then fold the empty side gently over the filled one. Cover the pan and cook on low heat just long enough to melt the cheese, if using. Slide the omelet onto a heated plate and serve immediately or keep warm, lightly covered, in a 200°F oven for a short a time.

VARIATIONS

Ingredients for 4 servings (four 9-inch omelets):

Beaten "Egg Whites":

1/2 CUP WATER

**2 TABLESPOONS ENER-G EGG REPLACER OR ORGRAN "NO
EGG" NATURAL EGG REPLACER (SEE PAGE 15)**

Batter:

**8 OUNCES (1 CUP) MEDIUM FIRM TOFU OR EXTRA-FIRM
SILKEN TOFU, DRAINED AND CRUMBLED**

1/2 CUP NONDAIRY MILK

1/2 CUP CORN FLOUR

1/4 CUP PLUS 2 TABLESPOONS NUTRITIONAL YEAST FLAKES

**2 TABLESPOONS GOLDEN FLAX SEED, GROUND FINE IN A
CLEAN, DRY COFFEE/SPICE MILL**

3/4 TEASPOON SALT

3/4 TEASPOON BAKING POWDER

2 PINCHES TURMERIC

VEGAN MARGARINE, FOR COOKING

Ingredients for 2 servings (two 9-inch omelets):

Beaten "Egg Whites":

1/4 CUP WATER

1 TABLESPOON ENER-G EGG REPLACER OR ORGRAN "NO EGG" NATURAL EGG REPLACER (SEE PAGE 15)

Batter:

4 OUNCES (1/2 CUP) FIRM TOFU OR EXTRA-FIRM SILKEN, DRAINED AND CRUMBLED

1/4 CUP NONDAIRY MILK

1/4 CUP CORN FLOUR

3 TABLESPOONS NUTRITIONAL YEAST FLAKES

1 TABLESPOON GOLDEN FLAX SEEDS, GROUND FINE IN A CLEAN, DRY COFFEE/SPICE MILL

3/8 TEASPOON SALT

3/8 TEASPOON BAKING POWDER

1 PINCH TURMERIC

VEGAN MARGARINE

Spinach-Filled Soufflé Roulade

FRANCE/AMERICA FUSION

Serves 6   GFO

I used to love soufflé roulades (or French rolled omelets) with vegetable fillings and a blanket of creamy sauce in my pre-vegan days, and often served them for holiday brunches. They are so versatile and impressive. After developing my French Tofu Soufflé Omelet recipe, I decided to try the batter for a roulade, and it worked beautifully, topped with a creamy vegan white cheese sauce. This is my one of my favorite fillings, but you can use anything that tickles your fancy – give your culinary imagination free rein.

1 RECIPE CREAMY VEGAN WHITE CHEESE SAUCE (PAGE 44)

2 POUNDS FRESH SPINACH, WASHED, TRIMMED AND SPUN DRY

2 1/2 CUPS MINCED FRESH MUSHROOMS (ANY KIND)

1/4 CUP MINCED GREEN ONION

2 TABLESPOONS VEGAN MARGARINE

1 PINCH GROUND NUTMEG

SALT AND FRESHLY GROUND BLACK PEPPER

1 RECIPE (6 SERVINGS) VEGAN SOUFFLÉ OMELET (PAGE 41), UNCOOKED

2 TABLESPOONS MELTED VEGAN MARGARINE, FOR BRUSHING

1 TO 2 CUPS FINE DRY BREADCRUMBS

1. Prepare the white cheese sauce before proceeding with the rest of the recipe.

2. To make the filling (this can be made ahead of the baking time), cut the spinach into 1/8-inch strips.

3. Heat a large skillet or pot over high heat and spray it with cooking oil from a spray pump. Add the spinach and immediately stir it around with a wooden spoon. If the spinach is very dry and does not immediately begin to exude its juice, add a few sprinkles of water from your fingertips. As soon as the spinach is wilted, remove the pan from the heat. Transfer the spinach to a colander in the sink and let it drain and cool.

4. When the spinach is cool enough to handle, squeeze it with your hands (a handful at a time) until it is as dry as you can get it. Transfer the squeezed spinach to a large bowl and fluff it up with your fingers. Set aside.

5. Heat a medium skillet over high heat, adding the vegan margarine. Add the mushrooms, green onions, and salt to taste and stir-fry, watching carefully. The mushrooms will exude liquid, but keep them moving until the liquid is absorbed again. Add the mushroom mixture to the spinach. Stir in 2 cups of the Creamy Vegan White Cheese Sauce and the nutmeg and stir

well to distribute. (Reserve the remaining sauce to reheat and serve with the baked roulade.) Add salt and pepper to taste. Set aside to cool. Several hours before serving time, line a 10 x 15-inch jelly roll pan or rimmed baking sheet) with baking parchment lightly brushed with melted margarine. Sprinkle the pan lightly with breadcrumbs. Preheat the oven to 350°F.

6. Prepare the omelet batter. With a non-metal spatula-bowl scraper, immediately scrape the batter onto the prepared baking sheet and smooth it out evenly. Bake for 12 to15 minutes or until the top feels firm.

7. Let the baking sheet cool on a rack for a few minutes. Meanwhile, lightly brush a 12 x 16-inch piece of baking parchment with a little melted margarine and then dust it lightly with breadcrumbs. Make sure that the breadcrumbs stick to the margarine. Carefully loosen the sides of the roulade from the baking parchment it was baked on with a thin spatula, but do not remove from the pan. Place the bread crumb-dusted side of the second piece of parchment over the roulade, then place another 10 x 15-inch baking sheet (it doesn't have to have a rim) over that and carefully invert the pan.

8. Remove the baking sheet now on the top and carefully peel away the parchment that the roulade was cooked on. Loosely and carefully roll up the roulade in the new parchment paper, rolling it right up inside the roulade. Set aside to cool completely. This step will facilitate easy rolling when you fill the roulade. (Do not refrigerate or the roulade will crack when unrolled!)

9. About 30 minutes before serving time, preheat the oven to 350°F. Carefully unroll the cooled roulade on a 10 x 15-inch baking sheet lined with baking parchment cut to fit and spread the roulade with the cooled filling (you may not be able to use it all – leave about an inch of the roulade uncovered all the way around). Carefully roll it up again (don't fret if it cracks in a spot

or two) like a jelly roll, using the parchment as a guide, not rolling it up with the roulade this time. Rest the roulade on the baking sheet seam-side-down.

10. Spray the top of the roulade with oil from a pump sprayer and bake for about 15 minutes. Gently reheat the remaining cheese sauce. Cut the baked roulade carefully into 6 thick slices, using a sharp serrated knife. Present each serving surrounded by some of the cheese sauce.

Important Tip: The sauce and filling can be made a day ahead but the roulade must be made several hours before serving, because it must cool in the rolled up parchment, then be unrolled, filled, re-rolled, and heated just before serving.

Tip: The filling should be at room temperature when filling the roulade so, if you make it ahead and refrigerate it, let it come to room temperature.

Creamy Vegan White Cheese Sauce

Makes 4 cups   GF, <30

This nearly fat-free sauce is deceptively rich and creamy, and also excellent on steamed vegetables or as a topping for lasagne, cannelloni, or moussaka.

2 RUSSET POTATOES (ABOUT 8 OUNCES TOTAL), PEELED
    AND CUT INTO 1-INCH CHUNKS
1 ONION, CUT INTO 1/2-INCH DICE
2 CUPS WATER
12 OUNCES (1 1/2 CUPS) MEDIUM-FIRM TOFU OR 1
    (12.3-OUNCE) BOX EXTRA-FIRM SILKEN TOFU, DRAINED
    AND CRUMBLED
1/2 CUP NUTRITIONAL YEAST FLAKES
2 TEASPOONS SALT
1/2 TEASPOON GARLIC POWDER
1 TO 2 TABLESPOONS FRESH LEMON JUICE, OPTIONAL

Combine the potatoes, onion, and water in a medium saucepan. Cover and simmer for about

10 minutes or until the potato is tender. Transfer to a blender with the remaining ingredients. (Make sure that air can escape from the blender lid, covering the air-hole with a folded clean kitchen towel. This will eliminate the danger of hot exploding sauce.) Blend until very smooth. Serve immediately or refrigerate, covered, for up to a week. Reheat over gentle heat.

Spanish Potato Omelet
Tortilla de Patatas

SPAIN

Serves 4 to 6

This Spanish potato omelet may become a staple in your house, as it is in ours. The Romesco sauce is a tangy, nutty, tomato-ey surprise. A "tortilla" in Spain is an omelet, not a bread. It's a bit like an Italian frittata (baked omelet), and traditionally contains potato. It's a perfect choice for potluck meals and picnics because it can be eaten at room temperature. It's also open to many variations – for instance, you might want to add sliced roasted red bell peppers or cooked artichoke hearts. The leftovers are good cold and can be made into a delicious sandwich on crusty bread.

1 TABLESPOON OLIVE OIL
8 OUNCES (1 CUP) FIRM TOFU OR EXTRA-FIRM SILKEN TOFU, DRAINED AND CRUMBLED
1/4 CUP NONDAIRY MILK
1/4 CUP CHICKPEA FLOUR (BESAN)
3 TABLESPOONS UNBLEACHED WHITE FLOUR OR 2 TABLESPOONS BROWN RICE FLOUR
1 TABLESPOON DRY SHERRY, WHITE WINE OR WATER
2 TABLESPOONS TOFU SCRAMBLER MIX (FOLLOWS)
1/2 TEASPOON BAKING POWDER
1/4 TEASPOON SALT
9 SLICES VEGAN HAM OR BACON CUT INTO THIN SLIVERS
1 LARGE ONION, THINLY SLICED
3 TO 4 COOKED THIN-SKINNED POTATOES, PEELED AND SLICED 1/4-INCH THICK
FRESHLY GROUND BLACK PEPPER
ROMESCO SAUCE (PAGE 46)

1. Preheat the oven to 450°F. Add the olive oil to a 10-inch cast iron skillet or pie pan and place the pan in the oven while the oven heats up.

2. In a food processor, combine the tofu, nondairy milk, both flours, sherry, scrambler mix, baking powder, and salt and blend until very smooth. Scoop the batter into a medium bowl and stir in the vegan ham or bacon.

3. Remove the hot skillet from the oven. Add the onion, salt lightly, and toss to coat with the oil, spreading it out evenly. Return the skillet to the oven and bake for about 5 minutes, then transfer the onion to the batter and fold it in. Reduce the oven temperature to 350°F.

4. Distribute the sliced cooked potatoes evenly in the same hot skillet, brushed with a little more olive oil and spread the batter evenly over the potatoes and out to the edges of the pan. Grind black pepper over the top.

5. Bake the tortilla for 20 to 30 minutes or until the batter is set. Cool the pan on a rack for 10 minutes, then loosen the bottom of the omelet carefully with a thin spatula and cut it into 6 wedges. Serve warm with the Romesco sauce on the side.

Tofu Scrambler Mix

Makes 1 3/4 cups   GF, SF, <30

1 CUP NUTRITIONAL YEAST FLAKES
5 TABLESPOONS PLUS 1 TEASPOON ONION POWDER
4 TEASPOONS CURRY POWDER
4 TEASPOONS SALT
4 TEASPOONS TURMERIC
4 TEASPOONS GROUND CUMIN

1. Blend the ingredients in a dry blender until well mixed. Store the mix in a covered jar.

2. Use 1/2 tablespoon of the mix for each 4 ounces of firm tofu, drained and crumbled or 2 tablespoons of the mix for each pound of firm tofu. (Shake or stir the mix before measuring.)

Romesco Sauce

Makes about 1 1/2 cups   GF, SF, <30

There are many versions of this classic Spanish sauce, which is usually served with seafood, but we use my personal version on the Spanish potato omelet, to our delight.

2 TABLESPOONS OLIVE OIL
1/4 CUP CHOPPED ONION
3 CLOVES GARLIC, CHOPPED
1/4 CUP SLIVERED BLANCHED RAW ALMONDS
1 LARGE ROASTED RED BELL PEPPER FROM A JAR, SEEDED, RINSED, AND PATTED DRY
4 LARGE OIL-PACKED SUN-DRIED TOMATO HALVES, RINSED WITH HOT WATER AND PATTED DRY
5 TABLESPOONS WATER
2 TABLESPOONS DRY SHERRY
1 TABLESPOON DRY RED WINE
1 TABLESPOON RED WINE VINEGAR
1 TEASPOON VEGETABLE BROTH POWDER
1 PINCH CAYENNE PEPPER

Heat the oil in a small skillet and add the onion and garlic. Sauté over medium heat until the onion is wilted, then transfer to a food processor along with the remaining ingredients. Process the mixture until smooth. Taste for salt. Serve at room temperature.

Chickpea Flour Omelet

Gujarati Chilla

INDIA FUSION

Serves 5   GF, SF, <30

This versatile recipe is adapted from a traditional recipe from the Indian province of Gujarat, but it lends itself to a variety of seasonings. The plain "omelets" can be filled with grilled vegetables for a special brunch dish if you wish, but I provide options for making "omelets" in several styles. For instance, I made the Italian-style version and topped the "omelets" with some leftover homemade spaghetti sauce, *sautéed oyster mushrooms, and a sprinkle of Walnut Parm (page 15) – talk about fusion!*

Basic Chilla:
1 1/2 CUPS COLD WATER
1 1/2 CUPS CHICKPEA FLOUR (BESAN)
1 TABLESPOON SUGAR
1 TEASPOON SALT
1/2 TEASPOON TURMERIC
3/4 CUP CHOPPED FRESH OR CANNED TOMATOES, DRAINED OR ROASTED RED BELL PEPPERS
Optional Flavor Choices:
Indian: 2 TABLESPOONS CHOPPED FRESH, SEEDED HOT CHILES OR PICKLED JALAPEÑOS; 1/4 CUP CHOPPED CILANTRO
Mexican: 2 TABLESPOONS CHOPPED FRESH OR PICKLED JALAPEÑOS; 2 TEASPOONS DRY OREGANO, 1/2 TEASPOON GROUND CUMIN
Italian: 2 TABLESPOON CHOPPED FRESH BASIL OR 2 TEASPOON DRIED, 2 CLOVES GARLIC, MINCED

1. **Basic Chilla:** In a blender or food processor, or using a whisk or immersion blender, combine the water, chickpea flour, sugar, salt, and turmeric and blend until smooth. The batter should be a similar consistency as crepe batter. Transfer the batter to a medium bowl and add the tomatoes and optional flavor choice, if using, stirring to mix well.

2. Heat an 8-inch skillet over medium-high heat. Spray it with oil from a pump sprayer before cooking each chilla. Cook just as you would a crepe, using 1/4 cup batter for each one. Quickly pour in the batter and swirl it in the pan to make an approximately round, fairly thin 6-inch round. Use the back of a spoon to smooth out the mixture and make it round, if you wish. (The batter is thin, so I just swirl it like crepe batter.)

3. When the bottom is golden-brown and there are little holes in the batter on top, carefully loosen it with a thin spatula-turner and turn it over. When the top is just dry, but not browned, remove the chilla from the pan, transfer it to a platter, and cover it with a clean kitchen towel.

Continue until all of the batter is used up. Stack the cooked chilla on top of each other and keep them covered with the towel.

4. You can roll them up, fold them in half, or leave them flat. They should be served hot. All varieties go well with potatoes.

SERVING SUGGESTIONS

Serve Indian-flavored omelets with plain soy or tofu yogurt or tofu sour cream (soy-free options, page 33) and any kind of chutney you prefer. They can also be filled or rolled around any sort of curried vegetables or legumes, such as dal.
Serve Mexican-style omelets with tofu or cashew sour cream (page 33) and your favorite salsa.
Serve Italian-style omelets with Vegan Besciamella (page 37) or Creamy Vegan White Cheese Sauce (page 44) or a marinara (simple tomato) sauce and/or shredded vegan white cheese.

Bell Pepper and Mushroom Quiche

FRANCE/NORTH AMERICA FUSION

Serves 6   GFO

This easy-to-make quiche is as smooth and rich-tasting as the egg-y version. One thing that's important to remember, however, is that this quiche must be made several hours before serving, because it needs thorough cooling in order to firm up for proper slicing. After it has cooled and set, it can be eaten cold, at room temperature, or gently reheated.

1/2 TABLESPOON OLIVE OIL
1/2 TABLESPOON DARK SESAME OIL
1/2 LARGE RED BELL PEPPER, THINLY SLICED
1/2 LARGE GREEN BELL PEPPER, THINLY SLICED
2 CUPS SLICED MUSHROOMS, ANY KIND
1 (9-INCH) PIE CRUST, UNBAKED (PAGE 172 OR GLUTEN-FREE)
1/4 CUP WALNUT PARM (PAGE 15)
1 3/4 CUPS NONDAIRY MILK
1/2 CUP (4 OUNCES) EXTRA-FIRM SILKEN TOFU, DRAINED AND CRUMBLED
1 TEASPOON VEGETABLE BROTH POWDER OR PASTE (PAGE 2)

Omelet Variations

There are no specific measurements for these variations – just wing it!

- **Japanese-Style Chickpea Flour Omelets:** Use the basic batter with no flavor options (and no tomatoes). This can be used instead of thin Japanese egg omelets to cut into strips for sushi.

- **Swiss-Style Omelets:** Use the basic batter with no flavor options (and no tomatoes). Fill the omelets with cooked, diced potatoes and onions, browned and crisped and top with a Creamy Vegan White Cheese Sauce (page 44) or Bésciamella Sauce (page 37), minced parsley, salt, pepper and soy bacon bits (or chopped vegan bacon or ham).

- **Spanish Omelets:** Use the basic batter with no flavor options (and no tomatoes). Fill with sautéed chopped onions, bell peppers, tomatoes and garlic. You can also add mushrooms to the sauté, if you like.

- **Kentucky Omelets** (these were a favorite of ours in pre-vegan days): Use the basic batter with no flavor options (and no tomatoes). Fill with sautéed onions, chopped green peppers and corn kernels, with a sprinkle soy bacon bits (or chopped vegan bacon or ham).

2 TABLESPOONS CORNSTARCH

1/2 TEASPOON AGAR POWDER

1/2 TEASPOON SALT

1 PINCH TURMERIC

1 PINCH NUTMEG

FRESHLY GROUND BLACK PEPPER

1 TABLESPOON SOY BACON BITS OR 1/4 CUP CHOPPED
VEGAN HAM OR BACON

1 TABLESPOON CHOPPED FRESH BASIL OR 1 TEASPOON
DRIED

SMOKED SWEET PAPRIKA (PIMENTÓN)

1. Heat the oils in a large skillet over medium-high heat. Add the bell peppers and mushrooms, salt lightly and stir-fry until softened. The vegetables will exude liquid, but keep them moving until the liquid is absorbed again. When they barely start to brown, spread them on a large platter or baking sheet and cool them to room temperature. (I speed this up by putting them in the freezer.)

2. Preheat oven to 425°F. Prebake the crust (pricked all over the inside with the tines of a fork) for 5 minutes. Remove from oven to a rack. Leave the oven on.

3. In a blender, combine the walnut parm, non-dairy milk, tofu, broth powder, cornstarch, agar, salt, turmeric, nutmeg, and pepper to taste. Process until smooth and well blended.

4. Spread the cooled vegetables over the bottom of the cooled pie crust and sprinkle evenly with the soy bacon bits and basil. Pour the blended mixture evenly over the vegetables in the crust. Sprinkle the top of the quiche evenly with a little smoked sweet paprika.

5. Bake for 30 minutes. If the edges of the crust start to brown too early, cover them with strips of aluminum foil. The quiche filling will have puffed up a bit, browned slightly on top, and be visibly bubbling. It may seem too liquid to you, but, it will set as it cools.

Important Tip: The quiche needs to be cooled at least to room temperature to firm up. Because this quiche contains agar, it can be reheated gently without getting runny, but we like it cold or at room temperature. I speed up the cooling by placing the quiche, right out of the oven, on a rack in the refrigerator. It should cool nicely within 2 or 3 hours. But it's best to make this early in the day before serving or the day before. It keeps well, refrigerated, for a few days.

VARIATIONS

You can make your own versions of this quiche, such as omitting the peppers and using diagonally-sliced roasted asparagus spears (page 36) or cooked broccoli. Other suggestions: Add sliced vegan ham or bacon or crumbled, browned veggie sausage, instead of the soy bacon bits; substitute any sautéed, roasted or steamed vegetables, or caramelized onions, for the peppers and mushrooms; substitute any dried or chopped fresh herbs that seem appropriate. Use your imagination! Just be sure the vegetables are not exuding liquid when the filling is placed in the crust.

Crostoni Benedict with Vegan Pesto Hollandaise

ITALY FUSION

Serves 4

This is an Italian-style vegan "Eggs Benny" – nutritious, delicious, out-of-the-ordinary, easy to make, and absolutely scrumptious! In this recipe, crostoni are used instead of English muffins. The creamy basil-flavored Hollandaise won't clog your arteries either! Note: Prepare the Hollandaise sauce first and keep warm in the top of a double boiler over barely simmering water or over an alcohol burner.

12 OUNCES SWISS CHARD, TOUGH STEMS REMOVED AND
THINLY-SLICED

6 OUNCES MUSHROOMS (ANY KIND), THINLY-SLICED

1/2 TABLESPOON OLIVE OIL

12 OUNCES FIRM TOFU, DRAINED AND CRUMBLED

3 TABLESPOONS TOFU SCRAMBLER MIX (PAGE 45)

8 (1/2-INCH) SLICES FRENCH BAGUETTE, CUT DIAGONALLY
    INTO 4-INCHES LONG SLICES
SALT AND FRESHLY GROUND BLACK PEPPER
VEGAN PESTO HOLLANDAISE SAUCE (PAGE 49)

1. Preheat the oven to 500°F. Steam the chard just until wilted. Set aside and keep warm.

2. Heat the oil in a large nonstick skillet over medium-high heat. Add the mushrooms, salt lightly, and sauté until they begin to brown a little. Set aside and keep warm.

3. Mash the tofu in a medium bowl, using a fork, a potato masher, or your fingers. Mix the tofu scrambler mix into the tofu evenly.

4. Cook the mashed tofu in a medium skillet, sprayed lightly with oil from a pump sprayer, over medium-high heat until it turns a nice yellow color and is the consistency you like. Use a non-metal spatula to keep the scramble moving around while it cooks.

5. While the tofu cooks, transfer the bread slices (crostoni) to a 12 x 17-inch oiled baking sheet and spray them with oil from a pump sprayer. When the oven temperature reaches 500°F, bake the crostoni for 3 minutes only. Watch carefully!

6. For each serving, transfer two crostoni to a warmed plate. Top the crostoni with one-fourth of the steamed chard and sprinkle with salt and pepper to taste. Top the chard with one-fourth of the mushrooms and then one-fourth of the tofu scramble. Top with warm Hollandaise and serve immediately with a knife and fork.

Vegan Pesto Hollandaise Sauce

Makes 2 cups   GF, SF, <30

This sauce is creamy-smooth and buttery. If you omit the pesto, you have a more traditional Hollandaise sauce.

1 1/2 CUPS NONDAIRY MILK, DIVIDED
1 TEASPOON SALT
1 DASH HOT PEPPER SAUCE
1/4 CUP VEGAN MARGARINE
3 1/2 TABLESPOONS CORNSTARCH
1 PINCH TURMERIC (LESS THAN 1/8 TEASPOON)
2 TABLESPOONS FRESH LEMON JUICE
2 TABLESPOONS TRADITIONAL-STYLE VEGAN PESTO (PAGE
    50) OR STOREBOUGHT

1. Heat 1 cup of the nondairy milk until not quite simmering. Pour it into a blender along with the salt and hot sauce and cover to keep it hot. Melt the margarine and cover to keep warm.

2. In a medium saucepan, combine the remaining 1/2 cup nondairy milk, cornstarch, and turmeric and whisk together well. Stir or whisk constantly over high heat until the mixture is thick and translucent and shiny yellow, not dull.

3. Scrape the cornstarch mixture into the blender container containing the hot milk and add the lemon juice and melted margarine. Blend until the mixture is pale yellow, frothy, and emulsified (you can't see any oil globules). Add the pesto and pulse briefly.

4. Serve immediately or, if it has cooled down, heat it briefly in the microwave on Low power or warm in the top of a double boiler over barely simmering water briefly before using.

"Crostoni" and "Crostini"

"Crostoni" and "Crostini" are two different things. Crostini are small slices of bread you can eat in one or two bites. Crostoni are bigger and you usually eaten with a knife and fork. Both words come from the Italian "crosta," meaning crust. Crostino (plural, crostini), is the Italian diminutive of crosta, meaning "small crust" while crostone (plural, crostoni) means "big crust."

Traditional-Style Vegan Pesto

Makes about 1 1/2 cups   GF, SFO, <30

- 4 CUPS PACKED-DOWN FRESH BASIL LEAVES
- 1/2 CUP EXTRA-VIRGIN OLIVE OIL (SEE BELOW FOR LOW-FAT VERSION)
- 1/4 CUP LIGHTLY-TOASTED PINE NUTS, CHOPPED WALNUTS, FILBERTS (HAZELNUTS), ALMONDS, BRAZIL NUTS, OR SHELLED, LIGHTLY-TOASTED SUNFLOWER AND/OR PUMPKIN SEEDS (FOR A NUT-FREE PESTO)
- 2 TABLESPOONS LIGHT-COLORED MISO (USE CHICKPEA MISO FOR A SOY-FREE VERSION)
- 2 TO 4 CLOVES GARLIC
- 1/2 TABLESPOON LEMON JUICE, OPTIONAL (TO PRESERVE COLOR)

Place all of the ingredients in a food processor and process until a paste forms. Place the paste in two or three small containers (the less air the pesto is exposed to, the better). Cover the pesto with a thin film of olive oil or a piece of plastic wrap (touching the pesto), to prevent discoloration, cover tightly and refrigerate. Use within two or three days (you can halve or even quarter the recipe, if you like). After that, you should freeze it in small containers or make frozen cubes of it, but don't leave it in the freezer for more than a month or so, as it loses flavor.

Tip: The garlic should not overwhelm the basil in authentic pesto.

VARIATIONS

Hemp Seed Pesto: Use only hemp seed oil, or 1/2 hemp seed oil and 1/2 olive oil. Omit the nuts or seeds and use 1/3 cup hemp seed butter instead. All other ingredients are the same.

Low-Fat Pesto: Omit all or some of the oil and substitute an equal quantity of mashed medium-firm or silken tofu, or mashed cooked or canned cannellini/white kidney beans (or use half tofu and half beans).

Winter Pesto: This is an authentic method of stretching expensive storebought fresh basil during the winter months. Use 2 cups of fresh basil and 2 cups fresh Italian parsley leaves, instead of 4 cups basil. It is traditional in Liguria to add 2 tablespoons of chopped fresh marjoram to this winter version.

Creole Grits and Grillades

NEW ORLEANS

Serves 4   SF

This heavenly braised vegan steak in a rich Creole sauce served over creamy corn grits would be a perfect Mardis Gras brunch dish, but it makes a good supper dish, as well. (Grillades are pronounced gree-yahds.) My version is much lighter in fat than the traditional one, but it is delicious. This is one of the best seitan "beef" dishes you'll ever have the pleasure of savoring. If you can't find grits, use very coarse polenta.

Grits:
- 1 1/3 CUPS COLD WATER
- 1 1/3 CUPS COLD NONDAIRY MILK
- 3/4 TEASPOON SALT
- 2/3 CUP CORN OR HOMINY GRITS (NOT INSTANT)
- 2 TO 4 TEASPOONS VEGAN MARGARINE

Grillades and Gravy:
- UNBLEACHED WHITE FLOUR, FOR DREDGING
- 4 SEITAN STEAKS (PAGE 134), SLICED IN HALF HORIZONTALLY TO MAKE VERY THIN STEAKS
- 2 TEASPOONS OLIVE OIL
- 1 TEASPOON DARK SESAME OIL
- 1 ONION, CHOPPED
- 6 GREEN ONIONS, CHOPPED, WHITE AND GREEN PARTS DIVIDED
- 1 GREEN BELL PEPPER, COARSELY CHOPPED
- 1 RIB CELERY, CHOPPED
- 2 TEASPOONS MINCED GARLIC
- 1/3 CUP CHOPPED FRESH RIPE OR CANNED PLUM TOMATOES, DRAINED
- 1 1/3 CUPS RICH MUSHROOM STOCK (PAGE 4) OR 1 CUP MUSHROOM BROTH PLUS 1/3 CUP OF DRY RED WINE
- 1 BAY LEAF
- 1/3 TEASPOON DRIED THYME
- 2 PINCHES CAYENNE PEPPER OR TO TASTE
- FRESHLY GROUND BLACK PEPPER

1 TEASPOON VEGAN WORCESTERSHIRE SAUCE (PAGE 13, REGULAR OR SOY-FREE OPTION)
1/4 CUP CHOPPEDFLAT-LEAF PARSLEY

1. **Grits:** Fill the bottom pan of a 1 to 2-quart double boiler halfway with water, set on the stove over high heat and bring to a boil. In the top pan of the double boiler, combine the 1 1/3 cups water, milk, and salt, and place onto a separate burner over high heat. Gradually sprinkle the grits into the liquids, stirring constantly with a wooden spoon or whisking, to prevent lumps from forming and to prevent the bottom from scorching. As soon as the mixture comes to a boil, transfer the top pan into the bottom pan of the double boiler, in which you have boiling water. Reduce the heat to a low simmer, stirring the grits with the wooden spoon until the water in the bottom pot is no longer boiling. Cover and simmer for 30 to 45 minutes, stirring occasionally. When the grits are creamy, stir in the margarine and remove the entire double boiler from the heat. Cover and keep warm over the hot water.

2. **Grillades and Gravy:** Lightly flour the seitan and shake off the excess flour. Heat both oils in a large nonstick, seasoned cast iron or anodized aluminum skillet over medium-high heat. Add the seitan and brown on both sides. Transfer to a baking sheet (any size) lined with paper towels or brown paper (to drain off excess oil) and set aside.

3. Add the onion to the hot skillet and sauté until it begins to soften, adding a spray of water as needed to keep the the onion from sticking. Add the chopped white part of the green onions (save the green part for garnish), bell pepper, celery, garlic, and tomatoes and continue stir-frying until the vegetables have started to wilt.

4. Add the broth, bay leaf, thyme, cayenne, black pepper to taste, and Worcestershire sauce, if using. Bring the mixture to a boil, add the browned seitan, then reduce the heat to a simmer, cover and braise the seitan in the tomato gravy for 30 minutes. Remove and discard the bay leaf before serving.

5. To serve: Have four dinner plates warmed. Spoon one-fourth of the grits onto each warm plate and partially cover with one-fourth of the grillades and gravy. Garnish each serving with some of the green onion tops and parsley. Serve immediately.

International Munchies

Appetizers, Sandwiches, and Wraps

This chapter offers a small sampling from the worldwide smorgasbord of tasty vegan bites to tempt the appetite, as well as small meals to eat on the run or take on picnics.

People of all nations and cultures love their snacks. I think one reason might be that in many countries dinner is eaten later than we North Americans are accustomed to. Consequently, an afternoon snack is essential. I know this to be the case in Peru, where my father was born and raised. We spent three months there when I was six years old, and I remember my father taking us (almost daily) to a café in Miraflores, Lima, where we were staying at my Abuelita's (grandmother's) large house. This was around four in the afternoon, and he would talk with the men and have a plate of seviche (fish "cooked" in the acid of the lemon or lime juice, with corn, sweet potato chunks, and other condiments), while my sister Karin and I enjoyed one of the very sweet Peruvian pastries and observed the passersby. Dinner for the adults would be around nine p.m. (we children had ours a bit earlier), so an afternoon snack after a nap was necessary.

The availability of tasty, cheap street food in most countries is another reason for the popularity of delicious snack foods. Working people often have to eat on the run, but that's no reason why the food can't be delicious! In Peru, it's often *camotes fritos* (sweet potato chips) and *anticuchos* (spicy kebabs). In the Middle East, it might be falafel in flatbread with all sorts of delicious condiments. In India, it could be dosas – the many varieties of "crepes" made from grain and bean flours, cooked in seconds over hot grills, and served with vegetables and chutneys. Suffice it to say that these "fast foods," even though some of them may be fried, are much more delicious and nutritious than the packaged or fast-foods so often within reach. No wonder we try to emulate them in our home kitchens!

International Munchies

Vegan Boursin-Style Spread

FRANCE/NORTH AMERICA

Makes 2 cups   GF, <30

This creamy vegan cheese spread is absolutely addictive and delicious on your favorite crackers, rye crisp, or crusty bread. My son-in-law once brought some Boursin® Cheese spread to our house on a visit. He wondered if it was possible to make a vegan version that tasted as rich and delicious. Always eager to prove that "it can be done" (especially to George, who good-naturedly teases me about being vegan), I developed this recipe. George loved my vegan spread, and he is definitely not a vegetarian, never mind a vegan. He said, "I would eat this every day!" The bonus: 2 tablespoons contains 86 calories, 8g fat, 0 cholesterol, 168mg sodium, and 2.4g protein. Two tablespoons of the "real thing" contain 120 calories, 13g fat, 35mg cholesterol, 180mg sodium, and 2g protein.

- 1 (12.3-OUNCE) BOX EXTRA-FIRM SILKEN TOFU, DRAINED AND CRUMBLED
- 1/2 CUP PLUS 2 TABLESPOONS RAW CASHEW PIECES, FINELY GROUND
- 1/2 CUP VEGAN MARGARINE
- 2 TABLESPOONS FRESH LEMON JUICE
- 3/4 TEASPOON SALT
- 1/2 TEASPOON LIGHT MISO PASTE
- 1 TO 2 MEDIUM CLOVES GARLIC, CRUSHED
- 1 TO 2 TEASPOONS MINCED FRESH CHIVES
- 1 TABLESPOON CHOPPED FRESH PARSLEY OR 1 TEASPOON DRIED
- 1/4 TEASPOON FRESHLY GROUND BLACK PEPPER

1. Place the crumbled tofu in a clean kitchen towel or piece of cotton sheeting, gather the ends up and twist, knead, and squeeze for a couple of minutes to extract as much of the water from the tofu as is possible. Transfer the squeezed tofu to a food processor. Add the cashews, margarine, lemon juice, salt, and miso and process until very smooth. Be patient—it has to be very smooth. You may have to stop the machine a couple of times and scrape the sides and push the ingredients that have accumulated under the blade. When as smooth as possible, add the garlic, chives, parsley, and pepper. Process again for a smooth, well-incorporated spread or pulse if you prefer small pieces of ingredient additions to be discernible.

2. Scoop into two straight-sided 1-cup ramekins (or three 3/4-cup ramekins), cover with plastic wrap, and refrigerate. They will firm up in a few hours.

VARIATIONS

Try any (or all) of these alternative flavoring ideas:

- Omit herbs and garlic and use more pepper.
- Use shallots instead of garlic.
- To the basic mixture, add 1 teaspoon dried basil or dill weed (or other favorite herb) or use 1 tablespoon chopped fresh herbs.
- To the basic mixture, add 2 tablespoons chopped roasted red pepper or sundried tomato.
- Make a sweet version with chopped nuts and dried fruit (Omit the garlic, chives, parsley, and pepper, of course). A holiday version of this might use chopped apple and dried cranberries, perhaps chopped toasted pecans and a pinch of cinnamon. Use no more than 1/4 cup of the chopped mixture, in total.

Smoky Levantine Eggplant Dip

Mutabbal

SYRIA/PALESTINE

Serves 8   GF, SF

This silky, garlicky Levantine spread is similar to Lebanese baba gannoush, but with less tahini and some chile heat. I actually prefer this to baba gannoush, because the eggplant is not overwhelmed by the tahini. The garnish of smoked hot paprika is not authentic, but it's a natural fit. I prefer the Middle Eastern way of serving spreads on a shallow platter rather than in a bowl. It looks more artistic, somehow, and it's easier for sharing. Serve this as an appetizer with sesame crackers, pita bread, pita chips, or slices of fresh crusty bread.

2 LARGE EGGPLANTS
1/4 CUP FRESH LEMON JUICE
3 TABLESPOONS TAHINI
1 TABLESPOON OLIVE OIL, PLUS MORE FOR GARNISH
2 CLOVES GARLIC, CRUSHED
1/2 TEASPOON SALT
HOT SAUCE, TO TASTE
SMOKED HOT PAPRIKA (PIMENTÓN)
KALAMATA OLIVES, OPTIONAL
2 TABLESPOONS CHOPPED FRESH PARSLEY, OPTIONAL

1. Remove the stem ends of the eggplants and make two horizontal cuts on each side of the eggplant. Place the eggplants under the broiler for 30 minutes or more, turning once, until the skin is almost burnt and they are soft inside.

2. In a small bowl, combine the tahini and lemon juice and whisk until smooth. Set aside.

3. Cut the cooked eggplants in half and scrape out the soft flesh with the side of a spoon. Discard the outer skin. Transfer the eggplant flesh to a plate and mash it well with a fork. (Do not puree it in a food processor—you don't want it that smooth.) Add the tahini/lemon juice mixture and mix well with the fork. Add the olive oil, garlic, salt, and hot sauce, and mix well.

4. Transfer the mixture to a shallow serving dish, spreading evenly. Drizzle the top lightly with olive oil and sprinkle with smoked paprika. Garnish with a few olives and parsley, if using.

Tip: Fresh hot green chiles are often used in this spread (though not always), but I don't always have them on hand. For that reason, I add a little hot sauce instead, but feel free to use minced fresh green chiles to taste, if you prefer.

"Who Needs Fois Gras?" Herbed Mushroom Pâté

FRANCE/NORTH AMERICA

Makes 2 pâtés   GF, SFO

I love watching carnivores try this for the first time – inevitably, eyes widen in delight and surprise. The title says it all. Don't be daunted by the long list of ingredients – this recipe is very easy to make. The pâté has a rich, deep flavor and a very smooth texture that belies the mundane ingredients. It makes an excellent spread on celery sticks, toast, crackers, rye crisp, crostini, Melba toast, bruschetta, or pita crisps, and is an elegant starter when served with crusty French bread on a bed of lettuce. It is also scrumptious in a sandwich.
Note: *You will need two nonstick 5 3/4 x 3 x 2 1/8-inch fruitcake/mini loaf pans for this recipe. Alternatively, you can use a 1.5-quart rectangular pâté mold or even an 8-inch round cake pan for the whole recipe.*

DARK SESAME OIL, TO OIL PANS
1 TABLESPOON OLIVE OIL
1 ONION (ABOUT 5 OUNCES), COARSELY CHOPPED
4 OUNCES CRIMINI OR PORTOBELLO MUSHROOMS, SLICED
1 CARROT, CUT INTO 1/2-INCH DICE
1 SMALL BAKING POTATO (4 OUNCES), PEELED AND CUT INTO 1/2-INCH DICE
1/2 CUP PLUS 2 TABLESPOONS WATER
1/2 CUP LIGHTLY TOASTED WALNUTS OR PECANS
1/2 CUP LIGHTLY TOASTED SUNFLOWER SEEDS
1/2 CUP CHICKPEA FLOUR (BESAN)
1/2 CUP NUTRITIONAL YEAST FLAKES
3 CLOVES GARLIC, PEELED
2 TABLESPOONS SOY OR RICE PROTEIN POWDER, OR SOY OR RICE MILK POWDER
2 TABLESPOONS DARK MISO PASTE (RED OR MUGI MISO)
1 TABLESPOON GROUND FLAX SEED
1 TABLESPOON TAHINI
1 TABLESPOON TOMATO PASTE
1 TABLESPOON BALSAMIC VINEGAR
1/2 TABLESPOON FRESH CHOPPED THYME OR 1/2 TEASPOON DRIED
1/2 TABLESPOON FRESH CHOPPED ROSEMARY OR 1/2 TEASPOON DRIED

1/2 TABLESPOON FRESH CHOPPED MARJORAM OR 1/2 TEA-
SPOON DRIED

1/2 TEASPOON SALT

1/4 TEASPOON WHITE PEPPER, OPTIONAL

PINCH FRESHLY GROUND NUTMEG

1. Preheat the oven to 350°F. Oil the pans with sesame oil and line the bottoms with baking parchment cut to fit. Oil the paper also.

2. Heat the olive oil in a large skillet over medium heat. When it is hot, add the onion, mushrooms, and carrot and cook, stirring, until the onions are softened, 5 to 7 minutes.

3. **Microwave Option:** Mix the vegetables with the oil in a microwave-safe pie plate or 2-quart casserole and cook on 100% power (default setting) for 6 minutes. The dish should be covered with a microwave-safe lid or plate.

4. Combine the cooked vegetables with all of the remaining batter ingredients in a large, heavy-duty blender or food processor and process until very smooth. (You may have to stop the blender and scrape down the sides from time to time.)

5. Fill the prepared pan(s) or mold and smooth the top(s) evenly. Cover the pan(s) with foil sprayed on the underside with oil from a pump sprayer (the side that will touch the pâté). Place the pans inside of an 8 x 12-inch baking pan with about an inch of hot water in the bottom. (If you use a long pâté mold you will need a 16-inch-long roasting pan.)

6. Bake for 1 hour (1 hour and 15 minutes for the long pâté mold). Cool the pâté(s) thoroughly on a rack, then carefully loosen the edges with a knife and invert them onto a serving platter or storage container. Cover the plate with plastic wrap and refrigerate for up to a week. If you would like to freeze the pâtés, cut them into whatever sizes are useful for you, wrap well with foil or plastic wrap, then transfer them to a zipper-lock bag, seal and freeze for up to three months.

Vegan Liverwurst and Braunschweiger

GERMANY

Makes 2 pâtés   GF, <30

I confess that I really liked liverwurst in pre-vegan days. And, judging by the recipes and info online, I am not alone. I devised a vegan recipe that tastes very much like it, in my opinion (and in the opinion of some real German testers), that is easy to make, can be frozen, and has a wonderful flavor. It makes good sandwiches, too and is great to have in the refrigerator during the summer, for a quick meal or an appetizer.

With an easy addition, it can be turned into braunschweiger. If you used to like braunschweiger, which is smoked liverwurst, just add a little liquid smoke (page 21) to taste, starting with a 1/2 teaspoon. The recipe is seasoned the way I like it, but some German testers also added a bit of ground cloves and cardamom. Note: You will need two nonstick 5 3/4 x 3 x 2 1/8-inch fruitcake/mini loaf pans for this recipe. Alternatively, you can use a 1.5-quart rectangular pâté mold or even an 8-inch round cake pan for the whole recipe.

DARK SESAME OIL, FOR OILING THE PANS

1 (12.3-OUNCE) BOX EXTRA-FIRM SILKEN TOFU OR 12
OUNCES MEDIUM-FIRM TOFU, DRAINED AND CRUMBLED

1 RUSSET POTATO (ABOUT 4 OUNCES), CUT INTO 1-INCH DICE

1/2 MEDIUM ONION (ABOUT 2.5 OUNCES), CUT INTO 1-INCH DICE

1/2 CUP RAW SUNFLOWER SEEDS

1/4 CUP WHOLE-WHEAT, SOY, OR CHICKPEA FLOUR (BESAN),
OR CORNMEAL

1/4 CUP NUTRITIONAL YEAST FLAKES

1/4 CUP SOY SAUCE

2 TABLESPOONS WARM WATER

1 1/2 TABLESPOONS FRESH LEMON JUICE

2 CLOVES GARLIC, PEELED

1/2 TEASPOON SUGAR

1/2 TABLESPOON CHOPPED FRESH THYME OR 1/2 TEASPOON
DRIED

1/2 TABLESPOON CHOPPED FRESH ROSEMARY OR 1/2 TEA-
SPOON DRIED

1/2 TABLESPOON CHOPPED FRESH MARJORAM OR 1/2 TEA-
SPOON DRIED
1/8 TEASPOON GROUND ALLSPICE
PINCH FRESHLY GROUND NUTMEG
FRESHLY GROUND BLACK PEPPER

1. Preheat the oven to 350°F. Oil the pans with dark sesame oil and line the bottoms with baking parchment cut to fit. Oil the paper also.

2. Combine all of the ingredients in a blender and process until very smooth. Fill the prepared pan(s) or mold and smooth the top(s) evenly. Cover the pan(s) with foil sprayed on the underside with oil from a pump sprayer (the side that will touch the "liverwurst").

3. Place the pans inside an 8 x 12-inch shallow baking pan with about 1-inch of hot water in the bottom. (If you use a long pâté mold you will need a 16-inch-long roasting pan.) Bake for 1 hour (1 hour and 15 minutes for the long pâté mold). Cool the "liverwurst" thoroughly on a rack, then carefully loosen the edges with a knife and invert onto a platter.

4. Cover the plate with plastic wrap and refrigerate for up to a week. To freeze the pâtés, cut them into whatever sizes are useful for you, wrap them well with foil or plastic wrap, then transfer them to a zipper-lock bag, seal and freeze for up to three months.

Sweet and Savory Afghan Squash

Kadu Bouranee

AFGHANISTAN

Serves 6 to 8   GF, SFO

Autumn brings one of my favorite vegetables, winter squash, and this unusual, spicy, sweet-and-savory dish is one of our favorite ways to enjoy it. Although it is meant to be served as an appetizer, I also some-

times serve it as an entrée (in which case it serves four). Serve this dish with basmati rice or Indian Flatbread (page 225).

1/4 CUP OLIVE OIL
2 POUNDS FRESH ORANGE WINTER SQUASH (HUBBARD, KABOCHA, OR BUTTERNUT) OR PUMPKIN, PEELED AND CUT INTO 2 TO 3-INCH CHUNKS
1 1/4 CUPS WATER
1/2 CUP SUGAR
1/4 CUP TOMATO PASTE
1 TABLESPOON CRUSHED GARLIC PLUS 1 SMALL CLOVE GARLIC, CRUSHED, DIVIDED
1 TABLESPOON GROUND CORIANDER
1/2 TABLESPOON PLUS 3/4 TEASPOON SALT, DIVIDED
1/2 TEASPOON GRATED FRESH GINGER
1/4 TEASPOON FRESHLY GROUND BLACK PEPPER
3/4 CUP TOFU YOGURT OR SOUR CREAM (PAGE 33), OR SOY-FREE ALTERNATIVE
2 TABLESPOONS CHOPPED FRESH MINT LEAVES OR 2 TEA-SPOONS DRIED

1. Heat the oil in a large skillet over medium-high heat. Add the squash and cook until lightly browned on both sides, turning once. Set aside.

2. In a medium bowl, combine the water, sugar, tomato paste, the 1 tablespoon crushed garlic, coriander, the 1/2 tablespoon salt, ginger, and pepper. Mix well and pour over the squash. Cover and cook 20 to 25 minutes over low heat, until the squash is cooked through and most of the liquid has evaporated.

3. In a small bowl, combine the yogurt, the crushed garlic clove, and the 3/4 teaspoon of salt, and mix well.

4. Spread half the yogurt sauce onto a shallow serving dish and arrange the cooked squash on top. Spread with remaining yogurt sauce and drizzle with any cooking juices left in the skillet. Sprinkle with the mint and serve.

Vietnamese-Style Mango Salad Rolls with Smoked Tofu

VIETNAM

Serves 4   GF, <30

Several years ago, I wanted to make a slightly different version of these popular summer rolls, so I added silky mango slices and replaced the usual bean sprouts with crunchy julienned cucumber, using smoked tofu for the protein. I also devised a creamy lower-fat peanut butter dipping sauce with plenty of flavor. These have become a summer staple in our house and are always a hit at potlucks.

Peanut Dipping Sauce:
1/3 CUP HOT WATER
3 TABLESPOONS SMOOTH NATURAL PEANUT BUTTER
2 TABLESPOONS SOY SAUCE
2 TABLESPOONS BROWN SUGAR
4 TEASPOONS UNSEASONED RICE VINEGAR
1 TEASPOON DARK SESAME OIL
1 TEASPOON SRIRACHA SAUCE, OR TO TASTE
2 TABLESPOONS CHOPPED GREEN ONION
Filling:
2 OUNCES RICE VERMICELLI NOODLES
8 (8 1/2-INCH) ROUND VIETNAMESE RICE PAPERS
8 CRISP MEDIUM-SIZED LETTUCE LEAVES (ANY KIND)
1 LARGE RIPE MANGO, PEELED, PITTED AND THINLY SLICED
12 TO 14 OUNCES SMOKED TOFU OR SMOKY BAKED TOFU
    (FOLLOWS), CUT INTO MATCHSTICKS
1/2 LARGE UNPEELED ENGLISH CUCUMBER, CUT INTO
    MATCHSTICKS
1 CUP FRESH BASIL LEAVES, SLICED 1/16-INCH THICK

1. **Peanut Dipping Sauce:** Mix the ingredients for the dipping sauce in a blender until smooth, transfer to a small bowl, cover and set aside in the refrigerator.

2. **Filling:** Transfer the rice vermicelli to a large bowl and cover with boiling water. Set aside to soak while you prepare the other ingredients.

3. Drain the noodles in a colander, rinsing under cold running water. Set them aside, still in the colander.

4. Have a large bowl of warm water ready and place a damp clean kitchen towel on a flat work surface. Working with only 2 rice papers at a time (keep the rest covered), immerse each round in the warm water, then quickly remove and smooth them out on the towel. The rice-paper rounds should be pliable within a few seconds.

5. Arrange one piece of lettuce over the bottom third of each round. On top of the lettuce place one-eighth portion each of the mango, tofu, noodles, and cucumber. Distribute the items evenly to the edges so that there won't be a bulge in the center of the roll. Roll the bottom third tightly toward the center once only. Arrange one eighth of the basil leaves over the folded part, then continue rolling to make a fairly tight cylinder. Repeat with the remaining ingredients. Transfer each finished roll to a platter and cover with a clean damp towel and then plastic wrap. Serve right away or refrigerate for several hours. Serve with the dipping sauce.

Smoky Baked Tofu

Serves 6   GF, <30

This is a yummy staple to have in your refrigerator to spark up your meals. It's an ideal inclusion in the salad rolls (above). Use a dark baking sheet, if possible, to bake the tofu, as food browns better on dark pans.

1 1/2 CUPS WATER
1/4 CUP SOY SAUCE
1 TABLESPOON MAPLE SYRUP OR BROWN SUGAR
1 TEASPOON LIQUID SMOKE (SEE PAGE 21)
1 1/2 POUNDS EXTRA-FIRM TOFU (NOT SILKEN), DRAINED,
    CUT INTO 1/4-INCH-THICK SLICES

1. In a shallow bowl or container, combine the water, soy sauce, maple syrup, and liquid smoke. Add the tofu to the marinade, cover, and refrig-

erate for several hours to several days.

2. When ready to bake, preheat the oven to 400°F. Transfer the tofu slices, removed from the marinade, to a nonstick or lightly-oiled 12 x 17-inch baking sheet in one layer. Bake until the undersides are golden, about 10 minutes. Turn the slices over and bake until the other side is golden, about 10 minutes. The slices can be used immediately or stored in a covered container in the refrigerator.

Tip: If you are in a hurry, try this: Instead of marinating the tofu slices, bake them at 400°F with half of the marinade poured over them in an 8 x 12-inch baking pan. Bake until all of the marinade is absorbed. Turn the slices over and bake until they firm up a bit.

Indian Semolina "Pizza"

Dosa

INDIA

Serves 6   SFO, <30

Semolina is the high protein wheat from which pasta is made. It makes a delicious, high-protein Indian snack bread, which children love. You can eat them plain with chutney, but we like them cooked for a few minutes with a crunchy, spicy topping. Serve with tofu yogurt or soy-free alternative (page 33) on the side. Note: If semolina flour (rava) is unavailable, use Cream of Wheat instead.

2 CUPS SEMOLINA FLOUR (RAVA) (SEE NOTE ABOVE)

1 CUP WATER

1 CUP NONDAIRY MILK

2 TEASPOONS FRESH LEMON JUICE

1 TEASPOON SALT

1 MEDIUM ONION, MINCED

1/4 CUP MINCED FRESH CILANTRO, BASIL, OR MINT, OPTIONAL

1 TABLESPOON CHOPPED FRESH HOT CHILE, OPTIONAL

1 TEASPOON BAKING SODA

TOPPINGS: FINELY CHOPPED BELL PEPPER, TOMATO, AND SHREDDED CABBAGE; LEFTOVER CURRIED VEGETABLES; OR SALSA AND VEGAN CHEESE (GOOD, IF UNAUTHENTIC)

1. In a bowl, combine the semolina flour, water, milk, lemon juice, salt, onion, and cilantro and/or chile, if using. Stir until well mixed. Let the batter sit while you heat an 8-inch nonstick skillet or a lightly oiled small cast iron griddle, over medium-low heat.

2. In a small bowl, combine the baking soda with a small amount of the batter, then fold it back into the main bowl.

3. To form the dosa, pour about 1/2 cup of batter into the center of the hot skillet or griddle and spread the batter outwards in concentric circles, with the bottom of the (metal or silicone) measuring cup or the bottom of a flat-bottomed spoon, until it makes a thick round crepe 7 or 8 inches in diameter. Cover and cook over medium-low heat for 5 minutes or until the bottom is golden-brown and crispy.

4. Sprinkle the topping ingredients sparsely over the top, cover and cook for another minute or so. Serve hot.

Grilled Eggplant and Red Pepper Panini

ITALY

Serves 4   SF, <30

There are so many varieties of the grilled Italian sandwich, panini, that whole books have been written about them. This is my current favorite vegan combination that bursts with creamy vegan cheese, roasted vegetables, baby kale, and pesto mayonnaise. I use an indoor/tabletop electric grill, but you can also use a special sandwich or panini grill, or even a waffle iron (traditional, not Belgian). Barring any of those possibilities, use a heavy skillet (this can be a grill pan, if you have one) over medium heat and

weigh the top of the sandwich down with a panini press or a flat-bottomed pot lid.

1/2 CUP TO 3/4 CUP VEGAN PESTO MAYONNAISE (FOLLOWS)
4 TO 8 SLICES (DEPENDING ON SIZE) BROILER-GRILLED EGG-
    PLANT (SEE SIDEBAR) OR GRILLED EGGPLANT SLICES
    FROM A DELI COUNTER
8 SLICES FIRM WHITE FRENCH OR ITALIAN-STYLE BREAD OR
    SANDWICH BREAD
1 CUP SHREDDED WHITE VEGAN CHEESE (OR 4 TO 8 THIN
    SLICES)
2 ROASTED RED BELL PEPPERS FROM A JAR, RINSED, PAT-
    TED DRY AND SLICED INTO 1-INCH WIDE PIECES
16 TO 24 TENDER BABY KALE LEAVES, SPUN DRY AND
    TOUGH STEMS REMOVED
OLIVE OIL

1. Have your grilling device or pan heating before you make the sandwich.

2. Spread the mayonnaise on both slices of bread. Sprinkle the shredded vegan cheese over one slice of bread (or use thin slices of vegan cheese) – the cheese will stick to the mayo.

3. Cover the second slice of bread with the cooked eggplant, cut to fit or overlapping, if necessary. Top the eggplant with roasted red pepper and then the kale.

4. Place the first bread slice, cheese-down, over the second slice. Press down gently. Spray or brush both sides of the sandwich lightly with olive oil. Repeat with remaining ingredients to make four sandwiches.

5. Transfer a sandwich to your heated grilling device and close the top. Grill until the bread is golden and slightly crispy and serve hot. Repeat with remaining sandwiches.

Vegan Pesto Mayonnaise
Makes 3/4 cup

Tip: *If you have some vegan pesto (page 50) handy, simply add it to the mayonnaise to taste.*

3/4 CUP VEGAN MAYO (PAGE 18)
1 LARGE CLOVE GARLIC, CRUSHED
1 1/2 CUP FRESH BASIL LEAVES, LOOSELY-PACKED

Blend all of the ingredients in a blender or food processor until the mayonnaise turns green and is fairly smooth. Use immediately, or transfer to a jar, cover and refrigerate until needed.

Broiler-Grilled Eggplant

Cut a medium eggplant into 3/4-inch slices and slice off the peels. Brush the eggplant slices on both sides with olive oil and place them in one layer on a 12 x 17-inch baking sheet. Place the baking sheet under a broiler 3 inches under heat source and broil until the slices are soft on the inside and slightly charred on the outside. Turn the slices over and broil a few minutes longer, until they start getting a bit charred on the second side. These can be eaten hot, at room temperature, or chilled.

Saigon Subs
Bahn Mi
VIETNAM

Serves 4   SFO

Vietnamese immigrants all over North America have opened quick luncheonettes featuring pho (noodle soup) and these crusty, thick sandwiches – a divine combination of Vietnamese fresh herbs and vegetables, meats, hot sauces, and crusty French baguettes. Vegans can use many types of meat substitutes, including veggie pâté and veggie "meatloaf" or grilled or sautéed portobello mushrooms. (It's a good way to use leftovers!) In Vietnam, often two or more meats are used. Fresh vegetables and herbs make the sand-wich healthful, crunchy, delicious, and fresh.

1/4 TO 1/2 CUP VEGAN MAYO (PAGE 18)
**2 SMALL FRENCH BAGUETTES, FRESHLY BAKED, SLICED IN
     HALF HORIZONTALLY**
**VIETNAMESE-STYLE BBQ (RECIPE FOLLOWS) OR OTHER
     VEGAN "MEAT" (SEE NOTE)**
1 CUP COARSELY CHOPPED FRESH BASIL, MINT OR CILANTRO
8 CRISP LETTUCE LEAVES
16 TO 20 THIN SLICES ENGLISH CUCUMBER SLICES
12 TO 16 FRESH RED RIPE TOMATO SLICES
**1/4 CUP THINLY-SLICED FRESH OR PICKLED HOT CHILES,
     OPTIONAL**
QUICK CARROT PICKLE (FOLLOWS)
VEGAN NUOC CHAM SAUCE (FOLLOWS)
SRIRACHA SAUCE

Spread mayo on the bottom half of each half-baguette. Place slices of BBQ or other vegan "meat" slightly overlapping, over the mayo. Top with the basil, lettuce, cucumber, tomato, and hot chiles, if using. Top with a spoonful of carrot pickle. Sprinkle the inside of the top half of each half-loaf with some nuoc cham sauce and a little sriracha. Cover the bottom half of the half-loaf with the top half. With a sharp serrated knife, slice each sandwich diagonally into 2 pieces and serve immediately.

VARIATIONS

Instead of the Vietnamese BBQ, you can substitute thin slices of any of the following (about 2 slices per sandwich, no further cooking needed) and add some of the Vietnamese Barbecue Sauce (recipe below) to the sandwich as well:

- Field Roast Classic Grain Meatloaf, thinly sliced
- Herbed Mushroom Pâté (page 56), thinly sliced
- Beefy Seitan (page 133), thinly sliced
- Crispy Marinated Tofu Slices (page 8)
- Smoky Baked Tofu (page 59), thinly sliced, or Asian-style baked tofu
- Commercial vegan deli slices

Vietnamese-Style BBQ

VIETNAM

Serves 4   SFO, <30

**LIGHT SEITAN CUTLETS (PAGE 5), CUT INTO MATCHSTICKS
     OR 2 CUPS RECONSTITUTED SOY CURLS (SEE PAGE 10)**
1/2 CUP SOY SAUCE
1/4 CUP DRY SHERRY OR RICE WINE
1/4 CUP BROWN SUGAR
8 CLOVES GARLIC, CRUSHED
**4 (1/8-INCH) SLICES GINGER, SMASHED WITH THE SIDE OF A
     KNIFE OR CLEAVER**
2 GREEN ONIONS, FINELY CHOPPED
1 TO 2 TEASPOONS SRIRACHA SAUCE
1 TEASPOON FIVE-SPICE POWDER
1 TEASPOON LIQUID SMOKE

1. Arrange the seitan in a shallow baking dish and set aside.

2. In a medium bowl, combine the soy sauce, sherry, sugar, garlic, ginger, green onions, sriracha, five-spice powder, and liquid smoke. Mix well.

3. Pour the marinade over the seitan and marinate for at least 1 hour. Preheat the broiler. Spread the marinated strips on a lightly-oiled 12 x 17-inch baking sheet and place 3 to 4 inches under the broiler. Broil the strips, watching carefully, until the tops start to char a bit. Remove from the oven. Serve hot or at room temperature.

Quick Carrot Pickle

Serves 4   GF, SF, <30

4 SMALL CARROTS, PEELED AND FINELY SHREDDED
3 TABLESPOONS UNSEASONED RICE VINEGAR
1 TABLESPOON SUGAR
1/2 TEASPOON SALT

In a bowl, combine the carrots, vinegar, sugar, and salt. Mix well and let stand 10 minutes or more before serving.

Vegan Nuoc Cham Sauce

Makes about 2/3 cup   GF, <30

There are many versions of this Vietnamese sauce. This is my own invention. There is such a thing as Vietnamese vegan "fish sauce" (nuoc mam chay) that can sometimes be found in Asian grocery stores. But it tasted like Bragg Liquid Aminos to me and Bragg is easier to find. Many people swear by Bragg, an unfermented sort of soy sauce, but I prefer naturally fermented soy sauce for general cooking and seasoning. It has a more complex flavor, so you can use less (and it's less expensive). You can also use the Soy-Free Sauce on page 12.

1/4 CUP BRAGG LIQUID AMINOS OR LIGHT SOY SAUCE
1/4 CUP WATER
1 TABLESPOON FRESH LIME JUICE
1 TABLESPOON UNSEASONED RICE VINEGAR
1 CLOVE GARLIC, CRUSHED
1 TABLESPOON MINCED FRESH BASIL, CILANTRO, OR MINT
1 TABLESPOON SUGAR
1/2 TEASPOON HOT RED PEPPER FLAKES, OR TO TASTE
1 TABLESPOON FINELY SHREDDED CARROTS

Combine all of the ingredients together in a small bowl. Cover and refrigerate until needed.

Baja-Style Tempeh Tacos

BAJA CALIFORNIA

Serves 6   GF

This is a vegan version of a popular Baja-style fried fish taco. My husband, who claims to dislike tempeh, threatened not to eat it if he didn't like it, but he ate three tacos! They are great with the Roasted Fresh Pineapple and Red Pepper-Chipotle Salsa. For this recipe, I used mild-tasting seven-grain tempeh and marinated it before oven-frying it in a crispy panko coating.

1 (8 OUNCE) PACKAGE 7-GRAIN TEMPEH OR OTHER TEMPEH,
    CUT INTO 12 SLICES
1 CUP SOY, HEMP, OR NUT MILK
1/4 CUP CHOPPED FRESH CILANTRO
1 TABLESPOON FRESH LIME JUICE
1 TO 1 1/2 TABLESPOONS HOT SAUCE
1/2 TEASPOON SALT
1 1/2 CUPS PANKO (JAPANESE BREADCRUMBS)
1/4 CUP UNBLEACHED WHITE FLOUR
12 CORN TORTILLAS (OR TACO SHELLS FOR AMERICAN-STYLE)
2 CUPS FINELY-SHREDDED CABBAGE
1 MEDIUM HASS AVOCADO, PITTED, PEELED AND CUT INTO
    1/2-INCH DICE AND TOSSED WITH 1 TABLESPOON
    LEMON OR LIME JUICE
SPECIAL TACO SAUCE (FOLLOWS)
ROASTED FRESH PINEAPPLE AND RED PEPPER-CHIPOTLE
    SALSA (FOLLOWS)

1. Arrange the tempeh slices in an 8 x 12-inch baking pan. In a bowl, combine the soy milk, cilantro, 1 tablespoon of the lime juice, hot sauce, and salt, and stir to combine. Pour the marinade over the tempeh. Cover and refrigerate for at least an hour or up to a day.

2. About 30 minutes before you are ready to serve, preheat the oven to 500°F. Line a 12 x 17-inch baking sheet with baking parchment. Transfer the panko to a large shallow bowl and set aside.

3. Remove the tempeh from the marinade. Mix the leftover marinade with the flour to make a batter. Coat the marinated tempeh slices in the batter and dredge them in the panko until coated all over. Place the coated slices at least 1 inch apart on the prepared baking sheet. Spray the slices with oil from a pump sprayer.

4. Bake the tempeh for about 15 minutes or until golden and crispy on top. Turn over, spray the tops with oil from a pump sprayer and bake for about 5 minutes longer. Remove from the oven and place the pan on a rack.

5. If you are using corn tortillas, reduce the oven to 300°F. Wrap the tortillas in aluminum foil, distributing them in 2 packets. Transfer the packets to the oven to warm while you assemble all of the components.

6. If you are using taco shells, reduce the oven to 350°F. Transfer the taco shells to a 10 x 15-inch baking sheet, slightly overlapping. Bake for

4 minutes only. Do this just before filling and serving the tacos.

7. To serve, spoon some cabbage into the bottom of each warmed tortilla or taco shell. Place a tempeh slice on top, then a large spoonful of Special Taco Sauce, a good dollop of the salsa, and a spoonful of diced avocado. Eat immediately with plenty of napkins.

Special Taco Sauce

GF, SFO, <30

1/4 CUP PLUS 2 TABLESPOONS VEGAN MAYO, (PAGE 18)
6 TABLESPOONS VEGAN SOUR CREAM (PAGE 33)
4 TEASPOONS FRESH LIME JUICE
1 TEASPOON FINELY GRATED ORGANIC LIME ZEST

In a small bowl, combine all the ingredients and mix until smooth and well blended. Cover and refrigerate until needed.

Roasted Fresh Pineapple and Red Pepper-Chipotle Salsa

Mexico/Hawaii

Serves 6   GF, SF, <30

I wanted this salsa to have a smoky nuance because I once tasted some dried smoked pineapple that my stepson had brought back from Hawaii. I loved the combination of smoky and sweet. This is an addictive salsa!

1/2 MEDIUM PINEAPPLE PEELED, CORED, AND SLICED ABOUT
    3/8-INCH THICK
1 MEDIUM RED BELL PEPPER, CUT INTO 1-INCH SQUARES
1/2 LARGE RED ONION, CUT IN 4 WEDGES AND SEPARATED
    INTO LAYERS
1/2 CUP DICED RIPE RED TOMATO (FRESH OR CANNED)
2 LARGE CLOVES GARLIC, SLICED
1 CANNED CHIPOTLE PEPPER IN ADOBO SAUCE, CHOPPED
1 TABLESPOON FRESH CHOPPED CILANTRO OR 1 TEASPOON
    DRIED
1 TEASPOON SALT
4 TEASPOONS FRESH LIME JUICE

1. Preheat the oven to 425°F. Combine the pineapple, onion, red bell pepper, tomatoes, and garlic on a 12 x 17-inch baking sheet lined with baking parchment. Spray the fruit and vegetables for a few seconds with oil from a pump sprayer. Roast in the oven for 15 minutes.

2. Turn the oven from Bake to Broil and place the pan 3 to 4 inches below the heat source. Broil for 5 minutes, turn the pineapple and veggies over, and broil 5 minutes more or until the pineapple starts to brown and the edges of the vegetables start to char. Transfer the contents of the pan into a food processor. Add the chipotle, cilantro, and salt. Pulse the mixture until it is well-chopped.

3. Transfer the mixture to a medium bowl and fold in the lime juice. Cover and refrigerate until serving time.

Tip: Please note that a medium pineapple weighs about 3 pounds, unpeeled.

Shwarma Wraps

THE LEVANT AND MIDDLE EAST

Serves 6   SFO, <30

Shwarma (other spellings are shawerma, shawarma, and, in North America, doner kabob) is a street food from the Levant. Meat is sliced, marinated in spices, and impaled on a spike, which is then rotated as it is barbecued. It is thinly sliced and served in flatbread or pita bread with yogurt, tomatoes, pickled chiles, and sometimes pickled eggplant. This is a delicious simplified vegan version.

4 SEITAN STEAKS (PAGE 134)
Marinade:
1/2 TEASPOON GROUND CORIANDER OR CARDAMOM
1/2 TEASPOON GROUND CINNAMON
1/2 TEASPOON GROUND CUMIN
1/4 TEASPOON FRESHLY GROUND NUTMEG
FRESHLY GROUND BLACK PEPPER

1 PINCH GROUND CAYENNE OR RED PEPPER FLAKES

1/4 TEASPOON SALT

4 CLOVES GARLIC, CRUSHED

3 GREEN ONIONS, MINCED

1 BAY LEAF

1/4 CUP WATER

1/4 CUP FRESH LEMON JUICE

1/4 CUP RED WINE VINEGAR

1 TABLESPOON DARK SESAME OIL

1 TEASPOON SUMAC, OPTIONAL (SEE SIDEBAR)

Accompaniments:

3 LARGE WHOLE-WHEAT PITA BREADS, HALVED (OR 6 SMALL
WHOLE-WHEAT TORTILLAS OR OTHER FLATBREAD)

2 RIPE, FIRM TOMATOES, CHOPPED OR SLICED

1 MEDIUM RED ONION, THINLY SLICED

6 CRISP LETTUCE LEAVES

1/3 CUP SLICED PICKLED HOT CHILES

1 CUP TOFU SOUR CREAM OR TOFU "YOGURT" OR SOY-FREE
ALTERNATIVE (PAGE 33)

1. **Seitan:** Slice the seitan into thin strips and transfer to a glass bowl or other container for marinating.

2. **Marinade:** Combine the spices, salt, garlic, onion, bay leaf, water, lemon juice and vinegar, stir well and pour it over the seitan. (If you are using the sumac, reserve it for after cooking.) Marinate the cutlet strips, covered, in the refrigerator for at least 2 hours.

3. Remove the strips from the marinade and pat dry. Grill them over a hot charcoal or gas fire until done (use a grill basket if necessary) or on a hot indoor grill or on a lightly-oiled 12 x 17-inch baking sheet placed about 3 to 4 inches directly under the broiler, until they are browned in some spots on both sides, turning often. If you are using the sumac, sprinkle it over the slices now.

4. **Serving:** Cut the pitas in half. Divide the seitan strips among the six pita bread halves or the tortillas, then a few tomato and onion slices, lettuce and pickled chiles, and a good dollop of tofu sour cream or tofu "yogurt."

Sumac

Sumac is deliciously tangy and sour with hints of lemon. Because of its flavor, it is used as a souring agent instead of, or in addition to, citrus juice or vinegar. Sumac is found in Middle Eastern stores or online.

Italian Chocolate Hazelnut Spread

Gianduia

ITALY

Makes about 2 1/2 cups   GF, SFO, <30

In Europe, chocolate is considered a food, and, indeed, it does contain valuable antioxidants. Combined with nuts, it makes a delicious (if high-fat) traditional Italian snack spread to use like peanut butter on toast or bread. I would recommend it as a treat; not an everyday commodity! Since most commercial brands of gianduia (pronounced "jahn-doo-ya") contain hydrogenated fats, dairy products, and non-organic chocolate, I make my own. It's easy to make, and the flavor is superior. If you have leftovers, you can swirl it into muffin batter or homemade vegan ice cream. You can also use it in sweet breads or as a chocolate panini filling with sliced bananas.

12 OUNCES VEGAN SEMISWEET CHOCOLATE CHIPS OR BAK-
ING CHOCOLATE, COARSELY CHOPPED

3/4 CUP NONDAIRY MILK, HEATED JUST TO THE BOILING POINT

3/4 CUP HAZELNUT BUTTER OR 4 OUNCES (1 CUP) PEELED,
TOASTED HAZELNUTS (SEE TIPS)

1 TABLESPOON COCONUT OIL (OMIT THE OIL IF YOU USE THE
HAZELNUT BUTTER)

2 TABLESPOONS CONFECTIONERS' SUGAR

1 TABLESPOON SOY OR RICE PROTEIN POWDER

1/2 TEASPOON PURE VANILLA EXTRACT

1. Place the chocolate in a food processor. Pulse the chocolate briefly and then let the machine run until the chocolate is ground into very small pieces.

2. Heat the nondairy milk to the boiling point, in a small pot on the stove over medium-high heat, or in a microwave in 2-cup microwave-safe pitcher, at 100 percent power for 1 minute.

3. With the machine running, pour the hot milk slowly through the open tube. The chocolate will melt as you run the processor. Quickly open the processor, scrape the chocolate down from the sides of the processor bowl and add the hazelnut butter. Process briefly to disperse it evenly throughout the chocolate. Scrape down the sides of the processor bowl once more. Add the remaining ingredients and process again until the mixture is very smooth.

4. The mixture will be thin and warm, but it will thicken up when refrigerated. Pour into 3 sterilized 1/2-pint canning jars, tighten the lids and refrigerate. They will keep, refrigerated, up to 1 month.

TIPS

- **If you're using whole hazelnuts,** grind the hazelnuts and oil to a paste in a food processor first. Scrape it out of the food processor into a cup, leaving as little behind as possible.

- How to peel and toast hazelnuts or filberts at the same time: Preheat oven to 400°F. Transfer the hazelnuts to a shallow baking pan in a single layer. Roast them until the skins are almost black, about 10 minutes. Wrap the hot hazelnuts in a clean kitchen towel and rub them in the towel until most of the skins have come off. Discard the skins.

The Common Pot

Soups

S oup is one of my favorite meals. It can be eaten anytime (yes, I even eat it for breakfast) and as a filling snack. That's one reason I like to keep soup on hand – my husband likes to snack, and a low-calorie, satisfying bowl of soup is a perfect solution.

My mother made soup about once a week, usually a lentil soup or a chickpea/vegetable soup. I have continued that habit – in fact, in fall and winter, I make soup almost every other day. My daughters also make soups, perhaps remembering my advice that making homemade soup is a great way to eat heartily on a tight budget, but perhaps also because they know that it tastes so much better than the commercial variety.

Canned and packaged soups certainly abound on supermarket shelves. But how many of those soups are vegan? And how many are as hearty and delicious as the television ads would have you believe? If you're not used to making your own soups, it will come as a nice surprise to learn how easy it is. Most of my soup recipes feed six or more because it's a time-saver to make more than you need and refrigerate or freeze the rest for a quick meal on another day.

For people (especially kids) who claim to dislike vegetables, grains and/or beans, soups are the perfect way to serve them these foods because they are more subtle when included in a tasty broth or perhaps even pureed. You can puree beans, potatoes, or grains to make soups creamy without cream. You can add some cooked beans and grains to a vegetable soup to make it a full-meal deal.

Every culture makes soup, and it was difficult to choose which recipes to include in this chapter. Soups have always been the mainstay of peasant cooking the world over – filling, warming, comforting, easy to stretch, and a good way to use up leftovers or whatever is in good supply in the garden. For good vegan soup, a tasty broth or stock is a must. There's no shame in using commercial vegan bouillon cubes, powders, or pastes. See pages 2-4 for advice on tasty vegan brands and also how to make your own.

The Common Pot

Georgian-Style Matzoh Ball Soup

REPUBLIC OF GEORGIA/JEWISH

Serves 5 to 6   GFO

With its delicate steamed walnut dumplings served in a light herbal mushroom broth, this soup is a lovely starter, especially for Passover. We enjoy it for a light meal any time of the year.

1 3/4 CUPS RAW WALNUTS, FINELY GROUND IN A DRY FOOD
    PROCESSOR
1 (12.3-OUNCE) BOX EXTRA-FIRM SILKEN TOFU, DRAINED
    AND CRUMBLED (SEE NOTE)
3/4 CUP MATZOH MEAL (CAN BE GF)
1 SMALL CARROT, FINELY SHREDDED
1/2 SMALL ONION, MINCED
1/2 TABLESPOON DRIED OREGANO
1 TEASPOON SALT
3/4 TEASPOON FRESHLY GROUND BLACK PEPPER
6 CUPS CHICKEN-STYLE VEGAN BROTH (SEE PAGE 2)
2 CUPS RICH MUSHROOM STOCK (PAGE 4)
1/4 CUP MINCED FRESH PARSLEY
1/4 CUP MINCED FRESH BASIL OR CILANTRO
1 1/2 TABLESPOONS CHOPPED FRESH DILL WEED OR 1/2
    TABLESPOON DRIED

1. Combine the ground walnuts, tofu, matzoh meal, carrot, onion, oregano, salt, and pepper in a food processor. Pulse at first, and then process until well mixed and fairly smooth. Transfer to a bowl, cover, and refrigerate for one hour.

2. Divide the dough into 32 equal pieces and roll them into smooth balls, using damp hands. You can cook the dumplings ahead of time and add them to the soup just before serving, if you wish, or make them just before serving.

3. Transfer the balls, not touching, to oiled steaming plates or baskets, with small holes in them, not grates. Steam the dumplings over gently boiling water, covered, for 10 minutes. If you make them ahead of time, they can be steamed again for a few minutes just to re-heat.

4. In a large pot, combine both broths, parsley, cilantro, and dill and heat to boiling, then reduce the heat to low.

5. To serve, transfer 4 or 5 warm dumplings each to warmed shallow soup bowls and gently ladle the hot broth over them. Serve immediately.

Note: I use silken tofu as a binder instead of the usual egg – it's the only thing that works and still results in a delicate dumpling. I understand that many vegan Jews choose to follow the Sephardic tradition for Passover cooking, even when they are of Ashkenazic ancestry, because it allows more choice within the vegan diet. Tofu is acceptable in the Sephardic Passover tradition.

Smoky Spicy Hominy Soup

Posole

MEXICO/U.S.A.

Serves 4   GF, SF, <30

I had been meaning to make a vegan version of the traditional, hearty Mexican soup posole for a long time, but this version was something of a spur-of-the-moment inspiration. I had to feed a crowd something fast and tasty. Those cans of hominy that I'd brought from my last visit to California called to me, and all the other ingredients were at hand for making this spicy, full-meal pot of goodness. Even my omni guests loved this thick, "meaty" soup.

1 TABLESPOON OLIVE OIL
12 MEDIUM GREEN ONIONS, SLICED 1/8-INCH THICK
3 CLOVES GARLIC, MINCED
2 TEASPOONS GROUND CUMIN
1 1/2 TEASPOONS SMOKED SWEET PAPRIKA (PIMENTÓN)
5 CUPS CHICKEN-STYLE VEGAN BROTH (SEE PAGE 2)
1 (29-OUNCE) CAN (3 1/2 CUPS) GOLDEN OR WHITE HOMINY,
    RINSED AND DRAINED (SEE NEXT PAGE)
4 CUPS RECONSTITUTED SOY CURLS (4 OUNCES OR 3 CUPS
    DRY; PAGE 10); OR 16 OUNCES LIGHT SEITAN CUTLETS
    (PAGE 5), CUT INTO STRIPS
1 CUP CANNED DICED TOMATOES AND JUICE OR SAUCE

1 SMALL CHIPOTLE CHILE IN ADOBO SAUCE, MINCED
1/2 CUP CHOPPED FRESH CILANTRO OR FLAT-LEAF PARSLEY
GARNISHES (ALL OR A FEW): TORTILLA CHIPS; AVOCADO
    CUBES TOSSED IN LEMON OR LIME JUICE; CHOPPED
    SWEET ONION; VEGAN SOUR CREAM; SHREDDED SAVOY
    CABBAGE; SLICED RADISHES; CHOPPED CUCUMBERS;
    TOASTED PUMPKIN SEEDS (PEPITAS); SHREDDED
    VEGAN CHEESE; CHOPPED RED BELL PEPPER; SLICED
    HOT CHILES; LIME WEDGES

Heat the oil in a soup pot over medium-high heat. Add the green onions, garlic, cumin, and smoked paprika. Sauté until the onion are wilted. Add the broth, hominy, Soy Curls or seitan, tomatoes, and chipotle. Bring to a boil, then reduce the heat to medium. Cover and simmer 15 minutes. Stir in the cilantro. Ladle the soup into large bowls and serve hot with the garnishes.

Hominy

Hominy is made from dried field corn that has been peeled by soaking and cooking it with calcium oxide, also known as "cal" in Spanish or "quick-lime" in English. It is popular in the Southern United States and Latin America. Look for "Mexican-style" hominy, but you can use "Southern-style" if necessary. If you can't find canned hominy, you can order dried posole (*pozole*) corn (also known as *mote*) from Rancho Gordo, or other online vendors. Soak 1 cup of dried posole corn in lots of water 6 to 10 hours, simmer for about four hours, then drain and add to the soup. You may have a bit more than 3 1/2 cups.

Peruvian Rice and Coriander Soup
Aguadito de "Pollo"
PERU

Serves 8   SFO, GFO, <30

This is a comfortingly thick soup (and a lot of it – but it freezes well) and very delicious, with colorful bits of bell pepper throughout and some hot pepper punch, if you want it. Years ago, the first recipe for this soup that I encountered was an Argentine recipe made with chicken. This is my vegan Peruvian version, that uses parsley and ground coriander instead of cilantro, with some tomato added. Originally, I used parsley and ground coriander because I couldn't find cilantro, but I still use them because I like the flavor of the coriander. You can use cilantro instead of parsley, if you prefer. **Gluten-Free/Soy-Free Opti**on: Use 3 cups canned or cooked chickpeas instead of the seitan or tofu.

1 TABLESPOON OLIVE OIL
1 MEDIUM ONION, CHOPPED
2 RED OR GREEN BELL PEPPERS (OR ONE OF EACH), CUT
    INTO 1/2-INCH PIECES
3 CLOVES GARLIC, CHOPPED
8 CUPS CHICKEN-STYLE VEGAN BROTH (SEE PAGE 2)
LIGHT SEITAN CUTLETS (PAGE 5) OR MARINATED, UNCOOKED
    CRISPY MARINATED TOFU SLICES (PAGE 8), CUT INTO
    STRIPS; OR 3 CUPS SOY CURLS, PAGE 10)
1 (28-OUNCE) CAN DICED TOMATOES, UNDRAINED
2 CUPS SHREDDED CABBAGE
1 1/2 TO 2 CUPS COOKED LONG-GRAIN BROWN RICE
1/2 CUP FROZEN PEAS
1 MEDIUM CARROT, DICED
1 CUP CHOPPED CELERY WITH LEAVES
1 LARGE THIN-SKINNED POTATO, SCRUBBED AND CUT INTO
    1/2-INCH DICE
2 TABLESPOONS CHICKEN-STYLE VEGAN BROTH POWDER
1/2 CUP CHOPPED PARSLEY OR CILANTRO
2 TABLESPOONS GROUND CORIANDER (OMIT IF USING CILANTRO)
SALT AND FRESHLY GROUND BLACK PEPPER TO TASTE
OPTIONAL: 1 TEASPOON AJÍ AMARILLO (PERUVIAN YELLOW
    CHILE) PASTE OR SRIRACHA SAUCE, OR TO TASTE

In a large soup pot, heat the olive oil over medium-high heat. Add the onion, peppers, and garlic and sauté until the onion softens, 3 to 5 minutes. Add the remaining ingredients, except for the salt and pepper and optional chile paste. Bring to a boil, then reduce the heat to low; cover and simmer 30 minutes. Taste for salt and pepper, add the chile paste, if using. Serve hot.

Sweet and Sour Pomegranate Soup

Shorbat Rumman

IRAQ

Serves 6   GF, SF, <30

This soup, called shorbat rumman in Iraq, is a beautiful soup in every way – sweet-sour delicious and a vibrant hot pink color with flecks of green. It's a meal in itself and very easy to make. Serve with plenty of Arabic-style flat breads, pita, or crusty bread.

1 TABLESPOON OLIVE OIL
1 CUP CHOPPED ONION
8 CUPS VEGETABLE BROTH
1 TABLESPOON YEAST EXTRACT PASTE, SUCH AS MARMITE
    (SEE PAGE 21)
1/2 CUP YELLOW SPLIT PEAS, PICKED OVER, RINSED AND
    DRAINED
3 MEDIUM BEETS, PEELED AND CUT INTO 1/2-INCH DICE
1 1/2 CUPS COOKED BROWN BASMATI RICE
1 SMALL BUNCH GREEN ONIONS, COARSELY CHOPPED
1/2 CUP MINCED FRESH PARSLEY
2 TABLESPOONS FRESH LEMON JUICE OR 3 TABLESPOONS
    LIME JUICE
2 TABLESPOONS POMEGRANATE MOLASSES (PAGE 73) OR 1
    CUP POMEGRANATE JUICE
2 TABLESPOONS SUGAR
1 POUND FRESH SPINACH, TRIMMED AND SLICED 1/4-INCH THICK
1/4 CUP MINCED FRESH CILANTRO, OPTIONAL
Garnish:
1 TABLESPOON DRIED MINT, CRUMBLED
1/4 TEASPOON GROUND CINNAMON
1/4 TEASPOON FRESHLY GROUND BLACK PEPPER

1. Heat the olive oil in a large pot over medium-high heat. Add the onions and sauté until the onions wilt, about 5 minutes. Add the broth, Marmite, and split peas to the pot and bring to a boil over high heat. Skim off any foam that gathers on top. Reduce the heat, cover, and simmer for 1 hour. Add the beets and cooked rice and cook 30 minutes.

2. Add the green onions, sugar, lemon or lime juice, parsley, and pomegranate molasses or juice. Simmer for 10 minutes. Bring the soup to a boil again and add the spinach, stirring as it wilts. Stir in cilantro, if you are using it. Add more broth if it seems too thick and taste for salt. Serve hot, sprinkling each serving with some of the garnish.

Persian New Year's Soup

PERSIA/IRAN

Serves 8   SFO, GFO

This is an unusual, nutritious, and delicious soup, made with a variety of dried legumes and flavored with a number of herbs. We serve it on Naw Ruz, the Persian New Year, which is on the Spring Equinox.

1/4 CUP DRIED CHICKPEAS, RINSED AND DRAINED
1/4 CUP DRIED BLACK-EYED PEAS, RINSED AND DRAINED
1/4 CUP DRIED SMALL RED BEANS, RINSED AND DRAINED
2 TABLESPOONS OLIVE OIL
4 CUPS THINLY SLICED ONION (2 TO 3 LARGE ONIONS)
5 CLOVES GARLIC, MINCED
FRESHLY GROUND BLACK PEPPER
1 TEASPOON TURMERIC
12 CUPS VEGETABLE BROTH
1/2 CUP DRIED LENTILS, RINSED AND DRAINED
1 1/2 TABLESPOONS DRIED DILL WEED
1/2 CUP COARSELY CHOPPED GREEN ONIONS
3 CUPS COARSELY CHOPPED KALE, COLLARD GREENS, OR
    SWISS CHARD, TOUGH STEMS REMOVED
1 POUND FRESH SPINACH, COARSELY CHOPPED
1 MEDIUM BEET, PEELED AND SHREDDED

8 OUNCES DRIED LINGUINE OR FETTUCCINE, BROKEN IN
    HALF (CAN BE GF)
2 TABLESPOONS FRESH LEMON JUICE
SALT
GARNISH:
1 TABLESPOON OLIVE OIL
1 LARGE ONION, THINLY SLICED
3 CLOVES GARLIC, MINCED
1 TEASPOON DRIED MINT
TOFU "YOGURT" OR CASHEW "YOGURT" (PAGE 33) OR
    STOREBOUGHT COCONUT YOGURT

1. Soak the dried beans and peas in hot water to cover for at least 2 hours. Drain in a colander.

2. In a large soup pot, heat the 2 tablespoons olive oil over medium-high heat. Add the onions and garlic and sauté until the onions soften, 5 to 10 minutes. Add the pepper and turmeric and stir into the onions. Add the soaked beans and the broth. Bring to a boil, cover, reduce the heat and simmer for 45 minutes, then add the lentils and simmer about 1 hour more.

3. Add the dill weed, green onions, kale, spinach, and grated beets. Simmer for 30 minutes longer. Add the pasta and cook for 10 more minutes, stirring often so that the pasta doesn't stick together, until the pasta is tender. Stir in the lemon juice and taste for salt and pepper.

4. For the garnish, heat the 1 tablespoon olive oil in a medium skillet. Add the onion and garlic and sauté over medium-high heat until the onion is softened and browned. Add the mint and stir well.

5. Serve the bowls of soup with a garnish of the sautéed minted onions and a dollop of yogurt.

Peruvian-Inspired Sweet Potato Chowder

Chupe

PERU

Serves 6   GF

Chupe is a hearty chowder, a favorite of my father, and a jewel in the crown of Peruvian cuisine. It is usually made with yellow potatoes and seafood, but I was inspired to make a vegan version with sweet potatoes as well as the usual yellow potatoes. It is a moderately spicy soup that can be served as a casual company meal with crusty bread and salad. It is typically made with ají amarillo *(Peruvian yellow chile paste), but you can use sriracha sauce instead.*

2 TABLESPOONS OLIVE OIL
2 CUPS MINCED ONION
2 LARGE CLOVES GARLIC, MINCED
1/2 CUP GOOD TOMATO SALSA (NO SUGAR)
1 TO 2 TABLESPOONS AJÍ AMARILLO (PERUVIAN YELLOW
    CHILE) PASTE OR SRIRACHA SAUCE TO TASTE
8 CUPS VEGETABLE BROTH
1/2 TABLESPOON CHOPPED FRESH OREGANO OR 1/2 TEA-
    SPOON DRIED
FRESHLY GROUND BLACK PEPPER
3 CUPS COOKED, PEELED SWEET POTATO, CUT INTO 1-INCH
    DICE
2 TEASPOONS SUGAR
1 TEASPOON TURMERIC
1 1/4 POUNDS YUKON GOLD POTATOES, STEAMED, PEELED
    AND CUT INTO 1-INCH DICE
1 1/2 CUPS COOKED BROWN BASMATI RICE
1 CUP FROZEN BABY PEAS (PETIT POIS), THAWED
2 CUPS FRESH SWEET CORN KERNELS OR 2 CUPS FROZEN
    (THAWED) SWEET CORN
8 OUNCES MEDIUM-FIRM REGULAR TOFU OR EXTRA-FIRM
    SILKEN TOFU, DRAINED AND CRUMBLED
1/2 CUP DRY WHITE WINE
1 1/2 TEASPOONS SALT
1/4 CUP MINCED FRESH PARSLEY
1 COOKED CORN ON THE COB, CUT INTO 2-INCH CHUNKS
6 GREEN GARLIC TOPS (SCAPES), TIED INTO KNOTS, OP-
    TIONAL

1. Heat the oil in a large pot over medium heat. Add the onion and garlic and sauté until the onion begins to soften – do not brown it at all. Add the salsa, chile paste, broth, oregano, bell pepper, sweet potato, sugar, and turmeric to the pot. Bring to a boil, then reduce the heat to low and simmer for 10 minutes.

2. Puree the soup right in the pot with an immersion/stick blender. (Alternatively, blend in batches in a blender or food processor. Make sure that air can escape from the lid of either machine, covering the air-hole with a folded clean kitchen towel. This will eliminate the danger of exploding hot soup.) Transfer the pureed soup back into the pot.

3. Add the cooked potato chunks, cooked rice, peas and corn. Cover and simmer for 10 minutes.

4. In a blender, combine the tofu, wine, and salt and blend until very smooth. Stir this into the soup and heat gently. Taste for seasoning.

5. Serve the soup hot in wide, warmed soup plates, garnished with the parsley and/or corn, and/or the garlic, and vegan shrimp, if using.

Velvety Brussels Sprout Crema

ITALY

Serves 4   GF, SF

"Velvety" is indeed the best description for this rich garden soup. The Brussels sprouts are bright green and still a bit crisp – a great combination of textures and flavors, which, believe it or not, was inspired by a dream! Perhaps I should have called it "Dreamy Brussels Sprout Crema" instead? Italians are experts at making nutritious, delicious creamed vegetable soups out of common vegetables – this soup is made in that spirit.

2 TEASPOONS PLUS 1 TABLESPOON VEGAN MARGARINE, DIVIDED

Pomegranate Molasses

Known as *dibs rumman* in Arabic, pomegranate molasses is an essential Middle Eastern ingredient. It has wonderful flavor and a heady aroma and keeps in the refrigerator almost indefinitely after opening. The uses for this tangy, piquant syrup are many. It blends well with walnuts, adds a tart and pungent flavor to beans and other savory dishes, and gives an astringent edge to salads and vegetables. It is delicious in glazes, dressings and marinades and it can even be diluted and used for tart drinks and sorbets. It is available from Middle Eastern, North African, Greek, and Turkish grocery stores and online vendors.

Alternatives: Neither of these has quite the distinctive tang of pomegranate molasses, but would do in a pinch. Do search out a source for pomegranate molasses; it's so delicious!

1. Combine equal parts light (or "fancy") molasses and tamarind paste.(Tamarind paste is easy to find in Asian grocery stores and in supermarkets that have a good Asian or Indian section.)

2. Mix 2 tablespoons light (or "fancy") molasses with 3 tablespoons lemon juice; boil down to a thicker syrup.

Note: Pomegranate molasses should not be confused with grenadine syrup, which is made from the same base but has sugar and other flavorings added.

1 MEDIUM ONION, COARSELY CHOPPED

2 RIBS CELERY, CUT INTO 1/4-INCH SLICES

1 CLOVE GARLIC, MINCED

2 MEDIUM RUSSET POTATOES (8 TO 10 OUNCES TOTAL),
    PEELED AND CUT INTO 1/2-INCH DICE

3 CUPS CHICKEN-STYLE VEGAN BROTH (SEE PAGE 2)

1/2 TEASPOON PLUS 1/4 TEASPOON SALT, DIVIDED

1 POUND FRESH BRUSSELS SPROUTS, TRIMMED, HALVED
    AND CUT INTO 1/8-INCH SLICES

4 GREEN ONIONS, SLICED 1/4-INCH THICK

1 1/2 TABLESPOONS CHOPPED FRESH DILLWEED OR 1/2
    TABLESPOON DRIED (PLUS MORE FOR GARNISH)

3/4 CUP NONDAIRY MILK

1/4 CUP RAW ORGANIC CASHEW PIECES SOAKED FOR 10
    MINUTES IN HOT WATER AND DRAINED

FRESHLY GROUND BLACK PEPPER

1 LARGE MILD-FLAVORED VEGAN SAUSAGE, THINLY-SLICED
    AND SAUTEED, OPTIONAL

1. In a medium nonstick pot over high heat, melt the 2 teaspoons vegan margarine. Add the onion, celery, and garlic, and sauté for 5 minutes, adding a sprinkling of water from your fingertips only as needed to keep it from sticking. Do not brown the vegetables.

2. Add the potatoes, broth, and 1/2 teaspoon salt to the pot and bring to a boil. Cover, reduce the heat to low and simmer for about 15 minutes or until the potatoes are tender.

3. In a large nonstick skillet, melt the 1 tablespoon vegan margarine over high heat. Add the sliced Brussels sprouts and green onion and stir-fry just until the sprouts are crisp-tender. Add the 1/4 teaspoon salt and dill and toss briefly. Remove from the heat and set aside.

4. Blend the nondairy milk and drained cashews to a smooth cream in a blender. Set aside.

5. Test the potatoes for doneness. When the potatoes are soft, puree the soup right in the pot with an immersion/stick blender. Alternatively, transfer all of the solids to a food processor or blender with a slotted spoon and puree until smooth. (Make sure that air can escape from the lid of either machine, covering the air-hole with a folded clean kitchen towel. This will eliminate the danger of exploding hot soup.) Add a small amount of the broth to the pureed mixture to make it pourable, then stir the pureed mixture back into the pot.

6. In a blender, combine the nondairy milk and cashews, and blend until very smooth. Stir the cashew cream into the soup. It should be velvety smooth. Season with salt and pepper to taste. Transfer half of the stir-fried Brussels sprouts to the soup and stir briefly.

7. To serve, ladle the hot soup into four wide soup plates, which have been warmed. Divide the reserved Brussels sprouts evenly among the four soup plates, mounding them in the middle, but slightly to one side of the soup plate. If you are using the optional sausage slices, spoon them into a small mound beside the Brussels sprouts. Garnish with dill weed as desired and serve hot.

Potato and Mushroom Miso Soup

JAPAN

Serves 4   GF, <30

There are many versions of miso soup, both in Japan and around the world. I love this particular combination of miso with mushrooms, potatoes, and onions for a hearty, but not heavy, soup. If you prefer (or for a start to a Japanese meal), omit the mushrooms, potatoes, and onions and serve the broth plain with a few cubes of tofu.

3 CUPS RICH MUSHROOM STOCK (PAGE 4)

1 CUP WATER

1 (4-INCH) PIECE OF DRIED KONBU (KOMBU) SEAWEED

4 OUNCES FRESH MUSHROOMS (ANY KIND), CUT INTO 1/4-
    INCH THICK SLICES

8 OUNCES THIN-SKINNED POTATO, SCRUBBED AND THINLY
    SLICED

1 MEDIUM ONION, THINLY SLICED

6 OUNCES EXTRA-FIRM SILKEN TOFU OR FIRM REGULAR
TOFU, DRAINED AND CUT INTO 1/2-INCH CUBES
1/3 CUP BROWN RICE OR BARLEY MISO PASTE
2 GREEN ONIONS, DIAGONALLY SLICED 1/8-INCH THICK

1. Combine the broth, water, konbu, mushrooms, potato and onion in a medium pot. Bring to a boil, then turn down to medium-low heat and simmer for about 15 minutes or until the potato is just tender. Remove and discard konbu.

2. Add the cubed tofu and simmer briefly again to heat. Remove the pot from the heat.

3. In a small bowl, whisk a little of the hot broth with the miso until smooth. Add this back to the soup, serve immediately and garnish each serving with green onions.

Vietnamese "Fisherman's Soup"

VIETNAM

Serves 6   GF

This fruity, fresh-tasting soup is, despite the long list of ingredients, very easy to put together. (If you are in a hurry, you can use chopped garlic and ginger from jars and shredded cabbage in a bag.) It is very low in calories and fat, but filling and spicy. You can use authentic Vietnamese ingredients or substitute more common North American ones suggested below, still with fabulous results. Mung bean sprouts are a must, though.

6 LARGE DRIED SHIITAKE (OR CHINESE BLACK FOREST)
MUSHROOMS
2 CUPS BOILING WATER
3 CUPS VEGETABLE BROTH
2 CUPS SHREDDED CABBAGE (I USE SAVOY)
1 (19-OUNCE) CAN UNSWEETENED PINEAPPLE TIDBITS,
UNDRAINED
1 LARGE ONION, COARSELY CHOPPED
2 CARROTS, CUT INTO MATCHSTICK PIECES
1 CUP CANNED OR FRESH DICED TOMATOES
3 TABLESPOONS SOY SAUCE
2 TABLESPOONS FINELY MINCED LEMONGRASS OR 1 TABLE-
SPOON FINELY GRATED ORGANIC LEMON ZEST
2 TABLESPOONS SUGAR OR 1 TABLESPOON AGAVE NECTAR
2 TABLESPOONS FINELY GRATED FRESH GINGER
2 TABLESPOONS DULSE OR NORI FLAKES OR SMALL PIECE
OF KONBU SEAWEED, OPTIONAL
2 CLOVES GARLIC, MINCED
1 TEASPOON SRIRACHA SAUCE
FRESHLY GROUND BLACK PEPPER
8 OUNCES FIRM REGULAR OR SILKEN TOFU, DRAINED AND
CUT INTO SMALL 1/2-INCH CUBES
2 TABLESPOONS CHOPPED FRESH MINT, BASIL, OR CILAN-
TRO (OR 2 TEASPOONS DRIED)
2 TABLESPOONS TAMARIND CONCENTRATE OR PASTE, OR
1/4 CUP FRESH LIME OR LEMON JUICE
2 PINCHES SALT
3 CUPS FRESH MUNG BEAN SPROUTS
6 GREEN ONIONS, CUT DIAGONALLY INTO 1/4-INCH THICK
SLICES

1. Soak the dried mushrooms for 30 minutes in the 2 cups boiling water, covered. Drain the mushrooms, reserving the soaking water. Discard the tough stems. Cut the mushroom caps into 1/8-inch slices.

2. In a large pot, combine the broth, cabbage, pineapple and juice, onion, carrot, sliced mushrooms, mushroom soaking water, tomatoes, soy sauce, lemon grass, sugar, ginger, optional seaweed, garlic, hot sauce, and black pepper. Bring the soup to a boil, then reduce the heat to medium-low and simmer, covered, just until the cabbage and carrots are crisp-tender, about 15 minutes. Add the tofu, stirring gently and simmer about 5 more minutes. Add the mint, tamarind concentrate, and salt. Taste for seasoning. Top each serving with a mound of fresh bean sprouts and green onions. Serve hot.

Tip: The minced lemongrass is from the tender inner white part of fresh or frozen lemon grass. The fresh white part does not need to be removed. However, if using dried lemon grass, leave it whole and remove after simmering.

Golden Cauliflower Dal Soup

BURMA

Serves 6   GF, SF

I devised this soup after having a delicious meal at the Mandalay Restaurant in Seattle. It's not an exact duplicate of what I had there, but pretty close.

- 4 CUPS VEGETABLE BROTH
- 1 1/2 CUPS WATER
- 1 1/2 CUPS DRIED SPLIT RED LENTILS, PICKED OVER, RINSED AND DRAINED
- 1 1/4 TEASPOONS TURMERIC, DIVIDED
- 1/2 LARGE CAULIFLOWER, TRIMMED, BROKEN INTO FLOWER-ETTES AND CUT INTO 1/4-INCH SLICES
- 2 TABLESPOONS COLD-PRESSED PEANUT OIL OR OLIVE OIL, DIVIDED
- SALT
- 1 LARGE ONION, MINCED
- 2 CLOVES GARLIC, CRUSHED
- 1 TABLESPOON GROUND CUMIN
- 1 TABLESPOON GROUND CORIANDER
- 1 TABLESPOON MILD OR HOT CURRY PASTE
- 1 TEASPOON GARAM MASALA
- 1 TEASPOON BLACK MUSTARD SEEDS

1. Preheat the oven to 400°F. Mix the broth, water, lentils and 1/4 teaspoon of the turmeric in a medium pot. Bring to a boil over high heat, skim off any foam that appears, then cover and reduce heat to a simmer.

2. Combine the cauliflower with 1 tablespoon of the oil and 1/4 teaspoon salt on a 10 x 15-inch baking sheet and place it in the oven. Roast, tossing the cauliflower occasionally, until the cauliflower is tender and a little charred in places, about 20 minutes. Remove from the oven and set aside.

3. Heat the remaining 1 tablespoon of oil in a large skillet or wok. Add the onion and garlic and stir-fry, turning the heat down a bit if necessary, until the onion is soft, but not brown, about 10 minutes. Add the spices, curry paste and salt to taste. Stir briefly, then transfer this mixture to the soup pot.

4. When the lentils are soft, puree the soup right in the pot with an immersion/stick blender until it is smooth. (Alternatively, blend the soup in batches in a food processor or blender and puree until smooth. Make sure that air can escape from the lid of either machine, covering the air-hole with a folded clean kitchen towel. This will eliminate the danger of exploding hot soup.) Add pepper to taste and add the roasted cauliflower last. Serve hot.

The Common Bowl

Salads

Imention my late father a lot in this book, I realize, but he was a gourmet of Italian descent and he influenced me greatly. Born in Peru, which has one of the most sophisticated cuisines in the world, my father insisted on a salad every night, which he would always eat last in the Italian style as a "digestive." Our salads were usually made with crispy California Romaine lettuce, sourdough garlic croutons (homemade with real garlic), and my mother's simple fresh lemon juice and olive oil dressing. I still love that salad, but I've branched out a bit.

Salads may not be quite as universally loved as soups, but they're close. In many countries, salads are cold dishes made with cooked foods (sometimes only very slightly cooked), rather than raw. We often enjoy this type of salad as the main dish during the summer, made not only with vegetables, but often with hearty whole grains, whole-grain pasta, legumes, potatoes, nuts, and fruit. It was very difficult to decide on which recipes to include in this chapter, but these are some of our favorites, and I hope you will add a few to your repertoire.

The Common Bowl

Red, White, (and Blue) Potato Salad

U.S.A./CANADA

Serves 6   GF, <30

This patriotic potato salad can be red, white, and blue for the American Fourth of July, or red and white (the colors of the maple leaf flag) for July 1st, Canada Day. It makes a colorful, fresh, and tangy counterpart to your favorite vegan burgers or links.

- 2 POUNDS NEW OR NUGGET POTATOES (USE HALF WHITE POTATOES AND RED POTATOES OR 12 OUNCES WHITE POTATOES, PLUS 10 OUNCES EACH OF RED AND BLUE POTATOES)
- 1/2 CUP VEGETABLE BROTH OR OIL SUBSTITUTE FOR SALAD DRESSINGS (PAGE 80)
- 2 TABLESPOONS OLIVE OIL
- 2 TABLESPOONS RED WINE VINEGAR
- 1 TABLESPOON BALSAMIC VINEGAR
- 1 TABLESPOON DIJON MUSTARD
- 1/2 TABLESPOON BROWN SUGAR
- 1/2 TEASPOON SALT
- 1 CLOVE GARLIC, CRUSHED
- FRESHLY GROUND BLACK PEPPER
- 1 SMALL RED ONION, FINELY CHOPPED
- 2 LARGE GREEN ONIONS, SLICED 1/8-INCH THICK
- 1 TABLESPOON CHOPPED FRESH DILLWEED OR 1 TEASPOON DRIED
- 1/2 CUP DRAINED AND CRUMBLED EXTRA-FIRM TOFU
- 1/4 CUP WALNUT PARM (PAGE 15)

1. Gently scrub the potatoes, but leave the skins on. Leave the potatoes whole if they are very small nuggets. Otherwise, cut into 1-inch dice. Steam the potatoes over simmering water until tender, about 15 minutes. Transfer to a serving bowl.

2. In a small bowl, combine the broth, oil, both vinegars, mustard, sugar, salt, garlic, and plenty of black pepper. Whisk together to blend well, then pour over the still hot potatoes. Add the red and green onions, dillweed, tofu, and Walnut Parm. Toss well to combine. Cover and refrigerate until serving time.

Peruvian Tri-Color Potato Salad Terrine

Causa Limeña

PERU

Serves 8   GF, SF

Causa Limeña *(pronounced kow-sah lee-men-ya) is very beautiful and makes an artistic and delicious centerpiece for a summer company meal. It's hard to describe, because, when you explain that it's "a potato salad made out of mashed potatoes," that doesn't sound very appetizing. But this unique cold salad is perhaps more clearly described as sort of terrine, with layers of savory, chile-laced filling and three colors of potatoes. The traditional recipe contains generous amounts of oil and is stuffed with seafood, but this version is much lower in oil and is, of course, vegan. Ají amarillo (Peruvian yellow chile paste) is available from online.*

Lemon Dressing:
- 1/2 TEASPOON SALT
- 2 SMALL CLOVES GARLIC, MINCED OR CRUSHED
- 1/2 CUP OIL SUBSTITUTE FOR SALAD DRESSINGS (PAGE 80)
- 2 TABLESPOONS OLIVE OIL
- 2 TABLESPOONS FRESH LEMON JUICE

Potato Layers:
- 1 POUND RUSSET POTATOES
- 1 POUND YELLOW POTATOES, SUCH AS YUKON GOLD, OR PINK-FLESHED POTATOES
- 1 POUND PURPLE OR BLUE POTATOES
- 10 1/2 TABLESPOONS LEMON DRESSING (SAVE REMAINING DRESSING FOR FILLING)
- 1/4 CUP PLUS 2 TABLESPOONS VEGAN MAYO (PAGE 18)
- 1/2 TABLESPOON SALT

Filling:
- 1 TABLESPOON OLIVE OIL
- 2 MEDIUM ONIONS, SLICED PAPER-THIN
- 3 CLOVES GARLIC, MINCED
- 2 MEDIUM BELL PEPPERS (YELLOW, ORANGE, AND/OR RED), CUT INTO MATCHSTICKS
- 10 OIL-PACKED SUN-DRIED TOMATO PIECES, CUT INTO MATCHSTICKS
- 1 CUP MARINATED ARTICHOKE HEARTS, DRAINED AND

SLICED 1/4-INCH THICK

1 TO 2 TABLESPOONS AJÍ AMARILLO (PERUVIAN YELLOW
CHILE) PASTE OR SRIRACHA SAUCE

REMAINING LEMON DRESSING (FROM ABOVE)

SALT AND FRESHLY GROUND BLACK PEPPER

Garnishes:

2 LARGE COBS SWEET CORN, COOKED, COOLED AND CUT
INTO 1 1/2-INCH-THICK ROUNDS

1 LARGE STEAMED OR BAKED ORANGE SWEET POTATO,
PEELED AND SLICED IN 6 TO 8 PIECES (COLD OR AT
ROOM TEMPERATURE)

18 TO 24 PERUVIAN ALFONSO OR KALAMATA OLIVES

Optional Garnishes:

AVOCADO CUBES, TOSSED IN LEMON JUICE

ROASTED, PICKLED OR RAW RED BELL PEPPERS, CUT INTO
STRIPS

PICKLED HOT PEPPERS

OIL-PACKED SUN-DRIED TOMATOES

CRISP LETTUCE LEAVES

1. **Lemon Dressing:** Mash together the salt and garlic to a coarse paste with the back of a teaspoon in a small round-bottomed bowl. (The salt grains will help mash the garlic to a paste and the garlic juice will dissolve the salt.) Whisk in the Oil Substitute, olive oil, and lemon juice with a fork or small wire whisk. This method of mixing is easy and convenient for small amounts made just before dressing the salad.

2. **Potato Layers:** Cook the three varieties of potatoes separately. You can peel and simmer the Russet and the yellow potatoes (cut into even-sized chunks) in water to cover until just tender, but the purple or blue potatoes fall apart easily, so I steam them with the skins on. I cut them into about 2-inch pieces and steam them in a covered microwave-safe 2-quart casserole with 3 tablespoons of water in the microwave for about

Oil Substitute for Salad Dressings

I use olive oil most of the time in my salad dressings, and, for uncooked dishes like these you should use a tasty extra-virgin olive oil. But I also prefer to cut down on the amount of oil in dressings, so I often use my Oil Substitute for Salad Dressings in place of most of the oil. This simple starch-based mixture makes a silky, slightly thickened, emulsified dressing, which is not possible if you use plain water, juice, or broth, and without the odd mouth-feel of added vegetable gums. Use this simple mixture in place of all or some of the oil in salad dressing.

Oil Substitute for Salad Dressings
Makes 1 cup

1 CUP COLD WATER OR LIGHT VEGETABLE BROTH

2 TEASPOONS CORNSTARCH OR POTATO STARCH

Whisk the ingredients together in a small saucepan. Cook, stirring constantly, until it is thickened and clear. Cornstarch will have to boil; potato starch does not.

Other Oil Substitutes: If you prefer, you can use the broth from cooking chickpeas instead of the starch mixture. Chickpea cooking broth jells like chicken broth when it chills, so it works well in salad dressings. If the dressing needs more thickening, adding a spoonful of Dijon mustard, pureed fruit, pureed cooked beans or vegetables, or roasted garlic adds more body.

10 minutes. If steamed on the stove, they will take 15 to 20 minutes. The other potatoes can also be steamed, if you like. To remove the skins of the blue or purple potatoes, hold them under gently-running cold water and the skins should slip off easily. Be careful not to saturate the potatoes with water.

3. Mash each batch of potatoes separately in its cooking pot or a bowl. When mashed, add the following to each separate batch of potatoes: 3 1/2 tablespoons of the lemon dressing, 2 tablespoons of the mayonnaise and 1/2 teaspoon of salt. Mash each batch of potatoes again until smooth. Reserve the remaining dressing for the filling. Set the mashed potatoes aside, covered.

4. **Filling:** Heat the olive oil in a large nonstick skillet over medium-high heat. Add the onions, garlic, and bell peppers and sauté until softened. Add the sun-dried tomatoes, artichoke hearts, chile paste, and the remaining dressing. Mix well, then taste for salt and pepper.

5. **To assemble:** Line a 9 x 5-inch loaf pan, a 2-quart round casserole or a 1.5-quart rectangular pâté mold with oiled plastic wrap, with an overlap over the sides and ends. Press one of the mashed potato mixtures onto the bottom of the pan. Add 1/2 of the filling, spreading evenly, then the second of the potato mixtures, followed by the remaining filling, and then the remaining potato mixture. Smooth the top, pressing down gently and evenly, fold the overlapping plastic wrap over, and refrigerate for several hours or days.

6. **To Serve:** Fold back the plastic wrap covering the top of the terrine. Carefully unmold the terrine onto a platter, removing the plastic wrap, and garnish attractively as desired. Carefully slice the terrine into 1-inch thick slices.

Hot German Potato Salad

GERMANY/U.S.A.

Serves 6   <30

My late mother-in-law, Ruth Stuhr Clark, was very fond of hot German potato salad, made with bacon and bacon fat. I had never heard of this salad before I married her son, my late husband Wayne, but I loved it years ago. Now I can have it again. I use dark sesame oil in place of bacon fat in this and other recipes, as it adds a rich, smoky flavor.

2 POUNDS RED POTATOES, PEELED OR UNPEELED
4 TO 5 OUNCES VEGAN BACON SLICES, CUT IN MATCHSTICKS
1 MEDIUM ONION, MINCED
1 TABLESPOON DARK SESAME OIL
2 TABLESPOONS ALL-PURPOSE FLOUR
1/2 CUP CIDER VINEGAR
1 CUP VEGETABLE BROTH
2 TEASPOONS SUGAR
1 TEASPOON CELERY SEEDS
3/4 TEASPOON SALT
FRESHLY-GROUND BLACK PEPPER
1/2 CUP MINCED FRESH PARSLEY

1. Cook the potatoes (whole if small or cut into 1 to 2-inch cubes) either by simmering in water just to cover or by steaming over simmering water until tender but still firm, about 20 minutes. Drain in a colander. Transfer the potatoes to the covered pot they were cooked in and place it over low heat for a few minutes to dry the potatoes out a bit. (Don't burn them!) Alternatively, microwave the potato cubes in a covered 2-quart microwave-safe bowl, with 3 tablespoons of water, on 100% power (default setting) for 10 minutes or until tender. Drain the potatoes in a colander until cool enough to handle. Cut them into 3/8-inch thick slices and set aside.

2. In a large, deep skillet (preferably nonstick or cast iron), heat the oil over high heat. Add the onion and sauté until lightly browned, about 5 minutes.

3. Sprinkle the flour over the onion and stir with a wooden spoon, then add the broth, vinegar, sugar, celery seeds, and salt and pepper to taste. Stir-fry over medium heat until thickened.

4. Add the vegan bacon and potatoes to the skillet and gently stir until well-coated. Cook gently until heated through and season with salt and pepper to taste. Transfer the salad to a serving bowl and sprinkle with the parsley. Serve warm.

Tip: If you cooked the potatoes with the skins on, you can leave them on, or hold the cooked potatoes under gently-running cold water and the skins should slip off easily. Be careful not to saturate the potatoes with water.

North African Potato and Zucchini Salad

Tirshi

<small>TUNISIA/NORTH AFRICA</small>

Serves 4   GF, SF, <30

North Africans are famous for their unusually delicious salads. This garlicky mashed salad was a big hit with my guests, despite its rather homely appearance. Tirshi is a mashed vegetable salad that is often made with pumpkin, but I prefer it with potatoes.

1 POUND ZUCCHINI (WHOLE)
2 MEDIUM BAKING POTATOES (SUCH AS RUSSETS)
DRESSING:
1 TABLESPOON FRESH LEMON JUICE
4 CLOVES GARLIC, CRUSHED
3/4 TEASPOON GROUND CUMIN
1/2 TEASPOON RED PEPPER FLAKES
1/2 TEASPOON SALT
2 TABLESPOONS OLIVE OIL

1. Preheat the oven to 500°F. Place the zucchini on an oiled 12 x 17-inch baking sheet and pierce it a few times in random spots with a fork. Bake it in the hot oven until it is soft inside, turning once or twice, 20 minutes or longer, depending on thickness. The peel will come right off. Mash the "flesh" of the zucchini coarsely and let it drain in a colander or sieve.

2. Peel the potatoes and cut them into approximately 2-inch pieces. Transfer the potatoes to a small saucepan, cover with water and bring to a boil. Turn the heat to medium, cover and cook just until tender, about 20 minutes. Drain the potatoes in a colander and transfer back to the saucepan. Mash the potatoes coarsely. Add the zucchini to the potatoes and mix well.

3. In a small bowl, combine the dressing ingredients, except for the oil. Stir the dressing into the vegetables, then transfer the mixture to a serving bowl and drizzle with the olive oil. Serve at room temperature.

Peruvian-Style Crispy Tofu and Cabbage Salad

Salpicón de Tofu con Col

<small>PERU</small>

Serves 4   GFO

This unusual cabbage salad, Salpicón de Tofu con Col (pronounced sal-pee-kohn day tofu kohn kohl), is not only delicious, filling, and refreshing – it's inexpensive and beautiful. Crispy fingers of pan-fried tofu cover a lemony wilted cabbage salad surrounded by colorful chunks of corn and sweet potatoes. It's hard to describe just how terrific this salad is – suffice it to say that there's never any left when I serve it. To keep the sodium down level down, I blanch the cabbage rather than the traditional method of wilting it with salt. We make this often for guests (this recipe is easily doubled).

Dressing:
1/4 CUP OIL SUBSTITUTE FOR SALAD DRESSINGS (PAGE 80)
2 TABLESPOONS OLIVE OIL

2 TABLESPOONS FRESH LEMON JUICE

1/2 TABLESPOON DIJON MUSTARD

1/2 TEASPOON SALT

1 SMALL CLOVE GARLIC, CRUSHED

1/8 TEASPOON WHITE PEPPER

Salad:

3 CUPS THINLY-SLICED OR SHREDDED SAVOY CABBAGE

1 MEDIUM RED BELL PEPPER, CUT INTO MATCHSTICKS

1 SMALL CARROT, CUT INTO MATCHSTICKS

1 SMALL SWEET OR RED ONION, THINLY SLICED (SEE TIP)

1 TABLESPOON CHOPPED FRESH DILLWEED OR 1 TEASPOON
   DRIED

1 SMALL STEAMED OR BAKED ORANGE SWEET POTATO,
   PEELED AND CUT INTO 4 PIECES (COLD OR ROOM
   TEMPERATURE)

12 KALAMATA OLIVES OR PERUVIAN ALFONSO OLIVES

Optional Garnishes:

1/4 CUP CUBED TOFU FETA (PAGE 101)

2 YELLOW POTATOES, PEELED, STEAMED AND SLICED 1/2-
   INCH THICK (COLD OR ROOM TEMPERATURE)

1 RIPE HASS AVOCADO, PITTED, PEELED AND CUT INTO
   1/2-INCH CUBES, TOSSED IN 1 TABLESPOON LEMON
   JUICE

12 CRISPY MARINATED TOFU SLICES (PAGE 8)

1. **Dressing:** Whisk the dressing ingredients together in a small bowl with a whisk. Set aside.

2. **Salad:** Blanch the cabbage for about 1 minute in a large pot of boiling water – just until wilted. Transfer it to a colander and rinse well under cold running water. Drain well.

3. In a large bowl, combine the cabbage, onion, bell pepper, carrot, and dill. Add the dressing and mix well. Mound the salad on a platter and surround with the sweet potato and olives. Cut the tofu slices into matchsticks and arrange on top of the salad along with any optional garnishes that you may prefer. Serve cold or at room temperature.

Tip: If you have no sweet onion or red onion: Use an ordinary yellow cooking onion, but peel and slice it paper-thin. Transfer it to a bowl and cover it with boiling water. Let it sit for about 5 minutes, then drain and rinse it, then drain

again. This removes the sharp raw onion flavor.

If you have cooked sweet potatoes and chunks of cooked corn leftover from the garnish, use them to make Peruvian-Inspired Sweet Potato Chupe on page 72.

Balinese-Inspired Spicy Green Bean Salad

BALI

Serves 3   GFO, <30

I wanted to make a vegan version of the Balinese salad "lawar," but what I ended up with is really quite different. Lawar is fairly complicated to make, and I didn't have access to some of the spices. And, to be honest, I knew it would be too spicy-hot for us. So this is a very simplified, North-Americanized version, but absolutely delicious.

16 OUNCES LIGHT SEITAN CUTLETS (PAGE 5), CUT INTO
   STRIPS; OR MATCHSTICK STRIPS OF MARINATED,
   UNCOOKED CRISPY MARINATED TOFU SLICES (PAGE 8),
   DRAINED; OR 4 CUPS RECONSTITUTED SOY CURLS (4
   OUNCES OR 3 CUPS DRY, OR ALTERNATIVE (PAGE 10)

3 TABLESPOONS FRESH LIME JUICE, DIVIDED

1 TABLESPOON FINELY GRATED FRESH GINGER

2 TEASPOONS THAI RED CHILE PASTE (FISH-FREE), DIVIDED

1 TABLESPOON COLD-PRESSED PEANUT OIL

1/2 TEASPOON DARK SESAME OIL

6 SMALL GREEN ONIONS, FINELY CHOPPED

6 CLOVES GARLIC, MINCED

1/4 TEASPOON RED PEPPER FLAKES

3 CUPS (12 OUNCES) YOUNG GREEN BEANS, STEAMED OR
   BLANCHED UNTIL CRISP-TENDER

1/4 CUP SHREDDED COCONUT

2 TABLESPOONS VEGETABLE BROTH

1/2 TEASPOON SALT

1. In a medium bowl, mix together the seitan strips, 2 tablespoons of the lime juice, ginger, and 1 teaspoon of the chile paste. Set aside.

2. In a large, nonstick skillet, heat the oils. Add

the green onions and garlic and stir-fry until softened. Add the remaining 1 teaspoon chile paste and red pepper flakes and stir-fry for a minute more. Add the seitan mixture to the skillet and stir-fry to combine the ingredients and heat through. Turn off the heat and add the cooked green beans, coconut, remaining lime juice, and salt. Mix well. Serve warm, at room temperature, or cold.

Moroccan Passover Spinach Salad

MOROCCO

Serves 4 to 6   GF, SF, <30

This North African salad would not win any beauty contests, but it's a super delicious way to prepare spinach.

2 POUNDS FRESH SPINACH, CLEANED, TRIMMED AND
    DRAINED
1 TABLESPOON OLIVE OIL
2 CLOVES GARLIC, CRUSHED
1 TEASPOON GROUND CUMIN
1 TEASPOON PAPRIKA
2 TABLESPOONS FRESH LEMON JUICE
SALT

1. Steam the spinach until just wilted. Drain the spinach in a colander and allow to cool.

2. Heat the olive oil in a medium skillet. Add the garlic and spices and stir-fry for a minute. Add the spinach to the oil and stir-fry for another minute. Stir in the lemon juice and salt to taste. Transfer to a serving bowl and allow to come to room temperature before serving.

Glazed Moroccan Carrot Salad

MOROCCO

Serves 4 to 6   GF, SF, <30

Moroccans are famous for their salads, and they do wonderful things with our common winter vegetable, the carrot. If you have access to a Middle Eastern or North African grocery store, you may be able to find jars of Moroccan preserved lemons, which lend a distinctive flavor to many Moroccan dishes.

1 1/2 POUNDS CARROTS, PEELED AND CUT INTO MATCH-
    STICKS
JUICE OF 1 LARGE LEMON (ABOUT 5 TABLESPOONS)
2 TABLESPOONS OLIVE OIL
2 TABLESPOONS MINCED PARSLEY
1/2 TEASPOON SALT
1/2 TEASPOON MINCED GARLIC
1/8 TEASPOON PAPRIKA
1/8 TEASPOON FRESHLY-GROUND BLACK PEPPER
Garnish:
4 TO 6 STRIPS OF MOROCCAN PRESERVED LEMON OR LONG
    SHREDS OF ORGANIC LEMON ZEST

1. Steam the carrot matchsticks just until crisp-tender. Transfer them to a colander and cool them off under cold running water. Drain well.

2. In a small bowl, whisk the lemon juice and olive oil with the remaining ingredients and then toss with the carrots. Transfer to a serving dish. Garnish with the preserved lemon peel or fresh lemon zest. Serve at room temperature.

Multi-Grain Sushi Salad
Bara-Zushi

JAPAN

Serves 4   SFO, GF

Urge your guests to eat this salad as "roll-it-yourself" sushi (temaki-zushi), by serving it with squares of toasted nori seaweed. Each diner scoops a little of

the sushi rice mixture into the nori square, wraps it up and eats it out of hand. (If you don't care for seaweed, use chopsticks or a fork.) The addition of millet to the brown rice in this dish raises the protein content and lowers the glycemic index rating. Add some vegan protein options to make a full meal. There are many kinds of sushi, but this is probably the easiest, because there is no rolling or shaping.

3/4 CUP SHORT GRAIN BROWN RICE

1/4 CUP MILLET, TOASTED (BELOW)

1 1/2 CUPS WATER

1/4 CUP RICE VINEGAR

1 TABLESPOON SUGAR

3/4 TEASPOON SALT

1 TABLESPOON DRY SHERRY, OPTIONAL

2 CUPS OF ADDITIONS (SEE LIST)

Accompaniments:

TAMARI OR SOY SAUCE (OR SF SAUCE, PAGE 12)

PICKLED GINGER

WASABI PASTE

Optional: 8 SHEETS TOASTED NORI SEAWEED SHEETS, CUT INTO 4 EQUAL PIECES

1. Combine the toasted millet and brown rice in a medium saucepan with a tight lid and add the water. Bring to a boil, then reduce the heat to

Toasting Millet

Toasting millet before cooking brings out a deeper flavor and helps avoid the millet being mushy on the outside and crunchy in the middle. If you toast millet before cooking, there's no need to rinse it, either. To toast, place the millet in a heavy dry skillet (such as cast iron) over medium heat and stir constantly with a wooden spoon for 3 to 4 minutes until you can detect a nutty aroma. Then remove from the heat and proceed with recipe.

low. Cover and cook for 40 to 45 minutes.

2. Transfer the hot cooked grains to an 8 x 12-inch or larger baking pan. Mix the sugar and salt with the vinegar and wine in a small bowl until it is dissolved and pour over the hot grains. Fold the seasoning mixture into the grains with a spatula (bamboo or wooden is traditional), using an over-and-under-motion, until the mixture is cool.

3. Add the additions that you are using and mound the rice attractively in a shallow bowl. Serve with any of the Accompaniments you wish or eat "as is." Sushi is served at room temperature.

ADDITIONS

Use 2 or more of these (2 cups, total):

- leftover steamed or stir-fried vegetables, chopped
- shredded carrots
- sautéed or grilled sliced mushrooms
- green onions, sliced 1/8-inch thick diagonally
- seasoned baked or smoked tofu, or Smoky Baked Tofu (page 59) chopped or sliced
- strips of seitan
- strips of grilled eggplant or summer squash
- baby peas (petit pois), thawed in hot water and drained well
- watercress or leafy herbs
- leftover scrambled tofu (page 45)
- strips of roasted or grilled bell peppers
- chopped cucumber or radish
- pickled onion or pickled eggplant
- thin strips of nori seaweed cut with kitchen shears
- Cavi-Art (a vegan "caviar" made of sea vegetables)

Tip: Don't make more than you can eat, because this shouldn't be refrigerated. The rice kernels harden when chilled.

Instead of the millet, you can use quinoa. Use only 1/2 cup short grain brown rice, cooked as instructed above with 3/4 cup water, and 1/2 cup quinoa, well-rinsed, cooked in a separate saucepan with 1 cup water for only 15 minutes and then left to sit off the heat for 5 minutes. Combine the two before adding the seasonings.

Fruity Tabouli

MIDDLE EAST/NORTH AMERICA

Serves 4 to 5   GFO, SF, <30

Don't let a lack of fresh tomatoes deprive you of enjoying a tabbouleh-like salad. This is a fruity and very refreshing variation on traditional tabbouleh.

3/4 CUP MEDIUM BULGUR WHEAT

3/4 CUP BOILING WATER

2 MEDIUM ORGANIC ORANGES

1 LARGE, RIPE MANGO, PEELED, PITTED, AND CUT INTO 1/4-INCH DICE

1 1/4 CUPS ENGLISH CUCUMBER, WASHED BUT NOT PEELED, CUT INTO 1/4-INCH DICE

1 CUP MINCED FRESH FLAT-LEAF PARSLEY (2 CUPS LOOSE-LY-PACKED LEAVES)

3/4 CUP MINCED FRESH MINT (1 1/2 CUPS LOOSELY-PACKED LEAVES)

1/2 CUP FINELY CHOPPED GREEN ONIONS (ABOUT 5 MEDIUM)

8 KALAMATA OLIVES, PITTED AND COARSELY CHOPPED

Dressing:

1/4 CUP FRESH LEMON JUICE

1/4 CUP VEGETABLE BROTH OR OIL SUBSTITUTE FOR SALAD DRESSINGS (PAGE 80)

2 TABLESPOONS OLIVE OIL

1/2 TEASPOON SALT

FRESHLY-GROUND BLACK PEPPER TO TASTE

OPTIONAL: 1 TO 2 TABLESPOONS AGAVE NECTAR OR SUGAR

1. Transfer the bulgur to a salad bowl and pour the boiling water over it. Cover and let stand for 30 minutes while you prepare the vegetables and dressing.

2. Shred the zest of one of the two oranges on top of the bulgur. Peel the two oranges (seed if necessary) and separate into sections. Cut each section in half or in thirds. (Another way to prepare oranges for salad is to slice off the peel with a sharp knife and then cut the orange into 1/2-inch chunks.) Place the orange chunks (and any juice) on top of the bulgur. Whisk the dressing ingredients together in a small bowl and set aside.

3. Add the vegetables and herbs to the soaked bulgur. Pour the dressing over the mixture and mix well. Cover and refrigerate until serving time.

Tip: The parsley, mint, and green onions can all be chopped together in a dry food processor.

Wheat-Free Substitutes for Bulgur and Couscous

For those with a wheat sensitivity (not a gluten allergy, however), there is now a kamut bulgur on the market that could be used in place of couscous, as well. From what I've read, it can be used just like wheat bulgur. If you must eat gluten-free, substitute quinoa for bulgur and couscous.

Universal Comfort Foods
Pasta, Potato, and Grain Mains

Being part Italian, I love pasta, and we serve it often. Over the years, we began to enjoy the improved quality of whole-wheat pasta that is now widely available, so we eat whole-grain pasta of one kind or another about ninety percent of the time. We also love our potatoes – no fear of complex carbs in our house. British Columbia is a big producer of potatoes, and we buy potatoes grown right here in the Comox Valley. Sometimes, when we're tired and hungry, we'll just have a salad and a baked potato with gravy (page 101) for dinner, and it couldn't be more satisfying.

I grew up having rice almost every day – it's a Peruvian thing. It was very dry, South American-style long-grain white rice. But now I can go to my pantry and find white and brown Basmati rice, white and brown jasmine rice, brown medium-grain and short-grain rice, white Japanese rice, Thai black rice, red rice, and sweet (glutinous/sticky) rice. Each variety has its own special qualities and uses – we enjoy them all. Besides the rice, I can also find three grades of bulgur wheat, millet, couscous (which is actually a type of pasta that we treat like a grain), pearl and pot barley, oats, and red and white quinoa, the Peruvian seed that we think of as a grain. What abundance!

These wonderful, nutritious comfort foods are the basis of the following collection of recipes that takes us on a trip around the world, from Singapore Noodles to Greek Nugget Potato and Kalamata Olive Stew and on to Mexican Tamale Pie. These carbohydrate-rich foods are great sources of fiber, vitamins, minerals, and also protein that sustained our hard-working ancestors over the centuries, and they sustain us today with a variety that our forebears could only imagine.

Universal Comfort Foods

Pasta with Cauliflower and Spicy Tomato-Creme Sauce

ITALY

Serves 4   GFO, <30, SFO

Do you think cauliflower and pasta is an odd combination? Give it a try – it's very down-home Italian. Best of all, you can make this satisfying, creamy, spicy pasta dish in the time it takes to boil the pasta. Any type of tubular pasta works well in this recipe, but I prefer penne rigate, which has little ridges in it to catch the sauce.

12 OUNCES PENNE OR OTHER TUBULAR PASTA
1 LARGE CAULIFLOWER, CUT INTO SMALL FLORETS AND
   SLICED ABOUT 1/2-INCH THICK
4 TEASPOONS OLIVE OIL
2 LARGE CLOVES GARLIC, MINCED
3/8 TEASPOON RED PEPPER FLAKES
2 1/4 CUPS CANNED DICED TOMATOES, UNDRAINED (2/3 OF A
   28-OUNCE CAN)
1/2 TEASPOON SALT
1/3 CUP NONDAIRY MILK
1/3 CUP CRUMBLED FIRM SILKEN TOFU
WALNUT PARM (PAGE 15)

1. Put a large pot of salted water on to boil. When it boils, add the pasta and set the timer for about 5 minutes. After 5 minutes, add the cauliflower to the pasta and cook 5 to 7 minutes, or until the pasta is al dente. Drain the cauliflower and pasta in a colander.

2. Heat the oil in a large nonstick skillet or stir-fry pan. Add the garlic and red pepper flakes over medium heat and sauté briefly. Add the tomatoes and salt. Mash the tomatoes a bit with a potato masher and simmer for 5 minutes.

3. In a blender, combine the nondairy milk and tofu and blend until smooth. Add the resulting cream to the pan and stir briefly to combine and heat through. Add the pasta and cauliflower and toss to coat with the sauce. Serve in pasta bowls with the Walnut Parm on the side.

Gluten-Free Option: use gluten-free pasta.

Soy-free Option: omit the tofu; use 3 tablespoons raw cashews plus 1/2 cup nondairy milk.

Farfalle with Sun-Dried Tomatoes and Oyster Mushrooms

ITALY

Serves 4   GFO, SFO

This luxurious pasta dish is easy enough for everyday but elegant enough for company. Instead of farfalle (bowtie pasta), another bite-sized pasta such as rigatoni, penne, or ziti may be used.

3/4 CUP PLUS 1/2 CUP BOILING WATER, DIVIDED
16 SUN-DRIED TOMATO PIECES (NOT OIL-PACKED)
1/4 CUP DRIED PORCINI MUSHROOMS
1 TABLESPOON OLIVE OIL
4 CLOVES GARLIC, MINCED
1/2 TABLESPOON MINCED FRESH ROSEMARY OR 1/2 TEA-
   SPOON DRIED
1/2 TABLESPOON MINCED FRESH THYME OR 1/2 TEASPOON
   DRIED
1 1/2 CUPS SLICED FRESH OYSTER MUSHROOMS
1/2 CUP NONDAIRY MILK
1/2 CUP EXTRA-FIRM SILKEN TOFU
1/2 TEASPOON SALT
FRESHLY GROUND BLACK PEPPER
12 OUNCES FARFALLE OR OTHER BITE-SIZED PASTA
1/4 CUP WALNUT PARM (PAGE 15) OR CHOPPED TOASTED
   WALNUTS

1. In a small heatproof bowl, pour the 3/4 cup boiling water over the sun-dried tomatoes. In a separate bowl, pour the remaining 1/2 cup boiling water over the dried mushrooms. Cover both bowls and set aside for 30 minutes. Remove the tomatoes from the water, squeeze them, and chop them. Set the tomato soaking water aside (don't discard it). Do the same with the mushrooms, saving the soaking water, but discard the sediment from the bottom of the bowl.

2. In a large nonstick skillet, combine the sun-

dried tomatoes, olive oil, garlic, and tomato soaking water over high heat. Stir for a few minutes to reduce the liquid. Add the soaked dried mushrooms, rosemary, thyme, and fresh oyster mushrooms. Stir until the mushrooms start to wilt, adding drops of water as necessary to keep from sticking. Add the mushroom soaking water and salt. Reduce the liquid a little more. Remove the pan from the heat.

3. Cook the pasta in a large pot of boiling salted water, until it is al dente, about 10 minutes. Drain the pasta in a colander.

4. In a blender, combine the soymilk and tofu and blend until smooth. Add the resulting cream to the pan with the mushroom mixture and cook over high heat just until it boils. Add salt to taste, then add the pasta and mix well. Grind pepper over the top.

5. Divide the pasta evenly among four warm plates or pasta bowls and sprinkle each serving with 1 tablespoon of Walnut Parm. Serve immediately.

Gluten-Free Option: Use gluten-free pasta.

Soy-Free Option: Omit the tofu and use 1/4 cup raw cashews blended until smooth in a blender with 3/4 cup nondairy milk.

Pasta ala Pescarese

ITALY

Serves 4   <30, GFO

If you are missing seafood dishes, this may just satisfy your cravings. I made this pasta when some of my granddaughters (none of them vegans) were visiting, and they loved it. It's seriously scrumptious, super-easy, and fast. Dulse is a sea vegetable and dulse flakes are available in natural food stores. For a gluten-free option, use gluten-free pasta.

8 OUNCES TEMPEH (I PREFER SEVEN-GRAIN TEMPEH)
8 OUNCES MEDIUM SHELL PASTA OR TUBULAR PASTA
1 CUP VEGETABLE BROTH

1 TABLESPOON DULSE FLAKES, OPTIONAL
1/4 CUP SEASONED FLOUR (PAGE 9) OR WHOLE-WHEAT FLOUR
2 TABLESPOONS EXTRA-VIRGIN OLIVE OIL
1 MEDIUM ONION, MINCED
2 CLOVES GARLIC, MINCED
1/8 TEASPOON RED PEPPER FLAKES
1 (14-OUNCE) CAN DICED TOMATOES, UNDRAINED
1/2 CUP FROZEN BABY PEAS (PETIT POIS)
2 TABLESPOONS DRY WHITE WINE OR WHITE VERMOUTH
1/2 TABLESPOON CHOPPED FRESH OREGANO OR 1/2 TEA-
    SPOON DRIED
1/2 TABLESPOON CHOPPED FRESH BASIL OR 1/2 TEASPOON
    DRIED
1/2 TEASPOON SALT
FRESHLY GROUND BLACK PEPPER
CHOPPED FLAT-LEAF PARSLEY

1. Cut the tempeh horizontally into 4 equal pieces. Cut each piece into 6 to 8 wedge-shaped pieces. In a medium skillet, bring the broth and dulse, if using, to a boil. Add the tempeh in a single layer, reduce the heat to low, cover and simmer for 10 minutes. Drain well.

2. Cook the pasta in a large pot of boiling salted water until al dente. Drain in a colander and set aside.

3. Heat 1 tablespoon of the oil in a large skillet over medium heat. Add the onion and sauté until softened, about 5 minutes. Add the garlic and red pepper flakes and sauté for 2 to 3 minutes. Add a few drops of water if it starts to stick. Add the tomatoes, peas, wine, herbs, and salt and simmer gently.

4. Toss the tempeh in the seasoned flour just to coat, then transfer to a plate.

5. Heat the remaining 1 tablespoon of olive oil in a medium nonstick skillet over high heat. Add the tempeh in a single layer and reduce the heat to medium-high. Brown the tempeh on both sides until crispy. Add the cooked pasta and tempeh to the skillet with the sauce, adding pepper liberally to taste. Serve hot in shallow pasta bowls with a garnish of chopped parsley.

Instead of tempeh, substitute one (or a combination) of these options:

- thawed frozen vegan "fish," cut into 1-inch cubes
- frozen vegan "shrimp" or "prawns," cut in half
- canned gluten "abalone," rinsed and drained
- canned Worthington "Skallops"
- smoked tofu cubes; or a combination – see Vegan "Seafood" sidebar

Tip: No need to precook the vegan "seafood" products before adding to the sauce.

Greek-Style Lasagne

GREECE

Serves 4 to 6   <30, GFO

A friend gave me a recipe years ago which I "veganized." I don't know if this is really a Greek dish – but it does have many Greek ingredients, including feta, eggplant, and kalamata olives. Since olive oil and olives are essential to the flavor of this dish, I use a fat-free béchamel and "grill" the eggplant under the broiler instead of frying it, producing a rich-tasting dish without too much fat. You can make the components for this deceptively simple dish days ahead and put it all together for a quick company meal at a later date. Serve with a simple green salad and crusty bread. Your guests will love it.

8 WHOLE-WHEAT DURUM SEMOLINA LASAGNA NOODLES (OR GLUTEN-FREE VARIETY)

2 EGGPLANTS (ABOUT 3 POUNDS), SLICED 1/2-INCH THICK

1 (28-OUNCE) CAN DICED TOMATOES, DRAINED

1 TABLESPOON OLIVE OIL

1 TEASPOON DRIED ROSEMARY

SALT AND FRESHLY GROUND PEPPER

2 CUPS QUICK "FETA" CRUMBLE (FOLLOWS)

OLIVADA (FOLLOWS)

VEGAN BÉSCIAMELLA SAUCE (PAGE 37), USING THE LOW-FAT VERSION WITH 1/4 CUP FLOUR

1. Preheat the oven to 350°F. In a large pot of boiling water, cook the lasagna noodles until al dente, drain in a colander, rinse them and lay them out flat on a baking sheet (any size) lined with baking parchment cut to fit.

2. Arrange the eggplant slices on an oiled 12 x 17-inch baking sheet in one layer, brush lightly with olive oil, and broil about 3 to 4 inches below your broiler heat source until slightly charred on the outside and soft on the inside, about 5 minutes per side. Set aside.

3. Spread the drained tomatoes on an oiled 12 x 17-inch baking sheet. Add the olive oil, rosemary and salt and pepper to taste and mix to combine. Place the baking sheet about 3 to 4 inches below the broiler's heat source and broil until the tomatoes begin to char, about 10 minutes. Set aside.

Vegan "Seafood"

Vegan seafood alternatives are a little harder to find than meat and cheese substitutes. Two products are Worthington Tuno (some people love it; some people hate it!) and Worthington Vegetable Skallops. You can order a dizzying array of delicious Chinese-style meat, poultry, and seafood substitutes, including "shrimp," from www.vegieworld.com and www.vegecyber.com. Some of these products are made from textured soy protein, gluten, or a combination of both. They are often available in Asian stores, usually in the frozen-food section.

4. Place four lasagna noodles in the bottom of an 8 x 12-inch baking pan lined with baking parchment cut to fit. Arrange half of the egg-plant slices, cut to fit the pan, over the noodles. Spread the roasted tomatoes over the eggplant, then sprinkle the feta over the tomatoes. Spread the olivada over the feta. Place the remaining eggplant slices over the olivada. Top with the last four noodles. Spread the top of the lasagna evenly with the béchamel sauce. Bake for 40 minutes. Cut into squares and serve piping hot.

Olivada

Makes 7/8 cup   GF, SF, <30

- 1 1/2 CUPS KALAMATA OLIVES, PITTED
- 1 CLOVE GARLIC, PEELED
- 3 TABLESPOONS OLIVE OIL

Transfer the olives and garlic to a food proces-sor. Pulse briefly, then process at full power. Add the olive oil in a stream while pureeing and pro-cess until the mixture becomes a thick, but not too smooth, paste.

Quick "Feta" Crumble

Makes 2 cups GF, <30

Use this in casseroles, dips and other dishes where you would use crumbled feta.

- 2 CUPS (ABOUT 12 OUNCES) DRAINED, CRUMBLED FIRM
      TOFU (NOT SILKEN)
- 2 TABLESPOONS LIGHT MISO PASTE
- 1 TABLESPOON FRESH LEMON JUICE

Mash all of the ingredients together well and use immediately.

Vushka Pyrogies

Ukraine

Serves 4 to 6   SFO

These delicate dumplings (similar to ravioli, though with thicker dough) are traditionally served for the Ukrainian Christmas Eve feast, which is vegan. The earthy mushroom filling contrasts beautifully with the caramelized onions and vegan sour cream. The recipe can be multiplied 2 or 3 times for a crowd, and it's fun to make with friends and family. The dough is basically an eggless pasta dough, the soy or chickpea flour adding flavor, color, nutrition, and cohesiveness.

Filling:
- 1 TABLESPOON VEGETABLE OIL OR VEGAN MARGARINE
- 1 SMALL ONION, MINCED
- 4 CUPS CREMINI OR BUTTON MUSHROOMS, CHOPPED (I USE
      A DRY FOOD PROCESSOR)
- SALT AND FRESHLY GROUND BLACK PEPPER
Dough:
- 3/4 CUP UNBLEACHED WHITE FLOUR
- 1/4 CUP (SCANT) SOY FLOUR OR CHICKPEA FLOUR (BESAN)
- 3/8 TEASPOON SALT
- 1/3 CUP WATER
To Serve:
- SLOW-COOKER CARAMELIZED ONIONS (PAGE 93)
- TOFU SOUR CREAM OR CASHEW SOUR CREAM (PAGE 33)

1. **Filling:** Heat the oil in a large skillet over me-dium-high heat. Add the onion and sauté until it is soft and slightly browned, lowering the heat a little if it is browning too fast. Add the mush-rooms to the pan with the onions. Sauté for 10 minutes or so, keeping them moving and add-ing a few drops of water or broth as necessary to keep them from sticking, but don't make the mixture too wet. The filling should not be exud-ing juice or the dough will get soggy. Evaporate all liquid in the mixture. Taste the mixture for salt and pepper and remove from the heat. Chill the mixture before filling the dumplings.

2. **Dough (by hand):** In a medium-sized bowl whisk the dry ingredients together. Add the

water, stirring it in with a fork until the dough gathers into a ball. On a lightly floured surface, knead the ball for about 5 minutes, adding a bit of flour if necessary, but don't over-do it. The dough will be stiff, but somewhat stickier than egg noodle dough.

3. **Dough (in a food processor):** Combine the flours and salt in a food processor and pulse to mix. With the motor running, pour in the water through the top. Knead 30 seconds. Remove the dough from the machine and hand-knead it on a lightly floured surface for 1 minute.

4. If possible, transfer the dough to a plastic bag and let it "rest" for about an hour or more before rolling out. This helps to "relax" the gluten and make it easier to roll.

5. Divide the dough into two parts and roll each out on a floured surface (or in a hand pasta machine, flouring well) to 1/8-inch thick. Cut each half of the dough into about nineteen 2 3/4-inch rounds with a cookie or biscuit cutter. (Cover the remaining half with a damp, clean kitchen towel.)

6. Place 1 teaspoon of filling in the center of each round. Moisten the edges of each round and fold one side over the other, making a "half-moon" shape. Pinch the edges well to seal. Be careful not to tear any holes in the dough. Place the finished dumplings, not touching, on baking sheets (any size) lined with baking parchment, cut to fit and sprinkled with flour. Cover the sheet with a clean dry kitchen towel while you work.

7. The formed dumplings can be frozen and cooked at a later date. Store them in rigid covered containers, layered between sheets of baking parchment sprinkled with flour or cornmeal.

8. Bring a large pot of water to a boil. Boil several dumplings at a time in the water, not crowding too much, for 3 minutes (timed from when the water comes back to a boil, if necessary). (Frozen dumplings need to cook about 7 to 8 minutes, timed from when the water comes back

Slow-Cooker Caramelized Onions

I must confess that although I love caramelized onions, I didn't make them very often because of the stirring time required to keep them from burning. Then I discovered an easy way to make a large amount of them in a large slow-cooker, so you can portion and freeze them to use in future recipes. What a concept – caramelized onions ready at a moment's notice.

Though many recipes advise using sweet onions, I use plain yellow onions, and they become very sweet with the long, slow cooking.

Here's what you do: You need a 6-quart slow-cooker. Peel and slice 6 to 8 large onions into 1/8-inch thick slices. To facilitate easy cleaning, line the bottom of your slow-cooker insert (and 1-inch up the sides, particularly in the corners) with baking parchment cut to fit. Arrange the onion slices on top of the parchment and drizzle with 2 to 3 tablespoons olive oil. Cover the pot and cook on Low for 8 hours. The onion aroma is quite strong, so I cook the onions overnight and plug the slow-cooker in out on my deck.

The onions keep, well-covered, in the refrigerator for about a week, but you'll probably want to freeze them in small containers for future use.

to a boil.) Remove the dumplings gently from the pot with a slotted spoon.

9. **To Serve:** Serve the dumplings with sautéed or caramelized onions and tofu or cashew sour cream.

Fresh Pineapple-Noodle Stir-Fry

SOUTHEAST ASIA

Serves 6   GFO, SFO, <30

This is a fresh-tasting and slightly spicy Asian-fusion dish, with a touch of Hawaii, that's very easy to make. A little bit sweet, a little bit spicy, chock-full of vegan "chicken," mushrooms, greens, and fresh pineapple, it's one of those dishes that you just don't want to stop eating. This recipe could also be made with strips of grilled or fried tempeh, or baked, seasoned tofu.

12 OUNCES SEMOLINA OR GLUTEN-FREE SPAGHETTI

2 LARGE PORTOBELLO MUSHROOMS, LIGHTLY RINSED AND
    PATTED DRY

1 TEASPOON COLD-PRESSED PEANUT OIL OR VEGETABLE OIL

12 OUNCES LIGHT SEITAN CUTLETS, CUT INTO STRIPS (PAGE
    5); OR STRIPS OF MARINATED, UNCOOKED CRISPY
    MARINATED TOFU SLICES (PAGE 8), DRAINED; OR 3
    CUPS RECONSTITUTED SOY CURLS (3 OUNCES OR 2 1/4
    CUPS DRY) OR ALTERNATIVE (PAGE 10)

2 CLOVES GARLIC, THINLY SLICED

1 TABLESPOON GRATED FRESH GINGER

3 CUPS FRESH PINEAPPLE, CUT INTO 1/2-INCH CHUNKS

2 TABLESPOONS DARK MOLASSES

6 CUPS THINLY SLICED SWISS CHARD, TOUGH STEMS RE-
    MOVED

1 CUP VEGETABLE BROTH

3 TABLESPOONS SOY SAUCE OR SOY-FREE SAUCE (PAGE 12)

2 TABLESPOONS FRESH LIME JUICE

1 TO 2 TABLESPOONS SRIRACHA OR OTHER ASIAN HOT
    SAUCE

2 TABLESPOONS TOASTED SESAME SEEDS

1. Cook the spaghetti in a large pot of boiling salted water until just tender, about 10 minutes. Drain and set aside.

2. Remove and discard the stems of the mushrooms. Scrape the dark-brown gills from the insides of the caps with the edge of a teaspoon. Halve the mushroom caps and cut them into 1/4-inch thick slices. Set aside.

3. Heat the oil over high heat in a large nonstick skillet or wok. Add the seitan and stir-fry briefly to brown. Add the garlic and ginger and stir-fry for another minute. Scrape the mixture into a large dish.

4. Add the pineapple chunks and molasses to the same skillet and stir-fry quickly over high heat until most of the molasses and juice are absorbed. Scrape the pineapple on top of the seitan. Add the sliced mushrooms and chard to the same skillet and stir-fry until wilted. Add the drained spaghetti.

5. In a bowl, mix together the broth, soy sauce, lime juice, and hot sauce, to taste. Quickly add the mixture to the skillet. Toss everything together quickly and continue cooking to allow the spaghetti to absorb most of the liquid. Add the pineapple mixture and mix gently and evenly. Serve hot, on a large platter, with a sprinkle of toasted sesame seeds on top.

Tip: Instead of spaghetti, you can use egg-free Chinese noodles, such as *gan mian* or *ji mian*.

Singapore Noodles

SINGAPORE

Serves 4   GFO, SFO, <30

This delicious, spicy, colorful rice noodle dish is a fantastic way to eat your veggies – you'll love it! I especially like the combination of seitan or Soy Curls and smoked tofu. This is also great made with strips of grilled tempeh or baked, seasoned tofu.

6 OUNCES RICE VERMICELLI (THIN RICE STICK NOODLES)

1 1/2 CUPS SMALL BROCCOLI FLOWERETTES

2 TABLESPOONS COLD-PRESSED PEANUT OIL

8 OUNCES LIGHT SEITAN CUTLETS, CUT INTO STRIPS (PAGE
    5); OR STRIPS OF MARINATED BUT UNCOOKED CRISPY
    MARINATED TOFU SLICES (PAGE 8), DRAINED; OR 2
    CUPS RECONSTITUTED SOY CURLS, DRAINED AND
    CHOPPED (2 OUNCES; 1 1/2 CUPS DRY); OR ALTERNA-
    TIVE (PAGE 10)

5 OUNCES SMOKED TOFU OR SMOKY BAKED TOFU (PAGE 59),
    DICED; OR VEGAN "SEAFOOD" (PAGE 91)

1 LARGE CLOVE GARLIC, MINCED

2 TABLESPOONS MINCED FRESH HOT OR PICKLED JALAPEÑOS

1 TABLESPOON MINCED FRESH GINGER

1 MEDIUM ONION, THINLY SLICED

1 SMALL CARROT, PEELED AND CUT INTO MATCHSTICKS

4 OUNCES ZUCCHINI, ANY COLOR, CUT INTO MATCHSTICKS

1 CUP JULIENNED BELL PEPPER, ANY COLOR

2 TABLESPOONS FINELY CHOPPED GREEN ONIONS

2 TEASPOONS GOOD QUALITY CURRY POWDER OR CURRY PASTE

1/2 TEASPOON TURMERIC

1 PINCH CAYENNE PEPPER

1/2 CUP VEGETABLE BROTH

2 1/2 TABLESPOONS SOY SAUCE OR SOY-FREE SAUCE (PAGE 12)

SALT

1/2 CUP CHOPPED UNSALTED ROASTED PEANUTS OR CA-
    SHEWS

1 LIME, CUT INTO WEDGES

1. Soak the rice vermicelli in warm water for 20 minutes. Steam the broccoli until tender-crisp, then place under cold running water to cool. Set aside.

2. Heat 1 tablespoon of the oil in a large non-stick skillet or wok over high heat. Swirl the oil around the pan. Add the seitan and smoked tofu (or alternates) and stir-fry for a couple of minutes. Remove from the pan and set aside. Heat the remaining 1 tablespoon oil. Add the jalapeños, garlic, and ginger and stir-fry for 30 seconds. Add the onion and stir-fry for 1 minute. Add the carrot and zucchini and cook 1 more minute. Add the broccoli, bell pepper, and green onions and stir-fry for another 2 minutes or so. Stir in the curry powder or paste, turmeric, and cayenne. Add the seitan and tofu back into the pan and stir well.

3. Drain the soaked noodles and add to the pan, along with the soy sauce and broth. Toss well. Cook until the noodles have absorbed most of the broth. Taste for salt. Transfer to a hot serving platter, top with the chopped nuts and surround with lime wedges. Serve hot.

Japanese Pan-Fried Noodles

Yaki Soba

JAPAN

Serves 4   SFO, GFO, <30

This is Japanese fast food and very good it is, especially for a tasty, quick family meal. If Japanese soba noodles are unavailable, regular vermicelli noodles (or angel hair pasta) can be used instead. Grilled tempeh or baked, seasoned tofu are good alternatives to the seitan.

6 OUNCES JAPANESE SOBA NOODLES OR SEMOLINA OR
    GLUTEN-FREE VERMICELLI

1 TABLESPOON EXPELLER-PRESSED PEANUT OIL

8 OUNCES LIGHT SEITAN CUTLETS, CUT INTO STRIPS (PAGE
    5); OR STRIPS OF MARINATED BUT UNCOOKED CRISPY
    MARINATED TOFU SLICES (PAGE 8), DRAINED; OR 2
    CUPS RECONSTITUTED SOY CURLS, DRAINED AND
    CHOPPED (1 1/2 CUPS DRY), OR ALTERNATIVE (PAGE 10)

2 SMALL CARROTS, CUT INTO MATCHSTICKS

2 CUPS SHREDDED CABBAGE

1 MEDIUM ONION, SLICED PAPER-THIN

1/2 CUP WATER

2 TABLESPOONS DRY SHERRY OR RICE WINE

1 PINCH SALT

1 TABLESPOON DARK SESAME OIL

5 TABLESPOONS VEGAN WORCESTERSHIRE SAUCE (PAGE 13)

Garnish:

2 TABLESPOONS NORI SEAWEED FLAKES

2 TABLESPOONS JAPANESE PICKLED GINGER, CHOPPED

1. Cook the noodles in a pot of boiling water until just tender. Drain well and set aside.

2. Heat the oil in a large nonstick skillet or wok over high heat. Add the seitan and stir-fry briefly, just to brown slightly. Add the carrots, cabbage, and onion and stir-fry briefly. Add the water, cover and cook on high heat, watching carefully, until the vegetables are just wilted, but still slightly crunchy. Add the sherry and salt, then the sesame oil and noodles. Toss over high heat. Add the vegan Worcestershire sauce and cook 1 minute more. Serve topped with the garnishes.

Baked Turkish Potatoes with Tomatoes and Peppers

Patates Oturtmasi

Serves 4

Patates Oturtmasi is a wonderful out-of-the-ordinary casserole that's great for company and potlucks. The combination of hot and sweet peppers, tomatoes, and herbs makes ordinary potatoes seem new and exotic.

- 3 POUNDS THIN-SKINNED POTATOES, SCRUBBED AND SLICED INTO 1/2-INCH-THICK ROUNDS
- 2 CUPS CHOPPED ONION
- 2 TABLESPOONS OLIVE OIL
- 6 OUNCES (ABOUT 1 CUP) GROUND "BEEFY" SEITAN (PAGE 133) OR COMMERCIAL VEGAN BURGER CRUMBLES
- 1 RED OR GREEN BELL PEPPER, CHOPPED
- 2 TABLESPOONS CHOPPED FRESH HOT CHILES OR PICKLED JALAPEÑOS
- 2 RIPE RED TOMATOES, CHOPPED (OR 1 CUP DICED CANNED TOMATOES, DRAINED)
- 1 TABLESPOON CHOPPED FRESH THYME OR 1 TEASPOON DRIED
- 1 TABLESPOON CHOPPED FRESH MARJORAM OR 1 TEA- SPOON DRIED
- SALT AND FRESHLY GROUND BLACK PEPPER
- 3/4 CUP CHOPPED FLAT-LEAF PARSLEY, PLUS MORE FOR GARNISH
- 1 CUP WATER
- 1 LARGE RIPE TOMATO, THINLY SLICED OR DICED CANNED TOMATOES
- 1 GREEN BELL PEPPER, CUT INTO 3/8-INCH THICK RINGS

1. Preheat oven to 400°F. Arrange the potato rounds on 2 oiled 12 x 17-inch baking sheets and spray them with olive oil from a pump sprayer or brush lightly with olive oil. Bake until golden brown on the bottom, then flip them over and bake until the other sides are browned.

2. While the potatoes bake, heat the oil in a large nonstick skillet over medium heat. Add the onion and cook until they begin to wilt and brown, about 5 minutes. Stir in the ground seit-an, then add the chopped bell pepper and chiles and cook for 1 minute. Add the tomatoes and herbs and simmer for 5 minutes. Add the 3/4 cup parsley and season with salt and pepper to taste.

3. When you remove the potatoes from the oven, reduce the heat to 350°F. In a 2-quart round cas-serole arrange half of the potatoes and sprinkle with salt and pepper. Spread half of the tomato/ burger mixture over them. Repeat layers. Add the water, dribbling it around the edge of the cas-serole. Top with tomato slices and bell pepper rings, cover and cook 40 to 50 minutes. Sprinkle with the parsley before serving. Serve hot.

Cheesy Potato Galette

Serves 6   GF, SF, <30

This version of a French casserole makes an elegant side dish of creamy, cheesy potatoes for a festive meal or a meltingly decadent main dish to serve with a variety of colorful vegetables. My omnivore guests devoured it.

- 2 POUNDS YUKON GOLD POTATOES (4 LARGE OR 6 MEDIUM), SCRUBBED
- 1/4 CUP OLIVE OIL
- 1 TO 2 TEASPOONS FRESH OR DRIED THYME OR ROSEMARY (OPTIONAL)
- KOSHER SALT
- FRESHLY GROUND BLACK PEPPER
- 1 CUP WALNUT PARM (PAGE 15)
- 1 RECIPE VEGAN GRUYERE (FOLLOWS) OR 1 1/2 CUPS SHREDDED WHITE VEGAN CHEESE

1. Preheat the oven to 375°F. Spray the inside of two 8-inch tart or cake pans with oil from a pump sprayer. Slice the potatoes as thinly as possible, about 1/16-inch thick. You can use the slicing device on a food processor or a mando-line (manual slicer). Combine the sliced po-tatoes in a mixing bowl with the olive oil and

thyme or rosemary, if using, coating well.

2. Cover the bottoms of the pans with a layer of overlapping potato slices, starting along the outside edge and moving inward until the bottom is covered. Sprinkle with a little kosher salt (about 1/8 teaspoon), pepper to taste, and 2 tablespoons of the Walnut Parm (for each pan). Thinly slice the Vegan Gruyere from the block with a cheese slice and lay slices over the Walnut Parm. (You just want a thin covering of the cheese, not too much). Repeat the layers 3 more times or until you have used up all of the ingredients.

3. Bake the galettes until the tops are golden brown and the bottom is crisp, the sides browned, and the potatoes tender when pierced with a fork, about 45 minutes. Let the galettes cool for 10 minutes before loosening the sides so that you can cut them into wedges to serve.

Vegan Gruyere

Makes 1 1/2 cups   GF, SF, <30

This easy homemade vegan "cheese" is tahini-and-cashew-based, but it is low in fat and calories. It has excellent, complex flavor and can be sliced and grated (while frozen). It melts well due to the different qualities of the two vegan seaweed-based gelatine used together. **Important:** *Please do not use more agar instead of the kosher gel or Genutine®.*

1 CUP WATER

2 TEASPOONS AGAR POWDER

2 TEASPOONS KOSHER GEL OR GENUTINE (SEE RESOURCES)

1/4 CUP RAW CASHEW PIECES, SOAKED IN HOT WATER FOR
    10 MINUTES AND WELL-DRAINED

1/4 CUP TAHINI

1 1/2 TABLESPOONS LIGHT MISO PASTE

1/2 TEASPOON ONION POWDER

1/4 TEASPOON GARLIC POWDER

1/2 TEASPOON SALT

3/4 TABLESPOON FRESH LEMON JUICE

2 TABLESPOONS NUTRITIONAL YEAST FLAKES

1. Mix the agar and kosher gel or Genutine with the water in a 1-quart microwave-proof bowl. Soak for 5 minutes. Microwave the mixture for 2 minutes on 100% power (default setting). Alternatively, you can stir constantly in a medium pot on the stove until the agar and kosher gel or Genutine is dissolved (it will feel silky and sticky rather than grainy when rubbed between your fingertips).

2. Transfer the hot mixture and cashews to the blender and blend until creamy-smooth. Add the remaining ingredients and process until very smooth. Pour into a rectangular mold or container that has been lightly sprayed with oil. Cover and chill until firm, at least 4 hours.

3. Invert onto serving platter. It can be sliced (even with a cheese slice) or spread. It also freezes well and can be grated while frozen.

Greek Nugget Potato and Kalamata Olive Stew

Greece

Serves 6   GF, SF, <30

This is my version of a delicious traditional Greek stew packed with umami-rich foods, such as tomatoes, olive, and wine. I love those little nugget potatoes, and they can be the basis for a nutritious, delicious meal with only a salad on the side (but crusty bread is good, too). Greek recipes are notoriously high in olive oil – up to 3/4 cup might be used in a recipe like this! Delicious as that might be, I can't afford the calories, especially as olives are an integral part of the dish and they contain a fair amount of calories and fat. So, I use much less oil, and the result is still very delicious.

2 TABLESPOONS OLIVE OIL

2 POUNDS BABY NUGGET POTATOES

3 LARGE ONIONS, SLICED 1/8-INCH THICK

6 CLOVES GARLIC, MINCED

1 (15-OUNCE) CAN CRUSHED TOMATOES

1 CUP PITTED KALAMATA OLIVES, SLICED 1/8-INCH THICK

1/2 CUP DRY WHITE OR RED WINE

1/2 CUP FLAT-LEAF PARSLEY, CHOPPED

1 TABLESPOON FRESH CHOPPED OREGANO OR 1 TEASPOON
    DRIED

1/4 TO 1/2 TEASPOON RED PEPPER FLAKES, OPTIONAL

SALT AND FRESHLY GROUND BLACK PEPPER

1. Preheat the oven to 350°F. Heat the olive oil in a large nonstick skillet over medium-high heat. Add the potatoes and quickly fry until golden on all sides, about 7 minutes. Remove the potatoes from the pan. Add the onions and cook, stirring occasionally, until softened, adding a few drops of water as needed to keep them from sticking, about 5 minutes. Add the garlic and cook 2 to 3 minutes longer.

2. Add the tomatoes, olives, wine, parsley, oregano, and pepper flakes, if using. Stir just to heat the mixture. Add the potatoes, combine well and then transfer the mixture to a large baking dish. Cover and bake for 30 to 45 minutes or until the potatoes are tender. Check half-way through the cooking time and add a little water (or wine) if the sauce is getting too thick. Season with salt and pepper to taste and continue cooking until tender. Serve hot.

Baked Lebanese Potato Kibbeh with Lentil Stuffing

LEBANON

Serves 6   SF

This is based on a traditional Lenten dish of the Levant region. I am crazy about potato and bulgur kibbeh, but it needs a lot of olive oil to do properly. The olive oil and the meltingly sweet, softly cooked onions really make the dish. Olive oil and onions are a common way to season simple peasant dishes in this area, and it's a revelation every time I taste such dishes.

I wanted to try a stuffed version, so I decided to

make a simple lentil stuffing. This allowed me cut the grain/potato mixture and the oil in half. The oil is spread out over more servings, and I don't have to feel guilty about enjoying it. You can serve this as part of a Middle Eastern dinner or in smaller servings as an appetizer, snack, or lunch dish. The lentil stuffing can be made ahead of time. Tip: To peel the hot cooked potatoes, hold under running cold water. The skin will peel off easily.

Lentil Stuffing:

1/2 CUP BROWN LENTILS, PICKED OVER, RINSED AND
    DRAINED

1 1/4 CUPS VEGETABLE BROTH

1/2 TABLESPOON OLIVE OIL

1 SMALL ONION, MINCED

2 CLOVES GARLIC, CHOPPED

1/2 TABLESPOON CHOPPED FRESH CILANTRO OR PARSLEY

1/8 TEASPOON GROUND ALLSPICE

1/8 TEASPOON GROUND NUTMEG

FRESHLY GROUND BLACK PEPPER

Kibbeh Mixture:

3/4 CUP BULGUR WHEAT (#2 OR MEDIUM-FINE)

1 TEASPOON SALT

1/2 SMALL ONION, SHREDDED

1/2 TABLESPOON CHOPPED FRESH BASIL OREGANO, MINT,
    OR CILANTRO

1/8 TEASPOON GROUND CINNAMON

1/8 TEASPOON FRESHLY GROUND BLACK PEPPER

2 MEDIUM RUSSET POTATOES (4 OUNCES EACH), COOKED
    UNTIL TENDER, THEN PEELED AND MASHED

1 LARGE ONION, SLICED PAPER-THIN

1/4 CUP PLUS 2 TABLESPOONS OLIVE OIL, DIVIDED

TAHEENA SAUCE (RECIPE FOLLOWS), OPTIONAL

1. **Lentil Stuffing:** Combine the lentils and broth in a medium pot and bring to a boil. Reduce the heat to a simmer, cover and cook until the lentils are tender, about 30 minutes.

2. While the lentils cook, heat the 1/2 tablespoon olive oil in a medium nonstick skillet. Add the onion and sauté over medium-high heat until it starts to wilt. Add the garlic to the cooked lentils and continue sautéing until the onion is soft, about 5 minutes. Add the onion

and garlic along with the cilantro, spices and pepper to taste. Set aside.

3. **Kibbeh Mixture:** Rinse the bulgur in a colander with cold water. With your hands, squeeze the water out of the moistened bulgur, sprinkle it with the salt and let it sit in a medium bowl, covered, for 20 minutes. Add the shredded onion, herbs, spices, and mashed potatoes to the bulgur, kneading it into a soft "dough." Moisten your hands with cold water while kneading to prevent the dough from sticking to you. Preheat the oven to 400° F.

4. To assemble, arrange the sliced onions in the bottom of a 9 x 9-inch square baking pan which has been sprayed or brushed with oil. Drizzle 3 tablespoons of the olive oil evenly over the onions.

5. Crumble half of the kibbeh "dough" evenly on top of the onions and smooth it out with your fingertips so that it completely covers the onions, with no gaps.

6. Spread the lentil stuffing evenly over the kibbeh mixture. Distribute the remaining mixture over the lentils and smooth it out with your fin-gertips so that it covers the onions, with no gaps. With a sharp knife, cut the kibbeh into diamond shapes only about 1/2-inch deep, not all the way through. Drizzle the remaining olive oil evenly over the top. Cover the pan with aluminum foil and bake for 25 minutes. Remove the foil. Continue baking until golden brown – about 20 to 30 minutes more. The onions at the bottom of the pan should be very soft and sweet.

7. Let the kibbeh cool until lukewarm, then cut into diamond shapes all the way down to the bottom of the pan with a sharp knife. Serve hot, warm, or at room temperature. Serve plain or with taheena sauce, if using. To store, cover with plastic wrap and refrigerate for up to a week.

Levantine Taheena Sauce

JORDAN/PALESTINE/SYRIA

Makes about 1 1/3 cups   GF, <30

This delicious sauce, ubiquitous in Lebanon, Syria, Jordan, Israel, and Palestine, is delicious on vegan "meats," grilled or fried eggplant and zucchini, falafel, and whatever else sounds good. According to

Kibbeh

A popular dish in the Levant, kibbeh is considered the national dish of Lebanon, Syria, Palestine, and Iraq. It is also a common food in North Africa, Turkey, the Arabian Peninsula, and parts of the Caucasus, such as Armenia and Georgia. Like hummus, everyone's mom makes it best!

Kibbeh is defined as a dish of minced meat with bulgur wheat and spices and has many variants, both raw and cooked. However, there are several popular vegan versions (often Lenten versions for Christians) made with potato, pumpkin, sweet potato and other vegetables, with plenty of onions for flavor. Many chefs are now experimenting with stuffed vegan kibbi, utilizing greens, legumes, pomegranate molasses, nuts, and herbs.

In its most common form, kibbeh consists of minced lamb mixed with bulgur and spices and stuffed inside a bulgur wheat crust. The shape, size, and ingredients vary between different types of kibbeh and between the recipes traditional in different areas. Recipes can include pine nuts and green herbs, among other things. It can be baked, fried, boiled, stuffed, or served raw. The mix of spices changes with nationality, as does the composition of the crust.

chef and researcher Sufian Mustafa, yogurt, as well as tahini, is used to make "white sauces" in Levantine cooking, so I mixed the two (using silken tofu and lemon juice instead of yogurt) to make a creamy, rich-tasting lower-fat version of this sauce.

6 OUNCES EXTRA-FIRM SILKEN TOFU, DRAINED

5 TABLESPOONS TAHINI

5 TABLESPOONS FRESH LEMON JUICE

1 TABLESPOON WATER

3 CLOVES GARLIC, PEELED

1 TABLESPOON CHOPPED FRESH MINT OR 1 TEASPOON DRIED

5/8 TEASPOON SALT

1/4 TEASPOON SUGAR

Mix all of the ingredients in a food processor or blender until very smooth. Transfer to a covered container and refrigerate. Bring the sauce to room temperature before using. If it seems too thick, add a little more water.

Vegan Poutine with Oven Fries

CANADA/QUEBEC

Serves 4   GF, <30

This is modern-day Quebeçois fast food (my husband, who is from Quebec City, tells me that he never saw this when he lived there) and you can get it in just about any fast-food place in Canada and many areas of the U.S.A. now. Of course, it is usually trans-fat laden and not vegan – the fries are covered in squeaky cheese curds (the ones used in cheese making, but unpressed and not aged). Outside of Quebec, and in big fast food chains, they just use grated cheese. Before serving, a gravy is poured over the whole thing. (In Canada, we like gravy on our fries – or chips, as we call them.)

My version features oven-baked fries, homemade vegan "fresh cheese" and fat-free vegan gravy. If you have a French fry cutter, you can make crispy oven French fries with very little oil in 25 minutes (this includes preparation).

4 LARGE (8 OUNCES EACH) RUSSET POTATOES, SCRUBBED

OLIVE OIL

2 CUPS TOFU "CURDS," CUT INTO 1/2-INCH CUBES (FOLLOWS)

1 RECIPE RICH BROWN YEAST GRAVY, VERY HOT (FOLLOWS)

1. Preheat the oven to 500°F. Select long potatoes, if you can. These can just be shaved a bit on their fat middles, so that they fit right into the feeder tube of your processor. Cut the potatoes in the food processor or, alternatively, cut the potatoes into French fry shapes using a sharp knife.

2. Spread the fries in one layer on 2 lightly-oiled or nonstick 12 x 17-inch dark baking sheets. (Dark baking sheets brown foods better than shiny ones.) Drizzle or spray on a small amount of olive oil and bake for 10 minutes, then flip them over and bake 10 minutes more. (If you have extra baking sheets, the quickest way to flip them over is just to place another nonstick or oiled baking sheet over the one with the fries, flip the whole thing over and remove the first sheet.) The fries should be golden and crispy. Season with salt to taste.

3. To serve, divide the hot fries among 4 warmed dinner plates. Sprinkle one-quarter of the tofu "curds" over each serving. Top each serving with a generous portion of hot gravy and serve immediately.

Tofu "Cheese Curds"

Makes 2 cups   GF, <30

This is very easy to make, especially with a microwave.

1 (12.3-OUNCE) BOX EXTRA-FIRM SILKEN TOFU, DRAINED AND CRUMBLED

2 TABLESPOONS PLUS 2 TEASPOONS WATER

4 TEASPOONS VEGETABLE OIL

2 TEASPOONS AGAR POWDER

3/4 TEASPOON SUGAR

1 TEASPOON SALT

2 TABLESPOONS FRESH LEMON JUICE

1. Blend the tofu, water, oil, agar, sugar, and salt in a food processor until very, very smooth. Transfer the mixture to a microwave-safe bowl and microwave on 100% power (default setting) for 3 minutes. Whisk briefly. Microwave 2 minute more. Alternatively, place the mixture in a small saucepan and stir constantly over medium heat until it bubbles for a few minutes and thickens. Whisk the lemon juice into the cooked mixture. (You add this last because the lemon juice can interfere with the jelling of the agar if cooked with it.) Pour the mixture into a flat 2-cup container, cover and chill until firm. Cut into 1/2-inch squares.

2. If you aren't using the cheese right away, refrigerate the squares in a jar of neutral vegetable oil. Make sure all of the cheese is covered in oil. Tighten the lid. The cheese will keep this way for several weeks. Rinse the oil off gently under warm water and pat dry before using.

VARIATION: TOFU "FETA"

Use 12 to 14 ounces regular firm tofu (not the silken variety). Use only 1/2 teaspoon salt and whisk in 1/4 cup plus 2 tablespoons of lemon after cooking the agar mixture. Make a fairly salty brine of water and salt (about 1 tablespoon salt per cup of water) boiled together for 5 minutes, cool it thoroughly and pour the brine over the chunks of "feta" to cover. The "feta" will keep for several weeks in a covered container in the refrigerator in this brine. If it starts getting too salty before you have used it up, remove from the brine and store it in a jar covered with vegetable oil. You can rinse off the oil before using.

Rich Brown Yeast Gravy

Makes 2 1/2 cups   GF, <30, SFO

This fat-free and delicious brown gravy will become a low-fat staple. It lends itself to many variations. If you don't have oat flour, simply grind rolled or quick oats in a dry blender or coffee/spice mill. Instead of

the oat and chickpea flour, you can substitute 1/3 cup unbleached white flour.

1/3 CUP NUTRITIONAL YEAST FLAKES
2 TABLESPOONS OAT FLOUR
1/4 CUP CHICKPEA FLOUR (BESAN)
2 TABLESPOONS SOY SAUCE (OR SOY-FREE SAUCE, PAGE 12)
2 1/2 CUPS WATER
1/2 TEASPOON SALT
1/4 TO 1/2 TEASPOON GRAVY BROWNER, SUCH AS KITCHEN BOUQUET (OPTIONAL)

1. In a 1 1/2 to 2-quart microwave-safe bowl or measuring pitcher, mix the flours and yeast. Toast this in the microwave on 100% power (default setting) for 2 to 3 minutes, uncovered. Whisk in the water, soy sauce, salt and gravy browner. Cover and cook again for 3 minutes. Whisk well. Cook again for 3 minutes. Whisk one last time.

2. Alternatively, in a small saucepan over high heat, whisk the yeast and flours together until they smell toasty. Remove from the heat briefly to whisk in the water, soy sauce, salt, and gravy browner, if using. Stir constantly over high heat until it thickens and comes to a boil. Reduce the heat and simmer for 2 to 5 minutes. This gravy can be made ahead and reheated.

Polenta Gratin with Mushrooms and Gruyere

NORTHERN ITALY

Serves 4   GF

Unlike me, my husband is not crazy about polenta, but he really liked this creamy dish, rich with sautéed mushrooms, garlic, sun-dried tomatoes, and fresh basil, and topped with a generous portion of homemade vegan gruyere. **Note:** *It is best to shred the "gruyere" when it is semi-frozen. (See "Three Easy Ways to Make Polenta" on page 103.)*

Polenta:

3/4 CUP POLENTA OR YELLOW CORNMEAL

2 1/2 CUPS COLD VEGETABLE BROTH

Filling:

1 TABLESPOON OLIVE OIL

8 OUNCES MUSHROOMS (ANY KIND), SLICED 1/4-INCH THICK

2 CLOVES GARLIC, MINCED

SALT

1/2 CUP VEGETABLE BROTH

1/2 CUP DRAINED AND CRUMBLED EXTRA-FIRM SILKEN TOFU

4 SUN-DRIED TOMATO HALVES (IN OIL), RINSED UNDER HOT
    WATER, DRAINED, AND CHOPPED

1/4 CUP CHOPPED FRESH BASIL

PINCH FRESHLY GRATED NUTMEG

FRESHLY GROUND BLACK PEPPER

3 (1/4-INCH) SLICES VEGAN GRUYERE (PAGE 97), BROKEN
    INTO BITS OR SHREDDED

2 TABLESPOONS WALNUT PARM (PAGE 15)

1. **Polenta:** Make the polenta a few hours (or days) ahead of time to allow it to firm up in the refrigerator. There are three ways to make polenta easily (see page 103). They are exactly the same for this recipe, except that you only need a 1 to 2- quart double boiler for the first method; a 1 to 2-quart deep heat-proof casserole, measuring pitcher or bowl for the Pressure-Cooker Method; and a 2-quart microwave-safe bowl, measuring pitcher or casserole for the Microwave Method (and cut the microwave cooking times in half).

2. Pour the cooked polenta into a well-oiled 5 3/4 x 3 x 2 1/8-inch fruitcake/mini loaf pan. Chill until firm (for several days, if you like). When you are ready to assemble, loosen the edges of the firmed polenta with a table knife. Turn the pan over with a bang onto a cutting board to remove it from the pan. Cut the polenta into 3/8-inch slices. Preheat the oven to 450°F.

3. **Filling:** Heat the oil in a large nonstick skillet over high heat. Add the mushrooms and garlic and sprinkle lightly with salt to taste. Reduce the heat to medium-high and sauté until the mushrooms have exuded their moisture and then most of it has evaporated.

4. Transfer the 1/2 cup broth and tofu to a blender or food processor (or use an immersion/stick blender) and blend until smooth. Add the tofu mixture to the cooked mushrooms, along with the sun-dried tomatoes, basil, nutmeg, and salt and pepper to taste. Stir well just to heat.

5. In an oiled 11 x 7-inch baking pan, layer half of the polenta slices. Cover with half of the filling. Repeat layering. Cover the whole thing with the "Gruyere" bits or shreds and finish with the Walnut Parm. Bake for 20 minutes and serve hot.

Authentic Tamale Pie

MEXICO

Serves 6   SFO, GFO

I love tamales, but I confess that I seldom make them because they are time-consuming to fill (they are really a food item that should be made in convivial company). This tamale pie with a delectable filling in Mexican red sauce has solved that dilemma for me. I wanted a company-worthy casserole that had the qualities of authentic tamales without all the stuffing and wrapping, and with a masa dough that was lower in fat than the traditional dough, but still moist and with plenty of flavor. It worked!

8 TO 10 DRIED CORN HUSKS (MEANT FOR TAMALES),
    COVERED WITH BOILING WATER IN A DEEP BOWL AND
    SOAKED FOR 1 HOUR (AVAILABLE IN THE PRODUCE
    SECTION OF LARGE SUPERMARKETS OR ONLINE)

Red Sauce:

1/2 TABLESPOON OLIVE OIL

4 CLOVES GARLIC, CRUSHED

1 SMALL ONION, MINCED

1/3 CUP NEW MEXICO RED CHILE POWDER (MILD, MEDIUM, OR HOT)

1 1/2 CUPS VEGETABLE BROTH

1/2 CUP CANNED CRUSHED TOMATOES

1/4 TEASPOON GROUND CUMIN

Filling:

1 MEDIUM ONION, CHOPPED

1 LARGE BELL PEPPER (ANY COLOR), CHOPPED

1/2 CUP SLICED MUSHROOMS OF ANY KIND

3 CLOVES GARLIC, MINCED OR CRUSHED

4 CUPS RECONSTITUTED SOY CURLS (4 OUNCES OR 3 CUPS
    DRY) OR ALTERNATIVE (PAGE 10); OR MATCHSTICK
    STRIPS OF MARINATED, UNCOOKED CRISPY MARINATED
    TOFU SLICES (PAGE 8), DRAINED; OR 16 OUNCES LIGHT
    SEITAN CUTLETS (PAGE 5), CUT INTO STRIPS

1/2 CUP SLICED PITTED CALIFORNIA OLIVES

1/4 CUP WATER

SALT AND FRESHLY GROUND BLACK PEPPER

2 CUPS SHREDDED VEGAN CHEESE (TRY VEGAN GRUYERE,
    PAGE 97, FROZEN AND SHREDDED), OPTIONAL

Corn-Laced Masa Dough:

2 CUPS MASA HARINA (CORN TORTILLA FLOUR)

1 1/2 CUPS BOILING VEGAN CHICKEN-STYLE BROTH (PAGE 2)

8 OUNCES FRESH OR FROZEN (THAWED) CORN KERNELS

1/4 CUP WATER

2 TABLESPOONS OLIVE OIL

1 TEASPOON DARK SESAME OIL

1 TEASPOON BAKING POWDER

1/2 TEASPOON SALT

1. **Red Sauce:** Heat the oil over medium heat in a large nonstick skillet. Add the garlic and onion and sauté until softened. Stir in the chile powder and stir for several minutes. Add the remaining ingredients, stirring until well-mixed, bring to a boil, then reduce heat to a simmer and cook for 10 minutes. Set aside.

2. **Filling:** Lightly oil a large nonstick skillet and

Three Easy Ways to Make Polenta

Double-Boiler Method; Set the bottom pan of a 2 1/2 to 3-quart double boiler, filled half-way with water, over high heat. While the water is heating, mix the cornmeal and 3 cups cold water in the top pan of the double boiler. Add the 3 cups boiling water, broth powder and salt. Place the top pan of the double boiler, with the cornmeal mixture, over high heat and bring to a boil quickly, stirring constantly with a whisk or wooden spoon, to prevent the polenta from sticking and clumping. As soon as the polenta boils, insert the top pan with the polenta in it into the bottom pan of the double boiler containing the simmering water. Simmer the polenta for 20 minutes over the simmering water, partially covered and stirring occasionally, until very thick and no longer gritty. Remove the top pan from the heat.

Pressure-Cooker Method: Mix the cornmeal and 3 cups cold water in a deep heat-proof casserole or bowl that will hold 2 1/2 quarts and fit into your pressure cooker. Stir in the 3 cups boiling water, broth powder and salt. Cover the bowl with aluminum foil. (Fold a long piece of heavy aluminum foil into a 2-inch-wide length and use that to lift the casserole/bowl in and out of the cooker.) Transfer the bowl to a rack over 1 to 2 inches of water in the bottom for your cooker and secure the lid. Bring to the pressure cooker 15 pounds pressure over high heat, then turn it down just enough to maintain this pressure and cook 10 minutes. Remove the cooker from the heat and allow to rest for 5 minutes, then quick-release the pressure under cold running water. Stir the polenta well.

Microwave Method: Whisk the cornmeal and 3 cups cold water together in a 3 to 4-quart microwave-safe bowl. Stir in the 3 cups boiling water, broth powder and salt. Cook on 100% power (default setting) for 5 minutes. Whisk the polenta very well, until no longer lumpy. Cook 3 more minutes. Stir well with a wooden spoon. Cook the same way again for 3 minutes more. Let stand 1 minute. (Taste the polenta and make sure that it doesn't have that rather unpleasant bitter taste of undercooked cornmeal. If it does, let it cook a little longer.)

heat over medium-high heat. Add the bell pepper, onion, mushrooms, and garlic and saute until tender, adding drops of water as needed to keep from sticking. Add the Soy Curls, olives, 1/2 cup of the reserved red sauce, water, and salt and pepper to taste. Stir to combine and heat through. Set aside.

3. **Masa Dough:** Mix the masa harina and boiling broth together in a large bowl or the bowl of your stand mixer. Puree the corn and water in a blender until quite smooth. Add the pureed corn and the remaining ingredient to the masa mixture. Beat with a sturdy wooden spoon or, if using the stand mixer, the beater attachment, not the dough hook, just until the dough is well mixed.

4. To assemble: Drain the soaked corn husks and pat dry. Preheat the oven to 350°F. Have ready an 8 x 12-inch baking pan. Brush a 2-quart covered casserole with vegan margarine. Line the bottom with half of the soaked corn husks. Spray the husks well with oil from a pump sprayer.

5. Spread half the masa dough over the bottom of the husk-lined casserole. Evenly spread the filling on top of the masa dough. (If you are using the vegan cheese, sprinkle it evenly over the filling at this point.) Spread the remaining masa dough over the filling. Use wet fingers to smooth it evenly. Cover the top with the remaining corn husks. Cover the casserole with the casserole lid or with baking parchment, covered by aluminum foil. Place the casserole in the baking pan and add hot water to the baking pan to go up the side of the casserole a couple of inches. Bake the casserole for 2 hours, adding water to the baking pan as needed, so that it doesn't go dry.

6. To serve: Heat the remaining red sauce. Uncover the casserole and carefully remove the top corn husks. Use the top husks to line the serving plates decoratively. Cut the casserole into 6 wedges and carefully loosen from the husks with a pie server. Transfer each wedge to a husk-lined plate. Drizzle each serving with red sauce.

Cheesy Grits and Sweet Potato-Arugula Gratin

FRANCE/SOUTHERN U.S.A.

Serves 4   GF, SF

I love corn, anything with corn, and I had an idea that pairing something corny and cheesy with sweet potatoes in a sort of Southern style would be good. It was! The arugula adds a little edge to the creamy casserole. You could stay with the Southern theme and use some chopped, cooked mustard or collard greens instead, if you wish. They are hard to find in my neck of the woods! This gratin can serve as a main dish or a side dish. If grits are unavailable, use coarse polenta cornmeal instead. The grits in this recipe are made firmer than usual so that they can firm up and be sliced.

2 1/4 CUPS COLD WATER
SALT
3/4 CUP OLD-FASHIONED (NOT INSTANT OR QUICK) STONE GROUND CORN GRITS
1/8 TEASPOON CAYENNE PEPPER
1 TABLESPOON VEGAN MARGARINE
12 OUNCES SWEET POTATO, PEELED, STEAMED UNTIL TENDER BUT FIRM AND SLICED 1/4-INCH THICK
1 CUP LOOSELY-PACKED FRESH ARUGULA
2 TEASPOONS OLIVE OIL
FRESHLY GROUND BLACK PEPPER
1/2 RECIPE SUISSE MELTY CHEESE, (PAGE 105)
1/2 CUP NONDAIRY MILK
1/2 CUP PANKO BREADCRUMBS
2 TABLESPOONS WALNUT PARM (PAGE 15)

1. Prepare the grits several hours ahead, as they need time to firm up in the refrigerator. Set the bottom pan of a double boiler, filled halfway with water, on the stove over high heat. Add the 2 1/4 cups water and 3/4 teaspoon salt to the top pan of the double boiler and place on the stove over high heat. Gradually pour the grits into the salted water, stirring constantly with a wooden spoon to prevent lumps and scorching. When the mixture comes to a boil, immediately insert it into the bottom pan of the double boiler

containing the boiling water. Reduce the heat to a low simmer, stirring with the wooden spoon until the water in the bottom pot is no longer boiling. Cover and simmer for 30 to 45 minutes over the simmering water, stirring occasionally. When the grits are creamy, stir in the margarine and remove the top pan from the heat.

2. Pour the grits evenly into an oiled 8 x 12-inch baking pan and smooth the top. Cover with plastic wrap and refrigerate until the grits are chilled and firm, about 1 to 2 hours (you can place the pan in the freezer). Cut the chilled grits into approximately 3-inch squares and carefully remove them from the pan with a small spatula. Slice the squares in half horizontally (it doesn't matter if they aren't even). Preheat the oven to 400°F.

3. Clean and dry the 8 x 12-inch baking pan and rub the inside lightly with vegan margarine. Place half of the sliced grits squares evenly on the bottom of the pan. Place half of the sliced sweet potatoes on top of the grits, season to taste with salt and black pepper and top with the arugula. Sprinkle the arugula with the olive oil and then spread half of the melty cheese evenly on top.

4. Layer with the remaining sliced grits, then arrange the remaining sweet potatoes on top and season with salt and pepper to taste. Spread the remaining melty cheese evenly over the top. Carefully pour the nondairy milk into the casserole along the edges only.

5. Mix the breadcrumbs and vegan parmesan substitute and sprinkle evenly on the casserole. Spray it with oil from a pump sprayer. Bake for 45 minutes. Cut into squares and serve hot.

Tip: Panko are flaky Japanese dried breadcrumbs that are great for making crunchy coatings without a lot of fat. It is widely available in Asian stores and large grocery stores.

Suisse Melty Cheese

Makes 1 1/4 cups   GFO, SFO, <30

This is a quick recipe which makes great vegan grilled cheese sandwiches and quesadillas, among other things, and can be used to make vegan cheese sauce (just add nondairy milk to taste). For a Soy-Free Option use chickpea miso.

1 CUP WATER
2 TABLESPOONS NUTRITIONAL YEAST FLAKES
1/4 CUP WALNUT PARM (PAGE 15), OPTIONAL
2 TABLESPOONS CORNSTARCH
1 TABLESPOON UNBLEACHED WHITE FLOUR (OR 2 1/2 TEA-
    SPOONS WHITE RICE FLOUR)
1 TABLESPOON LIGHT MISO PASTE
1 TABLESPOON TAHINI
1 TEASPOON FRESH LEMON JUICE
1/4 TEASPOON SALT
1/4 TEASPOON GARLIC POWDER
2 TABLESPOONS WATER

1. Combine all of the ingredients except for the last 2 tablespoons of water in a blender and blend until smooth. Pour the mixture into a small saucepan and stir over medium heat until it starts to thicken, then let it bubble for 30 seconds, whisking vigorously, then remove from the heat.

2. Whisk in the remaining 2 tablespoons water until smooth. Drizzle the cheese immediately on food and broil or bake it until a skin forms on top, or refrigerate it in a small rigid covered container for up to a week. It will get quite firm when chilled, but will still be spreadable. You can spread the firm cheese on bread or quesadillas for grilling or heat it gently to spread more thinly on casseroles and other dishes.

Jamaican-Style "Pumpkin" Rice

JAMAICA

Serves 4   GF, SF

This rice dish is traditionally served with Jamaican Curry, but it's delicious on its own. Our butternut or Hubbard squash make a good stand-in for the Jamaican pumpkin (calabeza). If a Scotch bonnet chile is unavailable, you can substitute a habañero – it's close in flavor and heat. Keep the pepper intact for a mildly spicy flavor, or trim, seed and mince it if you like more heat in your dish.

1 1/2 TABLESPOONS VEGAN MARGARINE OR OLIVE OIL
1 MEDIUM ONION, MINCED
3 GREEN ONIONS, CHOPPED
2 MEDIUM CLOVES GARLIC, MINCED
1 SMALL SCOTCH BONNET CHILE
2 2/3 CUPS VEGETABLE BROTH
6 OUNCES BUTTERNUT OR HUBBARD SQUASH, PEELED,
    SEEDED, IN 3/4-INCH CUBES
FRESHLY GROUND BLACK PEPPER
3/8 TEASPOON SALT
1 TEASPOON GROUND ALLSPICE
3/8 TSP DRIED THYME
1 CUP WHITE BASMATI RICE

In a large pot, heat the margarine over medium-high heat. Add both kinds of onions and the garlic and sauté until the onion wilts. Add the chile (intact or chopped), broth, squash cubes, and seasonings. Cover and simmer over low heat until the squash is just tender, about 10 minutes. Stir in the rice. Cover and cook on low for about 25 minutes, or until the rice is tender and dry. Serve hot.

Variation: For an Ital (Rastafarian) dish, use all or part coconut milk in place of the broth.

Korean Broccoli Fried Rice

Yachae Bap

KOREA

Serves 4   GF, <30

A good venue for using up cold cooked rice and leftover scrambled tofu, this spicy, homestyle recipe makes a great lunch as well as a side dish. If you don't have leftover scrambled tofu on hand, use 2/3 cup crumbled firm tofu seasoned with 3/4 tablespoon Tofu Scrambler Mix (page 45).

2 TEASPOONS VEGETABLE OIL
1 TEASPOON DARK SESAME OIL
4 GREEN ONIONS, CHOPPED
2 LARGE CLOVES GARLIC, MINCED
2 2/3 CUPS COLD COOKED RICE (BROWN BASMATI IS GOOD)
2 2/3 CUPS BROCCOLI, CUT INTO BITE-SIZED PIECES AND
    STEAMED UNTIL CRISP-TENDER
2/3 CUP PRE-COOKED SCRAMBLED TOFU (FROM THE CROS-
    TONI BENEDICT RECIPE, PAGE 48)
2 TEASPOONS SOY SAUCE
3/8 TEASPOON SALT
1/4 TEASPOON (OR MORE) RED PEPPER FLAKES
FRESHLY GROUND BLACK PEPPER

Heat both of the oils over medium-high heat in a large wok or skillet. Add the green onions and stir-fry until they start to soften, 1 to 2 minutes. Add the garlic and cold, cooked rice to the pan and continue stir-frying, breaking up clumps in the rice as you go. Add the broccoli and scrambled tofu, then add the soy sauce, salt, red pepper flakes, and plenty of black pepper. Stir-fry for 2 minutes more, or just until everything is well-mixed and hot. Serve immediately.

Beans Around the World

Legume and Vegetable Mains

If anything is central to the vegan diet, it's vegetables and legumes. All of us would do well to eat more of both. Every day, it seems that we hear about new vegetables and legumes (new to us, anyway!), or new varieties of old favorites, and our vegetable horizons keep expanding.

How many North Americans were familiar with black kale (dinosaur kale) or rapini twenty or even five years ago? Who knew that cannellini and gigante beans might become more popular than navy beans and kidney beans? It's hard to fathom how omnivores can shake their heads and wonder what we poor vegans have left to eat! As I've said many times, I couldn't live long enough to try all the vegan foods and combinations of vegan foods out there.

We are so fortunate to have this huge array of choices to cook with and savor. My pantry shelves are sagging with various protein and nutrient-rich lentils and dried beans just waiting to be used in a tasty bean dish from one of the four corners of the world.

Among the diverse global recipes in this chapter are Lebanese Gigante Bean Stew, Italian Polenta Loaf with Beans and Kale, Serbian Braised Sauerkraut and Seitan, and Sizzling Saigon Crepes. Cook up some beans, prepare some seasonal vegetable dishes, and introduce your meat-eating friends to a whole new world of gastronomy.

Legume and Vegetable Mains

Sizzling Saigon Crepes

VIETNAM

Serves 4   GFO, SFO

I have loved these crunchy crepes since the first time I tried them in a Vietnamese restaurant in Vancouver, BC. Since they are unavailable where I live, I've learned to make my own. In researching the recipe, I was intrigued with versions that contain ground mung beans in the batter rather than eggs, but I wanted to use more mung beans and less rice flour in the batter; to use whole grain flour; to reduce the fat; and, of course, to provide a spicy vegan filling in place of the usual meat. According to my husband, I was successful. The traditional way to make these is to sprinkle some of the filling over the batter and cook it with the pancake, but I like the taste of the filling when cooked separately and added later. It also gives the diners the freedom of adding the amount of filling they like.

Note: *Moong dal are split and skinned mung beans, available at Indian grocers or online.*

Crepe Batter:
1/4 CUP PLUS 2 TABLESPOONS (5.25 OUNCES) MOONG
    DAL (SEE NOTE ABOVE) PICKED OVER, RINSED AND
    DRAINED
1 CUP LITE UNSWEETENED COCONUT MILK
3/4 CUP BROWN RICE FLOUR
1/2 TEASPOON SUGAR
1/2 TEASPOON SALT
1/8 TEASPOON TURMERIC
Filling:
3 CUPS CHOPPED EXTRA-FIRM TOFU, SEITAN, OR TEMPEH
 2 1/4 TEASPOONS VEGAN NUOC CHAM SAUCE (PAGE 63),
    PLUS MORE FOR SERVING
2 LARGE CLOVES GARLIC, MINCED
1/8 TEASPOON SUGAR
FRESHLY GROUND BLACK PEPPER
2 TEASPOONS PLUS 2 TABLESPOONS COLD-PRESSED PEA-
    NUT OIL, DIVIDED
1 CUP THINLY SLICED MUSHROOMS (ANY KIND)
1 CUP THINLY SLICED SAVOY OR NAPA CABBAGE
1/2 LARGE ONION, THINLY SLICED
Accompaniments:

LETTUCE LEAVES (ANY KIND)
4 GREEN ONIONS, SLICED DIAGONALLY INTO 2-INCH PIECES
1/2 ENGLISH CUCUMBER, CUT INTO MATCHSTICKS
2 CUPS FRESH MUNG BEAN SPROUTS
3 CUPS FRESH MINT, BASIL, AND/OR CILANTRO LEAVES
SRIRACHA SAUCE

1. **Crepe Batter:** Cover the moong dal with water in a small bowl and soak for 30 minutes. Drain the dal and transfer to a blender with the remaining batter ingredients. Blend until very smooth. Set aside (in the blender container) in the refrigerator until time to cook.

2. **Filling:** Combine the tofu with the 2 1/4 teaspoons nuoc cham sauce, garlic, sugar, and pepper in a large bowl. Set aside for 30 minutes.

3. Heat the 2 teaspoons of oil in a large nonstick skillet or wok. Add the tofu and stir-fry to brown slightly. Add the mushrooms, cabbage, and onion and stir-fry until the vegetables are limp, but still a bit crunchy, adding water a few drops at a time as needed to keep from sticking.

4. Transfer the mixture to a platter and set aside (the filling can be served at room temperature). Have the vegetable and garnish platter prepared before you start the crepes and have everyone seated at the table as you cook them.

5. Blend the batter again briefly. Stir the batter before you measure it out each time. Heat an 8-inch nonstick crepe or omelet pan with 1/2 tablespoon of the remaining oil over medium-high heat. When the oil is hot, pour in 1/2 cup of the batter (which you have just blended or stirred). Quickly tilt the pan to make the batter run and form a round pancake.

6. Reduce the heat to medium and cover the pan. Cook about 5 minutes or until the bottom is golden brown and crispy. Flip the crepe over and cook for a few seconds. Fold the pancake in half and keep warm in the oven (at about 150°F) until the rest are cooked. Repeat with the remaining batter to make a total of four crepes.

7. To serve, each diner places a crispy crepe on a warm plate (sometimes over a lettuce leaf, but I prefer the lettuce on the inside), adds some filling and the vegetable accompaniments of choice. You can eat the crepe with a knife and fork or roll it up around the filling and eat it out of hand. Use the *nuoc cham* as a dipping sauce, with sriracha sauce added as you like.

TIPS

Use a nonstick 8-inch crepe or omelet pan – this will allow you to use 1/2 tablespoon of oil instead of the traditional 2 tablespoons per crepe. However, the crepe will still be crispy. (If you use no oil, the crepes will be soft.) You can make the batter a day ahead, but the crepes should be made fresh right before eating.

Italian Polenta Loaf with Beans and Kale

4 serving

(4 sp)

ITALY

Serves 6   GF, SF, <30

I think of this old country dish as "Italian Scrapple." (Scrapple is a Pennsylvania Dutch loaf of firm cornmeal mush, herbs, and pork scraps.) Both are cornmeal-based dishes that are cooled until solid, then sliced and browned, but the Italian version is naturally vegan. This delicious dish is inexpensive to make, low in fat and calories, and nutritious. Serve "as is" or with black pepper and Walnut Parm (page 15) and marinara sauce. Or, melt some vegan cheese on top, or sauce it with Rich Brown Yeast Gravy (page 101). Make the polenta using one of the three methods described on page 103.

8 OUNCES FRESH KALE, TOUGH STEMS REMOVED, CHOPPED

2 CLOVES GARLIC, MINCED

3 CUPS VEGETABLE BROTH

1/2 CUP CORNMEAL OR MEDIUM-GRIND POLENTA COOKED WITH 1/2 CUP COLD WATER

1 1/2 CUPS COOKED OR 1 (15-OUNCE) CAN PINTO, BORLOTTI, OR CRANBERRY BEANS, RINSED AND DRAINED

SALT AND FRESHLY GROUND BLACK PEPPER

OLIVE OIL

1. In a large pot, combine the kale, garlic, and broth. Cover and cook over medium-low heat until just tender, 7 to 10 minutes. Drain and set aside, reserving 1 1/2 cups of the broth.

2. Whichever way you cook the polenta, proceed as follows: Once the polenta is cooked, stir the drained beans and cooked, drained kale into the hot polenta and add salt and pepper to taste. Stir very well to distribute beans and kale the throughout the polenta. Transfer the mixture immediately to a well-oiled 9 x 5-inch loaf pan and smooth the top evenly. Cover and chill (you can refrigerate it for several days).

3. When the loaf is firm, cut it into 3/4-inch-thick slices. To pan-fry, heat a large nonstick skillet sprayed with olive oil from a pump sprayer over medium-high heat. Add the polenta slices and cook until browned on both sides, turning once, about 4 minutes per side. Or, to brown in the oven, transfer the slices to a 12 x 17-inch nonstick baking sheet, spray the tops with olive oil and broil 3 to 4 inches from the heat source until they are speckled with browned spots. Or, bake the polenta slices at 450°F for 10 to 15 minutes. Serve hot.

Cassoulette

FRANCE

Serves 4

At first glance, the classic French cassoulette appears to be a healthful dish—all those beans, after all. But the world-famous, traditional version is full of particularly fatty cuts of meat. In my version, sun-dried tomatoes, vegan sausage (try Field Roast or Tofurky brands), carrots, mushrooms, and more take the place of the fatty meats that are customarily used, resulting in a sophisticated complexity of flavor. The list of ingredients for this dish looks long, but it's really quite simple to make, especially if you use canned or pre-cooked beans. This makes a great company casserole (you can easily double it). It's even better when made ahead and reheated. Serve with crusty bread, a green salad, and fruit.

2 ITALIAN-STYLE VEGAN "SAUSAGES" SLICED DIAGONALLY INTO 3/4-INCH CHUNKS OR 1 CUP LIGHT SEITAN CUTLETS, CUT INTO STRIPS (PAGE 5) (OR HALF OF EACH)

1/2 TABLESPOON DARK SESAME OIL

5 FRESH SHIITAKE MUSHROOM CAPS, HALVED OR 1 SMALL PORTOBELLO MUSHROOM, SLICED 1/2-INCH THICK

2 OUNCES FRESH CHANTERELLE OR OTHER MUSHROOMS, SLICED 1/4-INCH THICK

1/4 CUP CHOPPED VEGAN BACON OR HAM OR 1 TABLESPOON SOY BACON BITS

1/2 TABLESPOON OLIVE OIL

1 LARGE ONION, CHOPPED

6 CLOVES GARLIC, CHOPPED

1 RIB CELERY (INCLUDING LEAVES), CHOPPED

1 BAY LEAF

1 MEDIUM CARROT, CUT DIAGONALLY INTO 1-INCH PIECES OR 1 CUP BABY CARROTS

2 1/4 CUPS COOKED OR CANNED CANNELLINI OR OTHER WHITE BEANS, RINSED AND DRAINED

8 OUNCES CANNED DICED TOMATOES WITH JUICE, OR FRESH PLUM TOMATOES, CHOPPED

1/2 CUP DRY RED WINE

1 CUP VEGETABLE BROTH

5 LARGE OIL-PACKED SUN-DRIED TOMATOES, RINSED UNDER HOT WATER

1 TABLESPOON SOY SAUCE

1 SPRIG FRESH ROSEMARY OR 1/2 TEASPOON DRIED

1 SPRIG FRESH THYME OR 1/2 TEASPOON DRIED

1 SPRIG FRESH SAGE OR 1/2 TEASPOON CRUMBLED DRIED

1 PINCH GROUND CLOVES

SALT AND FRESHLY GROUND BLACK PEPPER

1/2 CUP FRESH BREADCRUMBS

2 TABLESPOONS CHOPPED FRESH FLAT-LEAF PARSLEY

1 TABLESPOON GROUND FLAX SEED

1. Heat the oven to 350°F. Heat the sesame oil in a large nonstick skillet over high heat. Add the sausage or seitan and stir-fry until browned. Add both kinds of mushrooms and the vegan bacon and stir-fry until the mushrooms exude their liquid and it evaporates almost completely, adding drops of water or wine as necessary to keep the mixture from sticking. Transfer from the skillet to a shallow bowl.

2. Clean out the skillet, add the olive oil and heat over medium-high heat. Add the onion, garlic, and celery and cook until the onion starts to soften and brown slightly, then add the bay leaf and carrots. Continue to cook until the onion is soft, about 10 minutes. Set aside.

3. In a 2-quart casserole, combine the drained beans, mushroom mixture, sautéed vegetables, tomatoes, wine, broth, sundried tomatoes, soy sauce, rosemary, thyme, sage, and cloves. Season with salt and pepper to taste. Set aside.

4. In a small bowl, combine the bread crumbs, parsley, and flax seeds and mix well. (Double the amount if using a shallow baking dish.) Sprinkle the crumb topping evenly over the casserole. Bake for 1 to 1 1/2 hours or until bubbly and the ingredients have absorbed much of the liquid. Remove and discard the bay leaf before serving. Serve hot.

Note: I call this dish a "cassoulette" (which means "a small cassoulet") because it is a less complicated version of a traditional cassoulet.

"Drunken" Beans

Frijoles Borrachos

MEXICO

Serves 4 to 6   GF, <30

My guests were surprised that they loved this bean dish so much. They expected it to be boring, but kept asking for seconds. Pinto beans, which have such a creamy texture and naturally wonderful flavor, might be part of the reason for their enthusiasm. You can cook these beans in the oven or on the stovetop, but they did very nicely in the slow-cooker. It's important to soak the beans overnight and boil them briefly before slow-cooking, or they may not cook thoroughly,

(continued on page 114)

A Word (or Two) About Beans

Beans are so important, not only to a vegan diet, but to every diet in the world. They're important because of their nutritional value, of course, but also because they are so versatile and delicious in cooking. There is a lot of misinformation surrounding beans, and some myths, too. I'd like to address these issues here, so you know everything you need to know before you dig in to the bean recipes in this chapter.

To Soak or Not to Soak

I have encountered varying viewpoints on soaking beans before cooking. The food scientists say that it might speed up cooking a bit, and it might help with digestive problems, but you lose some nutrients. Mexican cooks don't soak their beans, and they eat beans three times a day (or so I'm told). Rick Bayless, Melissa Guerra, and Diana Kennedy (famous cookbook authors who specialize in Mexican or Tex-Mex cooking) don't soak. Food scientists also tell us that if you eat beans often, they don't have the same gaseous effect as on people who eat beans infrequently. So, a good case has been made for not soaking, if you don't feel like it or don't have the time.

Many cooks swear by the pressure cooker for cooking unsoaked beans. Pressure cookers, especially the modern versions, are indeed excellent for cooking any beans, unsoaked or not. Authors Lorna Sass and Jill Nussinow are great resources for using the pressure cooker for beans and grains.

I suspect that certain methods may be better than others, depending on the type and/or age of the beans and how you will be using them. (For instance, black beans generally take longer to cook than pinto beans.)

I was intrigued by the "Russ Parsons Method" of cooking unsoaked beans in a heavy, covered pot in the oven, with salted water or broth. (Russ Parsons is food editor for the *L.A. Times* and the author of *How to Read a French Fry*, Houghton Mifflin Harcourt, 2001.) You use less liquid than customary – 2 cups liquid to 1 cup dry beans – and bake in a low oven (325°F) for 75 to 90 minutes; at most, 2 hours. Many people have raved about it online, and long threads are dedicated to discussing this on the forums on eGullet.org.

Enthusiasts claim that this method produces a superior bean in terms of flavor, appearance, and texture, and a tastier bean broth. This sounded like a good thing for a vegan, I thought! So I adapted a favorite recipe, gave it a try, and I was very happy with the results. The beans cooked in 90 minutes and were soft and creamy inside and held their shape

well. (If the beans aren't done after 75 minutes, you should check them every 15 minutes and add a little more liquid if they are getting too dry for your preference.)

What does all this prove? That we have a lot of options with our bean cooking, and it sometimes pays to question the rules!

A Bean-Cooking Myth

A common myth about cooking beans is as follows: "Thou shalt not cook beans with salt or in salty broth or thine beans will be tough and take forever to cook." Well, I am here to tell you that this is not true. I have always cooked my beans with salt and/or bouillon and never had a problem, so I wondered why I was hearing and reading this everywhere. I have finally discovered the truth, thanks to *Cooks' Illustrated* magazine and food scientist Harold McGee, author of *On Food and Cooking: The Science and Lore of the Kitchen* (Scribner, 2004), and it looks like I was doing the right thing all along.

Not only does *Cooks' Illustrated* tell us that the long-held belief about cooking beans is a myth, they advise us to give the beans a long, salty soak before cooking them. I delved into Harold McGee's book to check on this, and he concurs. To make a long story short, it is acidity (from tomatoes and citrus juices, for instance), the magnesium and calcium content of your water, and sugar (such as the molasses in baked beans) that slow down the cooking of beans, not salt. But even so, it only slows them down a bit, and the slower absorption of liquid into the beans is not a bad thing. The slow cooking with any of the aforementioned elements can preserve the structure of the beans during long cooking, so they don't fall apart. I know this to be true, since I frequently cook beans with tomatoes and even orange juice.

McGee tells us that while salt in the cooking water does slow down the absorption of water, when the beans are presoaked in salty water, they actually cook faster. *Cooks' Illustrated* states that soaking the beans at room temperature for eight to twenty-four hours in water with salt added at the ratio of 2 teaspoons per quart – in effect "brining" the beans – yields better seasoned and more evenly cooked results.

You don't have to use this soaking technique, but you certainly don't have to wait until the end of cooking to add salt or bouillon cubes to your beans. This will definitely improve the flavor of your recipes, as it gives the salt and other flavors more time to meld and develop.

due to the acidity of the beer, which can impede the absorption of water into the beans.

1 POUND DRIED PINTO BEANS, PICKED OVER, RINSED AND
    DRAINED AND SOAKED IN PLENTY OF WATER (DO NOT
    OMIT THE SOAKING)
1 TABLESPOON OLIVE OIL
1 TEASPOON DARK SESAME OIL
1 MEDIUM ONION, FINELY CHOPPED
2 SLICES VEGAN BACON, CHOPPED
3 CLOVES GARLIC, MINCED
1 1/2 CHIPOTLE CHILES IN ADOBO SAUCE, CHOPPED
9 OUNCES BEER (CAN BE NON-ALCOHOLIC)
2 2/3 CUPS VEGETABLE BROTH
1 HEAPING CUP DICED TOMATOES WITH JUICE
1 TABLESPOON DRIED OREGANO
1/2 TEASPOON GROUND CUMIN
SALT

1. Drain the soaked beans and transfer them to a large pot with plenty of water to cover. Bring to a boil. Boil the beans at medium-high heat for 10 to 15 minutes. Drain them in a colander.

2. In a medium nonstick skillet, heat the two oils over medium-high heat. Add the onion, vegan bacon, garlic, and chipotles. Sauté the mixture, stirring often, until the onion is soft.

3. Transfer the beans, onion mixture, and the remaining ingredients into a slow cooker. Cook on Low for 8 to 10 hours or on High for 5 to 6 hours. Alternatively, you can simmer the beans over low heat in a covered pot on the stovetop, or bake in a covered casserole at 325°F, for about 1 1/2 hours, or until they are soft inside. Taste for salt before serving.

Persian Eggplant Stew with Yellow Split Peas and Lime

Egan Ghameih Badmejan

PERSIA/IRAN

Serves 4 to 6   GF, SF, <30

There are many versions of this unusual lime-scented eggplant stew. This is a vegan variation using chickpeas instead of meat. It's delicious served with Persian-Style Rice Pilaf with Edamamé (page 151).

1/4 CUP VEGAN MARGARINE
1 LARGE ONION, SLICED PAPER-THIN
2 CUPS COOKED OR CANNED CHICKPEAS, RINSED AND
    DRAINED
1 CUP VEGETABLE BROTH
1 (28-OUNCE) CAN PLUM TOMATOES, WITH JUICE
2 FRESH ORGANIC LIMES, WITH ZEST INTACT, CUT INTO
    QUARTERS AND SEEDED
1 TABLESPOON YELLOW SPLIT PEAS, SOAKED FOR 2 HOURS
    IN 1 CUP HOT WATER, THEN DRAINED
1/4 TEASPOON TURMERIC
1/4 TEASPOON FRESHLY GRATED NUTMEG
SALT AND FRESHLY GROUND BLACK PEPPER
1 1/2 POUNDS JAPANESE EGGPLANTS
OLIVE OIL

1. In a medium pot, heat the margarine over medium heat. Add the onion and sauté until transparent, about 10 minutes. Add the chickpeas, broth, tomatoes, limes, split peas, and turmeric. Bring to a boil, then cover, reduce the heat to low and cook for about 45 minutes. Add the nutmeg and salt and pepper to taste. Preheat the oven to 400°F.

2. Peel the eggplants lengthwise at 1/4-inch intervals, leaving equal strips of skin and strips without skin. Cut lengthwise into 1-inch thick slices and arrange on two 10 x 15-inch baking sheets lined with baking parchment cut to fit.

3. Lightly brush or spray the eggplant with olive oil. Bake for about 10 minutes, then turn over, brush the other side with olive oil and bake 10 to 15 minutes longer or until tender but not dry. Remove from the oven and reduce the heat to 350°F.

4. Transfer the eggplant to an oiled shallow 2-quart casserole. Spread the chickpea stew on top. Cover and bake for 45 minutes. Discard the limes before serving.

Lebanese Gigante Bean Stew

Fassolyah Bil-Lahmah

<small>LEBANON</small>

Serves 4   GFO, SFO

Introduce your family and friends to this wonderful bean with a fragrant and unusual Mediterranean stew. One of my favorite beans is the gigante, also called giant lima beans or, especially in the U.K., giant butter beans. They are available in Greek, Middle Eastern, and Mediterranean grocery stores and online. If you can't find them, substitute Great Northern Beans or white kidney beans rather than use small lima beans. Serve with crusty bread.

- 8 OUNCES DRIED GIGANTE BEANS, PICKED OVER, RINSED AND DRAINED AND SOAKED OVERNIGHT
- 2 CUPS RECONSTITUTED TEXTURED SOY PROTEIN CHUNKS (TSP, PAGE 10) OR BEEFY SEITAN, CUBED (PAGE 133)
- 1 SMALL ONION, SLICED PAPER-THIN
- 2 CLOVES GARLIC, MINCED
- 1 TABLESPOON VEGAN MARGARINE
- 1 MEDIUM RIPE TOMATO, CHOPPED
- 1 BAY LEAF
- 1/2 TEASPOON DRIED THYME
- 1/4 TEASPOON GROUND CINNAMON
- 1/8 TEASPOON GROUND ALLSPICE
- 1/8 TEASPOON FRESHLY GRATED NUTMEG
- 1 TABLESPOON TOMATO PASTE
- 1/2 TEASPOON YEAST EXTRACT PASTE, SUCH AS MARMITE (PAGE 21)
- 1 CUP VEGAN CHICKEN-STYLE BROTH (PAGE 2)
- 1 CUP RICH MUSHROOM STOCK (PAGE 4)
- 3 SMALL THIN-SKINNED POTATOES, WASHED AND CUT INTO 1-INCH CHUNKS
- SALT AND FRESHLY GROUND BLACK PEPPER
- 1 TABLESPOON FRESH LEMON JUICE

1. Drain the soaked beans and transfer them to a large pot with water to cover, about 2 to 3 inches above the beans. Bring to a boil, then reduce the heat and simmer, covered, until the beans are tender, but still hold their shape, 1 1/2 to 2 hours. Drain and return to the pot. Set aside.

2. In a medium nonstick skillet, heat the margarine. Add the onion and sauté over medium-high heat until it softens. Add the garlic and TSP chunks and sauté over high heat until the chunks start to brown. Transfer the mixture to the pot with the drained beans. Add the margarine, tomato, bay leaf, thyme, cinnamon, allspice, nutmeg, tomato paste, yeast extract, both kinds of broth, and the potatoes. Season with salt and pepper to taste and simmer for about 1 hour. Add the lemon juice and remove and discard the bay leaf. Serve hot.

Greek Gigante Bean and Chard Casserole

<small>GREECE</small>

Serves 4 to 6   GFO

Here is another fabulous dish featuring one of my favorite beans with greens and tangy tofu "feta." I use far less oil in this recipe than is used in traditional Greek recipes, but with no loss of flavor. This makes a delicious and unusual potluck dish. Serve with crusty bread and salad.

- 12 OUNCES GIGANTE BEANS (GIANT LIMA BEANS OR GIANT BUTTER BEANS), SOAKED OVERNIGHT
- 1 POUND SWISS CHARD, TOUGH STEMS REMOVED, WASHED AND TRIMMED
- 1 TABLESPOON OLIVE OIL
- 1 LARGE ONION, CHOPPED
- 1/2 BUNCH GREEN ONIONS, CHOPPED
- 1/4 CUP CHOPPED FRESH DILL WEED OR 4 TEASPOONS DRIED
- 2 CUPS VEGAN CHICKEN-STYLE BROTH (PAGE 2)
- 1 (14-OUNCE) CAN DICED TOMATOES, DRAINED
- 1/2 RECIPE TOFU FETA (PAGE 101), BROKEN INTO 1/2-INCH CHUNKS
- FRESHLY GROUND BLACK PEPPER
- TOPPING:
- 1 CUP FRESH BREADCRUMBS (CAN BE GLUTEN-FREE)
- OLIVE OIL FROM A PUMP SPRAYER

1. Drain the soaked beans and cover with fresh

water, with 2 to 3 inches water above the beans. Bring to a boil, then reduce to a simmer and cover. Simmer for about 1 hour or until the beans are al dente. Drain and set aside.

2. Steam the chard until just tender, then cool it off, squeeze it dry, and chop it. Set aside.

3. Heat the olive oil in a large nonstick skillet over medium heat and add the chopped onion and green onions. Sauté, stirring frequently, until the onions are softened and starting to brown.

4. Preheat the oven to 350°F. Oil a 2-quart baking dish or a 12 to 13-inch oval roaster. Add the beans, onion mixture, dill weed, chard, drained canned tomatoes, and broth. Mix well. Add the "feta" chunks and mix gently. Season with pepper to taste.

5. Bake, covered, until the beans are just tender, 1 to 2 1/2 hours, depending on the beans used. Top with the breadcrumbs and spray with a little oil from a pump sprayer. Bake for about 1/2 an hour more. If the topping isn't browned, place under the broiler for a few minutes (watch for burning).

Spicy Basque Garbanzo Bean Stew

Garbanzos con Chorizo

SPAIN/BASQUE REGION

Serves 4   GFO, SFO, <30

There are many versions of this common Basque stew. This one, thick with vegetables, chickpeas, and spicy vegan sausages, is super-simple and super-delicious. The recipe is easily doubled. This dish can be soy-free or gluten-free, depending on the type of sausage used. I especially like Field Roast Chipotle Sausages (which are soy-free) or vegan chorizo. Serve with steamed rice or crusty bread.

8 OUNCES DRIED CHICKPEAS, PICKED OVER, RINSED AND DRAINED AND SOAKED OVERNIGHT (SEE TIP)
1 TABLESPOON OLIVE OIL
1 SMALL ONION, CHOPPED
1 SMALL GREEN BELL PEPPER, CUT INTO 1/2-INCH DICE
1 SMALL RED BELL PEPPER, CUT INTO 1/2-INCH DICE
1 MEDIUM CARROT, CUT INTO 1/4-INCH-THICK ROUNDS
4 OUNCES VEGAN CHORIZO OR SPICY VEGAN SAUSAGE, COARSELY CRUMBLED OR CUT DIAGONALLY INTO 1/4-INCH SLICES
1 (14-OUNCE) CAN PLUM TOMATOES, WITH JUICE
1/2 CUP VEGETABLE BROTH
SALT

1. Drain the soaked chickpeas and put in a medium pot with water to cover, with 2 to 3 inches water above the beans. Simmer for 2 hours or until the chickpeas are tender. Drain them and set aside.

2. Use the same pot to heat the olive oil over medium-high heat. Add the onions, bell peppers and carrot and sauté until the onion starts to brown. Add the sausage and cook until browned, about 5 minutes. Add the tomatoes and juice, crushing the tomatoes between your fingers. Add the broth and bring the stew to a boil. Reduce the heat to a simmer and cook, covered, for about 30 minutes. Season with salt to taste and serve hot.

Slow-Cooker Variation: Increase the broth to 2 cups. Combine the ingredients into the slow-cooker insert and cook on Low for 8 hours or on High for about 4 hours. Serve as above. You can double the recipe for a large slow-cooker.

Tip: In the stovetop recipe, you can use approximately 3 1/4 cups drained cooked or canned chickpeas instead of cooking them from the dried state, if you like. In that case, omit the first step in the recipe.

Greek Bean and Orzo Stew

GREECE

Serves 4   GFO, SFO, <30

Orzo is a type of semolina pasta that resembles grains of rice, but there is a variation using barley at the end of the recipe. ("Orzo" is the Italian word for barley, by the way.) Either way, this "meaty" stew is very satisfying.

- 1 1/3 CUPS BEEFY SEITAN (PAGE 133), CUBED; OR RECONSTITUTED TEXTURED SOY PROTEIN CHUNKS (TSP) (PAGE 10), 3/4 CUP DRY
- 1/4 CUP WHOLE-WHEAT FLOUR (OR GLUTEN-FREE FLOUR)
- 1/2 TABLESPOON OLIVE OIL
- 1 SMALL ONION, CHOPPED
- 1 CLOVE GARLIC, MINCED
- 1/4 CUP DRY WHITE WINE
- 1/2 CUP VEGETABLE BROTH
- 1/2 (14-OUNCE) CAN DICED TOMATOES (WITH JUICE)
- 3/4 TEASPOON SOY SAUCE (OR SOY-FREE SAUCE, PAGE 12)
- 1/2 BAY LEAF
- 3/4 CUP COOKED OR CANNED WHITE KIDNEY, CANNELLINI, OR GREAT NORTHERN BEANS, RINSED AND DRAINED
- 3 TABLESPOONS FRESH CHOPPED MARJORAM OR 1/2 TABLESPOON DRIED
- 1/2 POUND ORZO PASTA
- SALT AND FRESHLY GROUND BLACK PEPPER
- WALNUT PARM (PAGE 15) OR TOFU FETA (PAGE 101), COARSELY CRUMBLED, OPTIONAL

1. Roll the seitan cubes in the flour to coat them and set aside.

2. Heat the oil in a medium nonstick skillet over high heat. Add the seitan, reduce the heat to medium-high and stir-fry until browned all over. Remove from the pan and set aside.

3. Add the onion and garlic to the hot skillet and stir-fry until they are soft and translucent, adding a few drops of water as needed to keep them from sticking.

4. Transfer the browned seitan, wine, broth, tomatoes (with juice), soy sauce, and bay leaf to the skillet with the onions and garlic. Bring the mixture to a boil, then turn it down to medium-low, cover and simmer for 1 hour. Add the drained beans and marjoram to the stew.

5. Cook the orzo in a medium pot of boiling salted water for 7 to 10 minutes or until al dente. Drain the orzo and pile it into a shallow serving bowl. Taste the stew for salt and pepper. Remove and discard the bay leaf before serving. Pour the stew over the orzo and top with Walnut Parm, if using. Serve immediately.

VARIATION

To substitute pearl barley for the orzo, bring 3 cups of vegetable broth to a boil in a medium saucepan, then stir in 8 ounces (about 1 1/2 cups) pearl barley. Cover and reduce the heat to low. Cook for 20 to 30 minutes or until tender.

Egyptian-Style Beans

Ful Medames

EGYPT

Serves 6   GF, SF, <30

Ful Medames *is the most common Egyptian bean stew, but there's a good reason for that – Ful (as it is often called) is tasty, satisfying comfort food. Ful is often eaten for breakfast and is also commonly sold by street vendors as a hearty snack or lunch – Egyptian fast food. I could not find small fava or brown beans, so I used small Mexican red or pink beans (please do not substitute kidney beans) because they are brown when cooked and have a similar creamy texture. I added a few split red lentils to thicken the broth. This was a successful substitution and a delicious and flavorful, yet simple, dish. So good with crusty bread, brown rice, or bulgur wheat pilaf, as well as the usual pita or Middle Eastern flatbread.*

- 1 POUND SMALL RED OR PINK BEANS (OR SMALL BROWN BEANS, IF YOU CAN FIND THEM), PICKED OVER, RINSED AND DRAINED AND SOAKED OVERNIGHT IN PLENTY OF WATER

1/4 CUP SPLIT RED LENTILS, PICKED OVER, RINSED AND
   DRAINED
5 CUPS WATER
2 TABLESPOONS OLIVE OIL
2 MEDIUM ONIONS, CHOPPED
4 CLOVES GARLIC, CHOPPED
1 TEASPOON GROUND CORIANDER
1 TEASPOON GROUND CUMIN
1/4 TEASPOON RED PEPPER FLAKES
2 TEASPOONS SALT
2 TABLESPOONS FRESH LEMON JUICE
FRESHLY GROUND BLACK PEPPER
OPTIONAL GARNISHES:
1/2 CUP CHOPPED FRESH CILANTRO, PARSLEY, OR MINT
1/4 CUP CHOPPED GREEN ONIONS
LEMON WEDGES
HOT SAUCE

1. Drain the soaked beans and transfer with the lentils to large pot with the 5 cups of water. Bring the water to a boil, skim off the resulting foam, then reduce the heat to a simmer. Cover and cook for 1 hour.

2. Heat the oil in a large nonstick skillet over medium-high heat. Add the onions and garlic and sauté until softened and beginning to brown. Add the coriander, cumin, and red pepper flakes, and stir briefly. Transfer the onion mixture, along with the salt, to the pot of beans after the beans have cooked for 1 hour.

3. Cook for 1 to 1 1/2 hours longer or until the beans are tender and the sauce has cooked down. Add the lemon juice and pepper to taste. Serve hot, with some of the optional garnishes.

Lentil and Rapini Stew with Spicy Vegan Sausage No¹.

ITALY

Serves 6   SFO

This is one of those peasant dishes that I crave in cold weather. This simple Italian-style stick-to your-ribs stew is delicious with a green salad and crusty bread to soak up the juices. Depending on the sausages used (try Tofurky Italian "Sausages" or soy-free Field Roast Chipotle "Sausages"), this can be made soy-free.

1/2 POUND (1 CUP PLUS 2 TABLESPOONS) DRIED BROWN
   LENTILS, PICKED OVER, RINSED, AND DRAINED
2 CUPS CANNED TOMATOES AND JUICE, CHOPPED
2 CUPS VEGETABLE BROTH
1 TABLESPOON OLIVE OIL
1 MEDIUM ONION, CHOPPED
4 CLOVES GARLIC, MINCED
2 SPICY VEGAN SAUSAGES, SLICED 1/4-INCH THICK
1 POUND RAPINI (BROCCOLI RAAB), TOUGH STEMS RE-
   MOVED, CUT INTO 1-INCH SLICES
1 TABLESPOON CHOPPED FRESH BASIL OR 1 TEASPOON
   DRIED
1 1/2 TABLESPOONS CHOPPED FRESH OREGANO OR MARJO-
   RAM, OR 1 1/2 TEASPOONS DRIED
1/2 CUP WALNUT PARM (PAGE 15)

1. Mix the drained lentils, tomatoes (with juice) and broth in a medium pot. (If you are using dried herbs, add them now). Bring the mixture to a boil, then reduce the heat to medium-low and simmer, covered, for 30 to 40 minutes.

2. Heat the olive oil in a medium nonstick skillet over medium-high heat. Add the garlic and onion and sauté them until translucent but not browned. Add the garlic and onions to the lentils.

3. Spray the same skillet with oil from a pump sprayer over medium heat. Add the sausage and cook until browned, about 5 minutes. Add the sausage to the lentils. Add the rapini and the fresh herbs (if you have not added the dried ones

already) to the lentils and cook an additional 5 to 7 minutes or until the rapini has wilted. Serve hot in shallow soup bowls, topped with the Walnut Parm.

Serbian Braised Sauerkraut and Seitan

Podvarak

SERBIA

Serves 4   GFO, SFO, <30

The original of this was a favorite dish in pre-vegan days. I made my own sauerkraut in those days and made Podvarak with chicken and bacon fat (!). When I tried it with a vegan chicken substitute in place of the chicken and a dark sesame oil/olive oil mixture in place of the bacon fat, I found that it needed more broth, as vegan proteins usually do, but it is just as delicious as the original and very low in calories. Boiled thin-skinned potatoes are an ideal accompaniment. Sauerkraut packed in wine is excellent in this recipe.
Tip: *If you prefer a less sour taste, rinse the sauerkraut first.*

1 TABLESPOON OLIVE OIL

1 TABLESPOON DARK SESAME OIL

12 OUNCES LIGHT SEITAN CUTLETS (PAGE 5), CUT INTO STRIPS OR 4 CUPS RECONSTITUTED SOY CURLS (4 OUNCES; 3 CUPS DRY) OR ALTERNATIVE (PAGE 10)

2 TO 3 MEDIUM ONIONS, MINCED

2 LARGE CLOVES GARLIC, MINCED

3 CUPS SAUERKRAUT, SQUEEZED

2 TEASPOONS CHOPPED PICKLED JALAPEÑOS OR FRESH, SEEDED HOT CHILES

FRESHLY GROUND BLACK PEPPER

1 1/2 CUPS (OR MORE) CHICKEN-STYLE VEGAN BROTH (SEE PAGE 2)

1. In a large nonstick skillet heat 1/2 tablespoon of the olive oil and 1/2 tablespoon of the sesame oil over high heat. Add the seitan and cook until browned, about 5 minutes. Remove from the pan.

2. Add the remaining 1/2 tablespoon each of both oils to the pan and add the onions and garlic. Cook over medium heat, stirring, until the onions are translucent, adding a bit of water or dry white wine as necessary to keep them from sticking. Add the prepared sauerkraut, jalapeños, and black pepper to taste. Mix together well.

3. Spread the seitan evenly over the sauerkraut mixture and pour the broth over all. Bring to a boil, then reduce the heat to a simmer, cover and cook for 30 minutes. If the mixture gets too dry, add a bit more broth. Serve hot.

Peruvian Squash and Vegetable Stew

Locro

PERU

Serves 6   GF, SF, <30

This is much more complex and delicious than it looks in print and very colorful. I usually make the simple vegetable version, but many Peruvians like the stew with cheese and/or olives added, so I have made those optional. Serve this colorful stew with steamed basmati rice (white or brown).

1/4 CUP OLIVE OIL

2 1/2 CUPS MINCED ONION

2 CLOVES GARLIC, MINCED

4 POUNDS WINTER SQUASH, (BUTTERNUT OR HUBBARD), PEELED, SEEDED, AND CUT INTO 1-INCH CUBES (ABOUT 10 CUPS)

2 LARGE RIPE TOMATOES, CHOPPED

1 TEASPOON DRIED OREGANO

1 1/2 TEASPOONS SALT

1/4 TEASPOON WHITE PEPPER

1/2 CUP WATER OR VEGETABLE BROTH

1 CUP FRESH OR FROZEN SWEET CORN KERNELS

1 CUP FRESH OR FROZEN SHELLED BABY PEAS (PETIT POIS)

1 TO 2 CUPS SHREDDED WHITE VEGAN CHEESE, OPTIONAL

PITTED KALAMATA OR PERUVIAN ALFONSO OLIVES, OPTIONAL

Heat the olive oil in a large pot over medium heat. Add the onion and garlic and sauté for about 8 minutes, or until softened. Add the squash, tomatoes, oregano, salt, pepper, and water. Cover and cook over low heat for 25 minutes. Add the corn and peas. Cover and cook just until the peas are done. Add the vegan cheese and/or olives, if using. Taste for salt and pepper. Serve hot.

Catalonian-Style Eggplant and Almond Stew

Spain

Serves 6   SFO, <30

My husband claims that he doesn't like eggplant, but he loved this stew! The eggplant almost disappears into the tasty mushroom broth and makes the stew silky-sensuous in texture. This stew is thickened by bread and almonds, a technique that goes back to medieval Europe and probably originated in the Middle East. This stew is not picture-pretty, but it's uncommonly delicious with crusty bread. The recipe can be made in a slow-cooker.

12 BLANCHED ALMONDS, LIGHTLY TOASTED
2 POUNDS EGGPLANT, PEELED AND CUT INTO 2-INCH CUBES
SALT
1/4 CUP OLIVE OIL
2 LARGE CLOVES GARLIC, THINLY SLICED
1 (1-INCH) SLICE FRENCH OR ITALIAN-STYLE BREAD, CRUST
    REMOVED
24 OUNCES LIGHT SEITAN CUTLETS (PAGE 5), CUT INTO
    STRIPS; OR 6 CUPS RECONSTITUTED SOY CURLS,
    DRAINED (4 1/2 CUPS DRY) OR ALTERNATIVE (PAGE 10)
ALL-PURPOSE FLOUR, FOR DREDGING
1 MEDIUM ONION, MINCED
1 CUP CANNED CRUSHED TOMATOES
3 CUPS RICH MUSHROOM STOCK (PAGE 4)

1. Process the toasted almonds in a food processor until they are fine crumbs. Leave in the food processor.

2. Sprinkle the eggplant pieces liberally with salt and let them drain in a colander for 30 minutes. Pat dry with paper towels.

3. Heat 1 tablespoon of the olive oil in a large nonstick skillet. Add the garlic and cook just until they begin to turn light golden, then remove from the skillet. Add the bread and fry it in the oil that remains in the skillet until golden on both sides. Set aside to cool. When cool, break up the bread and add to the almonds in the food processor along with the garlic. Pulse briefly and set aside.

4. Toss the seitan with flour lightly to coat. Heat 2 tablespoons of the oil in the same skillet over high heat. Add the seitan and stir-fry until starting to brown a little. Use a slotted spoon to transfer to a slow cooker or pot.

5. Add the remaining 1 tablespoon oil in the same skillet over high heat. Add the onion and reduce the heat to medium-high. Stir-fry until the onion is translucent, adding a few drops of water as needed to keep them from sticking. Scrape the onion into the slow cooker or pot and add the bread mixture, eggplant, mushroom broth, and crushed tomatoes. Stir gently and cover. If using a slow cooker, cook on High until the stew is bubbly, then turn to Low and slow-cook for 4 hours or until the eggplant has almost dissolved. If cooking in a pot on the stovetop, simmer the stew on low heat for about 1 1/2 hours, or until the eggplant has almost dissolved. Taste the stew for salt and serve hot.

Italian Rustic Squash and Kale Tart

Italy

Serves 4   SF

It's hard to believe that this vegetable filling can taste so "meaty," but it does in this absolute winner of a dish! The crispy olive oil pastry (a traditional, frugal peasant recipe designed to use as little expen-

sive olive oil as possible) is easy to make and low in fat (about 1/2 tablespoon of olive oil per serving). If you want to make a larger tart, double both the filling and the pastry recipes and bake it on a 14-inch pizza pan.

Pastry:

1 CUP UNBLEACHED WHITE FLOUR (DO NOT USE PASTRY FLOUR)

1/2 TEASPOON SALT

2 TABLESPOONS OLIVE OIL

1/3 CUP ICE-COLD WATER

Filling:

4 OUNCES KALE, TOUGH STEMS REMOVED, WASHED, DRAINED AND SLICED 1/4-INCH THICK

1 TABLESPOON OLIVE OIL

1 MEDIUM ONION, CHOPPED

4 TO 5 GREEN ONIONS, CHOPPED

6 OUNCES BUTTERNUT SQUASH (OR OTHER "MEATY" WINTER SQUASH), PEELED, AND CUT IN 1/2-INCH DICE

3 TABLESPOONS WALNUT PARM (PAGE 15) OR FINELY CHOPPED TOASTED WALNUTS

SALT AND FRESHLY GROUND BLACK PEPPER

1. **Pastry:** Whisk together the flour and salt in a medium bowl. Drizzle in the oil and mix with your fingers or a fork. Dribble in the cold water slowly, mixing with a fork as you go. When it holds together, knead it gently into a ball, cover with plastic wrap or a damp cloth and refrigerate for at least 30 minutes.

2. **Filling:** Steam the squash until just tender. Steam the kale until tender, then cool it under cold running water, drain it and then squeeze as much water out of it as you can. Chop the kale with a sharp knife.

3. Heat the olive oil in a large nonstick skillet over medium-high heat and add both kinds of onions. Stir-fry until tender. Add the kale and squash, Walnut Parm, and salt and pepper to taste. Set aside. Preheat the oven to 375°F.

4. On a lightly-floured piece of baking parchment, roll the pastry out into a thin 14-inch circle. Carefully transfer the rolled-out dough onto an oiled 10-inch pie pan (see Tip). Pile the filling in the middle of the dough and spread it out evenly. Bring up the edges around the filling to make a "freeform" pie, pleating the dough over the Filling and leaving an open circle of filling in the center.

5. Brush the dough with a little olive oil and cover the exposed filling with a circle of foil. Bake the tart for 30 to 45 minutes or until the dough is golden. Cut into wedges to serve. It's good hot, warm, or cold.

Tip: To transfer fragile pastry dough into a pan without tearing, flour the top of the circle lightly and then gently fold it in half and then in half again. Gently lift the pastry into the pie pan, letting the edges of the pastry overhang the edge of the pan. Carefully unfold the dough. Another way is to lightly flour the pastry and roll it up loosely around a rolling pin. Use the rolling pin to transfer the dough to the pan and unroll the pastry over the pan.

Ukrainian Stuffed Cabbage Rolls

Holubtsi

UKRAINE

Serves 6   GF, SF

My recipe is slightly different from the traditional version. I use brown rice, add a bit of garlic and thyme to the filling, and I don't cook the rolls for quite as long. I think this improves the flavor and texture. Freezing the cabbage ahead of time saves the work of pre-cooking the cabbage leaves, because the leaves are flexible after thawing. If you prefer, you can use pearl barley, buckwheat groats, or wheat kernels instead of the rice in the filling. They are all authentic variations. See the directions for using these grains at the end of the recipe.

1 LARGE GREEN CABBAGE (3 TO 4 POUNDS)
Filling:
2 OUNCES DRIED PORCINI MUSHROOMS
3 CUPS WATER
1 CUP VEGETABLE BROTH, AS NEEDED
2 CUPS (RAW) LONG GRAIN BROWN RICE
2 TABLESPOONS VEGAN MARGARINE
2 LARGE ONIONS, MINCED
2 CLOVES GARLIC, MINCED
1 TEASPOON DRIED THYME
SALT AND FRESHLY GROUND PEPPER
Cooking Liquid:
3 CUPS HOT WATER
1 (5-OUNCE) CAN TOMATO PASTE
1 TABLESPOON SUGAR
1 TABLESPOON VINEGAR OR FRESH LEMON JUICE
1/2 TEASPOON SALT

1. At least 48 hours before making the cabbage rolls, wrap the head of cabbage in plastic wrap and place in the freezer. The night before making the rolls, remove the cabbage from the freezer and set it in the sink to thaw out. The next day, carefully separate the thawed leaves. You should have 20 to 24 large, usable leaves. (The other leaves can be sliced or chopped and used in soup or in vegetable dishes.) Trim the hard thick stem ends out so that they will roll better. Set aside.

2. **Filling:** Combine the dried mushrooms and water in a medium saucepan and simmer for 1 hour. Drain the mushrooms and save the liquid, adding as much of the broth as needed to make 3 1/2 cups of liquid. Chop the mushrooms and set aside.

3. In a pot, bring the mushroom broth to a boil with salt to taste and add the brown rice. Bring it to a boil, then cover, reduce the heat to low and simmer for 45 minutes. Alternatively, you can use an electric rice cooker.

4. While the rice cooks, melt the margarine in a large nonstick skillet over medium-high heat. Add the onions and garlic and sauté until the onions are soft and slightly browned. Mix in the

cooked rice, mushrooms, and thyme. Add salt and pepper to taste. Preheat the oven to 350°F.

5. Whisk together the cooking liquid ingredients in a 1-quart bowl, making sure that the tomato paste is dissolved. Set aside.

6. Place about 1/4 cup of the filling (or whatever the leaf can comfortably hold, packed together lightly) in the middle of each cabbage leaf. Fold the sides of the leaf in toward the center, then roll up firmly. Place the rolls seam-side-down, close together, in one layer in a large oiled baking pan. Pour the cooking liquid over the rolls, cover and bake for 2 hours.

VARIATIONS

To use different grains in this recipe, follow the recipe instructions with these differences:

- **Pearl Barley or Buckwheat Groats (Kasha):** Use 2 cups of pearl barley or buckwheat groats in place of the brown rice. Add water to the mushroom broth to make 4 cups of liquid in total. Pearl barley only needs to cook for 20 to 30 minutes; buckwheat groats need to cook for 15 minutes and then are left to stand off the heat, covered, for another 10 minutes. Tip: Some cooks like to add 4 teaspoons margarine or olive oil to the buckwheat groats as it comes to a boil.

- **Wheat, Spelt, Kamut, or Farro Kernels:** Rinse and drain 2 cups of kernels. Add water to the mushroom broth to make 6 cups of liquid in total to cook the wheat kernels. The kernels will have to cook 1 to 2 hours. Alternatively, pressure-cook the kernels for 45 minutes.

"Meat of the Fields"
Soy and Seitan Mains

This chapter is home to many of my "celebration" centerpiece dishes that use soy foods and seitan to recreate international dishes for special occasions and feast days. You will be proud to serve recipes such as Seitan Wellington, Moroccan Savory Celebration Pie, and Pastry-Wrapped Russian Loaf to your family and friends. I hope that these recipes will inspire you to veganize some of your own family and national specialties to keep your traditions alive without sacrificing animals in order to do so.

In addition to special occasion recipes, this chapter also contains several quick-and-easy global family meals that satisfy the craving for hearty, "meaty" goodness. Among my favorites are General Tso's Stir-Fry, Jamaican Curry, Vegan Peruvian Kebabs *(Anticuchos)*, and Vegan *Coq au Vin*.

Many of the recipes provide more than one "meat of the field" option. For example, a recipe may call for seitan or tofu with one or two alternatives, such as tempeh or Butler Soy Curls, so that you can use whichever you prefer. Just in case you're not familiar with the various types of soy foods and seitan, see pages 5 to 10 for some helpful information.

Soy and Seitan Mains

Savory Layered Tortilla Pie

MEXICO/NORTH AMERICA

Serves 6   GFO, SFO

*Here corn tortillas are stacked and layered with
crispy tofu, hot chiles, vegan cheese, artichoke hearts,
and sun-dried tomatoes. The whole shebang is bathed
in a dark, rich, and fat-free, chile gravy – definitely
a few of my favorite things! This delectable casserole
assembles quickly and is just as quickly devoured.*

1 CUP WATER

1 1/2 TABLESPOON TOMATO PASTE

1 TABLESPOON ANCHO CHILE POWDER

1 TABLESPOON UNBLEACHED WHITE FLOUR (FOR GLUTEN-
    FREE, USE 2 TEASPOONS WHITE RICE FLOUR)

1/2 TEASPOON SOY SAUCE (OR SOY-FREE SAUCE, PAGE 12)

1/4 TEASPOON GARLIC POWDER

1/4 TEASPOON ONION POWDER

1/4 TEASPOON GROUND CUMIN

1/4 TEASPOON SALT

8 TO 10 CRISPY MARINATED TOFU SLICES (PAGE 8), COOKED
    (OR A VARIATION, BELOW)

8 (8-INCH) CORN TORTILLAS

3/4 CUP SUN-DRIED TOMATOES IN OIL, RINSED IN HOT WATER
    AND DRAINED AND SLICED 1/4-INCH THICK

3/4 CUP MARINATED ARTICHOKE HEARTS, RINSED IN HOT
    WATER AND DRAINED AND SLICED 1/4-INCH THICK

1 CUP TOFU FETA (PAGE 101)

1 (7-OUNCE) CAN WHOLE MILD GREEN CHILES (ANAHEIM OR
    CALIFORNIA GREEN CHILES), SEEDED, RINSED, AND
    DRAINED

3 OUNCES SHREDDED VEGAN CHEESE

2 TABLESPOONS CHOPPED GREEN ONIONS

MEXICAN HOT SAUCE

OPTIONAL GARNISHES: SLICED BLACK OLIVES, CASHEW OR
    TOFU SOUR CREAM (PAGE 33); OR SLICED RIPE HASS
    AVOCADO

1. Preheat the oven to 375°F. Lightly oil a 9-inch
pie pan and set aside. In a blender, combine the
water, tomato paste, chili powder, flour, soy
sauce, garlic powder, onion powder, cumin,
and salt, and blend until smooth. Transfer to a
medium saucepan and bring to a boil, stirring

frequently, then reduce the heat to medium-low
and simmer for 15 to 20 minutes, stirring frequently. Set aside.

2. Cut the tofu slices into 1/4-inch wide strips
and mix with 1/2 cup of the reserved gravy. Set
aside.

3. Layer 2 tortillas in the bottom of the prepared
pan. Cover evenly with the chiles and artichokes.
Cover that with 2 more tortillas, then the sun-
dried tomatoes and the crumbled "feta," then
2 more tortillas, and the tofu. Finish with the
last 2 tortillas, the remaining gravy, ending with
the shredded vegan cheese. Bake for 20 minutes
or until hot. Cut into wedges to serve. Sprinkle
with green onions, hot sauce, and optional garnishes, if using.

VARIATIONS

Instead of using the tofu, substitute 8 ounces
Light Seitan Cutlets (page 5) cut into strips, or 2
cups reconstituted Soy Curls (2 ounces or 1 1/2
cups dry; page 10), drained. Or substitute vegan
burgers (sliced or crumbled), vegan "shrimp" or
other mock seafood (page 91), vegan sausages
(Field Roast brand is soy-free), or canned or
cooked drained pinto or black beans.

Vegan Scottish Pot Haggis

SCOTLAND

Serves 4 to 6   GFO, SFO, <30

*This traditional Scottish dish, always served on Rob-
bie Burns' Night (January 25) or St. Andrew's Day
(November 30), is a mildly flavored oatmeal-laced
meatloaf made from (and stuffed into) – cringe –
sheep innards. These days, most Scottish haggis mak-
ers also offer vegan versions. This is my vegan take
on it (I spiced it up as much as I dared), made as a
"pot haggis," an authentic version that it is formed
in a bowl (or "pudding basin," as it is called in the
U.K.). I added shredded potato to firm up the loaf.
I think it is much tastier than the real thing (yes,*

I tasted it back in my pre-vegan days!) and can be served as a yummy gluten-free vegan meatloaf. Serve with gravy (page 101), and potatoes mashed with turnips (called "tatties 'n' neeps" in Scotland). For a modern touch, oven-roast the turnips instead of boiling them before mashing. You are supposed to drink Scotch whiskey with this as well, but I pass on that.

12 OUNCES (2 CUPS) COMMERCIAL VEGAN "BURGER
    CRUMBLES" (OR A VARIATION, SEE BELOW)
1/2 CUP OLD-FASHIONED ROLLED OR QUICK OATS
1 (4 OUNCE) POTATO, SHREDDED (ABOUT 2/3 CUP)
1 MEDIUM ONION, FINELY MINCED
2 TABLESPOONS SOY SAUCE (OR SOY-FREE SAUCE, PAGE 12)
2 TABLESPOONS KETCHUP
2 TABLESPOONS NUTRITIONAL YEAST FLAKES
1/2 TEASPOON SALT
1/2 TEASPOON GARLIC POWDER
1/2 TEASPOON DRIED THYME
1/2 TEASPOON DRIED SAVORY
FRESHLY GROUND BLACK PEPPER, TO TASTE
OPTIONAL: 1/4 TEASPOON EACH: CAYENNE PEPPER,
    GROUND CORIANDER, ALLSPICE, AND/OR NUTMEG

1. Combine all of the ingredients in a large bowl. Use your hands to mix well.

2. Pack the mixture into a 1-quart ceramic British pudding basin or heatproof casserole or bowl, very well-greased with vegan margarine, which will fit into a large pot. (You could even use a loaf pan, if necessary.) Cover the vessel with 2 layers of aluminum foil. Alternatively, line a small steaming basket with aluminum foil and pack the mixture into that, folding the excess foil over the top to cover completely. If you don't want the foil touching the food, line the inside with baking parchment cut to fit or line it with cheesecloth (see Tip).

3. Steam the haggis over simmering water for 2 hours. Loosen with a table knife (remove from the cheesecloth, if you used it) and invert it onto a plate. Cut into wedges to serve.

Gluten-Free Option: Use TSP (instead of seitan); Soy-Free Sauce; and gluten-free oatmeal.

TIPS

- To save time, use a food processor to mince the onion and shred the potato.

- For a more authentic appearance, line your steaming vessel or basket with cheesecloth. Tie it at the top to make a "bag."

- Make this the day before or the morning of the day you will serve it – it firms up best if cooled first and then reheated.

VARIATIONS

Instead of the vegan burger crumbles, use:

- 2 cups ground Beefy Seitan (page 133), with 2 tablespoons hot vegetable broth mixed with 1/2 teaspoon yeast extract paste, such as Marmite (page 21) or 1 teaspoon dark miso

- 1 1/2 cups dry textured soy protein granules (TVP or TSP) soaked with 1 1/4 cups hot water mixed with 1 teaspoon vegetable broth powder or paste (page 2), 2 teaspoons gravy browner (such as Kitchen Bouquet) and 1/2 tablespoon yeast extract paste or 1 tablespoon dark miso, until the liquid is absorbed.

Curried Vegan Meatloaf

Bobotie

SOUTH AFRICA

Serves 4   GFO

Bobotie (pronounced ba-boo-eh-tee) is a wonderfully spicy, fruity South African "meatloaf" with a savory custard topping. The origins of Bobotie can be traced back to the influence of the "Cape Malay" people. These Malaysian state prisoners of the Dutch landed on the shores of South Africa from Java and the neighboring Indonesian islands in the late 1600s up until 1749. These proud people brought with them the Muslim faith, fine architecture, and a unique style of cooking, which has had a great influence on

South African cuisine. My husband's late wife Ianthe was South African, so I was inspired to make this vegan version of the popular dish to celebrate my stepsons' maternal origins. Serve with your favorite chutney, *South African Yellow Rice (page 156)*, *Mielie Bread (page 215)*, and a green salad.
Note: *The tofu in this recipe must be frozen for at least 48 hours, then thawed and squeezed dry. (See page 8 about freezing tofu.) Thawing can be speeded up by placing the frozen tofu, in its storage bag or container, in a large bowl of boiling hot water.*

1 1/2 CUPS FRESH WHOLE-GRAIN BREADCRUMBS (CAN BE GLUTEN-FREE)

1/2 CUP NONDAIRY MILK

1/2 TABLESPOON OLIVE OIL

1/2 TABLESPOON DARK SESAME OIL

2 CUPS MINCED ONIONS (2 LARGE ONIONS)

4 CLOVES GARLIC, MINCED

1 1/2 TABLESPOONS GOOD-QUALITY CURRY POWDER

1 1/2 POUNDS (24 OUNCES) MEDIUM-FIRM TOFU, FROZEN FOR 48 HOURS, THEN THAWED, SQUEEZED DRY IN A CLEAN CLOTH, THEN CRUMBLED

1/4 CUP SOY SAUCE

1/4 CUP RAISINS

1/4 CUP GROUND TOASTED BLANCHED ALMONDS

2 TABLESPOONS KETCHUP, OPTIONAL

1 1/2 TABLESPOONS FRESH LEMON JUICE

1 1/2 TABLESPOONS MANGO, PEACH, OR APRICOT CHUTNEY

1/4 TEASPOON FRESHLY GROUND BLACK PEPPER

1 TEASPOON VEGAN GRAVY BROWNER, OPTIONAL

4 WHOLE BAY LEAVES

1/2 CUP SOY OR NUT MILK

1/2 TABLESPOON NUTRITIONAL YEAST FLAKES

1/2 TABLESPOON BIRD'S CUSTARD POWDER (PLAIN) OR CORNSTARCH WITH A PINCH OF TURMERIC

1/8 TEASPOON SALT

1. Preheat oven to 350°F. Oil a round shallow 1-quart baking dish and set aside. In a large bowl, combine the breadcrumbs and milk. Mix well and set aside.

2. In a large skillet, heat the oils over high heat. Add the onion and garlic and cook over medium heat, adding a little water as necessary to keep from sticking, until the onions are soft and be-ginning to brown, about 10 minutes. This is very important to the taste and texture of the dish, so don't undercook them. Add the curry powder to the onions and cook, stirring for a few minutes.

3. Transfer the onions to the large bowl with the soaked breadcrumbs, along with the thawed, squeezed tofu, soy sauce, raisins, almonds, ketchup (if using), lemon juice, chutney, pepper, and gravy browner, if using. Mix well. Pack the mixture into the prepared baking dish. Insert the bay leaves into the mixture in a circle, with the points sticking out the top. Bake for 30 minutes.

4. In a small saucepan, whisk together the soy milk, nutritional yeast, custard powder, and salt until smooth. Stir with a wooden spoon constantly over high heat until it has thickened, about 2 minutes. Pour the custard evenly over the loaf and bake 15 minutes more. Cut into 4 wedges and serve hot.

Moroccan Savory Celebration Pie

Bisteeya

MOROCCO

Serves 5 to 6

This makes a spectacular and unusual holiday entrée. This pie has a luxurious nut and "poultry" filling, with a scrambled egg mixture (scrambled tofu in this version, of course), sugar, and spices. I use the rather unusual (for this recipe) addition of fresh basil, because my husband doesn't care for cilantro, but you can use parsley or parsley and cilantro, if you prefer. I have reduced the fat of the traditional version as much as possible without losing the richness and flavor. Serve with a rice pilaf and two delicious Moroccan salads – Glazed Morocccan Carrot Salad and Moroccan Passover Spinach Salad (page 84). Almond Milk Custard with Rose Water, Saffron, and Berries (page 195) would make a lovely ending to the meal.
Tip: *You need two 10-inch pie plates or one 10-inch pie*

plate and one 12-inch pizza pan for this recipe.

Filling:

2 TABLESPOONS VEGAN MARGARINE

1 SMALL ONION, MINCED

2 CLOVES GARLIC, MINCED

3/4 TABLESPOON GRATED FRESH GINGER

8 OUNCES LIGHT SEITAN CUTLETS (SEE PAGE 5), CUT INTO
    STRIPS; OR 2 CUPS RECONSTITUTED SOY CURLS,
    DRAINED (2 OUNCES OR 1 1/2 CUPS DRY), OR ALTERNA-
    TIVE (PAGE 10)

1/2 TEASPOON GROUND CUMIN

1/2 TEASPOON GROUND CORIANDER

1/4 TEASPOON TURMERIC

1/4 TEASPOON CAYENNE PEPPER

FINELY GRATED ZEST OF 1 SMALL ORGANIC LEMON

JUICE OF 1 SMALL LEMON

2 TABLESPOONS VEGETABLE BROTH

1/4 CUP FRESH BASIL OR FLAT-LEAF PARSLEY LEAVES,
    CHOPPED

Scrambled Tofu:

1 (12.3-OUNCE) BOX EXTRA-FIRM SILKEN TOFU, DRAINED

3 TABLESPOONS NUTRITIONAL YEAST FLAKES

3/8 TEASPOON TURMERIC

3/8 TEASPOON ONION POWDER

1/8 TEASPOON GARLIC POWDER

1/4 TEASPOON SALT

1/4 CUP VEGETABLE BROTH

Almond Mixture:

3/4 CUP TOASTED SLIVERED ALMONDS

1 TABLESPOON SUGAR

1/2 TEASPOON GROUND CINNAMON

Pastry:

12 SHEETS PHYLLO PASTRY, THAWED

1/4 CUP VEGAN MARGARINE, MELTED

DECORATIVE TOPPING:

1/2 TABLESPOON CONFECTIONERS' SUGAR

1 TEASPOON GROUND CINNAMON

1. **Filling:** Heat the margarine in a large non-stick skillet over medium-high heat until the margarine is foamy. Add the onion, garlic, and ginger and sauté until the onions are translucent, about 5 minutes. Add the seitan along with the dry spices, lemon juice and zest, and broth. Sauté the mixture briefly. Remove from the heat and stir in the basil. Set aside to cool.

2. **Almond Mixture:** In a food processor, grind together the almonds, sugar, and cinnamon until the almonds are ground finely, but not to a paste. Set aside.

3. **Scrambled Tofu:** In a large bowl, combine the tofu, nutritional yeast, turmeric, onion powder, garlic powder, salt, and vegetable broth. Mash with a potato masher and then mix with a spoon to combine well. Heat a large nonstick skillet over medium-high heat and spray it with oil from a pump sprayer. Add the tofu mixture and turn it with a spatula until the mixture changes color, evaporates some of the liquid and looks like softly-scrambled eggs, about 5 minutes. Set aside.

4. To assemble: Preheat the oven to 350°F. Cut 12 sheets of phyllo in half horizontally with kitchen shears and keep them covered with a sheet of baking parchment covered with a damp kitchen towel. Have the melted margarine ready, along with a fine pastry brush. Oil a 10-inch pie plate. Working with 1 half-sheet of phyllo at a time, brush 12 half-sheets of the dough lightly with the melted margarine and arrange them in the pie plate, in an overlapping circular fashion, letting the edges hang over the side. Oil the second 10-inch pie plate or 12-inch pizza pan and set aside.

5. Sprinkle half of the almond mixture evenly over the dough inside the pan. Spoon half of the scrambled tofu over the almonds. Spread the filling evenly over the tofu. Spread with the remaining scrambled tofu. Sprinkle the tofu with the remaining almond mixture. Fold the overhanging dough up over the filling and brush with melted margarine.

6. Again working with 1 half-sheet of dough at a time, brush the dough lightly with melted margarine and arrange 12 half-sheets of dough over the filling in the same pinwheel manner as before. Tuck the overhang carefully under the pie.

7. Cover the pie loosely with baking parchment

Chai-Spiced Crepes with Citrus-Almond Ricotta, 40

Fresh Pineapple-Noodle Stir-Fry, 94

No-Knead Crusty Artisinal Bread, 226

Italian Pear Tart, 173

Thai Pineapple Fried Rice in a Pineapple Shell, 153

Smoky Spicy Hominy Soup *(Posole)*, 69

Italian Rustic Squash and Kale Tart, 120

Cranberry-Orange-Pecan Biscotti, 167

Fruity Tabouli, 86

Potato Fougasse, 220

Seitan Wellington, 132

Peruvian Squash and Vegetable Stew *(Locro)*, 119

Triple-Ginger Cake with Espresso Frosting, 185

Peruvian Tri-Color Potato Salad Terrine *(Causa Limeña)*, 79

Vegan Sponge Cake, 177

Fragrant Basmati Rice Pudding with Rose Water and Nectarines, 197

Clockwise from top: South African Mielie Bread, 215; South African Yellow Rice, 156; Curried Vegan Meatloaf *(Bobotie)*, 126

Vegan Soufflé Omelet, 41

Creole Grits and Grillades, 50

Balinese-Inspired Spicy Green Bean Salad, 83

Grown-Up Nanaimo Bars, 168

"Finnan Haddie" with Smoked Tofu, 146

Scandinavian Christmas Bread, 237

and then aluminum foil and refrigerate over-night. Do not press the foil onto the phyllo. Let it come to room temperature before baking. About 1 hour and 15 minutes before serving time, preheat the oven to 350°F.

8. Bake the pie for 20 minutes. Invert the second oiled pie plate or the oiled pizza pan over the pie and carefully turn the pie over onto the new pan (get someone to help you). Remove the first pie plate (now on top) and return the pie to the oven. Bake 20 to 25 minutes more or until golden brown. Invert the pie again (carefully) onto the original pan.

9. To decorate the pie before serving, sprinkle the top crust evenly with the confectioners' sugar, then make a decorative tic-tac-toe type grid over the confectioners' sugar with the cinnamon. (Use a stencil if you must.)

10. Let the pie cool for a few minutes, then carefully cut into 6 wedges with a very sharp knife. This is traditionally eaten with your fingers, but knives and forks are fine.

TIPS

- Make sure your hands are very dry when working with phyllo.
- You can double the recipe and make a large pie for company on a 14-inch pizza pan.

Levantine Molded Rice and Vegetable Casserole

Ma'aluba

PALESTINE/ISRAEL

Serves 8   GF, SFO

Ma'aluba means "upside down." This fragrant Middle Eastern layered and molded dish makes an excellent centerpiece dish for a company or holiday meal. It can be made with a variety of vegetables, including eggplant, but cauliflower seems to be very common. This is one of our all-time favorite dishes.

2 TABLESPOONS PLUS 1 1/2 TABLESPOONS OLIVE OIL, DIVIDED
2 LARGE ONIONS, THINLY SLICED
4 LARGE CLOVES GARLIC, CHOPPED
12 OUNCES LIGHT SEITAN CUTLETS (PAGE 5), CUT INTO STRIPS; OR 3 CUPS RECONSTITUTED SOY CURLS, DRAINED (3 OUNCES OR 2 1/4 CUPS DRY), OR ALTERNATIVE (PAGE 10)
1/2 TEASPOON GROUND ALLSPICE
SALT AND FRESHLY GROUND BLACK PEPPER
1 3/4 CUPS WHITE BASMATI RICE
3 CUPS PLUS 1/3 CUP CHICKEN-STYLE VEGETABLE BROTH (PAGE 2), DIVIDED
1 CUP FROZEN BABY PEAS (PETIT POIS), THAWED
1 CUP CANNED DICED TOMATOES, DRAINED OR 2 MEDIUM FRESH TOMATOES, CUT IN 1/2-INCH DICE
1 1/4 POUNDS (1/2 LARGE) CAULIFLOWER, TRIMMED, BROKEN UP INTO FLOWERETS AND SLICED 1/4-INCH THICK
KOSHER SALT
1 TABLESPOON VEGAN MARGARINE
1/2 CUP CHOPPED FRESH FLAT-LEAF PARSLEY

1. Preheat the oven to 400°F. Heat the 2 tablespoons olive oil over medium-high heat in a large nonstick skillet. Add the onions and garlic and cook until softened. Add the seitan and allspice and season with salt and pepper to taste. Set aside.

2. Mix the basmati rice in a medium pot with the 3 cups of broth. Bring to a boil, then reduce to a simmer, cover and cook for 15 minutes. (Alternatively, cook the rice in the broth in an electric rice cooker.) When the rice is done, remove from the heat and gently stir in the peas. Let the rice stand, covered for 5 minutes. Gently stir the tomatoes into the rice/pea mixture. Season with salt and pepper to taste. Set aside.

3. On a 12 x 17-inch shallow roasting pan or baking sheet (or two 8 x 12-inch baking pans or two 9 x 13-inch baking sheets with rims), mix the sliced cauliflower with the 1 1/2 tablespoons

olive oil and sprinkle generously with kosher salt. Roast the cauliflower for about 20 minutes, stirring once or twice until tender and slightly browned. Remove from the oven and set aside. Reduce the oven heat to 350°F.

4. To assemble: Generously grease a 2-quart round baking dish with vegan margarine. Spread half of the seitan mixture evenly in the baking dish. Top with half of the roasted cauliflower and then firmly pack in half of the rice mixture. Repeat these layers. Pack the last layer down gently. Dot with the margarine. Pour the 1/3 cup broth all around the edge of the baking dish.

5. Bake uncovered for 45 minutes. Remove from the oven and let sit for 10 to 15 minutes before unmolding. Loosen the sides gently with a table knife. Place a round serving platter upside down over the casserole. Then, using potholders, place one hand firmly over the plate and one hand (in an oven mitt) under the casserole (you may need another person to help with this) and carefully flip the casserole over so that the plate is on the bottom and the casserole is upside down on top. (Do this over a counter or table, just in case.) Rap the bottom of the casserole gently in a few places to loosen it further and carefully remove it from around the Ma'aluba.

6. Sprinkle with the parsley and bring it to the table. Cut it carefully into wedges to serve.

Pastry-Wrapped Russian Loaf

Coulibiac

Russia

Serves 8   SFO

This is my vegan (and lower-fat) version of an elegant dish that dates back to Tsarist Russia, but was also popular in France and in elegant restaurants in North America at the turn of the twentieth century. Coulibiac is spectacular and delicious, but easy to

make. The "salmon" is made at least one day ahead of time and then, providing you cook the rice early in the day, it goes together quickly. (You can actually make the entire filling the day before, if you wish.) I use phyllo dough instead of puff pastry, and brown basmati rice for extra fiber and nutrition. I serve this dish with a light vegan cream sauce laced with spring onions instead of the traditional herbed butter sauce. This makes a wonderful centerpiece for a vegan Easter dinner, accompanied by Hasselback Potatoes (page 160), roasted asparagus, and Russian Chocolate Torte (page 178).
Important: *Make the Vegan Salmon (page 131) at least one day ahead and refrigerate overnight.*

1/2 CUP BROWN BASMATI RICE

1 CUP VEGETABLE BROTH

2 TABLESPOONS VEGAN MARGARINE

1 POUND WHITE OR CRIMINI MUSHROOMS, SLICED 1/8-INCH THICK

1/2 TEASPOON SALT

2 TABLESPOONS DRY SHERRY, WHITE WINE, OR VEGETABLE BROTH

2 LARGE GREEN ONIONS, FINELY CHOPPED

1 LARGE ONION, MINCED

1/3 CUP FRESH CHOPPED DILL WEED OR 2 TABLESPOONS DRIED

2 TABLESPOONS FRESH LEMON JUICE

1 RECIPE VEGAN SALMON, (PAGE 131)

10 FULL SHEETS PHYLLO PASTRY, THAWED

1/4 CUP MELTED VEGAN MARGARINE OR 2 TABLESPOONS MELTED VEGAN MARGARINE AND 2 TABLESPOONS OLIVE OIL

3 GREEN ONIONS, MINCED

1 RECIPE VEGAN BESCIAMELLA SAUCE (PAGE 37, USING 2 TABLESPOONS FLOUR)

1. Early in the day, mix the rice and broth together in a small pot with a tight lid. Bring to a boil. Reduce the heat to low and cook, covered, for 45 minutes. Fluff the rice with a fork and transfer it to a plate to cool before using in the filling.

2. Heat the margarine in a large nonstick skillet. When the margarine is foamy, add the mushrooms, salt, and sherry. Stir-fry until the mushrooms exude their liquid, then add the onions

(both kinds) and sauté until the onions are soft and the mushrooms start to brown. Mix the mushrooms and onion in a large bowl with the cooked rice and dill weed. Combine well and add the lemon juice; mix again. Transfer the filling to the freezer to cool it quickly while you prepare to assemble the loaf.

3. Peel the nori sea vegetable wrapping off the two "salmon" loaves, being careful not to peel off too much of the loaf along with it. With a fork, flake the "salmon" into 1-inch chunks. Set aside. Preheat the oven to 350°F.

4. Arrange a long sheet of baking parchment on a 9 x 13-inch baking sheet. Have ready the melted margarine, a pastry brush, and a second 9 x 13-inch baking sheet.

5. Arrange a sheet of phyllo on the baking parchment-lined baking sheet. Brush it lightly with melted margarine. Repeat with the remaining 9 layers, leaving a little melted margarine for the top of the loaf.

6. Remove the filling from the freezer and transfer half of it to the middle of the phyllo. Shape the Filling into a rectangle 5 x 7 inches. Cover the filling evenly with the chunks of "salmon," pressing it gently into the rice mixture. Scoop the remaining rice filling evenly over the "salmon" and press it gently and evenly to make a solid mounded 5 x 7-inch rectangle.

7. Fold the edges of phyllo over the mound. Fold the two ends up like an envelope. Cover the loaf with 2 sheets of baking parchment (each cut 9 x 13 inches). Place the second 9 x 13-inch baking sheet upside-down over the parchment-covered loaf. Place one hand on the center of the top baking sheet, slide your other hand under the bottom baking sheet and flip the whole thing over carefully. Remove the baking sheet and the sheet of baking parchment now on top of the loaf. The loaf will be sitting on two layers of parchment. Brush the loaf all over with the remaining melted margarine. Tuck the ends of the phyllo under the loaf. Cut slashes into the loaf all the way through the phyllo with a very sharp knife, in a decorative pattern.

8. Bake for about 45 minutes, covering it loosely with foil if it is browning too fast or too much.

9. Add the chopped green onions to the sauce, and set aside. The sauce can be heated gently again before serving. When the loaf is done baking, carefully transfer it to a serving platter. Serve hot with the sauce.

NOTE: Cut the loaf lengthwise down the middle with a very sharp knife, then make 3 equidistant cuts across, making 8 servings. (Slicing all the way across without making the cut down the middle results in rather messy slices.)

Tip: The loaf can be refrigerated for an hour or so before baking.

Vegan Salmon

Makes two loaves   SFO, GFO, <30

This "salmon" is simple to make, can be frozen for future use, and can be used for more than a filling for Coulibiac. See serving suggestions at the end of the recipe. Dulse flakes are available in natural food stores. Tip: You will need two 5 3/4 x 3 x 2 1/8-inch fruitcake/mini loaf pans for this recipe.

"Salmon" Mixture:
1 CUP WATER
1 CUP TOMATO JUICE OR TOMATO-VEGETABLE JUICE
3/4 CUP SOY FLOUR, OR CHICKPEA FLOUR (BESAN)
1/2 CUP TEXTURED SOY PROTEIN GRANULES (TSP) (PAGE 10)
1/4 CUP CHICKPEA FLOUR (BESAN)
1 TABLESPOON OLIVE OIL
1 TEASPOON ONION POWDER
1/2 TEASPOON SALT
1 TABLESPOON DULSE FLAKES
Wrapping:
4 SHEETS NORI SEA VEGETABLE

1. Preheat the oven to 400°F. Blend all of the

"salmon" mixture ingredients in a food processor for about 1 minute. The mixture will be runny – don't worry.

2. Line 2 oiled 3 x 5-inch loaf pans (also known as fruitcake pans) with the sheets of nori, using 2 sheets per pan. Moisten the nori with wet fingers to make it more flexible and able to fit it into the pan. (The ends of the pans do not have to be covered, only the sides.) Overlap 2 of them on the bottom of each pan, with the sides overhanging the pan. The overhang should be long enough to fold over the loaf at the top, allowing some room for expansion (the loaf puffs up a bit as it cooks).

3. Pour the batter evenly into the pans and fold the over-hanging nori loosely over the tops. Spray the nori with oil from a pump sprayer. Bake the loaves for 40 minutes.

4. Cool the loaves completely on a cooling rack – don't plan on eating it straight out of the oven!

5. Wrap the cooled loaves in aluminum foil, then transfer the wrapped loaves to a zipper-lock bag and refrigerate. (You can also cut the loaves in half, wrap each half separately, bag them and freeze them.)

6. To serve (if not using in coulibiac): Slice the loaves in as many pieces as you wish and heat the slices in a microwave oven for a couple of minutes or brown the slices over medium heat in a lightly oiled nonstick skillet. If you like, you can wrap each slice with more nori, which will crisp up when heated. The slices also puff up a bit when cooked. Serve them with lemon wedges, tartar sauce, chili sauce, or other favorite condiment.

Note: The "salmon" can also be used as a pâté or spread, or you can mash it with a little vegan mayonnaise, chopped green onions, and celery for a tasty sandwich filling.

VARIATIONS

- **Soy-Free Version:** For a soy-free version, use coarse dry breadcrumbs to replace the TSP.
- **Gluten-Free Version:** Use gluten-free breadcrumbs. **Tip:** Make this at least 1 day before serving or using in the coulibiac and refrigerate.

Seitan Wellington

UNITED KINGDOM

Serves 10 to 12   SFO

Popular for over a century, a classic Beef Wellington is a filet of beef tenderloin coated with pâté de foie gras and mushroom duxelles, wrapped in puff pastry. Try this wonderful vegan version for a holiday dinner – my guests have raved over it. The main components (vegan pâté and Beefy Seitan roast) can be made weeks ahead and frozen. The duxelles (mushroom mixture) can be made in advance as well, and you can use a purchased vegan puff pastry (Pepperidge Farm brand is vegan), so this recipe is actually not difficult to make. Please read the recipe through before starting.

3 TABLESPOONS VEGAN MARGARINE
3/4 POUND WHITE OR CREMINI MUSHROOMS, RINSED, PATTED DRY, AND MINCED, PREFERABLY IN A FOOD PROCESSOR
SALT AND FRESHLY GROUND BLACK PEPPER
1 RECIPE BEEFY SEITAN (PAGE 133) MADE AHEAD AND COOLED THOROUGHLY
1/2 RECIPE "WHO NEEDS FOIS GRAS?" HERBED MUSHROOM PÂTÉ (PAGE 56) MADE AHEAD, OR 1/2 POUND PURCHASED SMOOTH VEGAN PÂTÉ OF CHOICE, REFRIGERATED
1 POUND VEGAN PUFF PASTRY, THAWED FOR 6 HOURS IN THE REFRIGERATOR
SOY OR NUT MILK, TO BRUSH PASTRY
MADEIRA GRAVY (PAGE 135)

1. Melt the margarine in a large nonstick skillet over medium heat. When the margarine is foamy, add the minced mushrooms. Sauté until

they exude liquid and continue to cook until the liquid is absorbed and the mixture is fairly dry. Season to taste with salt and pepper. Set aside to cool (or spread on a baking sheet and cool quickly in the freezer). Have the thawed puff pastry and cold pâté of choice ready in the refrigerator.

2. Use a very sharp knife to slice the cooked and thoroughly cooled seitan roast as thinly as you can without shredding it. Push the slices back together so that the roast resumes its original shape. With a measuring tape, measure how long, how thick, and how wide the reassembled loaf is and jot this down. Set aside.

3. Unroll the defrosted puff pastry and place on a lightly floured surface. Sprinkle rolling pin with flour and gently roll the puff pastry in one direction, away from you and then down towards you. Roll the pastry again in the opposite direction, to your left and to your right. Add more flour to the rolling pin if it starts to stick to the pastry. Continue to roll the pastry two or three times in each direction until it is the right size rectangle to enclose the roast completely, with some overlap (use your measurements). Smooth and patch any holes and tears that might appear – these are normal.

4. Sprinkle the cooled mushroom duxelles in the middle of the rolled-out pastry, in about the shape and size of your roast. Then, break up the pâté into small chunks and pat down over the duxelles, covering as much of the surface of the mushrooms as possible. Carefully place the sliced and reassembled roast over the pâté and duxelles. Brush the edges of the pastry with non-dairy milk, using a pastry brush.

5. Bring the long edges of the pastry up over the roast, overlapping them in the center and pinching the edge to seal. Bring the end pieces of the pastry up, using soy or nut milk to hold them in place. Carefully turn the wrapped roast over, seam-side down, on a 9 x 13-inch baking sheet lined with baking parchment cut to fit. Brush the pastry with soy or nut milk. Refrigerate the wrapped roast for 1 to 2 hours (no more). About 30 minutes before serving time, preheat the oven to 400°F.

6. Make some decorative cuts in the top of the pastry (half-way through) with a razor blade. You can also use bits of extra pastry to make decorative cutouts (such as leaves) and attach them to the top of the roast with nondairy milk.

7. Bake the roast in the center of the oven for 30 minutes, or until golden brown. Let the roast stand on a heated platter (transfer carefully with two spatulas) while you make the gravy. Garnish the roast with fresh herbs, if you have them. To serve, cut the roast into 1-inch-thick slices, preferably with a sharp serrated knife. Serve each slice drizzled with the Madeira Gravy.

TIPS

- The Beefy Seitan must be made at least the day before.

- Do not omit the slicing of the roast very thinly before proceeding with assembling the wrapped roast – this step makes the roast very tender to cut with a fork, whereas, if you left it in a big chunk, it would not be so tender.

- If you use a purchased vegan pâté, make sure that it is smooth, not coarse and crumbly.

Beefy Seitan

Makes 3 pounds; serves 10 to 12   SFO

This roast can be used on its own or as a pot roast or you can make it into delectable steaks (page 134). The tapioca bits make little "pockets" in the seitan, which add an interesting texture and the illusion of some "fattiness."

Dry Mix:
2 1/4 CUPS PURE GLUTEN POWDER (VITAL WHEAT GLUTEN)
1/2 CUP UNFLAVORED MINUTE OR INSTANT TAPIOCA

1/2 CUP UNSEASONED PINTO OR BLACK BEAN FLAKES OR
SOY FLAKES, OR OLD-FASHIONED ROLLED OATS (THE
OATS LIGHTLY TOASTED IN A DRY SKILLET), OR DRY
FLAKED OR GRANULATED TEXTURED SOY PROTEIN (TVP
OR TSP)

3 TABLESPOONS NUTRITIONAL YEAST FLAKES

1 1/2 TEASPOON ONION POWDER

3/4 TEASPOON GARLIC POWDER

Wet Mix:

1 1/2 CUPS COLD WATER

1/2 CUP DRY RED WINE (CAN BE NON-ALCOHOLIC)

1/3 CUP COMMERCIAL OR CHINESE-STYLE MUSHROOM "OYS-
TER" SAUCE (SEE SIDEBAR, PAGE 135)

2 TABLESPOONS SOY SAUCE (OR SOY-FREE SAUCE, PAGE 12)

Cooking Broth:

5 CUPS HOT WATER (YOU CAN USE DRIED MUSHROOM SOAK-
ING LIQUID FOR ALL OR PART OF THE WATER)

5 TEASPOONS YEAST EXTRACT PASTE, SUCH AS MARMITE
(PAGE 21) OR 2 TABLESPOONS PLUS 1 TEASPOON DARK
MISO

5 TABLESPOONS SOY SAUCE, DARK SOY SAUCE, OR MUSH-
ROOM SOY SAUCE (OR SOY-FREE SAUCE, PAGE 12)

5 TABLESPOONS KETCHUP

1 1/2 TABLESPOONS GRAVY BROWNER, SUCH AS KITCHEN
BOUQUET, OPTIONAL (FOR COLOR)

1. Combine the dry mix ingredients in the bowl of your electric mixer with dough hook attachment or place them in the bread machine pan in the order instructed for your machine. Combine the wet mix ingredients together in a measuring pitcher or bowl, pour into the dry mix and knead for about 10 minutes.

2. After this first kneading, let the seitan rest, covered, for at least 10 minutes, but preferably for 1 hour. You can make the cooking broth at this time and have it ready. After the dough has rested, knead it for 10 more minutes.

3. The twice-kneaded dough should be quite shiny and smooth. Avoid breaking it up when you take it out of the bowl. Form the dough into a roll that that will fit into your pan or oval slow cooker. Wet your hands occasionally to make the dough easier to handle. Oil the roast lightly and let it rest while you get the pot ready.

4. Oil the inside of a slow cooker or pan. It must to have room for the roast to expand. Pour in about 1 cup of the hot cooking broth, then place the roast in the cooker or pan. Pour in the rest of the broth. Cover with the lid and simmer on Low or bake in the oven at 200°F for 6 to 8 hours, turning once halfway through.

5. Cool the roast in the broth, then refrigerate it, well-wrapped. **Important:** if you are making the Wellington recipe, save the cooking broth for the Madeira Gravy. Seitan freezes well.

Seitan Steaks

Makes 16 steaks   SFO

These delectable steaks are used in Steak au Poivre (page 137), Seitan, Beer, and Carmelized Onion Stew (page 136) and Creole Grits and Grillades (page 50). Steaks can be cut into chunks or strips for stews and stir-fries.

Make the Beefy Seitan dough exactly as described in the main recipe. After the second kneading, cut the dough into 16 equal pieces, then flatten the pieces one at a time by stretching the dough with the palm of your hand on a damp flat surface. Keep your hands damp while doing this. Don't use flour. Make them as thin as possible without tearing them (you can re-fold them and start again if they tear too much, but let them rest a bit if you do that, to relax the gluten), because they will retract somewhat and should double in size when cooked.

You will need the same size slow cooker or pan as for the roast, so prepare it the same way as instructed in the main recipe. Pour all of the hot cooking broth into the pan (you will need more broth than for the roast – broth recipe follows) and slide in the steaks. You will have to layer some on top of each other, but that's fine. Cook the same as for the roast, also turning the steaks halfway through the cooking time.

Cool the steaks completely before browning by arranging them on cookie sheets and placing in the freezer to quickly cool. Or cool them in the broth for a longer period. Refrigerate or freeze the steaks in a covered container or zip-top bags.

Cooking Broth for Seitan Steaks

6 1/4 CUPS HOT WATER

2 TABLESPOONS YEAST EXTRACT PASTE, SUCH AS MARMITE (PAGE 21) OR OTHER YEAST EXTRACT, OR 3 SCANT TABLESPOONS DARK MISO PASTE

1/3 CUP PLUS 1 TABLESPOON SOY SAUCE, DARK SOY SAUCE OR MUSHROOM SOY SAUCE (OR SOY-FREE SAUCE, PAGE 12)

1/3 CUP PLUS 1 TABLESPOON KETCHUP

2 TABLESPOONS GRAVY BROWNER, SUCH AS KITCHEN BOUQUET (OPTIONAL)

Madeira Gravy

Makes 2 cups

The ease of preparation belies the delicious flavor of this gravy. Make it just before serving – it just takes a few minutes. If Madeira wine is unavailable, use marsala or a good medium-dry sherry instead.

1 1/2 CUPS RESERVED BEEFY SEITAN COOKING BROTH

1/2 CUP MADEIRA WINE

2 TABLESPOONS CORNSTARCH

1/4 CUP WATER

SALT AND FRESHLY GROUND PEPPER

Heat the broth and wine together in a medium skillet. Dissolve the cornstarch in the water and stir into the skillet over high heat and whisk until the gravy thickens and clears. Season with salt and pepper to taste. Serve immediately with the Seitan Wellington.

Mushroom "Oyster" Sauce

Makes 2 1/4 cups   SFO, GF, <30

Chinese oyster sauce is a versatile flavoring for many dishes. It's thick and rich-tasting and vegan versions made with mushrooms are available. One brand, Lee Kum Kee, is sold as "vegetarian stir-fry sauce." Other brands are labelled "mushroom oyster sauce." It is available in Asian markets, online, or you can make this homemade version in your own kitchen.

1 1/2 CUPS BOILING WATER

6 TABLESPOONS GROUND CHINESE DRIED MUSHROOMS (SEE NOTE)

4 TABLESPOONS BROWN MISO PASTE (SOY OR CHICKPEA) MIXED WITH 2 TABLESPOONS WATER

6 TABLESPOONS SOY SAUCE (OR SOY-FREE, PAGE 12)

7 TABLESPOONS BROWN SUGAR

1 TABLESPOON CORNSTARCH DISSOLVED IN 1 TABLESPOON COLD WATER

1. In a blender, combine the water, mushrooms, miso mixture, soy sauce, and brown sugar and blend until smooth. Transfer the mixture to a medium saucepan and heat to boiling over high heat. Add the dissolved cornstarch and stir until thickened, or microwave the mixture with the dissolved cornstarch in a 1-quart microwave-safe bowl and cook on 100% power (default setting) for 30 seconds, then whisk. Repeat until thickened.

2. Cool and store in a covered jar in the refrigerator where it will keep for several months.

Note: To grind dried mushrooms: use inexpensive dried Chinese mushrooms. Snap off the stems and discard, then grind the broken mushroom caps to a powder in a dry blender or spice grinder.

Seitan, Beer, and Caramelized Onion Stew

Carbonnade

BELGIUM

Serves 4   SFO

Carbonnade was a recipe I made quite often in my omnivore days. It is a classic Flemish recipe of beef in gravy fortified with brown ale. My boldly-flavored seitan chunks are a perfect foil for the ale. This stew, perfect for a winter meal, is often served with plain boiled or steamed new potatoes, but mashed potatoes are good with it as well. I like to serve it with potato pancakes, but it also pairs extremely well with Easy Homemade Spaetzle (page 160).

2 TABLESPOONS OLIVE OIL
2 TABLESPOONS DARK SESAME OIL
1 1/4 POUNDS OF BEEFY SEITAN ROAST OR STEAKS (PAGE 133), CUT INTO 1-INCH CHUNKS
1/4 CUP WHOLE-WHEAT FLOUR
4 LARGE ONIONS, VERY THINLY-SLICED
1 TABLESPOON BROWN SUGAR
1 TEASPOON SALT
2 CUPS LIGHTLY-SALTED VEGETABLE BROTH (SEE TIP)
1 (11.5-OUNCE) BOTTLE BROWN ALE (SEE TIP)
2 BAY LEAVES
1/2 TABLESPOON FRESH CHOPPED THYME OR 1/2 TEASPOON DRIED
1/4 TEASPOON GROUND ALLSPICE
SALT AND FRESHLY GROUND BLACK PEPPER
1/2 TABLESPOON DIJON MUSTARD
2 TABLESPOONS CHOPPED FRESH FLAT-LEAF PARSLEY

1. Preheat the oven to 350°F. In a large nonstick or cast iron skillet, heat 1 tablespoon of the olive oil and 1 tablespoon of sesame oil over medium-high heat. Toss the seitan chunks with the flour. Shake off any excess flour. Add the chunks to the hot oil and quickly brown on all sides. Remove from the skillet and set aside.

Tips for Making Seitan

To knead the seitan, use an automatic bread machine or a stand mixer with a dough hook. You can knead it by hand, but it's tougher than bread dough. If your bread machine has a dough cycle – two kneads with a long rest in between – use that cycle. Otherwise, just run it through the kneading cycle, unplug it and let it rest in the covered bread machine pan, as instructed above. Plug it in again for the second knead, then remove the pan from the machine.

If you don't have a large oval slow-cooker, use a covered roasting pan of a similar size in a 200°F oven or an electric skillet at 180°F (if you have a ceramic liner in yours, use that).

Timing the recipe: You can make the seitan in the morning and it will be done in the evening (figure about 10 hours total preparation and cooking time – most of that time you don't even need to be around). You could make it at night, but I like to turn it at least once during the cooking so that each side gets a chance to soak up the cooking broth and I don't want to get up in the middle of the night. It should be thoroughly cold when you slice it and use it in the Wellington recipe, so making it the day before you are serving is a good idea.

Leftover broth can be frozen for use in your next batch or to enhance sauces and gravies. You can keep this broth going as a "perpetual broth," the way Chinese cooks do with "red cooking"– just make sure you freeze the leftover broth in between cooking batches of seitan and strain off any seasonings. If the broth has gotten very strong, you may only have to add some water to it to use again or you can make another half-batch to add to it the next time.

---

2. Add the remaining oils to the skillet over high heat and when hot, add the onions, brown sugar, and salt. (Adding the salt at this point draws out some of the onion juice and the result is onions that are meltingly tender.) Toss the onions well and distribute them evenly over the pan with a wooden spoon. Reduce the heat to medium and cook, stirring often, until the onions soften and become nicely browned.

3. Scrape the contents of the skillet into a large pot or Dutch oven with a lid that can go into the oven (or use a small roaster). Add the seitan and broth, ale, bay leaves, thyme, allspice, and salt and pepper to taste. Combine well. Remove from the heat and cover with the lid. Bake for 2 hours. Check halfway through the cooking time. If the stew is too thick, add a bit more water, ale, or broth. Just before serving, stir in the mustard. Serve hot, sprinkled with parsley.

TIPS

- I use Superior Touch Vegan "Better Than Bouillon" No Beef Soup Base, which requires 1 teaspoon per cup of water to make broth.
- If you can obtain a Belgian ale, Chimay Blue and Leffe Radieuse are recommended for this dish. I could not find either one, so I used Newcastle Brown Ale, a British ale and it was lovely. Brown ale is what you want – dark stout is not the right choice for this stew.

Seitan Steak au Poivre

FRANCE

Serves 4   SFO, <30

This dish is a successful vegan version of a French classic. It's quick to make and so impressive. Serve it with a green salad, Oven-Fries (page 100), and a bottle of organic red wine for a really special meal. In the interests of keeping fat to a minimum, I tried this dish without the margarine, but it just doesn't

have the glossiness of the original. However, I did use far less than the butter called for in classic recipes and it's worth it for a treat now and then. The seitan steaks are low in fat to begin with, one serving (2 steaks) being less than 400 calories and only 20 percent calories from fat – not too bad!

2 TO 4 TABLESPOONS BLACK PEPPERCORNS, COARSELY CRUSHED
8 BEEFY SEITAN STEAKS (PAGE 134)
OLIVE OIL
1 1/3 CUPS DRY RED WINE
8 TEASPOONS VEGAN MARGARINE

1. Preheat the oven to 300°F. Spread half the crushed peppercorns evenly onto a plate. Press the steaks into the pepper until it coats the surface. Spread the second half of the crushed peppercorns on the plate, turn the steaks and repeat. Set aside. The steaks are moist and this helps the crushed peppercorns to "hang on."

2. Set a large heavy (preferably cast-iron) skillet over medium-high heat and add just enough olive oil to make a light film. When the oil is very hot, add the steaks, cooking until browned on one side, about 3 minutes. (If your pan is small, do this in 2 batches.) Turn the steaks over and brown the other sides. Remove to a hot serving platter and place in the oven to keep warm.

3. Place the skillet back on the burner over high heat. Add the wine and cook until reduced to 1/2 cup, scraping up the browned bits with a wooden spoon. Reduce the heat to medium-high. Whisk in the margarine a little at a time, whisking until completely melted. Drizzle the sauce over the steaks and serve immediately.

Tip: To coarsely crush peppercorns, use a mortar and pestle, the bottom of a cast iron skillet, or a mallet and pie pan.

Peruvian Kebabs

Anticuchos

PERU

Serves 6   SFO, <30

Anticuchos (ahn-tee-koo-chohs) are the "hot dogs" of Peru – served at every gathering and purchased from street vendors to be consumed right on the sidewalk. Homemade seitan chunks make a wonderful animal-friendly substitute for the traditional (cringe!) beef heart – it's the spicy marinade and sauce, redolent with chiles, cumin, garlic and red wine vinegar and vibrant red from achiote (annatto) paste, that really make the dish. Serve anticuchos in the traditional manner, with chunks of cooked sweet potato and corn on the cob. Ají amarillo (Peruvian yellow chile) paste is available online.

5 SEITAN STEAKS (PAGE 134), HALVED LENGTHWISE, THEN CUT INTO 12 CUBES
Marinade:
1 CUP RED WINE VINEGAR
12 LARGE CLOVES GARLIC, PEELED
1 TABLESPOON AJÍ AMARILLO (PERUVIAN YELLOW CHILE) PASTE OR SRIRACHA SAUCE
1 TABLESPOON GROUND CUMIN
1 TEASPOON SALT
FRESHLY GROUND PEPPER
Sauce:
3/4 CUP RESERVED MARINADE (ABOVE)
1 TABLESPOON RED PEPPER FLAKES
1 TABLESPOON ACHIOTE OR ANNATTO PASTE (OR USE 1 TABLESPOON PAPRIKA WITH A PINCH OF TURMERIC)
1/2 TABLESPOON OLIVE OIL
1/2 TABLESPOON DARK SESAME OIL
1 TEASPOON SALT
Garnishes:
CHUNKS OF COOKED SWEET POTATO AND CORN ON THE COB; PERUVIAN ALFONSO OR KALAMATA OLIVES; TOFU FETA (PAGE 101); COLORFUL PEPPERS (SWEET OR HOT)

1. Transfer the seitan cubes to a shallow container. Set aside. In a blender, combine the marinade ingredients and blend until smooth. Pour the marinade over the seitan. Cover and refrigerate for 8 to 24 hours, shaking the container once in a while. When ready to cook, soak 12 bamboo skewers in water for 15 minutes.

2. Drain the marinade from the seitan, reserving 3/4 cup. Mix the reserved marinade with the other sauce ingredients and toss the seitan with the sauce. Thread the cubes evenly onto the skewers. Grill or broil 3 inches from the heat until slightly charred on all sides, turning as needed and basting with the sauce several times. Serve hot, surrounded by the garnishes of your choice.

Peruvian Stir-Fry

Lomo Saltado

PERU

Serves 4   SFO, <30

Since my father was Peruvian, it was inevitable that I would "veganize" this dish at some point. It is not a traditional Peruvian dish (there are no recipes for it in my mother's Peruvian cookbooks from the 1950s, for instance), but it is now one of the most popular dishes in Peru, with good reason. It is colorful, quick and tasty, and it contains potatoes, a Peruvian staple, but is served, like most entrees in Peru, with rice. The cooking method reflects the influence of Peruvian/Chinese cuisine (called "chifa"). I lowered fat in this recipe by oven-frying the potatoes instead of deep-frying them. If you have a French fry cutter attachment on your food processor, use it to cut the potatoes into fries. Select longish potatoes, if you can. These can just be shaved a bit on their fat middles, so that they fit right into the feeder tube of your processor. Scrub the potatoes (I leave the skins on and trim only when necessary) and cut your fries.

1 POUND YUKON GOLD POTATOES
1 TABLESPOON OLIVE OIL
12 OUNCES SEITAN STEAK (PAGE 134), CUT INTO MATCHSTICK PIECES, OR ALTERNATIVE (PAGE 10)
1 LARGE ONION, THINLY SLICED

1/2 LARGE GREEN BELL PEPPER, SEEDED AND CUT INTO STRIPS

1 TABLESPOON MINCED GARLIC

3 TO 4 RIPE PLUM TOMATOES, CUT INTO EIGHTHS

1 TO 2 FRESH SMALL HOT CHILES, SEEDED, DE-VEINED AND
       THINLY SLICED (SEE NOTE)

1 TABLESPOON BALSAMIC VINEGAR

1 TABLESPOON SOY SAUCE (OR SOY-FREE SAUCE, PAGE 12)

1 TABLESPOON FRESH LIME JUICE

1 TEASPOON GROUND CUMIN

1 TEASPOON DRIED OREGANO

1/4 CUP CHOPPED FRESH FLAT-LEAF PARSLEY, OPTIONAL

3 TO 4 CUPS STEAMED WHITE OR BROWN BASMATI RICE

1. Preheat the oven to 500°F. Use the French-fry cutter on your food processor to cut the potatoes into fries. Otherwise, use a sharp knife to cut the potato into thin French-fry shapes. Spread the fries in one layer on 2 lightly-oiled or nonstick 12 x 17-inch dark baking sheets (dark baking sheets brown foods better). Bake for 10 minutes, then turn the fries over and bake 10 minutes more.

2. Heat the oil in a large nonstick skillet. When the oil is very hot, add the seitan strips and brown them a bit. Remove from the pan and set aside.

3. Add the onion, bell pepper, and garlic to the hot pan and toss until slightly wilted. Add the tomatoes and hot chiles. Stir-fry briefly. Add the browned seitan, oven-fried potatoes, and the seasonings. Stir-fry briefly just until everything is hot and serve with the rice.

TIPS

- Traditionally, each serving of rice is packed into a custard cup or ramekin with sloped sides and unmolded onto the plate. An indentation is made carefully (with the tip of your finger) in the top of the rice so that it looks a bit like a "volcano."

- Instead of using the fresh hot chile, use 1/2 teaspoon ají amarillo (Peruvian yellow chile) paste or sriracha sauce, or more to taste.

- If you have extra baking sheets, the quickest way to turn the fries over is to place another nonstick or oiled baking sheet over the one with the fries, hold them together at the ends (with oven mitts!), flip the whole thing over and remove the first sheet.) While they cook, you can cook the rice and prepare the other ingredients.

General Tso's Stir-Fry

CHINA/U.S.A

Serves 4

SFO, <30

The popular restaurant dish by this name is usually made with deep-fried chicken. This spicy, aromatic stir-fried vegan version is just as delectable and much lower in fat and sugar. I especially like using Soy Curls for this recipe, but strips of seitan also work well. Serve over freshly cooked rice.

3 TABLESPOONS DRY SHERRY

1 1/2 TABLESPOONS MUSHROOM "OYSTER" SAUCE (SEE PAGE 135)

3 1/2 TEASPOONS CORNSTARCH, DIVIDED

3 CUPS RECONSTITUTED SOY CURLS, DRAINED (PAGE 10)
       (2 1/4 CUPS DRY) OR ALTERNATIVE; OR 12 OUNCES
       LIGHT SEITAN CUTLETS (PAGE 5), CUT INTO STRIPS

1/4 CUP VEGETABLE BROTH

1 TABLESPOON UNSEASONED RICE VINEGAR

1 TABLESPOON SOY SAUCE (OR SOY-FREE SAUCE, PAGE 12)

1 TABLESPOON SUGAR

2 TEASPOONS DARK SESAME OIL

1 TABLESPOON MINCED GARLIC

2 TEASPOONS MINCED OR GRATED GINGER

2 GREEN ONIONS CUT INTO 1-INCH LENGTHS

1/4 TO 1/2 TEASPOON RED PEPPER FLAKES, TO TASTE

1/2 TABLESPOON CORNSTARCH

1 TABLESPOON COLD WATER

1. In a bowl, combine the sherry, "oyster" sauce, and 2 teaspoons of the cornstarch. Add the Soy Curls to the marinade and turn to coat. Let stand for 10 minutes.

2. In a small bowl, combine the vegetable broth, rice vinegar, soy sauce, and sugar. Set aside.

3. Heat the sesame oil in a large nonstick skillet over high heat until hot. Add the marinated Soy Curls and stir-fry for 2 minutes. Add the garlic, ginger, green onions, and red pepper flakes. Stir-fry for 1 minute. Add the reserved sauce and cook, stirring, for 1 minute.

4. In a small bowl, combine the remaining 1 1/2 teaspoons cornstarch with the 1 tablespoon water and quickly stir into the pan. Cook the mixture, stirring constantly, until the sauce boils and thickens. Serve immediately.

Crispy Tofu with Olives and Corn-Tomato Relish

Italy/U.S.A.

Serves 4   GFO <30

This is a stunning and absolutely delicious, but easy, summer dish to serve to guests. You can serve this hot, at room temperature, or cold.

Relish:
1 1/2 CUPS FRESH OR FROZEN (THAWED) SWEET CORN
    KERNELS
1/2 TABLESPOON OLIVE OIL
1/2 TABLESPOON DARK SESAME OIL
2 MEDIUM RIPE TOMATOES (ABOUT 12 OUNCES), DICED
2 GREEN ONIONS, CHOPPED
1/4 CUP FRESH BASIL, CHOPPED
1/4 CUP CHOPPED, PITTED KALAMATA OLIVES
1 TEASPOON BALSAMIC VINEGAR
1/2 TEASPOON SALT
FRESHLY GROUND BLACK PEPPER
12 OUNCES COOKED CRISPY MARINATED TOFU SLICES (PAGE 8)

Preheat the broiler. On a 12 x 17-inch baking sheet, combine the corn with the two oils. Place the baking sheet about 3 to 4 inches under the broiler and broil until the kernels start to brown. Toss them with a spatula and add the tomatoes. Broil the mixture until the tomato begins to look a little charred in places. Transfer the mixture to a bowl and add the green onions, basil, olives, vinegar, salt, and pepper to taste. Mix well. Divide the cooked tofu slices among four plates and top evenly with the relish.

Tahu Goreng with Edamame

Indonesia

Serves 6   GF, <30

This is my version of a vegan Indonesian dish, with the non-traditional addition of edamamé. It's quick, easy, and delicious – my husband often requests it. If you don't have Indonesian sweet soy sauce (ketjap manis), it's easy to make your own seriously good substitute (see page 141). Instead of edamame, you can use trimmed young green beans, which are lower in fat and more traditional, or even green baby peas. Serve over freshly cooked rice.

12 OUNCES FROZEN SHELLED EDAMAMÉ, THAWED
18 OUNCES FIRM TOFU, DRAINED AND PATTED DRY
1 1/2 TABLESPOONS VEGETABLE OIL
1 MEDIUM ONION, FINELY CHOPPED
6 CLOVES GARLIC, MINCED
1/4 CUP PLUS 2 TABLESPOONS KETJAP MANIS (PAGE 141)
1/4 CUP PLUS 2 TABLESPOONS WATER
3 TABLESPOONS TOMATO PASTE
3/4 TEASPOON SRIRACHA OR OTHER ASIAN HOT SAUCE
3/8 TEASPOON SALT

1. Blanch the edamamé in boiling water for 3 minutes. Drain and set aside. Cut the tofu into 1/4-inch thick slices, then cut the slices into 1-inch pieces.

2. Heat the oil in a large nonstick skillet over medium-high heat. Add the tofu to the skillet in one layer and fry until golden and crispy on both sides. Set aside on paper towels to drain.

3. In a bowl, combine the ketjap manis, water, tomato paste, hot sauce, and salt. Set aside. Add the onion and garlic to the same skillet and stir over high heat, adding a little water as necessary to keep from sticking. Stir-fry until the onion has softened, about 5 minutes. Add the tofu and

edamamé, and pour the reserved ketjap manis mixture over the tofu, tossing gently for a minute to coat the tofu and edamamé and heat the sauce. Serve immediately.

Indonesian Sweet Soy Sauce

Ketjap Manis

Makes 1 1/3 cups SFO, GF, <30

1 CUP SOY SAUCE (OR SOY-FREE SAUCE, PAGE 12)
3 TABLESPOONS MAPLE SYRUP OR AGAVE NECTAR
3 TABLESPOONS DARK MOLASSES

In a bowl, combine the soy sauce, maple syrup, and molasses, and mix well. Transfer to a tightly-capped bottle and refrigerate. This sauce keeps indefinitely in the refrigerator.

Thai Coconut Curry with Asparagus

THAILAND

Serves 4   GFO, SFO, <30

This is a quick meal that you would be proud to serve to company! Tender asparagus and strips of Soy Curls or seitan are bathed in a light but rich-tasting coconut curry sauce. Serve over steamed basmati or jasmine rice. **Gluten-Free Option:** *Use chickpea miso.*

1 CUP LITE COCONUT MILK
1/2 CUP CHICKEN-STYLE VEGAN BROTH (SEE PAGE 2)
1/2 TABLESPOON FISH-FREE THAI RED CURRY PASTE, OR
    MORE TO TASTE (SEE NOTES)
2 TEASPOONS MISO PASTE
1 TABLESPOON WATER
1 TABLESPOON BROWN SUGAR
1 POUND ASPARAGUS, CUT DIAGONALLY INTO 1-INCH PIECES
2 CUPS RECONSTITUTED SOY CURLS, DRAINED (PAGE 10) (1
    1/2 CUPS DRY) OR ALTERNATIVE; OR 8 OUNCES LIGHT
    SEITAN CUTLETS (PAGE 5), CUT INTO STRIPS
1 TABLESPOON FRESH LIME JUICE
SALT

In a deep 10-inch skillet, combine the coconut milk, broth, curry paste, miso, water, and brown sugar over medium heat and stir until dissolved and simmering. Stir in the asparagus and Soy Curls. Simmer for 5 minutes. Stir in the lime juice and season with salt to taste.

Tip: To remove woody stalks from asparagus, bend each stalk and the asparagus will naturally snap at the point where it becomes tough.

NOTES ON THAI CURRY PASTES

Many Thai curry pastes contain fish or shrimp products, so check your labels. However, there are several brands of good curry pastes (which last almost indefinitely in the refrigerator) that are vegan. For example, Taste of Thai is one widely available brand which is vegan, as are several Mae Ploy and Maesri curry pastes. I always keep some red, green, yellow, Penang, and Mussaman Thai curry pastes in my refrigerator for quick, tasty Thai curries. All are available online.

Vegan Coq au Vin

FRANCE

Serves 6   SFO

This vegan version of a traditional French recipe was developed, because I had 2 1/2 cups of dry red wine to use up. This rich-tasting vegan stew is nicely paired with egg-free wide noodles, tagliatelle, or steamed new potatoes, which showcase the roasted vegetable and wine gravy.

1 TABLESPOON DARK SESAME OIL
1 CUP CHOPPED ONIONS
1/2 CUP CHOPPED CARROTS
1 TABLESPOON CHOPPED GARLIC
2 TABLESPOONS UNBLEACHED WHITE FLOUR
6 CUPS RECONSTITUTED SOY CURLS, DRAINED (4 1/2 CUPS
    DRY) OR ALTERNATIVE (PAGE 10); OR 24 OUNCES LIGHT
    SEITAN CUTLETS (PAGE 5), CUT INTO STRIPS
2 1/2 CUPS DRY RED WINE
2 CUPS CHICKEN-STYLE VEGAN BROTH (SEE PAGE 2)

2 TABLESPOONS TOMATO PASTE

2 BAY LEAVES

1/2 TABLESPOON CHOPPED FRESH THYME OR 1/2 TEASPOON
DRIED

1/2 TABLESPOON CHOPPED FRESH MARJORAM OR 1/2 TEA-
SPOON DRIED

Roasted Vegetables:

2 CUPS PEARL ONIONS, TRIMMED

8 OUNCES WHITE OR CREMINI MUSHROOMS, CUT INTO 1/2-
INCH THICK SLICES

1/4 CUP DRY SHERRY

1 TABLESPOON OLIVE OIL

SALT AND FRESHLY GROUND PEPPER

1/4 CUP MINCED FRESH FLAT-LEAF PARSLEY

1. In a large nonstick skillet over medium-high heat, sauté the onions and carrots in the sesame oil until softened. Add the garlic and cook 1 minute longer. Add the flour and stir until it starts to turn golden. Stir in the Soy Curls and stir-fry briefly.

2. Add the contents of the skillet to a large pot along with the wine. Pour the broth into the same skillet along with the tomato paste and stir vigorously to mix in all of the flour that might have been left behind. Pour this mixture into the pot along with the herbs and bring to a boil, then cover, reduce the heat to a low simmer, and cook for 1 hour. Preheat the oven to 450°F.

3. In an 8 x 12-inch baking pan, combine the onions, mushrooms, olive oil, and sherry and toss to combine. Roast for 20 minutes or until the onions soften, stirring occasionally, then add to the stew. If the sauce has thickened after 1 hour, it needs no further cooking. If not, cook over medium heat, uncovered, stirring often, until it has thickened. Taste for salt and pepper and sprinkle with the parsley.

Indonesian Green Curry on Roasted Sweet Potatoes

INDONESIA

Serves 5   GFO, SFO, <30

This is an excellent and unusual way to enjoy sweet potatoes. The green coconut curry is fashioned after an Indonesian style, but the presentation is my own invention.

1 3/4 POUNDS SWEET POTATOES, PEELED AND CUT INTO 1
1/2-INCH CHUNKS

2 TABLESPOONS OLIVE OR PEANUT OIL

KOSHER SALT AND FRESHLY GROUND BLACK PEPPER

4 CUPS LIGHT SEITAN CUTLETS (PAGE 5), CUT INTO STRIPS;
OR RECONSTITUTED SOY CURLS, DRAINED (3 CUPS
DRY) OR ALTERNATIVE (PAGE 10)

2 TABLESPOONS (FISH-FREE) THAI GREEN CURRY PASTE

1 1/3 CUPS CHICKEN-STYLE VEGAN BROTH (SEE PAGE 2)

1 CUP LITE COCONUT MILK

1/3 CUP DRAINED AND CRUMBLED EXTRA-FIRM SILKEN TOFU
(OR VERY WELL-COOKED SHORT GRAIN WHITE RICE)

4 TO 5 DRIED KAFFIR LIME LEAVES OR ZEST FROM 1 OR-
GANIC LIME OR LEMON

1/4 CUP CHOPPED FRESH CILANTRO

1. Preheat the oven to 400°F. Toss the sweet potato chunks with the oil and salt and pepper to taste. Spread on a 12 x 17-inch baking sheet and bake for about 25 minutes or until soft inside and browning on the outside.

2. Combine the seitan and curry paste in a medium bowl. Heat a large nonstick skillet over medium heat. Add the seitan and sear the strips a bit. Add the broth. Blend the coconut milk and tofu in a blender until smooth, then add to the skillet, along with the kaffir lime leaves or zest.

3. Bring to a boil and then turn down to a simmer. Simmer until the sauce thickens. Add the cilantro. Divide the roasted sweet potatoes among 5 warm plates. Top each mound of sweet potatoes with some of the curry.

Peruvian Stew with Peppers and Walnut Sauce

Ají de Gallina

PERU

Serves 6   <30

Based on a traditional Peruvian chicken dish, this stew features an intriguing walnut sauce thickened in a very old-fashioned way – with bread! I have drastically reduced the fat in the nut-rich sauce, but it is still absolutely delicious. Ají amarillo (Peruvian yellow chile) paste is available online.

1 RECIPE CRISPY MARINATED TOFU SLICES (PAGE 8), FRESHLY COOKED AND KEPT WARM IN A LOW OVEN

1 TABLESPOON OLIVE OIL

2 LARGE ONIONS, CHOPPED

6 CLOVES GARLIC, CRUSHED

3 SLICES FRESH VEGAN WHITE BREAD (ABOUT 4 1/2 OUNCES), TORN INTO PIECES

2 CUPS WATER

1 3/4 CUPS NONDAIRY MILK

1/2 CUP WALNUT PIECES

1/3 CUP WALNUT PARM (PAGE 15)

3 TABLESPOONS TO 1/4 CUP AJÍ AMARILLO (PERUVIAN YELLOW CHILE) PASTE OR SRIRACHA SAUCE

1 ROASTED ORANGE BELL PEPPER, OPTIONAL (TO ADD MORE ORANGE-YELLOW COLOR TO THE SAUCE)

4 TEASPOONS CHICKEN-STYLE VEGAN BROTH POWDER OR PASTE (PAGE 2)

SALT AND FRESHLY GROUND BLACK PEPPER

1 1/2 POUNDS YUKON GOLD POTATOES, STEAMED AND CUT INTO 3/8-INCH THICK SLICES (KEPT WARM)

PERUVIAN ALFONSO OR KALAMATA OLIVES, FOR GARNISH

FRESH PARSLEY AND OR CILANTRO SPRIGS, FOR GARNISH

1. Heat the oil in a large nonstick skillet over medium heat. Add the onions and garlic and sauté until the onions begins to soften, about 10 minutes. Do not brown.

2. Process the bread into fine bread crumbs in a dry food processor or blender. Set aside.

3. In a blender, combine the water, nondairy milk, walnuts, Walnut Parm, ají Amarillo, bell pepper, if using, and broth powder or paste. Blend until very smooth.

4. Add the blended mixture to the skillet with the cooked onions and garlic. Bring the sauce to a simmer and add the bread crumbs. Stir until the sauce is fairly thick. Season with salt and pepper to taste.

5. Arrange the potato slices on a warmed platter. Cover with the crispy tofu slices and spoon the sauce over both. Garnish with the olives and parsley and/or cilantro.

Persian Stew with Spinach and Prunes

PERSIA/IRAN

Serves 4 to 6   SFO, GFO

This delectable stew is a snap to make and chock-full of nutrition. It features a typical Persian combination of sweet spices and fruit with savory vegetables and "meat." Serve with steamed basmati rice.

1/4 CUP OLIVE OIL

2 LARGE ONIONS, THINLY SLICED

3 CUPS RECONSTITUTED (1 3/4 CUPS DRY) TEXTURED SOY PROTEIN CHUNKS (PAGE 10); OR 1-INCH SEITAN CUBES

1/2 CUP SEASONED FLOUR (PAGE 9)

2 TEASPOONS TURMERIC

1 TEASPOON GROUND CINNAMON

1 TEASPOON SALT

FRESHLY GROUND BLACK PEPPER

3 CUPS VEGETABLE BROTH

1 POUND FRESH BABY SPINACH

2 CUPS CHOPPED GREEN ONIONS

1/4 CUP FRESH LEMON JUICE

12 TO 16 PITTED PRUNES (DRIED PLUMS)

1. Heat 2 tablespoons of the olive oil in a large nonstick pot over medium heat. Add the onions and cook until softened and slightly browned, about 7 minutes. Transfer the onions to a medium bowl.

2. Add the remaining 2 tablespoons of olive oil to the same pot over medium-high heat. Dredge the TSP chunks in the seasoned flour and brown in the oil, stirring frequently. Add the turmeric, cinnamon, salt, and pepper to taste, stirring briefly. Add the sautéed onions, broth, spinach, green onions, lemon juice, and prunes. Bring to a boil, then reduce the heat to a simmer. Cook, covered, for 30 minutes. Serve hot.

Jamaican Curry

JAMAICA

Serves 6   GFO, SFO

This is another old favorite from pre-vegan days that I have "veganized" and made lower in fat. The delicious, spicy stew can be made with seitan or TSP chunks. Be sure to make the distinctive Jamaican curry powder for this recipe. Serve with cooked greens, steamed basmati rice, your favorite chutney, and hot pepper sauce.

    4 1/4 CUPS 1-INCH SEITAN CHUNKS (PAGE 133) OR RECON-
        STITUTED TEXTURED SOY PROTEIN (PAGE 10) CHUNKS
        (3 CUPS DRY)
    1/2 CUP WHOLE-WHEAT FLOUR (OR GLUTEN-FREE FLOUR)
    2 TABLESPOONS OLIVE OIL
    3 MEDIUM ONIONS, CHOPPED
    3 CLOVES GARLIC, CHOPPED
    1 TABLESPOON GRATED FRESH GINGER
    2 TABLESPOONS JAMAICAN CURRY POWDER (FOLLOWS)
    1/2 TEASPOON SALT
    1 BAY LEAF
    2 SMALL YUKON GOLD POTATOES, CUT INTO 1/2-INCH DICE
    2 CUPS CHICKEN-STYLE VEGAN BROTH (SEE PAGE 2)
    1 CUP BEER (CAN BE NON-ALCOHOLIC)
    1 CUP LITE COCONUT MILK
    1 1/2 TABLESPOONS SOY SAUCE (OR SOY-FREE SAUCE, PAGE 12)
    2 TABLESPOONS FRESH LIME JUICE
    FRESHLY GROUND BLACK PEPPER
    2 TABLESPOONS DARK RUM, OPTIONAL
    1/4 CUP TOASTED SHREDDED COCONUT

1. Coat the seitan with the flour. Heat the oil in a large heavy skillet. Add the seitan and cook until browned all over, then remove from the pan.

2. In the same pan, add the onions, garlic, and ginger, and stir-fry until softened, adding a little water as needed to keep from sticking. When the onions soften, add the curry powder and salt and stir-fry for a few minutes

3. Microwave Option: Cook the onions, garlic and ginger in a covered microwave-safe 2-quart casserole, on 100% power (default setting) for about 7 minutes or until the onion has softened. When the onions soften, add the curry powder and salt and microwave for about 30 seconds.

4. In a large pot, combine the seitan, onion mixture, bay leaf, potatoes, broth, beer, coconut milk, and soy sauce. Bring to a boil, then reduce to a simmer. Cover and cook for 1 1/2 hours. Stir in the lime juice. Taste for salt and add black pepper to taste. Add the rum, if using. Remove and discard the bay leaf before serving. Serve hot, sprinkled with coconut.

Jamaican Curry Powder
Makes about 1/2 cup   GF, SF, <30

If you can't find this product (a popular brand is Grace), you can make your own version. This one is quite hot! Jamaican curry powder always contains allspice and cumin.

    5 TEASPOONS GROUND TURMERIC
    4 TEASPOONS WHOLE CORIANDER SEEDS
    1 TABLESPOON CAYENNE PEPPER
    1 TABLESPOON FENUGREEK SEEDS
    2 TEASPOONS CUMIN SEEDS
    2 TEASPOONS WHOLE BLACK PEPPERCORNS
    2 TEASPOONS STAR ANISE
    2 TEASPOONS YELLOW MUSTARD SEEDS
    2 WHOLE CLOVES
    1 TEASPOON GROUND DRIED GINGER
    1 TEASPOON GRATED NUTMEG
    1 TEASPOON WHOLE ALLSPICE

Combine the ingredients in a dry blender and blend until it becomes a powder. Transfer to a small jar with a tight lid to store.

 ## Ugandan-Style Peanut Butter Stew

UGANDA

Serves 4   GF

An adaptation of an old family favorite chicken recipe, this velvety stew is easy to make, spicy, colorful, nutritious, and rich in texture and flavor. Serve over steamed rice with braised or sautéed greens.

12 OUNCES LIGHT SEITAN CUTLETS (PAGE 5), CUT INTO STRIPS; OR 3 CUPS RECONSTITUTED SOY CURLS (2 1/4 CUPS DRY), DRAINED; OR ALTERNATIVE (PAGE 10)

1 LARGE ONION, SLICED

2 TO 4 CLOVES GARLIC, MINCED

1 LARGE GREEN OR RED BELL PEPPER, SLICED

1 LARGE RIPE TOMATO, SLICED (OR 4 DRAINED CANNED TOMATOES, CHOPPED)

1/2 TEASPOON SALT

1 TO 3 TEASPOONS CURRY POWDER

1/4 TO 1/2 TEASPOON RED PEPPER FLAKES

1 1/2 CUPS CHICKEN-STYLE VEGAN BROTH (SEE PAGE 2)

1/4 CUP NATURAL CRUNCHY PEANUT BUTTER

1/4 CUP HOT WATER

1. Heat a large nonstick skillet sprayed with oil from a pump sprayer over medium-high heat. Add the seitan and cook until lightly browned. Remove from the pan and set aside.

2. Add the onion, garlic, bell peppers, and tomato to the same pan and stir-fry over medium heat, adding water if necessary to prevent sticking, until the onion starts to soften. Stir in the salt, curry powder, and red pepper flakes. Add the broth and seitan, cover, and simmer for 30 minutes.

3. Whisk the peanut butter with the hot water in a small bowl to make a soft paste. Add to the pan and stir until the sauce is smooth. Taste for salt. Serve immediately.

Deep, Dark Stew a La Sicilia

SICILY

Serves 4 to 6

This stew is perfect for cold weather – it has a rich, deep, dark flavor that I just can't get enough of! I like it on tagliatelle pasta, but polenta or mashed potatoes would be good, too. The stew contains the medieval touch of raisins soaked in wine, as well as a "mystery ingredient." I thought it was absolutely delicious and my husband remarked, "This is the kind of meal you don't want to end!" What is the mystery ingredient? Dark cocoa! Cocoa and chocolate have been used for centuries in savory cooking in Central America and Mexico, of course, but also in Europe, particularly parts of France and Italy. It provides a touch of acidity and adds a natural thickness to sauces, while enhancing the other flavors. Instead of soy chunks, you can use diced seitan.

2 CUPS RECONSTITUTED TEXTURED SOY PROTEIN (1 CUP DRY) CHUNKS (PAGE 10); OR 1-INCH SEITAN CUBES (PAGE 133)

1/4 CUP WHOLE-WHEAT FLOUR

2 TABLESPOONS OLIVE OIL, DIVIDED

1 TEASPOON DARK SESAME OIL

1 LARGE ONION, HALVED AND THINLY SLICED

3 MEDIUM CARROTS, CUT INTO 1/4-INCH DICE

1 CUP CHOPPED CELERY, WITH LEAVES

4 CLOVES GARLIC, FINELY CHOPPED

6 OUNCES MUSHROOMS, SLICED 1/2-INCH THICK

1 (28-OUNCE) CAN PLUM TOMATOES WITH JUICE, CHOPPED

2 CUPS RICH MUSHROOM STOCK (PAGE 4)

1/2 CUP DRY OR MEDIUM DRY SHERRY

1/4 CUP UNSWEETENED COCOA POWDER

1 TABLESPOON SOY BACON BITS

1 TABLESPOON SUGAR

1 TABLESPOON SOY SAUCE

1/2 TABLESPOON YEAST EXTRACT PASTE, SUCH AS MARMITE (PAGE 21)

1 TEASPOON DRIED ROSEMARY

1 TEASPOON DRIED SAGE

1 TEASPOON DRIED THYME

1 LARGE BAY LEAF

1/2 TEASPOON SALT

1. Toss the TSP chunks in the flour and shake off any excess.

2. Heat 1 tablespoon of the olive oil and the sesame oil in a large pot over high heat. Add the TSP chunks and cook until browned all over, stirring often. Reduce the heat if they brown too fast. Transfer to a plate and set aside.

3. Add the remaining 1 tablespoon of olive oil to the pot. Add the onion, carrots, celery, and garlic. Sauté over medium-high heat until the onion starts to wilt. Add the mushrooms and sauté until the mushrooms are cooked, about 5 minutes. Add the tomatoes, broth, sherry, cocoa powder, soy bacon bits, sugar, soy sauce, yeast extract, rosemary, sage, thyme, bay leaf, and salt. Stir well and bring to a boil. Reduce the heat to a simmer and cover. Simmer for about an hour. Remove and discard the bay leaf before serving. Taste for seasoning and serve hot.

"Finnan Haddie" with Smoked Tofu

SCOTLAND

Serves 6   GF, <30

The "fishy" version of this, made with smoked haddock, was a winter favorite of mine when I was a child. My mother made it according to her Grandmother Colwell's recipe, and that side of the family was of Scottish ancestry. Finnan Haddie is a form of smoked haddock, named for the Aberdeen fishing village of Findon, Scotland – locally pronounced "Finnan" – where it was originally cold-smoked over peat. Finnan Haddie was often served poached in milk for breakfast, which I assume was the origin of this type of recipe. Try this delicious and comforting vegan version. Use commercial smoked tofu, if you prefer.

4 CUPS NONDAIRY MILK
1/4 CUP CHICKEN-STYLE VEGAN BROTH POWDER (SEE PAGE 2)
1 TEASPOON SALT

1 TEASPOON LIQUID SMOKE
2 (6 X 4-INCH) PIECES OF KONBU SEAWEED
2 BAY LEAVES
2 MEDIUM ONIONS, THINLY SLICED
8 MEDIUM THIN-SKINNED POTATOES, SCRUBBED AND QUARTERED
1 POUND SMOKY BAKED TOFU, THINLY SLICED (PAGE 59)
FRESHLY GROUND BLACK PEPPER
CHOPPED FRESH PARSLEY, FOR GARNISH

1. In a large shallow pot, combine the nondairy milk, broth powder, salt, and liquid smoke. Add the konbu, bay leaves, onion, potatoes, and tofu. Bring to a boil, then reduce the heat to medium-low simmer, covered, until the potatoes are tender, about 15 minutes. The milk will have thickened into a sauce.

2. Remove the pot from the heat, taste for salt and add plenty of freshly ground pepper. Remove and discard the bay leaves and konbu before serving. If you want a richer stew, add a pat of vegan margarine to each serving. Serve in bowls, sprinkled with chopped parsley.

Peruvian Crispy Fried Tofu

Chicharrón

PERU

Serves 4

Chicharrón, which formerly referred only to what is known in North America as "cracklings," now refers to any crispy fried food in Peruvian cuisine. I got the idea for the quinoa coating on this dish from the beautiful (but definitely not vegan) book, The Art of Peruvian Cuisine by Tony Cussler, who derived his idea from Peruvian Chef Chucho La Rosa. It's a great example of Novoandino (New Andean) cuisine. I thought the idea of a crispy quinoa coating was genius and it was! I used tofu in my Crispy Marinated Tofu marinade instead of fish or chicken and "veganized" the coating. The quinoa makes a very pretty golden crust. You can use your favorite salsa

instead of the salsa in this recipe, if you prefer. In addition to serving 4 as a main dish, this recipe also serves 6 to 8 as a starter.

Tofu and Marinade:
3/4 POUND (12 OUNCES) FIRM TOFU (NOT SILKEN), DRAINED
3/4 CUP WATER
2 TABLESPOONS SOY SAUCE
1/2 TABLESPOON NUTRITIONAL YEAST FLAKES
1 TEASPOON DRIED SAGE LEAVES, CRUMBLED
1/4 TEASPOON DRIED ROSEMARY
1/4 TEASPOON DRIED THYME
1/4 TEASPOON ONION POWDER

Quinoa:
1 CUP QUINOA, WELL-RINSED
2 CUPS WATER
1/2 TEASPOON SALT

Other Ingredients:
1/2 CUP WHOLE-WHEAT FLOUR, FOR DREDGING
1 CUP SOY, NUT, OR HEMP MILK (THESE NONDAIRY MILKS
    WILL CURDLE LIKE DAIRY MILK)
1 TABLESPOON FRESH LEMON JUICE
CANOLA OR PEANUT OIL FOR FRYING

Salsa:
2 LARGE FRESH RIPE FIRM TOMATOES
1 TABLESPOON CHOPPED HOT CHILES OR PICKLED JALAPE-
    ÑOS
1 TABLESPOON CHOPPED FRESH CILANTRO, BASIL, OR
    FLAT-LEAF PARSLEY
1 TEASPOON OLIVE OIL
1/2 TEASPOON SALT
FRESHLY GROUND BLACK PEPPER

1. **Tofu:** Slice the tofu into "fingers" approximately 3/4 x 1/2 x 2 1/2 inches. Mix together the marinade ingredients and immerse the tofu in the marinade in a covered container. Marinate overnight in the refrigerator or even for several days.

2. **Quinoa:** Bring the quinoa, water and salt to a boil in a medium saucepan with a tight lid. Turn the heat down to low and cook for 15 to 20 minutes or until the quinoa is tender, has absorbed all of the water and you can see the little "tails" in the grains. Spread the cooked quinoa out on a 12 x 17-inch baking sheet. Cool thoroughly in the refrigerator, then set it on the counter to air-dry for a few hours, stirring occasionally.

3. **Frying:** I use a miniature deep-fryer or a wok to save on oil. Have the oil (3 inches deep will be enough) heated to 375°F. If you are going to fry the tofu only once in the usual way, plan to have your guests seated and ready to eat while you fry. Otherwise, you can use the "Twice-Frying" technique (see sidebar).

4. Remove the tofu from the marinade, pat gently with a clean cloth and dredge in the flour on all sides. Arrange the tofu pieces, not touching, on a 12 x 17-inch baking sheet.

5. Mix together the nondairy milk and lemon juice in a shallow bowl (such as a large, flat soup or pasta bowl). Coat each flour-coated "finger" in curdled nondairy milk and then roll it in the quinoa to coat thoroughly, pressing the quinoa into the coating. Set the coated "fingers" on baking sheets (any size) lined with baking parchment cut to fit or, ideally, have someone else coating the tofu as you fry it. Fry the tofu "fingers" in the hot oil until crispy and golden brown. Drain on paper towels and serve hot with the salsa.

Tip: You can cook the quinoa well ahead of time – in any case, it should be cooled and a bit air-dried before using in this recipe, so it's best to make it a few hours ahead.

The Secret of Twice-Frying

This is an old favorite Chinese and also French way of pre-frying foods so they can be (conveniently) partially pre-cooked and then fried briefly again to heat. The method also allows the food to be very crispy without being greasy. First of all, the food is fried at 350°F until it is a pale golden color. The food is removed and drained on paper. This can be done early in the day it is to be served.

Just before serving, the oil is heated to 425°F. (Make sure to use peanut or canola oil for this, as these oils have high smoking points and are therefore safer to use at high heat.) The pre-fried food is added to the hot oil and fried again until crisp and golden brown, then drained and served immediately. The second frying actually decreases the amount of oil that is absorbed.

The Side of the Plate

Uncommonly Good Global Go-Withs

When you need an interesting side dish to go with a special meal or to add interest to a ho-hum entrée, have a look at the recipes in this chapter. Whether it's a fragrant rice pilaf, such as Persian-Style Rice Pilaf with Edamame; gussied-up French mashed potatoes disguised as Sicilian; minty braised Italian squash; or Nepalese Green Beans with Coconut, diners at your table will appreciate the time and effort you took to make the "sides" so much more than mundane. Green and Gold Quinoa Pilaf, South African Yellow Rice with Raisins, and Roasted Sweet Potatoes with Moroccan Spices can brighten up any plate and any palate.

The Thai Pineapple Fried Rice makes a magnificent centerpiece dish, but is actually very easy to prepare. Buttery layered Lentil and Raisin Rice Pilaf is sure to become a family favorite. The golden Hasselback Potatoes "fans" and tender mushroom-filled Chremslach take potatoes to a whole new level, and the spaetzle recipe enables you to serve tender homemade noodles with minimal time and effort. Several of these dishes are substantial and delicious enough to serve as main dishes themselves.

Uncommonly Good Global Go-Withs

Italian-Style Braised Winter Squash

ITALY

Serves 4 to 6   GF, SF, <30

This is one of my favorite ways to prepare winter squash – it has a clean, savory flavor that is quite different from the usual American sweet preparations. It's a very easy dish to make, once you get the squash peeled.

- 2 TABLESPOONS OLIVE OIL
- 1 1/2 POUNDS BUTTERNUT OR HUBBARD SQUASH, PEELED AND CUT INTO 1-INCH CUBES
- 2 CLOVES GARLIC, CHOPPED
- SALT AND FRESHLY GROUND BLACK PEPPER
- 2 TABLESPOONS CHOPPED FRESH BASIL OR FLAT-LEAF PARSLEY

Heat the oil in a large nonstick skillet or sauté pan. Add the squash cubes and garlic and toss to coat. Reduce the heat to medium-low and cover tightly. Cook until the squash is tender, turning occasionally with a spatula, about 20 minutes. It should get somewhat browned and caramelized. If it is sticking too much, add a splash of water or dry white wine. When it's tender, season with salt and pepper to taste and stir in the basil or parsley. Serve immediately.

Peeling Winter Squash

You need a very sharp knife to peel the squash – a Chinese cleaver works well, if you have one. Some winter squash are so hard to open that I have used a small axe on them. Or, you can drop the squash on pavement or a brick (covered with a clean plastic garbage bag) to split it.

Persian-Style Rice Pilaf with Edamamé

PERSIA/IRAN

Serves 6   GF

This dish appears in many versions in Iraq and Iran. The original dish contains white basmati rice, fresh fava beans or lima beans, and lots of butter. I thought it would work well with less fat, brown basmati rice, and edamamé, and it did. It's a lovely spring-green dish, which you could use as an unusual alternative to mashed potatoes on an Easter menu. You can substitute frozen baby lima beans for the edamame, if necessary.

- 1 TABLESPOON VEGAN MARGARINE
- 1 MEDIUM ONION, MINCED
- 2 CLOVES GARLIC, MINCED OR CRUSHED
- 3 CUPS COOKED BROWN BASMATI RICE (SIDEBAR PAGE 154)
- 4 TABLESPOONS CHOPPED FRESH DILL WEED OR 4 TEASPOONS DRIED
- 1 1/2 CUPS FROZEN SHELLED EDAMAME
- SALT AND FRESHLY GROUND BLACK PEPPER

1. Preheat the oven to 350°F. In a large nonstick skillet, melt the margarine over medium heat. Add the onion and garlic and sauté until the onion is soft, about 7 minutes, adding drops of water as necessary to keep it from sticking. You don't want the onion to brown, but you want it to be soft. Mix in the rice, dill, edamamé, and salt and pepper to taste. Toss well.

2. Transfer the mixture to an oiled 2-quart covered casserole or 13-inch oval covered roaster. Bake for 20 to 30 minutes or until the edamamé are cooked and the rice is dry and fluffy. Serve hot.

Roasted Sweet Potatoes with Moroccan Spices

MOROCCO

Serves 5 to 6   GF, SF

Fragrant roasted sweets with the crunch of whole spices and a touch of maple syrup – trust me, there won't be any leftovers.

- 1 1/2 POUNDS SWEET POTATOES, PEELED, HALVED LENGTH-WISE AND CUT CROSSWISE INTO 1/2-INCH-THICK SLICES
- 1 TABLESPOON MELTED VEGAN MARGARINE
- 1 TABLESPOON OLIVE OIL
- 1 TABLESPOON MAPLE SYRUP
- GRATED ZEST OF 1/2 MEDIUM ORGANIC LEMON
- 1/2 TABLESPOON CORIANDER SEEDS
- 1/2 TABLESPOON CUMIN SEEDS
- 1/2 TABLESPOON MUSTARD SEEDS
- SALT AND FRESHLY GROUND BLACK PEPPER

1. Position a rack in the bottom third of the oven and preheat the oven to 375°F. Spray a 12 x 17-inch rimmed baking sheet or a shallow baking pan, with oil from a pump sprayer.

2. Combine the sweet potato slices, margarine, oil, maple syrup, lemon zest, and spice seeds on the baking sheet. Toss to coat, then spread out evenly. Sprinkle with salt and pepper to taste. Roast the sweet potatoes until tender and golden brown, stirring occasionally, 30 to 45 minutes. Taste for seasoning and serve hot.

Egyptian Okra and Tomato Stew with Green Beans

Bamiya

EGYPT

Serves 6   GF, SF, <30

There are many versions of this delicious vegetable dish. I wanted to use only okra, but my husband claims not to like it, so I mixed in green beans and

he liked the dish! Okra is a great source of soluble fiber, by the way. If you prefer, you can omit the green beans and use 1 pound of okra instead.

- 2 TABLESPOONS OLIVE OIL
- 8 OUNCES YOUNG OKRA (USE FROZEN, THAWED, IF FRESH IS UNAVAILABLE)
- 8 OUNCES FRESH YOUNG GREEN BEANS OR SMALL WHOLE FROZEN GREEN BEANS, THAWED
- 1 LARGE ONION, CHOPPED
- 2 TABLESPOONS CHOPPED FRESH DILL WEED OR 2 TEA-SPOONS DRIED
- 1 TABLESPOON CHOPPED FRESH SAGE LEAVES OR 1 TEA-SPOON CRUMBLED DRIED (NOT GROUND)
- 1 TEASPOON SUGAR
- 1 TEASPOON SALT
- 1 (28-OUNCE) CAN DICED TOMATOES, DRAINED (JUICE RESERVED)
- FRESHLY GROUND BLACK PEPPER

Heat the oil in a large nonstick skillet over medium-high heat. Add the okra and green beans and stir-fry until they have browned a bit. Add the onion and sauté until softened, about 5 minutes. Add the dill, sage, sugar, salt, tomatoes, and pepper to taste. Bring to a boil, then cover and reduce the heat to low. Simmer for about 15 minutes or until the beans are tender, adding a bit of the reserved tomato juice if the mixture is too dry. Serve hot or at room temperature.

Nepalese Green Beans with Coconut

NEPAL

Serves 6   GF, SF, <30

This is a simplified version of a traditional dish. The fragrant ginger and mustard seeds are a great contrast with the fresh beans and mild coconut flavor. It makes a wonderful accompaniment to many Asian meals.

- 1 1/2 POUNDS YOUNG GREEN BEANS, TRIMMED, OR FROZEN YOUNG, WHOLE GREEN BEANS, THAWED
- 2 TABLESPOONS OLIVE OIL OR PEANUT OIL

1/2 TABLESPOON BLACK MUSTARD SEEDS

1 SMALL ONION, CHOPPED

1 TABLESPOON GRATED GINGER

1 PINCH CAYENNE

1/2 CUP UNSWEETENED SHREDDED COCONUT

1 1/2 TABLESPOONS DRIED CURRY LEAVES, CRUMBLED,
    OPTIONAL (SEE TIP)

JUICE OF 1 LEMON

SALT AND FRESHLY GROUND BLACK PEPPER

Heat the oil over high heat in a large deep skillet or wok. Add the mustard seeds. When the seeds start to pop, add the onion and sauté over medium heat until softened, about 5 minutes. Add the ginger, cayenne, and green beans and toss to coat. Add the coconut and curry leaves, if using. Reduce the heat to medium, cover and cook until the beans are tender but still slightly crunchy. Add the lemon juice and season with salt and pepper to taste. Serve hot.

Tip: Purchase curry leaves in Asian grocery stores or online. According to my research, ou can substitute bay leaves, basil leaves, or kaffir lime leaves, but all have a different flavor. Do not substitute curry powder!

Braised Baby Bok Choy and Shiitake Mushrooms

JAPAN/ASIA

Serves 4   GF, SFO

This is a terrific vegetable side dish that goes well with many Asian menus. Prepare everything ahead of time and it can be put together quickly.

6 LARGE DRIED SHIITAKE OR CHINESE BLACK MUSHROOMS [FRESH]

1/2 TABLESPOON DARK SESAME OIL

1 LARGE CLOVE GARLIC, SLICED

1 POUND BABY BOK CHOY, SLICED ABOUT 1-INCH THICK

2 GREEN ONIONS, SLICED DIAGONALLY ABOUT 1/2-INCH THICK

1 TABLESPOON SOY SAUCE (OR SOY-FREE SAUCE, PAGE 12)

1/4 TEASPOON KOSHER SALT

FRESHLY GROUND BLACK PEPPER

1 TABLESPOON TOASTED SESAME SEEDS

1. Place the mushrooms in a bowl, cover with boiling water, cover and set aside to soften, about 30 minutes. Drain the mushrooms. When cool enough to handle, remove and discard the stems and cut the mushrooms into 1/2-inch thick slices. Set aside.

2. Heat the sesame oil in a large deep nonstick skillet or stir-fry pan over high heat. Add the garlic and stir-fry until golden, just a few seconds. Do not brown. Add the mushrooms, bok choy, green onions, soy sauce, and salt. Reduce heat to low, cover and cook until bok choy is tender but not mushy, about 10 minutes. Season to taste with salt and pepper. Sprinkle with the toasted sesame seeds and serve immediately.

Thai Pineapple Fried Rice in a Pineapple Shell

THAILAND

Serves 4 to 6   GF

This dish is quick and easy to make, but delicious enough for company. Thai dishes are traditionally made with white jasmine rice, but I make this with long grain brown jasmine rice. Brown jasmine rice is so fragrant that it perfumes the whole house while it cooks. This recipe serves 4 as a main dish or 6 as a side dish. You can use any kind of mushrooms in this recipe, but oyster mushrooms or lobster mushrooms are a plus!

1 LARGE RIPE PINEAPPLE

2 TABLESPOONS EXPELLER-PRESSED CHINESE PEANUT OIL
    OR LIGHT SESAME OIL

1 MEDIUM ONION, CHOPPED

2 CUPS THINLY SLICED MUSHROOMS

4 CLOVES GARLIC, MINCED

1/2 TEASPOON RED PEPPER FLAKES

1 TABLESPOON GRATED FRESH GINGER

4 CUPS COLD COOKED FRAGRANT LONG GRAIN BROWN RICE
    (SEE SIDEBAR)

1 CUP YOUNG GREEN BEANS, STEAMED OR BOILED UNTIL
    CRISP-TENDER

4 OUNCES FIRM TOFU, PATTED DRY AND CUT INTO 1/2-INCH
  CUBES
1/2 CUP TOASTED CASHEWS
3 TABLESPOONS SOY SAUCE
1 TEASPOON SUGAR
FRESHLY GROUND BLACK PEPPER
2 GREEN ONIONS, THINLY SLICED DIAGONALLY
2 TABLESPOONS TOASTED SHREDDED OR FLAKED COCONUT,
  OPTIONAL

1. Halve the pineapple lengthwise, leaving the leafy top intact and cutting through it. Hollow out each half (a serrated, curved grapefruit knife works well). Chop 1 cup of the fruit very small and set aside for the rice. Cut the remaining pineapple into 1/2-inch cubes and set aside for garnish.

2. Crumble the cold rice between your fingers to separate the grains and set aside.

3. Heat 1 tablespoon of the oil in a large non-stick skillet or wok over high heat, swirling to spread it in the bottom of the pan. Add the onion and mushrooms and stir-fry until they start to soften. Add the garlic and red pepper flakes and stir-fry for about 1 or 2 minutes. Add the ginger and stir-fry for another minute.

4. Add the remaining tablespoon of oil and the cold rice to the pan. Stir-fry for 2 or 3 minutes over high heat, then add the green beans, tofu, and the 1 cup of chopped pineapple and stir-fry for 2 or 3 minutes more. Add the cashews, soy sauce, and sugar and stir-fry until the ingredients are well combined and rice is heated thoroughly, about 5 minutes. Turn the heat down a little if it seems to be sticking and browning. Add black pepper to taste. Remove the pan from the heat and fill each half of the prepared pineapple evenly with the hot rice. Garnish with extra chunks of the pineapple, the sliced green onions, and coconut, if using. Serve immediately.

TIPS

• Fried rice is best when made with cold rice, so it's a perfect dish for using leftover rice. If you cook rice especially for this dish, make it the day before or early in the day and refrigerate it.

• If you are in a hurry, spread the hot cooked rice on a baking sheet and place it in the freezer just long enough to cool the grains.

• 1 1/2 cups dry rice will make a little over 4 cups cooked.

Fragrant Long-Grain Rice

A fragrant rice is an important component of the Thai Pineapple Fried Rice in a Pineapple Shell and other Thai rice dishes. I especially like brown jasmine rice. If you can't find brown jasmine rice, there are several other varieties of fragrant long-grain rice available, such as brown basmati, Calmati or Texmati rice. Brownish-red Wehani rice is also fragrant and would be lovely in this dish, by itself or mixed with jasmine rice or brown rice.

How to cook long grain brown rice: If you are using an electric rice cooker, use 1 part rice and 2 parts water. If you cook this on a stovetop, use a sturdy pot with a tight lid. Use 1 part rice and 11/2 parts water, bring it to a boil, then turn down to low, cover and cook for 45 minutes.

Tip: If you soak the rice in the cooking water for 8 hours before cooking time, the rice will only take 20 minutes to cook.

Gujarati-Style Stewed Tomatoes

INDIA

Serves 6   SF, <30

This slightly hot tomato stew, fragrant with spices, is the perfect partner for tender, sweet South Indian Steamed Corn Bread (page 215). Together, they make a wonderful luncheon dish, as well as a substantial snack. This is my version for Western kitchens. Gujarat is a province in India which has a primarily vegetarian cuisine, extremely varied, and often not as hot as other Indian cuisines. Many Gujarati dishes are sweet, salty, and spicy at the same time, and this combination is somewhat representative of that.

3 TABLESPOONS OLIVE OIL

1/2 TEASPOON CUMIN SEEDS

1 TEASPOON BROWN OR BLACK MUSTARD SEEDS

1/2 TEASPOON RED PEPPER FLAKES

1 CLOVE GARLIC, CRUSHED

1 SMALL ONION, MINCED

1 (28-OUNCE) CAN ITALIAN PLUM TOMATOES, UNDRAINED OR 2 POUNDS CHOPPED FRESH PLUM TOMATOES

1 TEASPOON SALT

1 TEASPOON GRATED FRESH GINGER

1/2 TABLESPOON BROWN SUGAR

FRESHLY GROUND BLACK PEPPER

1 TABLESPOON CHICKPEA FLOUR OR CORN FLOUR PLUS 2 TABLESPOONS WATER

Heat the oil in a skillet or shallow saucepan over medium-high heat. When the oil is very hot, add the cumin and mustard seeds. As soon as the mustard seeds begin to pop, add the red pepper flakes. After a few seconds, add the onions and garlic and sauté until the onions wilt. Add the tomatoes and stir briefly, then add the salt, ginger, brown sugar, and pepper to taste. Cover and simmer gently for about 10 minutes. Combine the flour and water in a small bowl and mix to a paste, then stir into the pot, stirring until it thickens. Serve hot.

Tip: If using fresh tomatoes in this recipe, don't bother to seed or peel them. Food scientists have found that much of the tomato flavor is in the seeds and "jelly" around the seeds.

Persian Lentil and Raisin Rice Pilaf

Adas Polow

PERSIA/IRAN

Serves 4 to 6   GF, SF

This delightful rice dish is served as a side dish at special meals, but it makes a lovely main dish on its own. Persian rice is very buttery, but I use only a little vegan margarine for a buttery taste with less fat. I use the steaming method for cooking the rice, rather than boiling and draining it, to preserve nutrients. Some cooks mix the rice and lentils in this dish, some layer them, which I chose to do.

1 3/4 CUPS BROWN LENTILS, PICKED OVER, RINSED AND DRAINED

4 1/2 CUPS PLUS 1/2 CUP WATER, DIVIDED

1/2 TEASPOON SALT

3 CUPS WHITE BASMATI RICE

2 TABLESPOONS OLIVE OIL

2 MEDIUM ONIONS, CHOPPED

12 OUNCES GROUND SEITAN (PAGE 133), VEGAN "BURGER CRUMBLES," OR GROUND FIELD ROAST CLASSIC MEATLOAF

1/4 TEASPOON GROUND CINNAMON

1/4 TEASPOON NUTMEG

1/4 TEASPOON TURMERIC

SALT AND FRESHLY GROUND BLACK PEPPER

1 CUP RAISINS (OR A MIXTURE OF RAISINS, CHOPPED DATES, AND/OR CURRANTS)

2 TABLESPOONS MELTED VEGAN MARGARINE (OR MORE)

1. Cook the lentils in a small pot with water to cover and a pinch of salt until they are tender. Cover the pot as they cook. Add more water as needed to keep from sticking, but not too much. When the lentils are tender but not mushy (they

should still hold their shape), drain in a colander and set aside.

2. Bring the 4 1/2 cups of water to a boil in a medium pot with the 1/2 teaspoon of salt. When it boils, slowly add the rice. When it comes to a boil again, cover tightly, turn the heat to low and cook for 20 minutes. Take the lid off, fold up a small kitchen towel and place it over the rice, then cover tightly again. (This makes the rice nice and dry.) Let rice stand off the heat while you prepare the filling. Preheat the oven to 350°F.

3. Heat the oil in a large nonstick skillet over medium heat. Add the onions and saute until soft, about 7 minutes. Add the seitan, cinnamon, nutmeg, turmeric, and the 1/2 cup water. Cover the skillet and cook over medium heat until all of the water is absorbed. Season with salt and pepper to taste. Set aside.

4. To assemble, uncover the rice and fluff it with a fork. Transfer to a large bowl and add the lentils. Carefully toss the rice and lentils together – you want to see the lentils in the rice and not mash them so that they coat the rice.

5. Layer half of the lentil/rice mixture in a shallow 2-quart casserole or 8 x 12-inch baking dish. Spread the filling over the rice, distribute the raisins evenly over the filling and then top evenly with the rest of the rice. Drizzle the margarine over it. Cover the casserole with a lid or with aluminum foil and bake for about 20 minutes, until hot and steamy.

South African Yellow Rice

Geel Rys

Sᴏᴜᴛʜ Aꜰʀɪᴄᴀ

Serves 6   GF, SF

Bake this aromatic, fruity rice in the oven alongside Bobotie (page 126) – it's the traditional accompaniment. This recipe calls for the same amount of cooking time as the bobotie, so you can bake them together.

2 CUPS BROWN BASMATI RICE
3 CUPS VEGETABLE BROTH
2 TABLESPOONS VEGAN MARGARINE OR OLIVE OIL
2 CUPS MINCED ONIONS (2 MEDIUM ONIONS)
2 CLOVES GARLIC, MINCED
1 TEASPOON TURMERIC
1/2 TO 3/4 CUP RAISINS
2 TABLESPOONS SUGAR
1 (6-INCH) CINNAMON STICK

1. Eight hours before cooking the rice, combine the rice with the vegetable broth in a medium covered pot or bowl. Allow to soak until it's time to cook the rice. Preheat the oven to 375°F.

2. Heat the margarine or oil over high heat in a 2 to 3-quart ovenproof pot or Dutch oven with a tight lid. (See Note below) Add the onions and reduce the heat to medium. Sauté until the onions are quite soft, about 10 minutes adding drops of water as necessary to keep it from sticking. You don't want the onions to brown. Add the garlic and turmeric and sauté for a few minutes longer. Add the soaked rice and broth and the remaining ingredients to the pot, combine well and cover with a tight lid. Bake for 45 minutes. Serve hot.

Note: If you don't have an ovenproof pot or a casserole that can be heated on top of the stove, use the microwave option below, or use a large skillet for sautéing, and then transfer the sautéed mixture to an ovenproof 2 or 3-quart covered casserole. Add the remaining ingredients to the casserole, combine well, and cover with a tight lid.

Microwave Option: In a covered microwave-safe 2 to 3-quart casserole, cook the onions in the margarine or oil on 100% power (default setting) for about 7 minutes or until the onions have softened. When the onions have softened, add the turmeric and microwave for about 30 seconds. Add the remaining ingredients to the casserole, combine well and cover with a tight lid.

Green and Gold Quinoa Pilaf

U.S.A.

Serves 4   GF, SF, <30

This is a lovely vegetable and whole-grain side dish to accompany almost any meal, any time of the year! The squash and herbs can vary from season to season.

> 3/4 CUP QUINOA, WELL-RINSED
> 1 1/2 CUPS CHICKEN-STYLE VEGAN BROTH (PAGE 2)
> 1 TEASPOON CHICKEN-STYLE VEGAN BROTH POWDER OR
>   PASTE (PAGE 2)
> 1 TABLESPOON OLIVE OIL OR VEGAN MARGARINE
> 1 CUP GREEN AND/OR YELLOW SQUASH, CUT INTO 1/2-INCH
>   DICE (SEE TIP BELOW)
> 1/2 CUP CHOPPED LEEKS OR GREEN ONIONS
> 1/2 MEDIUM ONION, CHOPPED
> 1 RIB CELERY, CHOPPED
> 1 TABLESPOON SINGLE OR MIXED FRESH HERBS (SEE NOTE
>   BELOW) OR 1 TEASPOON DRIED
> 1/2 CUP FRESH OR FROZEN BABY PEAS
> 1/2 CUP FRESH OR FROZEN SWEET CORN KERNELS
> 2 TABLESPOONS WALNUT PARM (PAGE 15)
> FRESHLY GROUND BLACK PEPPER

1. Toast the quinoa in a dry skillet (such as cast iron) over medium-high heat until it smells toasty, stirring continually with a wooden spoon. Remove from the heat and transfer to a medium saucepan, along with the broth and broth powder or paste. Bring the broth to a boil and then reduce the heat to low. Cover and simmer for 15 minutes.

2. In a nonstick skillet, heat the olive oil over medium-high heat. Add the squash, leeks or green onions, onion, and celery, and sauté until the vegetables soften. Add the herbs and sauté for a few seconds. Add this to the quinoa while it cooks. After the quinoa has cooked for 15 minutes, add the peas and corn and cook 5 minutes longer or until the quinoa is cooked and the mixture is drier. Gently stir in the Walnut Parm and pepper to taste. Fluff the quinoa with a fork before serving.

Tip: In the summer, use dark green or yellow zucchini, scallopini, crookneck, or patty pan squash; in the winter use peeled golden-fleshed winter squash, such as acorn, Gold Nugget, or Sweet Dumpling.

Note: In the summer, fresh basil, cilantro, parsley, and mint are all winners; in the winter, dried thyme, marjoram, oregano, tarragon, or dill are good choices.

Sicilian-Style Mashed Potatoes with Orange

Pommes Siciliennes

France

Serves 4 to 6   GF, SF

This is my version of an old French recipe – I suspect that the orange flavor is what makes it "Sicilian." The original recipe was full of cream and butter, which I replaced with my homemade Almond "Ricotta." In addition, Yukon Gold potatoes contribute a "buttery" look and flavor. I steam the potatoes rather than boil them because steaming reduces the chance of having "gluey" mashed potatoes. It also saves nutrients.

> 2 POUNDS YUKON GOLD POTATOES, PEELED AND CUT INTO
>   1-INCH CHUNKS
> 1/2 CUP ALMOND "RICOTTA" (PAGE 40, WITHOUT THE CITRUS
>   FLAVORING), GENTLY WARMED (SEE TIP)
> 1/4 CUP PLUS 2 TABLESPOONS FRESH ORANGE JUICE,
>   GENTLY WARMED
> GRATED ZEST OF 1 LARGE ORGANIC ORANGE
> 1/2 TEASPOON SALT

1. Place a metal colander or steamer insert in a large pot or Dutch oven. Add enough water to barely reach the bottom of the colander. Bring the water to a boil over high heat. Transfer the potato chunks to the steamer/colander, cover the pot and reduce the heat to medium-high. Cook the potatoes for 20 to 25 minutes or until the

potatoes are soft and the tip of a paring knife inserted into a potato chunk meets no resistance.

2. Set a potato ricer or food mill over the now-empty pot. Working in batches, transfer the potatoes to the hopper of the ricer or food mill and press or grind them through the holes, removing any potatoes that stick to bottom. Press all the potatoes through the ricer or food mill into the pot. If you do not have a ricer or a food mill, transfer the potatoes to the pot, which has been drained of water, and mash them with a potato masher.

3. Stir in the grated orange zest and salt until well-mixed. Stir in the warm "Ricotta" and orange juice and beat the potatoes with a wooden spoon until they are smooth and fluffy. Serve hot.

Tips

- The "ricotta" and orange juice can be placed in cups and the cups set in bowls of hot water to warm them while you cook the potatoes.
- Using a potato ricer or a food mill makes mashed potatoes extra fluffy.

Mashed Potatoes with Sautéed Chard and Garlic

MEDITERRANEAN

Serves 6   GF, SF

This is a delicious Mediterranean take on the Irish potato and cabbage dish, colcannon. I like to serve it with a Mediterranean-style Christmas menu.

2 POUNDS YUKON GOLD POTATOES, PEELED AND CUT INTO
    CHUNKS (SEE TIP)
2 TABLESPOONS OLIVE OIL
3/4 POUND GREEN SWISS CHARD, TOUGH STEMS REMOVED
    AND CUT INTO 1/4-INCH THICK SLICES
6 CLOVES GARLIC, THINLY SLICED
1/2 CUP HOT NONDAIRY MILK
1/2 TEASPOON SALT
FRESHLY GROUND BLACK PEPPER

1. Place a metal colander or steamer insert in large pot or Dutch oven. Add enough water to barely reach the bottom of the colander. Bring the water to a boil over high heat. Transfer the potato chunks to the steamer/colander, cover the pot and reduce the heat to medium-high. Cook the potatoes for 20 to 25 minutes or until the potatoes are soft and the tip of a paring knife inserted into a potato chunk meets no resistance.

2. While the potatoes cook, sauté the garlic and chard in hot olive oil in a large skillet over medium-high heat. Keep stirring, adding a tiny bit of water or broth if necessary, but the chard should exude its own liquid. When all of the liquid has evaporated and the garlic and chard are tender (but still bright green), remove from heat and set aside with a lid over the skillet to keep it warm. (The chard can be cooked ahead of time and briefly reheated before adding to the potatoes to serve.)

3. Set a potato ricer or food mill over the empty pot. Working in batches, transfer the potatoes to the hopper of the ricer or food mill and press or grind them through the holes, removing any potatoes that stick to the bottom. Press all the potatoes through the ricer or food mill into the pot. If you do not have a ricer or a food mill, transfer the potatoes to the pot, which has been drained of water and mash with a potato masher.

4. Stir in the salt until well-mixed. Stir in the hot milk and beat the potatoes with a wooden spoon until they are smooth and fluffy. Add the chard and garlic and lots of black pepper. Mix well and taste for salt. Serve immediately.

Tip: Yukon Gold potatoes contribute a "buttery" look and flavor without using much fat. I steam the potatoes rather than boil them because steaming reduces the chance of having "gluey" mashed potatoes. It also saves nutrients. Using a potato ricer or a food mill makes mashed potatoes extra fluffy.

Mushroom-Stuffed Potato Balls

Chremslach

NORTHERN-EUROPE/JEWISH

Serves 6   GFO, SF

Chremslach means many things, I have learned, and often refers to a type of pancake. But these particular ones are fried filled potato balls. My filling is a simple but extremely tasty mushroom mixture (which can also double as a spread).

This dish was a big hit at my table and can be served at any time of the year. I think it makes a great starter for a winter meal, as well as a side dish. The chremslach need to be refrigerated for several hours before cooking. It is preferable to make the chremslach the day before and fry it just before serving. You can actually make the potato mixture and the filling several days ahead, then put the chremslach together a day ahead of time. On the day you plan to serve them, you can simply fry them just before serving. This will save time and fuss at meal time.

2 POUNDS RUSSET OR OTHER BAKING POTATOES, PEELED
    AND CUT INTO 1-INCH DICE
1 TABLESPOON DARK SESAME OIL
1/2 MEDIUM ONION, MINCED
8 OUNCES WHITE OR CREMINI MUSHROOMS, MINCED (I USE A
    FOOD PROCESSOR)
SALT
1/2 TEASPOON YEAST EXTRACT PASTE, SUCH AS MARMITE
    (PAGE 21)
1 TABLESPOON HOT WATER
1/2 CUP PLUS 1 TABLESPOON MATZOH MEAL, DIVIDED, PLUS
    MORE FOR COATING (CAN BE GLUTEN-FREE)
FRESHLY GROUND BLACK PEPPER
2 TABLESPOONS GOLDEN FLAX SEEDS, GROUND FINE IN A
    CLEAN DRY BLENDER OR COFFEE/SPICE MILL
VEGETABLE OIL, FOR FRYING

1. Place a metal colander or steamer insert in large pot or Dutch oven. Add enough water to barely reach the bottom of the colander. Bring the water to a boil over high heat. Transfer the potato chunks to the steamer/colander, cover the pot and reduce the heat to medium-high. Cook the potatoes for 20 to 25 minutes or until the potatoes are soft and the tip of a paring knife inserted into a potato chunk meets no resistance.

2. Heat the sesame oil in a large nonstick skillet over medium-high heat. Add the onion and sauté until it is soft. Add the mushrooms, a little salt and the Marmite dissolved in the hot water. Cook, stirring frequently, over high heat until the mushrooms exude their liquid, then absorb it again. Mix in the 1/2 cup matzoh meal and season with salt and pepper to taste. Spread the mixture thinly on a cookie sheet and place in the freezer to cool quickly. Check on it frequently.

3. When the potatoes are done, set a potato ricer or food mill over the now-empty pot. Working in batches, transfer the potatoes to the hopper of the ricer or food mill and press or grind them through the holes, removing any potatoes that stick to the bottom. Press all the potatoes through the ricer or food mill into the pot. If you do not have a ricer or a food mill, transfer the potatoes to the pot, which has been drained of water and mash them with a potato masher.

4. Add 1 tablespoon matzoh meal, ground flax seed and 1 teaspoon salt and beat the ingredients together well. It should be like pliable dough – add a little more matzoh meal, if necessary. Transfer it to a bowl and refrigerate until completely cool.

5. Divide the potato "dough" into 12 equal pieces and form into balls. Flatten each ball in the palm of your hand and place about 1 tablespoon of the mushroom filling in the center. Enclose the filling completely in the potato dough, leaving no holes. It should form a ball. Repeat with the rest of the mixture. Roll each ball in matzoh meal and press it into the dough. Place the balls on a cookie sheet and refrigerate (uncovered) for several hours or overnight.

6. When you are ready to cook and serve, heat at least 3 inches of the oil to 375°F. Fry the

chremslach about 4 at a time, a few minutes on each side, turning until golden-brown all over. Drain them on paper towels and keep them warm in a 250°F oven while you fry the remainder. Serve hot.

Hasselback Potatoes

SWEDEN

Serves 4   GF, SF

This recipe is adapted from one served at Stockholm's popular old Restaurant Hasselbacken. It's so easy to make and, at the same time, a good way to "fancy up" ordinary potatoes. Choose oblong potatoes of uniform size.

4 MEDIUM ALL-PURPOSE POTATOES, SUCH AS YUKON GOLD (6 OUNCES EACH)
3 TABLESPOONS VEGAN MARGARINE, MELTED
1/2 TEASPOON SALT
2 TABLESPOONS FRESH BREADCRUMBS
2 TABLESPOONS WALNUT PARM (PAGE 15)

1. Preheat the oven to 425°F. Peel the potatoes, transferring them to a large bowl of cold water as peeled (to prevent browning). Working with 1 potato at a time, cut a thin slice lengthwise on one side of the potato (the flattest side, if there is one) to make it lie flat on your work surface. Arrange 2 wooden, square-cut chopsticks (the kind you get in restaurants) on your work surface, parallel to each other. Place a prepared potato lengthwise on top of chopsticks, which are slightly spread apart to allow the potato to sit squarely between the two chopsticks.

2. Using a sharp knife, make crosswise cuts 1/8-inch apart, down to chopsticks, not all the way through (except on the narrow ends of the potatoes) or the slices will fall off. You want the potato in lots of thin slices, but still connected on the bottom, so that the potato holds its original shape. Transfer the potatoes back into the cold water after cutting. Placing the potato between

two chopsticks prevents you from accidentally cutting all the way through the bottom of the potato.

3. Arrange potatoes spoke-fashion in a 10-inch pie plate which has been brushed with margarine. Drizzle 2 tablespoons melted margarine evenly over the potatoes and then sprinkle with salt.

4. Bake potatoes on middle oven rack for 30 minutes. Sprinkle the breadcrumbs evenly over the potatoes, then drizzle with the remaining 1 tablespoon melted margarine. Bake 20 more minutes.

5. Sprinkle the Walnut Parm over the potatoes and baste with the melted margarine in the baking dish. Bake for 5 more minutes or until potatoes are golden. Serve hot.

Tip: All-purpose potatoes have a less starch than starchy baking potatoes, but not so much that they completely fall apart when cooked. They will work for most potato dishes.

Easy Homemade Spaetzle

GERMANY, AUSTRIA, HUNGARY

Serves 6   SF

I was introduced to these by my late friend, Roberta Bishop Johnson, who was my editor when I worked on the La Leche League cookbook, Whole Foods for the Whole Family. Spaetzle is the German name for these drop noodles, which means "little sparrows." Roberta called them "Galloping Galuska" ("Galuska" being the Hungarian name for this noodle and the "galloping" referred to the speed of preparation, because she dispensed with the "resting" process.) Traditional German and Hungarian recipes contain a lot of eggs, so this was a challenge, but my vegan version is very tasty and easy. I think you're going to like this recipe and I think any kids you have around will enjoy making and eating it, too.

1 3/4 CUPS UNBLEACHED WHITE FLOUR OR WHITE WHOLE-WHEAT FLOUR (SEE TIP)

◇ ◇ ◇ ◇ ◇ ◇

1 CUP CHICKPEA FLOUR (BESAN OR CHANNA FLOUR) OR
FULL-FAT SOY FLOUR
1/2 TEASPOON SALT
FRESHLY GROUND BLACK PEPPER, OPTIONAL
1 1/2 CUPS NONDAIRY MILK

1. Combine the flours, salt, and pepper, if using, and whisk together in a small bowl. Pour the milk into a medium bowl and whisk in the flour mixture until smooth. It should be like a thick pancake batter. (Add a bit of water if it's too thick.) Beat it until it gets kind of "gluey." This is to develop the gluten. Now, cover it and let it rest for about 30 minutes.

2. When you are ready to cook the spaetzle, have the large pot of water boiling and whatever apparatus you are going to use to make the spaetzle (see sidebar). Place some batter into the receptacle and slide, turn or push the batter through the holes, depending on which kind you are using.

Spaetzle Makers

You will need a spaetzle maker to make the drop noodle recipe. You can improvise by laying a flat rough (large-holed) grater across the top of the pot of boiling water and pushing the batter through the holes into the pot with a plastic dough scraper. If you have a food mill (mouli), you can use that to push the batter through the medium or large-holed plate. Another option is a potato ricer, which will push the batter through the holes into the pot, making somewhat longer noodles. You can buy an inexpensive sliding spaetzle maker, or the round type (with a handle) that is dotted with holes and fits on top of the pot – you push the batter through the holes with a dough scraper – at many cookware shops or online.

As soon as the spaetzle float to the top, scoop them out with a slotted spoon into a colander and continue until all of your batter is used up.

SERVING SUGGESTIONS

The simplest way to serve them is coated with melted vegan margarine (it can be a whipped or lower-fat variety) or a tasty oil and serve plain with a vegan stew or hearty sauce. You can sauté them a little in the margarine or oil, or let them cool and use them in a casserole, as you might with ordinary pasta. You can bake them with vegan cheese. Let your imagination take flight with these "little sparrows." I like to combine spaetzle with hearty fall and winter vegetables and fruits, such as apples, pears, and parsnips, as in the recipe for Whole-Grain Spaetzle with Browned Parsnips, page 162.

TIPS

- To measure flour: Lightly spoon the flour directly into the measuring cup from the container or bag. Do not shake the cup or pack the flour down.

- You can substitute 1 1/2 cups white whole-wheat pastry flour plus 1/4 cup semolina flour for white or regular whole-wheat flour

- Experiment with adding herbs to the batter or using pureed cooked vegetables in place of some of the milk.

Sicilian Winter Squash with Mint and Garlic

SICILY

Serves 4 to 6   GF, SF, <30

This traditional recipe was meant for Italian pumpkin, zucca, which actually closely resembles our butternut or Hubbard squash, so use whichever one you prefer. I have cut down considerably on the amount of oil that is used in Sicily for this recipe. It was received with great enthusiasm by my guests.

- 1/4 CUP OLIVE OIL
- 9 CLOVES GARLIC, CRUSHED
- 1 1/2 POUNDS BUTTERNUT OR HUBBARD SQUASH, PEELED AND SLICED ABOUT 1/4-INCH THICK
- 4 1/2 TEASPOONS SUGAR
- 3 TABLESPOONS RED WINE VINEGAR
- SALT AND FRESHLY GROUND BLACK PEPPER
- 4 OR 5 TEASPOONS CHOPPED FRESH MINT

1. In a large nonstick skillet, heat the olive oil over medium-high heat. Add the garlic and brown lightly – be careful not to burn it. Remove the garlic immediately and set it aside.

2. Add the squash to the same skillet and brown it in the oil, stirring constantly with a spatula. Increase the heat a bit if necessary. Add the lightly-browned garlic back to the skillet, along with the sugar and vinegar. Bring to a boil and stir while you cook it down to a syrup, about 2 or 3 minutes. Arrange the squash on a platter, season with salt and pepper to taste, and sprinkle with the mint. This dish can be served hot or at room temperature.

Whole-Grain Spaetzle with Browned Parsnips

Serves 4   SF

This is a lovely side dish that is excellent served with a vegan meatloaf or hearty, savory bean dish.

- 1/2 RECIPE VEGAN SPAETZLE (PAGE 160), USING WHOLE-WHEAT FLOUR INSTEAD OF WHITE, COOKED AND DRAINED
- 3 CUPS PEELED PARSNIPS, CUT INTO 1/2 TO 1/4-INCH DICE
- 1 CUP CHICKEN-STYLE VEGAN BROTH (PAGE 2)
- 1/4 CUP MEDIUM OR DRY SHERRY
- 1/2 TEASPOON DRIED THYME LEAVES
- 1/2 TEASPOON DRIED ROSEMARY
- SALT AND FRESHLY GROUND BLACK PEPPER
- 1 TABLESPOON VEGAN MARGARINE

1. Set aside the cooked and drained spaetzle. Lightly oil a large nonstick skillet. Add the diced parsnips and cook until browned, over high heat. Add a spray of water when necessary to keep from sticking. Keep them moving with a spatula.

2. When the parsnips are browned, add the broth, sherry, thyme, and rosemary. Cover the pan and turn heat to medium. Let the parsnips cook until most of the broth is absorbed. Reduce the heat to low. Stir in the margarine and season with salt and pepper to taste.

3. Pour hot water over the drained, cooked spaetzle and drain again. Add to the skillet with the parsnips and stir gently. Heat through and serve.

Sweets from the Global Oven

It's funny – even though I have baked cakes, cookies, and pies for my family for years, and no one ever complained, I never considered myself a very good dessert baker. Breads, yes, but cakes, pies, and cookies? Well, I could follow a recipe. Now that I look back, I realize that although my mother was an excellent cook, she rarely baked. Baking out of cookbooks from a young age, I never developed the confidence of a truly experienced baker.

Oddly enough, it was with vegan baking that I gained my confidence. The rules were different (nonexistent when I started!) and so were many of the ingredients. I had to find my own way, discover food science, and begin many recipes from the ground up. This is how I "found my feet." So, truly, if I can do it, you can do it – and maybe even take it to the next level!

Desserts may not be the most important part of our diets, but they certainly are the most appreciated. My philosophy is, "Don't eat sweets often, but when you do, make them worth every calorie!" I hope you'll agree that every recipe in this small sampling of international and fusion treats is worth the calories.

One of our favorites from this chapter is the Almond Café Latte Cake, which I developed for my son Tim. He's not a dessert fan, so I wanted something special, but not too sweet. It's the one cake he really likes, and I make it often for birthdays. It seems to be foolproof, with a tender, light crumb to the cake and just enough chocolate to satisfy (coffee is the primary flavor).

From the humble but delicious Blueberry-Maple Poor Man's Pudding, a jazzed up version of a "pudding-cake" my husband grew up with, to vegan South American "Three Milks" Cake, to the versatile Vegan Sponge Cake, and much more, I'm hopeful that you'll discover some recipes here that can become your own family favorites.

Sweets from the Global Oven

Soft Molasses Cookies

Eastern U.S.A./Canada

Makes 5 dozen   SF

The heady sweet scent of molasses, cinnamon, ginger, and allspice heralds the winter holiday season like nothing else. These soft, chewy cookies are an old East Coast favorite, but we appreciate them out West, too, especially the vegan variety! Do not use regular whole-wheat flour, or the cookies may be tough.

1 CUP VEGAN MARGARINE
1 CUP SUGAR OR BROWN SUGAR
1 CUP MOLASSES (ANY KIND)
4 CUPS WHOLE-WHEAT PASTRY FLOUR
1/2 TEASPOON SALT
1 TABLESPOON GROUND CINNAMON
1 TABLESPOON GROUND GINGER
1 TABLESPOON GROUND ALLSPICE
1 TABLESPOON BAKING SODA DISSOLVED IN 1/4 CUP WATER

1. Preheat the oven to 375°F. In a large bowl or the bowl of a stand mixer, cream together the margarine and sugar, then blend in the molasses. In a separate bowl, sift together the flour, salt, cinnamon, ginger, and allspice. Add the dissolved soda to the wet mixture, then add the wet mixture to the dry mixture, stirring to mix well. Chill the dough until it is easy to roll out.

2. Roll out dough on a floured surface to 1/4-inch thickness. Cut out with a 2 1/2-inch round cutter. Arrange the cookies on nonstick or greased baking sheets (any size) and bake for 8 to 10 minutes or until the tops spring back when touched lightly. Cool on racks; store in a tightly-covered container after thoroughly cooled.

Flour for Cakes and Pastries

Important – Please read before you start!

I use pastry flour (white or whole-wheat) in much of my non-yeast baking because fat coats the gluten and makes it more tender, but I prefer to use only moderate amounts of fat in baking, if possible. Pastry flour, made from soft wheat, has a lower gluten content than either all-purpose flour or bread flour, so you can use less fat and still have a tender product.

In this chapter, when I call for "unbleached white flour" or "whole-wheat flour," I am referring to "all-purpose flour," which contains 9 to 12 percent gluten (wheat protein) in the USA (13 percent in Canada). But, if I call for "pastry flour" (either white or whole-wheat) be sure that pastry flour (or "cake flour" or "cake and pastry flour") is what you use, or the recipe may not turn out as you expect. American cake flour is typically 7-9 percent protein; pastry flour ranges from 9-10 percent. British cake and pastry flour also ranges from 7-10 percent. In Australia, cake and/or pastry flour is apparently hard to come by, but plain flour (all-purpose) is only in the range of 7-10 percent, so it should work in recipes that call for pastry flour. Read your labels. For a handy chart of different types of flour and protein contents in Europe, check out the King Arthur flour website.

Tip: *Do not use* self-rising flour in these recipes, as it contains salt and leavenings.

Important for All Baking: To measure flour correctly, you need calibrated measuring cups made for measuring dry ingredients. Do not use a coffee cup or drinking glass. For consistent results, lightly spoon the flour directly into the measuring cup from the container or bag. Do not shake the cup and don't pack the flour down.

Swedish Ginger Balls

Pepparkakor

SWEDEN

Makes 7 dozen   SF

There are many versions of these traditional spicy cookies – feel free to use the spice combination that you prefer. "Peppar" is Swedish for pepper, which provides additional "bite." These are often made as a very thin rolled cookie, but I prefer them this way. Note: Do not use regular whole-wheat flour, or the cookies may be tough.

- 1 CUP VEGAN MARGARINE
- 1 CUP SUGAR OR BROWN SUGAR, PLUS MORE TO COAT COOKIES
- 1 CUP MOLASSES (ANY KIND)
- 3 1/2 CUPS WHOLE-WHEAT PASTRY FLOUR
- 1 TEASPOON BAKING SODA
- 1/2 TEASPOON SALT
- 1 TEASPOON GROUND CINNAMON
- 1 TEASPOON GROUND GINGER
- 3/4 TEASPOON FRESHLY GROUND BLACK PEPPER
- 1/2 TEASPOON GROUND CLOVES
- 1/2 TEASPOON FRESHLY GROUND NUTMEG
- 1/2 TEASPOON GROUND ALLSPICE
- 1/4 TEASPOON GROUND CARDAMOM

1. Preheat the oven to 350°F. In a large bowl or the bowl of a stand mixer, cream together the margarine and sugar, then blend in the molasses. In a bowl, sift together the flour, baking soda, salt, and spices. Add to the molasses mixture and mix well. Chill the dough until it is easy to roll out.

2. Roll the chilled dough into walnut-sized balls. Coat the balls in sugar before baking. Arrange on nonstick or greased baking sheets and bake for 12 to 15 minutes. Cool the cookies on the baking sheets for 1 minute, then transfer to racks to cool. Store in airtight containers after thoroughly cooling.

Lemon-Ginger Pistachio Biscotti

ITALY

Makes about 20 biscotti   SF

Who can resist the lure of a buttery, lemon-scented biscotti studded with candied ginger and pistachios; or a biscotti perfumed with orange zest and bursting with jewel-colored cranberries and toasty pecans? Not me! I make these twice-baked treats every Christmas, but you don't have to wait for the holidays to enjoy

---

Cookie Baking in Batches

It's not advisable to place cookie dough on hot baking sheets, but what do you do if you have only 2 baking sheets, and you're baking lots of cookies? I took the advice of baking guru Sarah Phillips of baking911.com. While the first batch of cookies is baking, shape the dough for the second batch in advance on baking parchment cut the same size as your sheet. This means that you don't have to clean the baking sheets before reusing them, and the second batch of cookies won't stick to the sheet or spread too much. Place sheets of baking parchment on upside-down baking sheets or on large pieces of cardboard to keep the cookies from bending. Shape the cookies and refrigerate or freeze until needed. You don't need to thaw the cookies before baking. When one batch of cookies is done, just slide the parchment off the baking sheet onto a cooling rack and let the sheets cool. When it's cool, slide a new batch of cookies, with the parchment they are resting on, onto the baking sheets and bake.

---

them with coffee, tea, hot cocoa, or wine.

These biscotti are larger, a little richer, and more "buttery" than the biscotti in my book, Nonna's Italian Kitchen. *They are scrumptious on their own, whereas the drier biscotti are best when dunked into one of the above-mentioned beverages. When the biscotti are completely cooled, you can sift a little confectioners' sugar over them, if you like.* **Note:** *Do not use regular whole-wheat flour or the biscotti will be tough.*

1 1/2 CUPS WHOLE-WHEAT PASTRY FLOUR
1 1/2 CUPS UNBLEACHED WHITE FLOUR
1 TABLESPOON BAKING POWDER
1/2 TEASPOON SALT
1 1/2 CUPS SUGAR
3/4 CUP SMOOTH UNSWEETENED APPLESAUCE
1/4 CUP MELTED VEGAN MARGARINE
1 TEASPOON PURE VANILLA EXTRACT
FINELY GRATED ZEST OF 2 MEDIUM ORGANIC LEMONS
1 1/2 CUPS WHOLE SHELLED UNSALTED PISTACHIOS
3/4 CUP CHOPPED CANDIED GINGER (ORGANIC, IF POSSIBLE)

1. Preheat the oven to 325°F. Line a 12 x 17-inch baking sheet with baking parchment cut to fit.

2. In a large bowl, whisk together both flours, baking powder, and salt. In a medium bowl, whisk together the sugar, applesauce, margarine, and vanilla. Stir the wet mixture into the dry mixture, along with the lemon zest, pistachios, and ginger. Mix thoroughly with a wooden spoon.

3. With floured hands, shape the dough into one 6-inch-wide "log," about 3/4-inch thick, with the ends squared off. Place this log on the lined baking sheet. Bake for 25 minutes. Remove the pan from the oven to a cooling rack and reduce the oven heat to 300°F.

4. Cool the log on the rack for 15 minutes. Cut the log carefully with a sharp knife straight across into 1/2-inch-wide slices. Place the slices cut-side-down on the baking sheet (you can re-use the parchment). Bake the slices for 10 minutes or until just golden on the bottom. Turn the slices over and bake 10 minutes longer or

until golden on the bottom. Transfer the biscotti to cooling racks. Store the biscotti in an airtight container for up to two weeks (or freeze them in tightly-sealed rigid freezer containers).

VARIATION

Cranberry-Orange-Pecan: For this version, add the following ingredients instead of the lemon zest, pistachios, and ginger:

FINELY GRATED ZEST OF 1 LARGE ORGANIC ORANGE OR 2 MEDIUM ORGANIC ORANGES
1 1/2 CUPS CHOPPED TOASTED PECANS
1 CUP DRIED CRANBERRIES

Tip: Using baking parchment keeps these biscotti from burning, which is a danger because of the generous dried fruit content.

ANZAC Biscuits

AUSTRALIA/NEW ZEALAND

Makes 24 cookies   SF, GFO

Both New Zealand and Australia claim these popular brown sugar oat cookies, or biscuits, as they are called, with the tropical crunch of coconut as their own. I provide the option of replacing the traditional golden syrup (a type of cane syrup that's hard to find in the U.S.A.) with agave nectar, and I use less fat, unsweetened coconut, and whole-wheat pastry flour for a more nutritious cookie. This is a perfect recipe to try with gluten-free flour mixes and gluten-free oats. We love these cookies! They are tasty enough for a holiday cookie (especially with ruby-red dried cranberries added), but easy and inexpensive enough to serve as an everyday tea or nondairy milk dunker.

Note: *Do not use regular whole-wheat flour, or the cookies may be tough.*

1 CUP OLD-FASHIONED ROLLED OATS
1 CUP WHOLE-WHEAT PASTRY FLOUR OR GLUTEN-FREE

FLOUR MIX

1 CUP PACKED BROWN SUGAR

1/2 CUP SHREDDED UNSWEETENED COCONUT

1/2 TEASPOON BAKING SODA

1/4 CUP MELTED VEGAN MARGARINE

3 TABLESPOON WATER

2 TABLESPOONS AGAVE NECTAR OR GOLDEN SYRUP

1. Preheat oven to 325°F. In a bowl, combine the oats, flour, sugar, coconut, and baking soda and stir to mix well. Add the margarine, water, and agave nectar. Stir well and then mix with your hands.

2. Form level tablespoons of dough into balls and place them 2 inches apart on two 10 x 15-inch baking sheets, either nonstick or lined with baking parchment cut to fit. Flatten the balls with the flat bottom of a glass which has been dipped in cold water.

3. Bake the cookies for 12 minutes or until the cookies are almost set. Remove the baking sheets from the oven to racks and let stand for 2 to 3 minutes or until the cookies firm up. Place the cookies on wire racks to cool completely. They keep for several weeks in airtight containers.

Variation

Holiday version: add 1/2 cup chopped dried cranberries, chopped mixed dried fruits, or dried cherries to the dry ingredients.

The ANZAC Biscuit Story

ANZAC Biscuits (cookies) are similar to many older British biscuit recipes that are designed to produce crisp, hard, and nutritious cookies that keep well. These were known as Soldiers' Biscuits (thousands were sent to the front by loving mothers, wives, and sisters), but after the Gallipoli landings in 1915, they became known as ANZAC Biscuits. (ANZAC is the acronym for Australian and New Zealand Army Corps.)

The traditional ANZAC Biscuit is hard and flat – ideal for dunking into hot tea. Over the years, the cookies have become softer and chewier. ANZAC biscuits are quite popular here in Canada and in other parts of the Commonwealth, and they are so good that they deserve to be better-known in the U.S.A. ANZAC Biscuits have always been egg-free, by the way. This may be because eggs were in short supply during the First World War.

Grown-Up Nanaimo Bars

CANADA

Makes 30 squares   SFO, GFO

If you are Canadian or live near the Canadian border, you already know about sweet, gooey, coconut-and-chocolate-laden Nanaimo Bars! I have always found them too sweet, so I developed this "grown-up" vegan Nanaimo Bar recipe. The addition of the cocoa nibs in the base gives the bars extra crunch and a slightly bitter edge that counteracts the sweetness. Dark chocolate ganache and coffee liqueur add the "grown-up" elements. I also cut the fat content and use flax seed as an egg replacer, which adds more nutrients. No one notices the nutrition, though – they are too busy oohing and ahhing over the contrasting flavors and textures!

Base:

1/4 CUP WATER

1 TABLESPOON FLAX SEED

1/3 CUP VEGAN MARGARINE

1/4 CUP BROWN SUGAR

2 1/2 TABLESPOONS AGAVE NECTAR, MAPLE SYRUP, OR BROWN RICE SYRUP

5 TABLESPOONS UNSWEETENED COCOA POWDER

1 TEASPOON PURE VANILLA EXTRACT

2 CUPS VEGAN GRAHAM CRACKER CRUMBS (SEE PAGE 170)

1/2 CUP UNSWEETENED SHREDDED COCONUT

1/2 CUP CHOPPED ROASTED COCOA NIBS (SEE NOTE)

1/2 CUP CHOPPED WALNUTS OR ALMONDS, TOASTED

Filling:

1/2 CUP VEGAN MASCARPONE OR SOY-FREE CREAM
   CHEESE-MASCARPONE (PAGE 202), OR VEGAN CREAM
   CHEESE

2 TABLESPOONS VEGAN MARGARINE

2 TABLESPOONS PLAIN BIRD'S CUSTARD POWDER OR
   CORNSTARCH

1 TABLESPOON COFFEE LIQUEUR OR COFFEE-FLAVORED
   ITALIAN SYRUP (PAGE 171)

1/4 TABLESPOON PURE VANILLA

2 CUPS CONFECTIONERS' SUGAR

Ganache Topping:

4 OUNCES VEGAN SEMISWEET CHOCOLATE, ROUGHLY
   CHOPPED, OR CHOCOLATE CHIPS (2/3 CUP)

1/3 CUP NONDAIRY MILK

1/4 CUP EXTRA-FIRM SILKEN TOFU

1 TABLESPOON LIQUID ESPRESSO, COFFEE LIQUEUR, OR
   COFFEE-FLAVORED ITALIAN SYRUP

1. **Base:** Process the water and flax seed in a blender until it is thick and foamy. Set aside.

2. In a saucepan over low heat, combine the margarine, brown sugar, syrup, cocoa, and flax seed mixture. Stir until the consistency is thick and custard-like. Stir in the vanilla. Set aside.

3. In a medium bowl, combine the graham cracker crumbs, coconut, cocoa nibs, and nuts. Add to the mixture in the saucepan, and mix well. Pack the mixture into an oiled 9-inch square cake pan lined with baking parchment cut to fit. Set aside.

4. **Filling:** Cream together the mascarpone, margarine, custard powder, liqueur, and vanilla. Add the confectioners' sugar. Beat until it is creamy, then spread it over the crumb base. Refrigerate until the filling has set, at least 30 minutes.

5. **Ganache Topping:** Process the chocolate finely in a dry food processor. Leave the chocolate in the processor. Whip the nondairy milk and tofu together in a blender or with an immersion/stick blender in a deep, narrow container until smooth – this is the vegan cream.

6. Heat the vegan cream in the top of a double

The Origin of Nanaimo Bars

These popular no-bake bars originated in the 1950s in the city of Nanaimo, just an hour south of where I live on Vancouver Island (and where celebs Diana Krall and Kim Cattrall were born). As popular legend has it, a local housewife submitted the recipe with the name "Nanaimo Bars" to a magazine for a recipe contest. Her recipe won, giving it substantial publicity. It made its way throughout the province's communities. The earliest confirmed printed copy of the recipe "Nanaimo Bars" appears in a publication entitled "His/Hers Favorite Recipes," compiled by the Women's Association of the Brechin United Church, in the 1950s. Nanaimo Bars are a must at many a dessert table during the winter holiday season.

boiler over simmering water until almost to the boiling point. Alternatively, you can cook the cream in a microwave-safe bowl for about 1 minute at 50 % power or until it is very hot, but not boiling. (If the mixture curdles, blend it again until smooth.)

7. With the motor running, pour the hot cream into the chocolate in the food processor through the feed tube. Process until smooth. Add the liqueur and process again briefly. When the ganache mixture has cooled slightly, but is still pourable, spread it evenly over the chilled filling. Refrigerate until the ganache is solid.

8. To serve: Score the ganache with a very sharp knife into 30 squares and then cut the squares all the way to the bottom of the pan. Loosen the squares along the sides of the pan with a table knife. The bars will keep refrigerated for a month (well-covered).

Soy-Free Ganache: Omit the tofu and nondairy milk and use 1/2 cup coconut nondairy creamer or nut milk instead.)

Note: Cocoa nibs are simply broken or crushed pieces of cocoa beans. Traditionally, the beans are roasted, cracked and de-shelled. Cocoa nibs are the dry-roasted pieces of the cocoa bean, and they are labeled as "roasted." Raw cocoa nibs are made from cocoa beans which have gone through the fermentation process (which precedes drying and roasting) and are dried and then peel and crushed.

Vegan Graham Crackers

Some bulk graham cracker crumbs are vegan – check the label or ask your grocer to let you see the original bag. The following are vegan:

- Keebler Original and Cinnamon Graham Crackers (but not their graham crumbs)
- Murray Cinnamon Grahams
- Nabisco Original Graham Crackers
- Nabisco Teddy Grahams (Chocolate and Cinnamon)
- Kinnikinnick Foods S'moreable Graham-Style Crackers (gluten-free)

Health Valley makes three kinds of vegan graham crackers:

- Original Oat Bran Graham Crackers
- Original Amaranth Bran Graham Crackers
- Original Rice Bran Graham Crackers (gluten-free)

Peruvian Caramel-Filled Pastries

Alfajores

PERU

Makes 30   SFO

Think of meltingly delicious caramel-y filling sandwiched between rounds of ultra-tender, flaky pastry, with a generous dusting of confectioners' sugar, and you have traditional alfajores (pronounced ahl-fah-hor-ays). These delicate sweet pastries are served at every special occasion in Peru. I only make alfajores once or twice a year, which makes them a much-anticipated treat! The traditional pastry is made with lard and eggs and the sweet, golden filling is "manjar blanco" (mahn-har blahn-ko), which my aunts made by boiling a can of sweetened condensed milk for three hours! This produced a creamy caramel which is known as dulce de leche everywhere else in Latin America. This recipe is a wonderfully sweet way to introduce vegan Peruvian cuisine. To ensure tender pastry, do not use all-purpose white or whole-wheat flour.

"Manjar Blanco" Filling:
1 1/3 CUPS BROWN RICE SYRUP (HALF OF A 22-OUNCE JAR; SEE TIP)
1/4 CUP BROWN SUGAR
2 TABLESPOONS SOY OR RICE PROTEIN POWDER
Flaky Pastry:
1 1/4 CUPS WHITE PASTRY FLOUR
1 1/4 CUPS WHOLE-WHEAT PASTRY FLOUR
1/2 TEASPOON BAKING POWDER
1/2 CUP FROZEN VEGAN MARGARINE, CUT INTO SMALL PIECES
1/2 CUP VERY COLD NON-HYDROGENATED VEGETABLE SHORTENING, CUT INTO SMALL PIECES
1/2 TABLESPOON ENER-G EGG REPLACER POWDER OR OR-GRAN "NO EGG" (SEE PAGE 15)
1 TABLESPOON WATER
1/4 CUP COLD WATER OR 3 1/2 TABLESPOONS WATER PLUS 1/2 TABLESPOON PISCO (PERUVIAN GRAPE BRANDY) OR BRANDY OR WHITE RUM
1/8 TEASPOON SALT
To assemble:
1 CUP CONFECTIONERS' SUGAR

1. **Filling:** In a mixing bowl, combine the brown rice syrup and brown sugar, stirring until the sugar has dissolved, then stir in the protein powder until the mixture is smooth. Cover and refrigerate until it has thickened.

2. **Pastry:** Sift the flours and baking powder together in a medium bowl. Add the frozen margarine and cold shortening pieces. Use your fingertips to gently work the margarine into the flour mixture until the mixture resembles breadcrumbs. Mix together the egg replacer, water, brandy, if using, and salt and stir it into the flour mixture. You want a fairly soft dough – add more (very cold) water by the drop if necessary. It should be like soft pie dough. Divide the dough in half and gently shape into two discs. Wrap each disc in plastic wrap and refrigerate at least 1 hour or up to 2 days.

3. When you are ready to make the alfajores, remove one disc of pastry from the refrigerator. Let it sit at room temperature for 5 to 10 minutes in order to soften just enough to make rolling out a bit easier. Roll out the dough with a rolling pin on a work surface covered with a lightly-floured sheet of baking parchment, to about 1/8-inch thick. As you roll out the dough, check to see if the dough is sticking to the parchment at all. If necessary, add a few sprinkles of flour underneath the dough, but avoid using too much flour.

4. Preheat oven to 400°F. Cut the dough into circles with a 2-inch round cookie cutter. Carefully transfer the rounds (should be about 30) to two 12 x 17-inch baking sheets lined with baking parchment cut to fit and prick them all over with a fork. Refrigerate the first batch of pastry rounds while you repeat the procedure with the remaining disc of dough. (See the sidebar on page 166 for how to handle the dough if you only have 2 12 x 17-inch baking sheets.) You should end up with 60 circles. Bake the pastries in two batches for about 6 minutes or until pale golden. Thoroughly cool the pastries on the baking sheets on cooling racks.

5. **To assemble:** Spread the flat side of 30 of the rounds with a little of the chilled "manjar blanco" filling. Don't use too much filling or it will ooze out the sides when you sandwich it between two of the pastry circles. Cover with the remaining 30 rounds (flat side down). Dredge the little "sandwiches" in confectioners' sugar in a flat dish, covering them completely with confectioners' sugar.

6. Place the alfajores on cooling racks placed over two 12 x 17-inch baking sheets until serving time, at which time you can transfer them to serving platters. Alfajores will keep in the refrigerator for 3 days or in the freezer in rigid containers for 3 months.

Tip: If using a 22 ounce jar of brown rice syrup, here's an easy way to measure what you need: Microwave the jar (with the lid removed!) at 50 percent power for 1 to 2 minutes. Alternatively, place the jar in a deep bowl of hot water, until the syrup very warm and pourable. Measure out half the jar of syrup into a small bowl.

Italian Flavored Syrups

Italian syrups, which are used to make special coffees and Italian sodas, make a great non-alcoholic substitute for liqueurs, adding concentrated flavor where it's needed. Monin or Torani are two premium brands, with over 100 flavors and 80 flavors, respectively. Look for these syrups in well-stocked supermarkets, gourmet groceries, or online.

Pecan Pie

U.S.A.

Serves 8   SF

I have always loved real pecan pie. The sweet, clear custard (a variant of the old English "Chess Pie," filled with a "custard" of beaten eggs, sugar, and butter) contrasting with the flaky crust and richly toasty pecans always seemed to me to be the epitome of the word "treat." But I wasn't satisfied with my old vegan pecan pie recipe – it was too sweet and it was unreliable – sometimes it set and sometimes it didn't! I developed a new version that is reliable, but has the customary taste, texture, and look of a real pecan pie, without eggs or even egg replacer; without lots of fat; and also without corn syrup. I believe I came up with a keeper! Serve with your favorite vanilla vegan "ice cream" or whipped topping, such as Almond Crème Whipped Topping (page 207), Soyatoo Whippable Soy Topping Cream, or soy-free MimicCreme Healthy Top.

1 (9-INCH) PIE CRUST, UNBAKED (FOR LOW-FAT PIE DOUGH, PAGE 173), OR YOUR FAVORITE

SWEETENER OF CHOICE: 3/4 CUP WATER PLUS 3/4 CUP SUGAR PLUS 1/2 CUP BROWN SUGAR; OR 1 1/2 CUPS MAPLE SYRUP (CHOOSE ONE OPTION)

3/4 CUP WATER

1/4 CUP CORNSTARCH

1/4 CUP PLUS 1/2 TABLESPOON COLD WATER

PINCH SALT

2 TABLESPOONS VEGAN MARGARINE

1 TEASPOON PURE VANILLA EXTRACT

1 TO 2 CUPS TOASTED, UNSALTED PECAN HALVES

1. Preheat the oven to 400°F. Pierce the pie crust all over with the tines of a fork and pre-bake it for 3 minutes. Remove from the oven to a rack.

2. In a medium saucepan, combine the sweetener (either the water/sugar mixture or the maple syrup) with the second 3/4 cup water. Bring to a boil and boil it for 5 minutes. Dissolve the cornstarch in the 1/4 cup plus 1/2 tablespoon of cold water and add to the sweet mixture along with the salt, whisking vigorously. Cook, stirring, over high heat just until the mixture thickens and looks clear. Remove the saucepan from the heat and stir in the margarine and vanilla, stirring until the margarine has melted. The mixture will still be fairly liquid.

3. Pour the mixture into the pre-baked pie shell. Arrange the pecan halves on top, pressing them down into the mixture a little. Place the pie in the middle of the oven and immediately reduce the heat to 350°F. Bake for 30 minutes. The filling will still be "jiggly"– don't worry! It will set as it cools. Cool the pie on a rack for about 1 1/2 hours, then refrigerate until thoroughly cooled and set.

VARIATIONS

• **For Quebec "Sugar Pie"** (Maple Syrup Pie): Use the maple syrup and use lightly-toasted walnuts or no nuts at all.

• Instead of pecans, use roasted salted mixed nuts, roasted salted macadamia nuts or toasted shredded or flaked coconut.

- **For a "Spiked" Pecan Pie:** Use rum, bourbon, or Jack Daniels instead of the 1/4 cup plus 1/2 tablespoon water used to dissolve the cornstarch for the filling.

Tip: See page 211 for how to toast nuts, seeds, and coconut.

Low-Fat Pie Dough

Makes 1 crust   SFO, <30

This crust contains about half the fat of ordinary pie pastry dough. I use oil, rather than solid shortening, and half whole-wheat flour. I have used this crust for many years and is the only pie crust that doesn't give my husband indigestion! The pastry flour and non-dairy "buttermilk" make a tender, crispy crust, rather than a flaky one, but I have never heard complaints. The recipe can be doubled or tripled, etc., as needed. Do not use regular whole-wheat flour or it will be tough.

1/2 CUP UNBLEACHED WHITE FLOUR
7 TABLESPOONS WHOLE-WHEAT PASTRY FLOUR
3 TABLESPOONS SOY, HEMP OR NUT MILK
1/2 TEASPOON LEMON JUICE OR CIDER VINEGAR
3 TABLESPOONS OIL (OLIVE OIL FOR SAVORY PIES; CANOLA OR SUNFLOWER FOR SWEET PIES)
3/8 TEASPOON SALT
3/8 TEASPOON BAKING POWDER
3/8 TEASPOON SUGAR

Mix the 2 flours together in a medium bowl with the salt, baking powder and sugar. In a small cup, mix together the nondairy milk with the lemon juice or vinegar. Whisk in the oil until it is emulsified (you can't see any oil globules). Pour this mixture into the dry ingredients and mix the dough gently with a fork until it holds together in a ball. (If it's too dry, sprinkle with a tiny bit of water.) If you have time, place the dough in a plastic bag and refrigerate it for 30 minutes to an hour before rolling out. Roll out and bake the pastry as you would an ordinary crust.

Tip: Roll the dough out on a lightly floured sheet of baking parchment – it never sticks!

Italian Pear Tart

Crostata di Pere

ITALY

Serves 12   SF

A perfect autumn dessert – fresh, sweet pears and jam in a crunchy corn pastry. The pears and corn crust are perfect together, and it's not overly sweet or heavy after a big meal. My choice to accompany this tart would be a vanilla, pecan, or almond vegan ice cream. This is a very simple dessert to make, so you can make it the morning of the day you serve it. You need a 14-inch pizza pan for this recipe.

CORN FLOUR PASTRY FOR A DOUBLE CRUST (SEE PAGE 174)
5 FIRM SWEET PEARS, PEELED AND SLICED ABOUT 3/8-INCH THICK
1/3 CUP SUGAR
2 TABLESPOONS FRESH LEMON JUICE
1/2 CUP PEACH OR APRICOT JAM

1. Roll out all of the pastry into a 15-inch circle. Transfer it carefully to a 14-inch pizza pan and flute the edges. Refrigerate the crust until you have prepared the pears. Preheat the oven to 350°F.

2. Place the pear slices in a large bowl. In a small bowl, combine the sugar and lemon juice, stirring to dissolve, then pour over the pear slices. Use your hands to gently toss the sugar mixture with the pears, so that the pear slices do not break. Cover and set aside for 30 minutes.

3. Carefully transfer the pears to a colander, with a large bowl under it to catch the juice.

4. When the pears have drained thoroughly, combine the juice with the jam and press the mixture through a sieve. Set aside.

5. Arrange the pear slices in concentric circles over the pastry in an attractive pattern. Spread the jam mixture evenly over the pears. Bake the tart for about 25 minutes or until the pastry is golden and the pears are tender. Cool on a rack. Serve at room temperature.

Corn Flour Pastry

Makes one crust   SFO

*This is a version of the Low-Fat Pie Dough on page 173. I was playing around with corn flour in various low-fat recipes to add a "buttery" taste, and it occurred to me that it might be a taste-enhancer in pastry made with oil. Since corn contains no gluten, I wondered if, mixed with some regular wheat flour, it might also make a tender pastry. It succeeded on both counts! Although this crust does contain fat, it has about half that of ordinary pastry, and it uses oil rather than solid fat. I tried using pastry flour instead of the all-purpose flour in this recipe, but it was very hard to handle – not enough gluten, is my guess. Even so, this dough is a little harder to handle than the all-wheat version, but it works fine if you chill it before rolling and roll it between two sheets of baking parchment. (**Note:** To make a double crust, simply double the ingredients.)*

1/2 CUP UNBLEACHED WHITE FLOUR (DO NOT USE CAKE OR
    PASTRY FLOUR)
1/2 CUP CORN FLOUR (SEE SIDEBAR)
3 TABLESPOONS VEGETABLE OIL
3 TABLESPOONS SOY, HEMP, OR NUT MILK
1/2 TEASPOON LEMON JUICE OR VINEGAR
3/8 TEASPOON SALT
3/8 TEASPOON BAKING POWDER
3/8 TEASPOON SUGAR

1. Mix the 2 flours together in a medium bowl with the salt, baking powder and sugar. In a small cup, mix together the nondairy milk with the lemon juice or vinegar. Whisk in the oil until it is emulsified (you can't see any oil globules). Pour this mixture into the dry ingredients and mix the dough gently with a fork until it holds together in a ball. (If it's too dry, sprinkle with water by the drop.) Transfer the dough to a zipper-lock bag and refrigerate it for at least an hour before rolling out (you can refrigerate it overnight).

2. Roll it out as for ordinary pastry (about 1/8-inch thick) between 2 sheets of baking parchment for easy handling. Flour the parchment lightly as necessary. If cracks appear, smooth them together with damp fingers, pressing firmly. (If you are using a pie pan to bake a tart, bring the pastry to the inside edge of the pan and flute the edge inside the pan, not on the rim like an American pie, to make a shallow shell.) Trim the top edge neatly. Flute the edge with your fingers

About Corn Flour

Corn flour is very finely ground yellow cornmeal. Corn flour is not the same as cornstarch (confusingly, what we call "cornstarch" in North America is referred to as "corn flour" in the U.K.). Corn flour creates a pale yellow "buttery" or "egg-y" color in the finished product that is much more appetizing than using turmeric for color (which tends to have a greenish cast). Corn flour also contributes a "buttery" flavor and has more nutritive value than cornstarch. It blends to a creamy smooth texture after it's cooked in liquid and then blended with more liquid. You can also create soy-free vegan sauces and spreads using corn flour. Corn flour mixtures also cook well in the microwave. It is usually available in the Asian or Indian section of well-stocked supermarkets, in Asian or Indian markets, and natural food stores.

To make your own corn flour, grind the finest yellow cornmeal you can find in a clean, dry coffee/spice mill until it is powdery (this is important). If you own an electric grain mill, grind yellow cornmeal on the finest setting (I had to run it through mine twice).

or press down with the tines of a fork. Bake according to the recipe instructions for the pie.

Note: The recipe for one crust will make 12 small tart shells (cut 4-inch circles). To bake unfilled shells, pierce the bottoms of the shells with a fork and bake at 425°F for 8 to 10 minutes.

3. To pre-bake or bake "blind" an unfilled crust, preheat the oven to 425°F. Prick the bottom and sides of the crust with a fork. Place a square of aluminium foil over the dough and weight it down with a layer of dried beans. Bake for 6 minutes. Remove beans and foil and bake 8 minutes more. Cool the pastry on a rack.

VARIATION

Sweet Crust: For one crust, use 2 tablespoons sugar and add 1/2 teaspoon pure lemon extract and 1/4 teaspoon pure vanilla extract to the liquid ingredients. For two crusts, use 1/4 cup sugar and add 1 teaspoon pure lemon extract and 1/2 teaspoon pure vanilla extract to the liquid ingredients.

Ginger Treacle Tart

UNITED KINGDOM

Serves 6 to 8

The classic, gooey English tart is vegan by nature, as long as the pastry is vegan. I added ginger for a little "edge," as a counterpoint to the sweetness. This is an easy and inexpensive dessert and delicious with a scoop of vanilla vegan "ice cream."

1 (9-INCH) PIE CRUST (SEE PAGE 173)
1 1/3 CUPS GOLDEN SYRUP (SEE PAGE 176) OR 1 CUP LIGHT
    CORN SYRUP PLUS 1/3 CUP FANCY (LIGHT) MOLASSES
3 OUNCES FRESH BREADCRUMBS
1/4 CUP CHOPPED CANDIED GINGER (PREFERABLY ORGANIC)
GRATED ZEST OF ONE LARGE ORGANIC LEMON
2 TABLESPOONS FRESH LEMON JUICE

1. Preheat the oven to 375°F. Bake the pastry

"blind" (empty) according to direction #3 in the Corn Flour Pastry recipe (except for oven temperature).

2. In a medium bowl, combine the syrup, breadcrumbs, ginger, lemon zest, and juice, and mix well. Pour the filling mixture into the prepared pastry, spreading it evenly. Bake the tart for about 30 minutes. Transfer the pie to a cooling rack. Cool for at least 10 minutes. Serve hot, cold, or at room temperature.

Tip: Organic candied ginger has a stronger flavor than ordinary candied ginger.

Maple-Chocolate Shoofly Pie

U.S.A.

Serves 8   SF

Think Chocolate Pecan Chess Pie (a modern version of Southern sugar custard pie) crossed with a Pennsylvania Dutch Shoofly Pie (a sort of crumb cake with a runny molasses layer, encased in a pie shell). I've been making Shoofly Pie for many years and it is egg-free, which makes it vegan-friendly. It's so delicious that I wanted to devise a lower-fat and more healthful version (the original often contains as much as 3/4 cup shortening in the filling alone). I couldn't leave well enough alone, so I combined it with some of the elements of the chocolate chess pie and – voila – a winner! My guests couldn't get enough of it. Serve with a scoop of vanilla vegan ice cream.

3/4 CUP BOILING WATER
1/2 CUP MAPLE SYRUP
1 TABLESPOON BOURBON, DARK RUM, OR CHOCOLATE OR
    COFFEE LIQUEUR, OPTIONAL
1 TEASPOON PURE VANILLA EXTRACT
1/2 TEASPOON BAKING SODA
3/4 CUP WHOLE-WHEAT FLOUR (ALL-PURPOSE OR PASTRY
    FLOUR)
1/2 CUP BROWN SUGAR
1/2 CUP VEGAN SEMISWEET CHOCOLATE CHIPS
1/2 TEASPOON SALT
1/4 TEASPOON GROUND CINNAMON

1/8 TEASPOON GROUND NUTMEG
1/8 TEASPOON GROUND GINGER
1/8 TEASPOON GROUND CLOVES OR ALLSPICE
1 (9-INCH) PIE CRUST (YOUR FAVORITE OR SEE PAGE 173)

1. Preheat oven to 350°F. In a small bowl, whisk together the boiling water, maple syrup, bourbon, if using, vanilla, and baking soda. In a larger bowl, combine the flour, brown sugar, chocolate chips, salt, cinnamon, nutmeg, ginger, and cloves.

2. Pour 1/3 of the maple syrup mixture into the pie crust and sprinkle it evenly with 1/2 of the crumb mixture. Repeat this layering, ending with the last 1/3 of the maple syrup mixture. Bake the pie for 30 minutes. Transfer the pie to a cooling rack. Serve warm or at room temperature.

Rose-Scented Baklava

MIDDLE EAST

Makes 30 pieces   SFO

Do you wait to visit a Middle Eastern restaurant to enjoy the bliss of multi-layers of crispy pastry encasing nuts and drenched in syrup? Well, be advised that baklava is surprisingly easy and extremely satisfying to make in your own kitchen. I prefer my baklava flavored with rose water, which is more subtle than the usual cinnamon or cloves. Some cooks vehemently insist on cinnamon and, don't get me wrong, I think cinnamon is lovely, if it is used moderately. But cinnamon is often added with a heavy hand, whereas rose water is so gorgeously subtle and unexpected! I use kitchen shears to cut the phyllo – it cuts just like paper.

Rose Water Syrup:
1 1/2 CUPS SUGAR
3/4 CUP WATER
2 TABLESPOONS ROSE WATER (PAGE 196)
Nut Filling:
2 CUPS CHOPPED RAW WALNUTS (OR RAW HAZELNUTS OR
      UNSALTED SHELLED PISTACHIOS)
1/2 CUP SUGAR
2 TABLESPOONS ROSE WATER
To assemble:
1 CUP VEGAN MARGARINE, MELTED
1 POUND PHYLLO PASTRY, CUT IN HALF TO MAKE 9 X 13-
      INCH SHEETS

1. **Rose Water Syrup:** Boil the water and sugar together in a medium saucepan for 2 minutes. Stir in the rose water. Cool the syrup a bit and then refrigerate.

2. **Nut Filling:** Grind the nuts, sugar, and rose water together in a food processor until it is almost, but not quite, a paste. Preheat the oven to 350°F.

3. **To assemble:** To keep the melted margarine warm, place the bowl inside of a larger bowl of very hot water. Brush a 9 x 13-inch baking pan with a little of the melted margarine. Place a half-sheet of phyllo in the pan, brush it with margarine and continue until you have used up half of the phyllo and half of the margarine. Distribute the filling evenly over the top. Layer the rest of the phyllo and margarine in the same manner, brushing the top layer with margarine. Keep the phyllo you are not working with covered with a sheet of baking parchment covered with a damp kitchen towel.

4. Cut through the baklava the length of the pan with a sharp knife in 1-inch-wide strips, through

---

┌─────────────────────────────────┐
│   **About Golden Syrup**   │
│   │
│ This amber-colored liquid sweetener is popular among British and British Commonwealth cooks. It's made by evaporating sugar cane juice until it is thick and syrupy. Popular brands include Lyle's Golden Syrup, Steen's Pure Cane Syrup, and Rogers, which is made Canada. It is also called "cane syrup" and "light treacle." │
└─────────────────────────────────┘

to the bottom of the pan. Then make cuts (all the way through) on the diagonal across the straight cuts, 1 inch apart, to make diamond shapes.

5. Bake the baklava for 30 minutes, then reduce the heat to 300°F and bake for about 10 minutes more or until the pastry is golden brown and puffy.

6. Re-cut the baklava where you have already cut it, then pour the cooled rose water syrup over the whole thing. It will look like it is sitting in a pool of syrup, but it gets absorbed as it cools. Let it cool on a rack at room temperature for several hours before serving.

7. You can freeze the baklava, either baked or unbaked, if necessary. Bake frozen unbaked baklava at 350°F for 1 hour and then at 325°F for 1 more hour or until the pastry is golden brown and puffy. To thaw baked baklava before serving, thaw previously-baked pieces of baklava at room temperature.

Vegan Sponge Cake

UNITED KINGDOM

Serves 6 to 8   SF

This light vegan sponge cake has a myriad of uses (such as for Scottish Sherry Trifle, page 198), but we also enjoy it plain with berries and other fruit. The sponge cake is thought to be one of the first of the non-yeasted cakes. The earliest recorded sponge cake recipe in English is mentioned in a book by English poet and author Gervase Markham, written in 1615 and entitled The English Huswife, Containing the Inward and Outward Virtues Which Ought to Be in a Complete Woman. *Do not use all-purpose flour or the cake will be tough! Note: Pan choices for this cake are either a small tube pan (9 inches across the top, 6 inches across the bottom and 3 inches deep); or 4 mini tube pans (each 4 to 4 1/2 inches across and 2 inches deep). If you are making this cake for a trifle, use three 8-inch round cake pans.*

3 TABLESPOONS ENER-G EGG REPLACER POWDER OR

ORGRAN "NO EGG" (SEE PAGE 15) (THE ONLY BRANDS THAT WHIP FIRMLY ENOUGH FOR THIS RECIPE)
3/4 CUP COLD WATER
1 1/2 CUPS WHITE PASTRY FLOUR OR 3/4 CUP WHITE PASTRY FLOUR AND 3/4 CUP WHITE WHOLE-WHEAT PASTRY FLOUR
1 1/2 TEASPOONS BAKING POWDER
1/2 TEASPOON SALT
1 1/4 CUPS SUGAR
1/2 CUP NONDAIRY MILK
2 TABLESPOONS VEGETABLE OIL
1 TEASPOON PURE VANILLA EXTRACT
1/4 TEASPOON PURE ALMOND EXTRACT

1. Preheat the oven to 350°F. Combine the egg replacer powder and water in a medium mixing bowl or the bowl of a stand mixer. Beat with a hand-held electric mixer or the whip attachment of the mixer, scraping the sides often at first, for about 10 minutes or until the mixture looks like beaten egg whites that will hold a soft peak. Set aside.

2. In a medium bowl, combine the flour, baking powder, and salt and set aside.

3. In a blender or food processor combine the sugar, nondairy milk, oil, vanilla, and almond extract and blend until the sugar is almost dissolved. Add the blended mixture to the flour mixture and mix well, but briefly, until the mixture is smooth, but without beating it.

4. Transfer the beaten "egg white" mixture into the batter with a silicone spatula and fold and turn the mixture carefully into the batter (do not stir it in) until it is homogenous (no "blobs" of white remain) and the mixture is a light, airy batter. (The batter may look beige in color, but, don't worry, the cake turns out white!)

5. Spray the pan(s) well with baking spray or brush with Generic Pan Coating (page 184) or grease the pans well with margarine and then flour it, tapping the bottom of the pan to remove any excess flour. Transfer the batter into the prepared pan(s), smoothing the top(s) evenly.

6. Bake for about 1 hour or until the cake is golden and springy to the touch (use a cake tes-

ter, too, to make sure that it is cooked all the way through). Bake the mini tube pans or the 3 round cake layers for about 20 minutes.

7. Transfer the pan(s) to a cooling rack to cool for 5 minutes. Loosen the sides of the cake with a thin table knife. Place a piece of baking parchment cut to fit over the surface of the cake. Turn a serving plate upside-down over the parchment-topped cake and hold it in place firmly as you turn it over. Place the plate on your work surface with the cake pan upside down on it. Give the bottom of the pan a whack with a wooden spoon to loosen it. Remove the baking pan and place the plate on the rack to cool the cake completely.

Russian Chocolate Torte

Tort Shokoladnyi

RUSSIA

Serves 16   SFO

A very decadent, moist three-layer dark chocolate almond cake swathed in fluffy, light chocolate frosting and topped with a generous portion of chocolate curls...mmmm! Apparently, it is a common torte to serve with afternoon tea in Russian tea rooms and restaurants. It is a perfect company cake – easy to make and a sure crowd-pleaser.

Cake:
Dry Ingredients:
- 1 1/2 CUPS PLUS 2 TABLESPOONS WHITE CAKE OR PASTRY FLOUR (DO NOT USE ALL-PURPOSE FLOUR)
- 1/2 CUP UNSWEETENED COCOA POWDER
- 1/2 CUP FINELY-GROUND LIGHTLY-TOASTED ALMONDS
- 1 1/2 CUPS SUGAR
- 2 TEASPOONS BAKING POWDER
- 1/2 TEASPOON BAKING SODA
- 3/4 TEASPOON SALT

Wet Ingredients:
- 1/4 CUP PLUS 2 TABLESPOONS VEGAN MARGARINE
- 1 CUP WATER
- 3/4 CUP NONDAIRY MILK

- 1 TABLESPOON FRESH LEMON JUICE
- 1 TABLESPOON PURE VANILLA EXTRACT

Frosting:
- 1 CUP NONDAIRY MILK
- 5 TABLESPOONS WHITE UNBLEACHED FLOUR
- 1/2 TEASPOON AGAR POWDER
- 3 TABLESPOONS VEGAN MARGARINE OR NON-HYDROGENAT- ED SHORTENING OR A COMBINATION
- 1 CUP SUGAR
- 3 TABLESPOONS UNSWEETENED COCOA POWDER
- 1 TEASPOON PURE VANILLA EXTRACT
- 1/8 TEASPOON SALT
- CHOCOLATE CARAQUE (CHOCOLATE CURLS FOR TOP OF CAKE) SEE SIDEBAR PAGE 180.
- 4 OUNCES VEGAN SEMISWEET CHOCOLATE OR CHOCOLATE CHIPS

1. **Cake:** Preheat the oven to 350°F. Line a 10 x 15-inch nonstick baking pan with a rim (jelly roll pan) with baking parchment cut to fit. If you don't have a nonstick pan, spray it with baking spray or brush with Generic Pan Coating (page 184), or grease the pan well with margarine and then flour it, tapping the bottom of the pan to remove any excess flour before lining with the parchment.

2. Whisk the dry ingredients together in a large bowl or the bowl of a stand mixer. Add the margarine and water and beat with a hand-held electric mixer or the whip attachment of your mixer for one minute. Mix the milk in a small bowl with the lemon juice. Add this to the batter in the large bowl, along with the vanilla and beat for one more minute. Smooth the batter into the prepared pan, making the middle of the cake slightly concave so that it doesn't "hump" in the center when baked. Bake the cake for about 30 minutes or until a toothpick inserted in the center of the cake comes out dry.

3. Cool the cake on a rack for 30 minutes. To remove the cake from the pan, run a thin table knife around the edge of the pan to loosen the cake. Place a sheet of baking parchment over the cake itself. Turn a second 10 x 15-inch baking

sheet upside-down over the parchment-topped cake and, with a hand on each end, grasping both pans together, both ends at once, quickly invert. Gently shake or tap the bottom of the pan with a wooden spoon handle to help remove the cake.

4. Carefully peel the parchment off the side the cake was baked on and turn cake right-side-up on another parchment-lined baking sheet (using the same instructions as above). Place on a cake rack to cool.

5. **Frosting:** Whisk the milk into the flour and agar in a small saucepan until smooth. (You can use an immersion/stick blender if you wish or even run it through the blender before transferring it to the saucepan.) Stir the mixture over medium-high heat until it boils and thickens. Remove from the heat.

Microwave Option: Whisk the milk into the flour and agar in a medium microwave-safe bowl until smooth. (You can use an immersion/stick blender if you wish or even run the mixture through the blender before transferring it to the bowl.) Microwave the mixture for 45 seconds at 100% power (default setting), whisk it vigorously and repeat the procedure twice or until thick.

6. Cool the thickened mixture thoroughly by transferring it to a small bowl and placing it inside of a larger bowl of ice-cold water or ice cubes. (Don't let water get into the mixture.) The mixture will get quite stiff – don't worry!

7. With a hand-held electric mixer or the whip attachment of your stand mixer, beat the margarine, sugar, cocoa, vanilla, and salt until light and fluffy – this takes several minutes. Beat in the cooled flour paste and beat again until smooth and fluffy. Chill the frosting thoroughly before frosting the cake.

8. To assemble the cake: Cut the cooled cake rectangle vertically into three equal-sized loaf-shaped pieces– use a ruler or measuring tape to cut the pieces exactly the same size. Place one piece top-side-down on an oval or rectangular serving platter. Spread it evenly with 1/3 of the frosting. Place another layer on top of that and spread 1/3 of the icing over it. Top with the last cake layer.

9. Cut 4 plastic drinking straws to the same height as the cake. Stick them into the cake, forming the corners of a square in the center. This keeps the layers from slipping. Spread the rest of the frosting over the top (the sides are not frosted). Distribute the chocolate caraque artistically over the top. Refrigerate the cake until serving time. To serve, cut the loaf into 8 thick slices and then cut each slice vertically in half.

Important: To measure flour correctly, you need calibrated measuring cups made for measuring dry ingredients. Do not use a coffee cup or drinking glass. Lightly spoon the flour directly into the measuring cup from the container or bag. Do not shake the cup or pack the flour down.

Tip: You can grind blanched almonds easily and quickly in a small (clean, dry) electric spice or coffee grinder or a mini-chopper.

South American "Three Milks" Cake

Pastel de Tres Leches

NICARAGUA

Serves 12 to 18

This rich, dense yellow cake soaked in the "Tres Leches/Three Milks" (sweetened condensed milk, evaporated milk, and whole milk or cream) and topped with whipped cream, is ubiquitous in Latin America. It seems to have originated in Nicaragua, but my Peruvian cousins serve it and tell me that the dessert has traveled all over South America. For me, fresh fruit is a must to accompany this cake. I find that the fruit offsets the sweetness and allows you to serve a smaller piece without looking stingy! If you don't mind using some alcohol, adding a small amount to the "Tres Leches" mixture adds a little edge to the über-sweetness, as well! **Important:** Make the components for the cake the day before serving. Soak the cake with the "Three Milks" the morning of the day you are serving it.

The Cake:
PLAIN CAKE VARIATION OF LEMON-ALMOND-CARDAMOM CAKE (PAGE 201), BAKED IN AN 8 X 12-INCH PYREX OR CERAMIC BAKING PAN AND THOROUGHLY COOLED
"Three Milks" or "Tres Leches":
HOMEMADE SWEETENED CONDENSED SOY MILK (PAGE 181)

┌─────────────────────────────────┐

Chocolate Caraque

Important: Place a 10 x 15-inch baking sheet in the freezer.

Chop the chocolate into little pieces with a sharp knife (or use chocolate chips). Melt the chocolate in the top of a double boiler over hot, not simmering water. Stir until smooth. Microwave Option: Microwave on 50% power in a microwave-safe bowl or measuring pitcher for 2 to 4 minutes or just until the chocolate is shiny. Stir it well.

Using a frosting spatula/bent icing knife, a large palette knife or a plastic spackle or putty knife, spread the melted chocolate as thinly and evenly as possible on the frozen baking sheet, spreading the knife back and forth to get a smooth and level finish. Refrigerate until the chocolate is just set but not hard. Hold a medium-sized sharp knife at a 45° angle to the chocolate and draw the knife towards you across the surface of the chocolate to remove thin layers that form into long curls. Place the curls into a container lined with baking parchment and keep in a cool dry place until needed.

└─────────────────────────────────┘

1 3/4 CUPS COMMERCIAL VEGAN COFFEE CREAMER
1 CUP SOY OR NUT MILK
1/3 CUP BRANDY, RUM, OR FRUIT SCHNAPPS, OPTIONAL
1 RECIPE ALMOND CREAM WHIPPED TOPPING (PAGE 207), MADE SEVERAL HOURS BEFORE AND CHILLED, OR SOYATOO WHIPPABLE SOY TOPPING CREAM, OR MIMIC-CREME HEALTHY TOP
4 CUPS FRESH SLICED FRUIT (BERRIES, MANGOES, PEACHES, OR NECTARINES)
Garnishes:
TOASTED COCONUT FLAKES
TOASTED PECANS
Optional Garnish:
VEGAN MANJAR BLANCO (PERUVIAN DULCE DE LECHE, PAGE 170); VEGAN CHOCOLATE SAUCE, SUCH AS WAX ORCHARDS FUDGE SAUCE

1. Make the cake as specified above. Loosen it on the sides with a table knife and pierce in several places with a fork or skewer. Set aside.

2. In a bowl, whisk together the condensed soy milk, vegan coffee creamer, nondairy milk, and optional liquor, if using.

3. Pour this mixture over the cooled cake (still in the cake pan). Cover and transfer to the refrigerator to allow it to soak and absorb the "three milks" during the day. If the cake doesn't soak up all of the "tres leches," pour off any excess, strain it, and save it to use as a dessert sauce or to sweeten coffee.

4. When ready to serve, spread the whipped topping over the top of the cake. Decorate the cake or surround it, with the fresh fruit of your choice and decorate it with toasted coconut and/or pecans. Cut the cake into 18 pieces and serve each square with some of the fruit.

5. To further "gild the lily" (this is optional), use a squeeze bottle to drizzle vegan manjar blanco or chocolate sauce thinly and decoratively around each serving of cake or on top of the whipped topping.

Sweetened Condensed Soy Milk

Makes 1 2/3 cups   GF, <30

This lusciously thick and sweet, fast, and easy-to-make product can be used in sweet coffee beverages, baking, and candy-making instead of the dairy product. It keeps in the refrigerator for several weeks. Sweetened condensed milk and evaporated milk have been available in cans since the mid-1800s, and they became staples in countries where it was difficult to keep milk products fresh. Canned sweetened condensed and evaporated milks are now part of Latin American culture. My late father, Alejandro Urbina, laced his many cups of tea with the dreaded canned evaporated milk, a habit from his upbringing in Peru. Sweetened condensed milk is the basis for manjar blanco *(as* dulce de leche *is called in Peru), the thick caramel sauce used in many South American desserts. Fortunately, we vegans have alternatives!*

Note: *Soy milk powder and isolated soy protein powder are available in natural food stores.*

1 CUP SUGAR

2/3 CUP BOILING WATER

1/4 CUP PLUS 2 TABLESPOONS SOY MILK POWDER

5 TABLESPOONS UNFLAVORED ISOLATED SOY PROTEIN POWDER

1 TABLESPOON MELTED VEGAN MARGARINE

Combine all of the ingredients in a blender and blend until the sugar has dissolved and the mixture is quite thick (it will thicken more when chilled). Pour it into a clean jar, seal, and refrigerate.

Yellow Semolina Cake with Lemon Syrup

Sfoof

LEBANON

Serves 8   SF

I took the liberty of adding fragrant lemon zest and a lemony syrup to this traditional Lebanese semolina cake, which is colored with antioxidant-rich turmeric. Soaking cake in syrup is a common Middle Eastern practice and lemon added just the right amount of tang.

*Semolina is a high-protein wheat flour used in making pasta and sometimes in breads and cakes, particularly in Italy and the Middle East. It is also used for breads and pancakes in Indian cuisine. If you can't find semolina flour (*rava *is the Indian term), use Cream of Wheat cereal. If your semolina is coarse, grind it in small batches in a clean, dry coffee/spice grinder until it is more powdery and then measure it again.*

Syrup:

3/4 CUP SUGAR

3/4 CUP WATER

GRATED ZEST OF 1 MEDIUM ORGANIC LEMON

JUICE OF 2 MEDIUM LEMONS

Cake:

1 1/2 CUPS SEMOLINA FLOUR (RAVA) OR CREAM OF WHEAT

1/2 CUP WHITE OR WHOLE-WHEAT PASTRY FLOUR (DO NOT USE ALL-PURPOSE FLOUR)

1 TEASPOON TURMERIC

1 1/2 TEASPOONS BAKING POWDER

1/2 TEASPOON SALT

1 1/4 CUPS SUGAR

1 CUP NONDAIRY MILK

GRATED ZEST OF 1 MEDIUM ORGANIC LEMON

1/2 CUP OLIVE, SUNFLOWER, OR CANOLA OIL

1/4 CUP BLANCHED SLIVERED RAW ALMONDS

1. **Syrup:** In a small saucepan, mix together the water, sugar, and lemon zest. Bring to a boil, then turn the heat down and simmer for 10 minutes. Add the lemon juice and stir well. Pour into a shallow bowl and refrigerate.

2. **Cake:** Preheat oven to 350°F. Use a 9-inch round cake pan at least 2 inches deep. Spray the inside with baking spray or brush with Generic Pan Coating (page 184), or grease the pan well with margarine and then flour it, tapping the bottom of the pan to remove any excess flour.

3. In a small bowl, combine the semolina, flour, turmeric, salt, and baking powder. Set aside.

4. In a large bowl or the bowl of a stand mixer, beat together the milk, lemon zest, and sugar with a hand-held electric mixer or the whip attachment of your stand mixer until sugar is dissolved. Add the reserved flour mixture and the oil and beat at medium speed for 5 minutes. Do not shorten this time– it's important to beat air into the batter.

5. Pour the batter into the prepared cake pan. Sprinkle the top of the batter evenly with the almonds. Bake for 35 minutes or until it tests done.

6. Cool the cake on a rack for 10 to 15 minutes, then carefully loosen the sides with a table knife and place a flat plate over the cake pan. Carefully flip the plate over, grasping the cake pan along with it with both hands, so that the cake ends up on the plate. Remove the pan. Place a large serving plate over the cake and flip it over again, so that the almond-studded side is up. Pierce the cake all over with a bamboo skewer. Pour the cooled lemon syrup over the cake. Let it cool and soak up the syrup. This cake keeps well for several days.

Almond Café Latte Cake

Italy/North America

Serves 12   SFO

This light and tender espresso-flavored cake, with a rich layer of Vegan Mocha Ganache, Coffee "Buttercream," and toasted nuts, is our current first choice for birthday cakes.
Important: *To measure flour correctly, you need cal-*

ibrated measuring cups made for measuring dry ingredients. Do not use a coffee cup or drinking glass. Lightly spoon the flour directly into the measuring cup from the container or bag. Do not shake the cup or pack the flour down. Do not use all-purpose flour to make this cake.

Espresso Cake:
2 1/2 CUPS PLUS 2 TABLESPOONS WHITE CAKE OR PASTRY FLOUR
1 1/2 CUPS SUGAR
2 TEASPOONS BAKING POWDER
1/2 TEASPOON BAKING SODA
3/4 TEASPOON SALT
1/4 CUP PLUS 2 TABLESPOONS VEGAN MARGARINE
1 CUP NONDAIRY MILK
3/4 CUP ESPRESSO, FRESHLY-BREWED OR MADE WITH
    INSTANT ESPRESSO POWDER
1 TABLESPOON COFFEE OR ALMOND LIQUEUR OR COFFEE
    OR ALMOND-FLAVORED ITALIAN SYRUP (PAGE 171)
1 TABLESPOON PURE VANILLA EXTRACT
Coffee Buttercream Frosting:
1/4 CUP VEGAN MARGARINE
1/4 CUP NON-HYDROGENATED SHORTENING
12 OUNCES CONFECTIONERS' SUGAR, SIFTED, OR MORE IF
    NEEDED
5 1/2 TEASPOONS NONDAIRY MILK
1 TABLESPOON INSTANT ESPRESSO GRANULES OR 2 TABLE-
    SPOONS INSTANT COFFEE GRANULES
1/2 TABLESPOON ALMOND LIQUEUR PLUS 1 TEASPOON
    VANILLA EXTRACT, (OR 2 TEASPOONS PURE VANILLA
    EXTRACT PLUS 1/2 TEASPOON ALMOND EXTRACT)
Mocha-Soy Ganache:
6 OUNCES EXCELLENT-QUALITY VEGAN SEMISWEET EATING
    CHOCOLATE OR 1 CUP CHOCOLATE CHIPS
1/4 CUP SOY, COCONUT, HEMP, OR NUT MILK
1/4 CUP ESPRESSO, FRESHLY-BREWED OR MADE WITH
    INSTANT ESPRESSO POWDER
1/3 CUP EXTRA-FIRM SILKEN TOFU
1 TEASPOON VANILLA OR CHOCOLATE EXTRACT OR 1 TABLE-
    SPOON COFFEE OR ALMOND LIQUEUR
Garnish:
1 CUP TOASTED SLIVERED ALMONDS
1/2 CUP GRATED VEGAN BITTERSWEET OR SEMISWEET
    CHOCOLATE

1. Preheat oven to 350°F. Prepare two round 8-inch layer cake pans by spraying with baking

spray, brushing with Generic Pan Coating (see page 184), or grease the pan well with margarine and then flour it, tapping the bottom of the pan to remove any excess flour. Line the bottoms of the pans with baking parchment cut to fit.

2. **Cake:** Mix the flour, sugar, baking powder, baking soda, and salt together with a whisk in a large mixing bowl or the bowl of your stand mixer. Add the margarine and milk and beat with a hand-held electric mixer or the whip attachment of the mixer for one minute. Add the remaining cake ingredients and beat for one more minute. This batter is quite runny, but don't worry. Divide the batter equally between the two prepared cake pans. Bake for 25 to 30 minutes or until the cakes test done.

3. Cool the cakes on racks for 10 minutes and remove from pans to finish cooling or the delicate cakes might crack and fall apart. To remove from pans, loosen the edges of the cake layers with a thin table knife. Place a wire rack over the top of one layer and, grasping the cake pan and the rack with both hands, quickly invert. Repeat with the other layer. Gently tap the bottoms of the pans with a wooden spoon handle to help remove the cake layer. Carefully peel off the parchment and carefully turn cake layer right-side-up to cool on the wire cake rack. Cool the cake thoroughly before icing.

4. **Coffee Buttercream:** Cream the margarine and shortening until very smooth in a large bowl or the bowl of your stand mixer, using the mixer's whip attachment or a hand-held electric mixer. Add 2 cups of the confectioners' sugar and the remaining ingredients. Keep beating until very creamy. The mixture may look curdled – don't worry! Add the remaining confectioners' sugar, a little at a time, beating all the while, until the frosting holds its shape well and you can see "trails" in it from the beaters. Refrigerate until it's time to ice the cake.

5. **Mocha-Soy Ganache:** Chop the chocolate

with a large, sharp knife or cleaver and process it very finely in a dry food processor. Leave the chocolate in the processor.

6. Process the milk, espresso, and silken tofu together in a blender or in a deep, narrow container with an immersion/stick blender until very smooth. Heat the blended mixture in the top of a double boiler over simmering water until almost to the boiling point. Or cook the mixture in a medium microwave-safe bowl for about 1 minute at 50% power or until very hot, but not boiling. (If the mixture seems to curdle at all, blend it again until smooth.)

7. With the motor running, pour the very hot soy cream into the processor with the ground chocolate through the feed tube. Process until the mixture is smooth. Refrigerate the ganache until it is time to ice the cake.

Notes on Ganache: The quality of your ganache depends upon the quality of the chocolate you use. Make the ganache well-ahead of time so that it is spreadable by the time you ice the cake. If it gets too firm, leave it out at room temperature to soften.

Soy-Free Option: Omit the tofu. Use 1/2 cup coconut nondairy creamer or nut milk plus 1 tablespoon espresso powder.

8. To assemble: Transfer one cake layer to a serving plate. Spread it evenly with the ganache. Place the second layer firmly over the ganache. Frost the top and sides of the cake with the buttercream. Sprinkle the top of the cake with the toasted almond slivers, leaving a circle in the center. Distribute the grated chocolate in the center. Refrigerate until serving time. Cut the slices with a sharp serrated knife.

Chocolate-Hazelnut Praline Lava Cakes

FRANCE-NORTH AMERICA

Makes 4 small cakes to serve 8

These incredibly decadent and moist individual chocolate cakes have a soft center of melted hazelnut praline filling that erupts from the cakes when you dig into them. Originally, "lava cakes" were French egg-based, flourless cakes that formed a molten center when the cakes were deliberately under-baked. More often than not, these days (due to concerns about undercooked eggs) a rich cake batter containing flour is used and a frozen chocolate mixture is placed between layers of batter before baking. This is the type that I started with to make my vegan version. My batter, however, has very little fat in it, yet it is rich, tender, and chocolatey. The hazelnut praline filling contrasts perfectly with the dark chocolate cake, and the result is rich enough that half a cake is plenty for one serving, especially when served with a scoop of vegan vanilla ice cream on top of or alongside each serving.

Generic Pan Coating

You can buy commercial versions in cake supply stores or specialty cooking shops, but it's easy and cheap to make. You'll want to keep some in your refrigerator at all times!

Beat together equal parts of non-hydrogenated shortening, canola or sunflower oil, and all-purpose flour. An immersion/stick blender works well for this. Store the mixture in a tightly closed container in the refrigerator, but let come to room temperature before using. Use a pastry brush to apply the coating on the inside of your pan and there will be no need to flour the pan.

To bake these cakes, you will need 4 ramekins, bowls, little soufflé dishes, giant muffin tins, ceramic coffee cups – anything that holds 1 cup (8 ounces). I have successfully used a variety of vessels.

Hazelnut Filling:
2 TABLESPOONS VEGAN MARGARINE
7 TABLESPOONS TOASTED AND CHOPPED HAZELNUTS OR FILBERTS
1/4 CUP PLUS 2 TABLESPOONS BROWN SUGAR
1 1/2 TABLESPOONS COMMERCIAL VEGAN COFFEE CREAMER OR NUT CREAM (PAGE 197)
1 TABLESPOON SUGAR

Chocolate Cakes:

Wet Mix:
1/2 CUP (4 OUNCES) FIRM SILKEN TOFU OR MEDIUM-FIRM TOFU
1/2 CUP PLUS 2 TABLESPOONS STRONG LIQUID COFFEE OR ESPRESSO
1 TABLESPOON CANOLA OIL
1 CUP BROWN SUGAR, PACKED
2 TEASPOONS ENER-G EGG REPLACER POWDER OR ORGRAN "NO EGG" (SEE PAGE 15)
1/2 TABLESPOON VINEGAR
1/2 TABLESPOON PURE VANILLA OR CHOCOLATE EXTRACT OR CHOCOLATE, COFFEE OR HAZELNUT LIQUEUR

Dry Mix:
1/2 CUP PLUS 2 TABLESPOONS WHITE CAKE OR PASTRY FLOUR OR SIFTED WHOLE-WHEAT PASTRY FLOUR (DO NOT USE ALL-PURPOSE FLOUR)
1/2 CUP UNSWEETENED COCOA POWDER
1/2 TEASPOON BAKING POWDER
1/2 TEASPOON BAKING SODA
1/4 TEASPOON SALT

1. **Hazelnut Filling:** Melt the margarine in a small saucepan over medium heat. Add the remaining ingredients and bring to a boil. Boil for 2 minutes and remove from the heat.

Microwave Option: Place the margarine in a medium microwave-safe bowl and microwave on 100% (default setting) power until melted, about 30 seconds. Add the remaining ingredients and microwave on full power for 1 1/2 to 2 minutes.

2. Pour the mixture onto a 10 x 15-inch baking sheet lined with baking parchment cut to fit and place the sheet in the freezer to cool until you can handle it like candy. Watch it carefully. Divide the "candy" into 4 equal portions and roll each portion into a ball. Place the balls, not touching, back on the parchment and transfer to the freezer while you make the cake batter.

3. **Chocolate Cakes:** Preheat the oven to 350°F. Generously brush 4 ramekins or other 1-cup baking dishes with vegan margarine.

4. Combine the wet mix ingredients in a food processor or blender and process until smooth. In a medium bowl, whisk together the dry mix ingredients. Pour the wet mixture into the dry mixture and whisk briefly to make a smooth batter.

5. Divide half of the batter evenly into the prepared cups or ramekins. Carefully place one of the semi-frozen hazelnut praline balls in the center of each cup of batter and gently press it down into the batter slightly, then divide the remaining batter evenly between the 4 cups, smoothing it over the top. Place the filled cups/ramekins/dishes in an 8 x 12-inch baking pan or on a 9 x 13-inch jelly roll pan (baking sheet with a rim all around).

6. Bake the cakes in the center of the oven until the cakes are puffy and set, about 35 minutes. Use a cake tester or toothpick to test one of the cakes between the center and the side of the cake cakes, not in the center. Let the cakes cool on the pan for 10 minutes, then loosen the edges of each cake carefully with a thin table knife and invert them onto a 9 x 13-inch or 10 x 15-inch baking sheet lined with baking parchment. To serve, cut each cake carefully in half. With a spatula or cake server, transfer each half to a small dessert plate, still warm.

Tip: Leftovers can be refrigerated, wrapped in plastic wrap and then reheated, uncovered, in the microwave for 1 minute at 33% power or in a 350°F oven, covered loosely with foil, for about 10 minutes.

Triple-Ginger Cake with Espresso Frosting

NORTH AMERICA

Serves 9   SF

This ginger cake is the cosmopolitan cousin of the familiar gingerbread many of us grew up with. The cake itself is very light in texture (you would definitely not call this "bread"!) and infused with a generous amount of both fresh and ground dried ginger. Topped off with a fluffy espresso frosting and plenty of sweet-hot candied ginger, this cake always gets rave reviews at potlucks and community get-togethers. Tasters are pleasantly surprised at the pairing of coffee and ginger and keep going back for more. But, really, how many times have we enjoyed a cup of coffee with a ginger cookie or a piece of gingerbread? It seems like a match made in heaven.

Wet Mixture:
1/2 CUP BOILING WATER
1/2 CUP FANCY (LIGHT) MOLASSES
1/2 CUP SOFT BROWN SUGAR, PACKED
1/4 CUP VEGAN MARGARINE OR OIL
1/4 CUP UNSWEETENED SMOOTH APPLESAUCE
1/4 CUP NONDAIRY MILK
3 TABLESPOONS FINELY GRATED FRESH GINGER
Dry Mixture:
3/4 CUP UNBLEACHED WHITE FLOUR
3/4 CUP WHOLE-WHEAT PASTRY FLOUR (DO NOT USE REGULAR WHOLE-WHEAT FLOUR)
1 TEASPOON BAKING SODA
1 TEASPOON GROUND GINGER
1 TEASPOON GROUND CINNAMON
1/2 TEASPOON SALT
1/2 TEASPOON GROUND ALLSPICE
Espresso Frosting:
1 1/2 TEASPOONS BOILING WATER
1 TABLESPOON INSTANT ESPRESSO GRANULES (OR 2 TABLESPOONS INSTANT COFFEE GRANULES)
2 TABLESPOONS SOFTENED VEGAN MARGARINE

2 3/4 TABLESPOONS NONDAIRY MILK
2 CUPS CONFECTIONERS' SUGAR
Garnish:
1 CUP CHOPPED CANDIED GINGER

1. Oil a 9-inch square cake pan and line the bottom with baking parchment cut to fit. Preheat the oven to 350°F. In a large heatproof bowl, pour the boiling water over the margarine and whisk until smooth. Whisk in the molasses, brown sugar, applesauce, milk, and fresh ginger.

2. In another bowl, stir together the flours with the baking soda, ground ginger, cinnamon, salt, and allspice. Add to the molasses mixture in two additions, stirring until smooth. Transfer the batter into the prepared pan and bake for 30 to 40 minutes or until a cake tester comes out clean when inserted into the center. Cool thoroughly on a rack.

3. **Espresso Frosting:** Pour the boiling water into a large mixing bowl or the bowl of a stand mixer. Add the espresso or coffee granules and stir to dissolve. Add the margarine and milk. Whisk together well. With a hand-held electric mixer or the whip attachment to your mixer, gradually beat in the confectioners' sugar until the frosting is creamy and smooth. Spread it immediately over the top of cooled cake (not the sides) so that icing drips over the sides but does not cover them completely. Sprinkle the top evenly with the chopped candied ginger. Cut into 9 squares to serve.

Tip: Organic candied (or crystalized) ginger has a stronger ginger flavor and "bite" to it than the ordinary variety, so if you really like ginger, look for it!

Chocolate Stout Cake

United Kingdom/Ireland/North America

Makes 16 slices

My friend and fellow vegan cookbook author Julie Hasson and her husband, Jay, once took us to a great little microbrewery/pub in Portland, Oregon. They urged us to try the chocolate stout, which was delicious. I couldn't wait to use it in a vegan chocolate stout cake. In this vegan version of a very rich-tasting, dense cake, you can use any dark stout or porter (they are both brewed from roasted grains), and if you have a locally brewed one, especially a chocolate stout, that's the best. I used whole grains in my cake (they disappear nicely in a dense, dark cake) and cut way back on the fat with no loss of flavor. This is a dense cake, so small slices are advised! Do not use regular whole-wheat flour in this cake.

1/2 CUP PLUS 2 TABLESPOONS VEGAN CHOCOLATE STOUT OR VEGAN DARK STOUT (DON'T INCLUDE FOAM WHEN MEASURING)
1/3 CUP COOKING MOLASSES
3/4 CUP PLUS 1 1/2 TABLESPOONS WHOLE-WHEAT PASTRY FLOUR
1/4 CUP PLUS 2 TABLESPOONS UNSWEETENED COCOA POWDER, PLUS MORE FOR DUSTING
2 TABLESPOONS OAT BRAN
3/4 TEASPOON BAKING POWDER
1/4 TEASPOON BAKING SODA
1/4 TEASPOON SALT
1/4 CUP PLUS 2 TABLESPOONS SMOOTH UNSWEETENED APPLESAUCE
1/4 CUP VEGAN MARGARINE, SOFTENED AT ROOM TEMPERATURE
3/4 CUP PACKED BROWN SUGAR
3 OUNCES FIRM OR EXTRA-FIRM SILKEN TOFU OR MEDIUM-FIRM REGULAR TOFU
1 TABLESPOON ENER-G EGG REPLACER POWDER OR ORGRAN "NO EGG" (SEE PAGE 15)
3 OUNCES VEGAN SEMISWEET CHOCOLATE, CHOPPED
Chocolate Glaze:
3 TABLESPOONS VEGAN COFFEE CREAMER, FULL-FAT SOY MILK, OR NUT MILK
1 1/2 OUNCES VEGAN SEMISWEET CHOCOLATE, CHOPPED

1. Preheat oven to 350°F. Grease a 6-cup Bundt cake pan (7 1/2 x 3 inches) with shortening and lightly dust it with sifted unsweetened cocoa powder. Tap out the excess cocoa.

2. Bring the stout and molasses to a simmer in a small saucepan. Remove it from the heat and set aside. In a medium bowl, whisk together the flour, oat bran, cocoa powder, baking powder, baking soda, and salt.

3. In a food processor, process the applesauce, margarine, and brown sugar until light and fluffy. Add the tofu and egg replacer and process again. Transfer the mixture into a medium mixing bowl or the bowl of a stand mixer.

4. With the electric mixer or stand mixer (with whip attachment) on low speed, alternate between adding the flour mixture and the stout mixture to the sugar mixture, beginning and ending with the flour mixture, with about 3 additions of each. Scrape down sides of bowl and then beat for another 20 seconds or until smooth.

5. Stir in the chopped chocolate (don't beat in). Spoon the batter into prepared pan, spreading evenly. Run a knife through the batter to eliminate air pockets.

6. Bake the cake in the center of the oven for about 1 hour and 10 minutes or until a cake tester or toothpick comes out with only a few moist crumbs clinging to it.

7. Let the cake cool in the pan on a rack for 20 minutes, then loosen the sides carefully with a thin table knife and invert it onto a serving plate. Transfer the plate to a rack to cool until just barely warm.

8. **Chocolate Glaze:** In a small saucepan, bring the vegan coffee creamer to a boil over high heat. Remove the pan from heat and add the chocolate. Whisk until the chocolate is melted and smooth. Let the mixture cool for 5 minutes before drizzling it over the cake.

9. If you are making the cake ahead, do not glaze it until just before serving. Wrap it in plastic wrap and refrigerate or freeze it.

Sticky Toffee Pudding

22 SP/65w

UNITED KINGDOM

Serves 8 to 9   SF

This is a "pudding" that is actually a cake – a light, tender cake, laced with a generous portion of meltingly-sweet dates, bathed in sweet, buttery brown sugar sauce. It's one of the most popular desserts in

---

Vegan Stout and Porter for Chocolate Stout Cake

You may have noticed by now that I like to find out the origin of recipes, if I can. But, try as I have, I cannot discover the origin of this cake. I have heard that it comes from Ireland, but I could not verify that. It is popular in the U.K. and North America, especially on St. Patricks Day, so perhaps it is a North American recipe that was developed to celebrate an Irish holiday.

In the U.K., beer (bitter) has commonly been fined (meaning "refined") using isinglass, which is a fish product. But this is changing and many bottled bitters and most lagers are vegan, using a new refining technique. (Guinness Stout, unfortunately, is still not suitable for vegans, even though vegan-friendly companies such as Samuel Smiths and Pitfield Brewery have shown that fish-free vegan stout is possible.) The best resource for finding vegan wines, beers, and other alcoholic beverages is http://barnivore.com.

the U.K. and is now growing in popularity elsewhere. My vegan version is much lower in fat than the original, but with all the rich flavor and spongy texture. This is best served fresh, but if you make the cake and sauce ahead, each portion can be heated briefly in the microwave, or simply heat the sauce in a small saucepan and portion it over the room-temperature cake servings. Do not refrigerate the cake before serving. Do not use regular whole-wheat flour.

Cake:
6 OUNCES PITTED DATES
1 CUP BOILING WATER
1 TEASPOON BAKING SODA
2 TABLESPOONS ENER-G EGG REPLACER POWDER OR ORGRAN "NO EGG" (SEE PAGE 15) NOTE: THESE ARE THE ONLY BRANDS THAT WILL WHIP ENOUGH FOR THIS RECIPE.
1/2 CUP WATER
3 TABLESPOONS APPLESAUCE
1 TABLESPOON MELTED VEGAN MARGARINE
3/4 CUP SUGAR
1 TEASPOON VANILLA EXTRACT

Dry Mixture:
1 1/2 CUPS WHOLE-WHEAT PASTRY FLOUR
1 1/2 TEASPOONS BAKING POWDER
1/4 TEASPOON SALT

Sauce:
1/3 CUP CORN SYRUP, BROWN RICE SYRUP, OR GOLDEN SYRUP (SEE PAGE 176)
1/2 CUP PLUS 2 TABLESPOONS BROWN SUGAR
2 TABLESPOONS VEGAN MARGARINE, SOFTENED
1/8 TEASPOON SALT
1/3 CUP FULL-FAT SOY MILK, NUT MILK, OR VEGAN COFFEE CREAMER
1/4 TEASPOON PURE VANILLA EXTRACT

1. **Cake:** Preheat the oven to 350°F. Spray an 8-inch square pan with baking spray, or brush with Generic Pan Coating (page 184), or grease the pan generously with margarine and then flour it, tapping the bottom of the pan to remove any excess flour.

2. Chop the dates coarsely with a sharp knife and mix them in a small saucepan with the boiling water. Bring to a boil, then reduce heat to me-

dium and simmer for 5 minutes. Remove from the heat, stir in the baking soda and set aside. In a small bowl, mix together the dry ingredients and set aside.

3. Combine the egg replacer and 1/2 cup water in a large, deep bowl or the bowl of a stand mixer. Beat it with a hand-held electric mixer or in your stand mixer with the whip attachment (this is preferable, since it takes so long) at high speed for 10 to12 minutes or until it forms soft peaks.

4. Mix together the applesauce, margarine, sugar, and vanilla, using an immersion/stick blender or a hand-held mixer in a deep medium bowl or a food processor. Mix it until it is quite fluffy, for several minutes. (If you are using a food processor, scrape the mixture into a medium bowl.) Stir in the dry mixture and the chopped dates. Stir only until mixed – do not beat the batter. Fold in the beaten egg replacer with a spatula, using an over-and-under motion, just until it is all folded in, no more. Scrape the batter into the prepared pan and smooth the top evenly. Bake for 35 minutes or until the cake tests done.

5. **Sauce:** Bring the syrup, brown sugar, margarine and salt to a boil in a medium saucepan and boil it over medium heat, stirring constantly, until it is the consistency of heavy syrup. Remove it from the heat and cool it for about 10 minutes. Heat the soy milk, nut milk, or creamer just until warm. Whisk it into the syrup along with the vanilla.

6. To serve, cool the cake on a rack for at least 5 minutes, then cut into 8 or 9 pieces. Place each piece on a dessert plate and spoon some of the hot sauce over it. Add a scoop of your favorite vanilla vegan ice cream to each serving or pass vegan coffee creamer for each diner to drizzle over the cake.

Blueberry-Maple "Poor Man's Pudding"

Pudding au Chômeur

CANADA/QUEBEC

Serves 8   SF, <30

I've jazzed up this saucy Quebeçois pudding-cake with maple syrup, blueberries, and walnuts and used nutty whole-wheat pastry flour instead of the usual white. The original dessert, sometimes called "unemployed pudding," because of its inexpensive ingredients, became very popular in Quebec during the Great Depression and remains a favorite in many French Canadian homes to this day. It may be an "everyday" dessert, but there's nothing ordinary about it! Each bite of fluffy nutmeg- and lemon-scented cake delivers juicy blueberries and toasty walnuts, comfortingly drenched in a slightly buttery maple syrup sauce. Serve hot or warm with your favorite vegan vanilla ice cream or simply some vegan coffee creamer or nut cream (page 197). Do not use regular whole-wheat flour.

1 CUP WHOLE-WHEAT PASTRY FLOUR
1/2 CUP SUGAR
2 TEASPOONS BAKING POWDER
1/4 TEASPOON SALT
1/4 TEASPOON FRESHLY GROUND NUTMEG
3/4 CUP NONDAIRY MILK
1 TEASPOON FINELY GRATED ORGANIC LEMON ZEST
3/4 CUP FRESH BLUEBERRIES
1/2 CUP CHOPPED TOASTED WALNUTS
1 1/2 CUPS WATER
1 CUP PURE MAPLE SYRUP (GRADE B IS FINE)
1 TABLESPOON MELTED VEGAN MARGARINE
1 TEASPOON CORNSTARCH

1. Preheat oven to 350°F. Spray an 8-inch square baking pan with oil from a pump sprayer.

2. In a medium bowl, whisk together the flour, sugar, baking powder, and nutmeg. In a separate, smaller bowl, whisk together the milk, oil, and lemon zest and pour it over the flour mixture. Sprinkle in the blueberries and walnuts and stir just until combined. Spread the batter evenly in the prepared baking pan.

3. In a small mixing bowl, whisk together the water, maple syrup, melted margarine, and cornstarch and pour the mixture slowly and evenly over the batter. Bake the cake in the center of the oven until the batter has risen to the top and is golden and firm to the touch, 40 to 45 minutes.

Everyone Has a Sweet Tooth

More Desserts from Around the World

Who doesn't enjoy a good dessert now and then? We don't have dessert often at our house, but, when we do, I like it to be truly worth the effort!

There were too many desserts to choose from for this book, so I had to divide them into two categories. The preceding chapter consisted only of desserts from the oven, and only cakes, cookies, and pies at that. This chapter consists of non-baked desserts, that is, those that use a variety of other cooking methods. Some are simmered or microwaved; some are steamed; some are layered creations of cake, fruit, and creamy mixtures; some are even boiled (Ukrainian Cherry Dumplings).

Take, for instance, puddings. I've got a recipe for you that will open a new vista on your rice-pudding horizon: Basmati Rice Pudding with Rose Water and Nectarines. It is fluffy, fragrant, and fruity. And, while I'm on the subject of rice puddings, Chinese Eight-Treasure Steamed Rice Pudding makes a spectacular fruit- and nut-studded ending to any special vegan meal. No special skills are needed!

Although candy-making is definitely not my forte, I have included two unusual candy recipes – my version of Turkish Delight, made with luscious pomegranate and walnuts, and Chocolate Panforte, a unique Italian confection.

Italian Baked Fruit-Stuffed Peaches, fruity Peruvian Purple Corn Pudding, Chocolate-Orange Sorbetto, and two creamy cappuccino puddings (espresso and chai) are easy enough to make for every day, but elegant enough for company. If you are really trying to impress, there are two spectacular trifles (one Scottish and one with Indian spices and mangoes) and two varieties of creamy, decadent vegan tiramísu. If that's not enough, how about a Chocolate Soufflé with Vanilla Sauce?

More Desserts from Around the World

Chinese Eight-Treasure Steamed Rice Pudding

CHINA

Serves 8   GF, SF

This pudding is quite easy to make and absolutely beautiful to look at. The original version contains a hefty portion of lard, suet, and/or shortening. This lighter, modern version contains only a little oil. The "eight treasures" are the dried or candied fruits and/or nuts used to decorate the pudding. The filling is traditionally a sweet red bean paste, which can be bought in cans in Asian grocery stores, but it can be replaced by a date paste that is more compatible with Western notions of dessert. Serve this to end a special feast (and it doesn't have to be a Chinese feast)!

1 TABLESPOON COLD NON-HYDROGENATED VEGETABLE
    SHORTENING (FOR GREASING THE BOWL)
1/2 TO 1 CUP ASSORTED COLORFUL DRIED FRUITS AND NUTS
    (SEE NOTE)
2/3 CUP CANNED CHINESE SWEET RED BEAN PASTE OR DATE
    PASTE (SEE SIDEBAR)
1 CUP WHITE GLUTINOUS ("SWEET" OR "STICKY") RICE
1 CUP WATER
2 TABLESPOONS SUGAR
2 TABLESPOONS CANOLA, SUNFLOWER, OR PEANUT OIL
Syrup:
1 TEASPOON CORNSTARCH
1/2 CUP WATER
1/4 CUP SUGAR
1 TEASPOON PURE ALMOND EXTRACT

1. Generously grease a 3 to 4-cup heatproof bowl with the shortening. Arrange the fruits and nuts in an attractive pattern on the bottom (and the sides, too, if you like) of the bowl, sticking them onto the cold shortening. Place the bowl in the refrigerator while you prepare the pudding.

2. Bring the water and rice to a boil in a small covered saucepan. Cover and cook over low heat for 15 minutes. Stir in the sugar and oil. Spread two-thirds of the rice mixture over the bottom and part way up the sides of the bowl, pressing it against the bowl firmly and carefully so as not to disturb the stuck-on fruit and nuts. Transfer thet red bean paste or date paste into the rice "lining" – it should come to within 1/2-inch of the top of the rice. Cover the paste with the remaining rice mixture, spreading it to the edge of the rice "lining." Cover the bowl with aluminium foil.

3. Steam the pudding on a rack or balanced on 2 or 3 canning jar rings over boiling water in a covered pot. (See advice on steaming arrangements on page 23.) Steam the pudding over moderate heat for 1 hour. If you make the pudding ahead of time, it can be reheated by steaming again for 30 minutes. The pudding should be served hot.

4. Loosen the top edges of the pudding gently with a table knife, place a serving plate over the top of the bowl, flip it over (holding the plate firmly with one hand and the bottom of the bowl with the other) and set the plate on a work surface with the bowl upside-down. Give the bottom of the bowl a sharp whack with a wooden spoon if the pudding doesn't loosen immediately. The pudding should come out in one piece with a lovely pattern of fruits and nuts on top. If any decorations were left behind, re-attach them to the pudding carefully and smooth the rice if it was disturbed.

5. **Syrup:** Dissolve the cornstarch in the water and mix it with the sugar in a small saucepan.

Date Paste

To make date paste, combine 1 cup whole pitted dates in a small saucepan with 1 cup water over high heat and cook, stirring constantly until the dates break down, the water is absorbed, and the mixture resembles a paste. Remove from heat. This makes approximately 2/3 cup.

Stir it over high heat until the sugar dissolves and the sauce is slightly thickened. Stir in the almond extract. Pour this over the pudding to make a shiny glaze. Carefully cut into wedges to serve.

Note: Choose from among these dried fruits and nuts for this recipe: sliced whole dates, golden raisins, dried apricots, dried prunes, dried mango, dried papaya, dried pineapple, dried cherries, whole raw almonds, pecan or walnut halves

Tip: You need plenty of shortening to "glue" the decorations to the bowl and also to facilitate removing the pudding from the bowl after steaming.

Mexican Bread Pudding

Christmas Capirotada

MEXICO

Serves 8   SFO, GFO

Mexican bread pudding is quite different from our typical North American varieties – it contains no milk or eggs, but it does contain cheese. This version uses vegan mozzarella-type cheese, and I added dried cranberries for a Christmas touch. For the bread, use a baguette or similar crusty bread. This version is lower in fat than most and is very easy to make. It's always a hit! For a soy-free version use soy-free Earth Balance and Daiya cheese.

6 CUPS (1/2-INCH) FRESH BREAD CUBES
1 TABLESPOON MELTED VEGAN MARGARINE
1/2 TEASPOON GROUND CINNAMON
1 CUP DRIED CRANBERRIES
1 1/2 CUPS MAPLE SYRUP
1/2 CUP WATER
8 OUNCES SHREDDED VEGAN WHITE CHEESE
1 TABLESPOON GRATED ORGANIC ORANGE ZEST
2 TABLESPOONS FRESH LEMON JUICE
1 CUP CHOPPED LIGHTLY TOASTED PECANS

1. Preheat the oven to 350°F. Spread the bread cubes onto two 10 x 15-inch baking sheets and toast them for 10 minutes. Toss the bread cubes

with the melted margarine and cinnamon. Combine them with the remaining ingredients, saving 1/4 cup of the pecans to sprinkle on top.

2. Spread the mixture into an oiled 2-quart round casserole. Sprinkle the remaining pecans on top. Bake the casserole, covered, for 35 minutes. Let the pudding stand, covered, for about 15 minutes before serving with Rich Vegan Cream (see sidebar) or your favorite commercial vegan creamer.

Peruvian Purple Corn Pudding

Mazamorra Morada

PERU

Serves 6   GF, SF, <30

This uniquely beautiful Peruvian pudding is in the Northwestern style, which is traditionally made with purple corn and sweet potato starch. Since purple corn is hard to come by, I use blueberries (which grow locally) for the color, and cornstarch for the thickener. It tastes very authentic and is a refreshing, unusual dessert. It's quick to make in the microwave, but I provide stove-top instructions as well.

Rich Vegan Cream

Makes 1 cup   SFO, GF, <30

1 CUP RICH, FULL-FAT SOY MILK OR NUT MILK
5 TEASPOONS SUGAR
1 TEASPOON PURE VANILLA EXTRACT
1/3 CUP VEGETABLE OIL

Mix the milk, sugar, and vanilla in a blender. With the machine running, slowly add the oil in a thin stream. When all the oil is added, the milk will thicken. Pour the thickened mixture into a container and refrigerate.

Fruit Mixture:

1 CUP FRESH OR THAWED FROZEN BLUEBERRIES

3 CUPS WATER

3/4 CUP SUGAR

1 (2-INCH) STICK CINNAMON

2 WHOLE CLOVES

3 PRUNES (DRIED PLUMS), CHOPPED

3 DRIED APRICOTS, CHOPPED

3 TABLESPOONS GOLDEN RAISINS

1 SMALL MILDLY TART RED APPLE, SUCH AS ROME BEAUTY, PEELED AND CHOPPED

GRATED ZEST AND CHOPPED FLESH OF 1 SMALL ORGANIC ORANGE

GRATED ZEST OF 1/2 SMALL ORGANIC LIME

GRATED ZEST OF 1/2 SMALL ORGANIC LEMON

Starch Mixture:

1/2 CUP COLD WATER

3 TABLESPOONS CORNSTARCH

Pineapple Mixture:

1 CUP DICED FRESH OR UNSWEETENED CANNED PINEAPPLE, WELL-DRAINED

1 TABLESPOON FRESH LIME JUICE

1 TABLESPOON FRESH LEMON JUICE

Microwave Method: Combine the fruit mixture ingredients into a large microwave-safe bowl and microwave on 100% power (default setting) for 7 minutes. Whisk the starch mixture ingredients together well in a small bowl and stir the mixture into the hot mixture. Cook it on 100% power for 2 minutes, stir it well and cook for 2 minutes more. The pudding should be thick and clear.

Stovetop Method: Combine the fruit mixture ingredients in a medium pot. Bring it to a boil over high heat, stirring with a wooden spoon, then turn it down to a simmer and cook, partially covered, for about 20 minutes or until the apple and the dried fruits have softened. Whisk the starch mixture ingredients together well in a small bowl and stir the mixture into the hot mixture. Stir over high heat until the mixture is thickened and clear.

Whichever way you cook it, stir the pineapple and lemon and lime juice into the pudding and combine well. Spoon the pudding into 6 serving bowls or glasses. Cover them with plastic wrap and chill for several hours before serving. It should be cold and pudding-like.

Almond, Rose Water, and Saffron Custard with Berries

MIDDLE EAST

Serves 8   GF, SFO

Custard desserts are a favorite in the Middle East, and this recipe is based on a Persian version. The corn flour adds a delicate almost "eggy" taste, along with adding its thickening properties to the cornstarch and agar. The custard tastes much richer when made with homemade almond milk and it's easy to make. Important: Make the custards the day before serving. (See the soy-free option at the end of recipe.)

3 CUPS HOMEMADE ALMOND MILK (SEE PAGE 197)

1 TEASPOON AGAR POWDER

1/4 CUP PLUS 2 TABLESPOONS PLUS 2 TEASPOONS CORN FLOUR (SEE PAGE 174)

3 TABLESPOONS PLUS 1 TEASPOON CORNSTARCH

1/4 TEASPOON SPANISH SAFFRON

1 SCANT CUP SUGAR, DIVIDED

1 CUP (8 OUNCES) EXTRA-FIRM SILKEN TOFU

2 TO 3 TABLESPOONS PLUS 1 TABLESPOON ROSE WATER OR ORANGE FLOWER WATER (PAGE 196), DIVIDED

1 TEASPOON LEMON JUICE

1/4 TEASPOON GROUND CARDAMOM

PINCH SALT

8 LARGE FRESH STRAWBERRIES, SLICED

1 CUP FRESH OR THAWED FROZEN MIXED BERRIES, (SLICED, IF LARGE)

2 TABLESPOONS TOASTED ALMOND SLIVERS

1. Generously oil eight 1/2-cup ramekins and set aside. In a 1-quart saucepan or microwave-proof bowl (depending on whether you use the stovetop or microwave method), combine 2 cups of the almond milk, the agar, corn flour, and cornstarch, and whisk together well. Let the mixture stand for about 5 minutes. In a small bowl, combine the saffron and 1/2 teaspoon of the sugar and grind together with the back of a spoon.

2. In a saucepan, heat the remaining 1 cup almond milk, 2/3 cup of the sugar, and saffron/sugar mixture until it is not quite simmering (or heat it briefly a microwave oven, if you like). Pour the hot mixture into the blender along with the tofu. Cover the blender to keep hot while you go on to the next step. (Do not blend yet!)

3. Stir the almond milk/agar mixture in the saucepan constantly over high heat until it is thick and holding together in a mass. Or you can instead cook the mixture in the 1-quart microwave-proof bowl on 100% power (default setting) for 45 seconds. Whisk it well. Repeat the cooking and whisking two or three times or until the mixture is thick and holding together in a mass.

4. Scrape the cooked mixture into the blender containing the hot milk and tofu. Add the 2 to 3 tablespoons of rose water, lemon juice, cardamom, and salt. Remove the middle insert of the blender lid and cover it loosely with a folded clean kitchen towel (hold it on with your hand), to prevent the hot mixture from exploding. Blend well, until the mixture is very smooth.

Pour the mixture evenly into the oiled ramekins. Refrigerate for several hours or until firm.

5. When the custards are firm, place the bottoms of the ramekins in hot water for a minute to loosen them, then carefully run a table knife around the edge of each custard to loosen. Carefully invert each custard onto a small serving plate. Keep the custards refrigerated until serving time.

6. Combine the berries, 1/4 cup of the sugar, and the remaining 1 tablespoon of rose water in a medium bowl. Cover and let stand at room temperature until ready to serve. When you are ready to serve, top each custard with the some of the berries and sprinkle with some of the toasted almonds.

Soy-Free Option: Omit the tofu and use 3 1/2 cups almond milk (in total) plus 1/2 cup raw cashews.

Rose Water and Orange Flower Water

Rose water is made from rose petals and is used to flavor food throughout Europe, Asia, and the Middle East. In the Arab world and India, rose water is used to flavor milk and dairy-based dishes, such as rice pudding. In Malaysia and Singapore, it is used in sweet drinks, and in Lebanon, Israel, and Palestine it is a common, flavorful addition to lemonade. In Western Europe, rose water and orange flower water are sometimes used to flavor both marzipan and madeleine, a petite scallop-shaped French sponge cake. American and European bakers used rose water in their baking until the nineteenth century when vanilla became popular.

Orange flower water, or orange blossom water, is made from fresh bitter-orange blossoms. It has traditionally been used in many French and Mediterranean dessert dishes. It has more recently been included in Western cuisine – in France to flavor madeleines, in Mexico to flavor little wedding cakes, and in North America to make orange blossom scones. It has long been a traditional ingredient in Middle Eastern and North African cooking.

These essential flower waters are inexpensive and can be purchased in international grocery stores and online. After opening, they keep indefinitely in the refrigerator.

Fragrant Basmati Rice Pudding with Rose Water and Nectarines

INDIA

Serves 6   GF, SFO

I have always made rice pudding with short-grain rice, so I was surprised at how wonderfully soft and delicate a pudding could be when made with leftover basmati rice. Make extra rice next time just for this dessert – it's a lovely treat! You can substitute peaches, mangoes, plums, berries, or other soft fruit for the nectarines.

3 CUPS COOKED WHITE BASMATI RICE
2 CUPS SOY MILK OR OTHER NONDAIRY MILK
1/2 CUP (4 OUNCES) EXTRA-FIRM SILKEN TOFU
1/2 CUP SUGAR
1 1/2 TABLESPOONS VEGAN MARGARINE, OPTIONAL
1 TABLESPOON BIRD'S CUSTARD POWDER OR CORNSTARCH WITH A PINCH OF TURMERIC
1 PINCH SALT
3 PODS CARDAMOM, CRUSHED, SEEDS SET ASIDE AND PODS DISCARDED
1 (3-INCH) CINNAMON STICK
2 TABLESPOONS ROSE WATER (PAGE 196)
3 RIPE NECTARINES, WASHED, RUBBED DRY AND THINLY SLICED

Homemade Nut Cream and Nut Milk

Once you make the nut cream, you can then dilute it with more water to make nut milk. (See page 198 for how to remove the skins.) Homemade nut milks and creams are delicious on desserts, cereal, and fruit and in beverages. If you're making nut cream for cooking purposes, omit the syrup and salt.

Nut Cream

Makes 1/2 cup   GF, SF, <30

1/4 CUP CHOPPED BLANCHED RAW ALMONDS, RAW CASHEW PIECES, RAW SKINNED BRAZIL NUTS, OR HAZELNUTS (FILBERTS)
1/2 CUP WATER
1 TEASPOON MAPLE SYRUP OR OTHER SWEETENER
1 PINCH SALT

Process everything for 3 minutes (don't cheat!) in a blender (not in a food processor).

NUT MILK: Add 1/2 cup of water to the nut cream. It will make 1 cup.

NUT "BUTTERMILK": Curdle the nut milk or cream with a bit of lemon juice to use instead of buttermilk in cooking and baking.

You can use cashew or Brazil nut cream and milk "as is." You might prefer to strain the almond or hazelnut (filbert) cream or milk through fine cheesecloth (squeeze every last drop out and use the resulting pulp in granola or even as a facial scrub). Keep the liquids in tightly sealed jars in the refrigerator. Raw nut milks and creams don't last long and should be made fresh, in small quantities, every 2 to 3 days if you use them regularly.

Tip: Nut milk and cream will separate in the refrigerator – just shake the jar before use.

1. Preheat the oven to 325°F. Generously grease a 1 1/2 to 2 quart casserole and set aside. In a blender combine the nondairy milk, tofu, sugar, margarine, custard powder or cornstarch, salt, and crushed cardamom seeds. Blend until very smooth, then combine with the cooked rice in the prepared casserole. Insert the cinnamon stick into the mixture. Bake for 50 minutes. Allow the pudding to cool to room temperature.

2. Transfer the pudding to small dessert dishes and drizzle each serving with a teaspoon of rose water. Garnish with nectarine slices.

Soy-Free Option: Omit the tofu and use 1/4 cup raw cashews and 1/4 cup more nondairy milk instead. Use soy-free vegan margarine.

How to Remove Skin from Raw Nuts

For hazelnuts (filberts) and Brazil nuts: Bring 2 cups water to boil with 3 tablespoons baking soda. Add the nuts and blanch for 3 to 4 minutes. Drain and rinse the nuts in a colander under cold running water – the skins will slide off.

For almonds: Place the almonds in boiling water for 1 minute, then drain in a colander and plunge into cold water. Squeeze each almond between your thumb and forefinger and the almond will pop out of the skin (be careful or they will shoot across the room!).

Scottish Sherry Trifle

Typsy Laird

<small>SCOTLAND</small>

Serves 12

Trifles are easy to make and always received well. This lovely trifle is traditional for Christmas and Robbie Burns Day (January 25), but it can be enjoyed any time of the year for any occasion. The cake and whipped topping can be made at least a day (even several days) ahead of time and the trifle assembled the morning of the day you are going to serve it.

Important: *Bake the cake in three 8-inch round cake pans, as instructed in either cake recipe.*

> VEGAN SPONGE CAKE (PAGE 177) OR PLAIN CAKE VARIATION OF LEMON-ALMOND-CARDAMOM CAKE (PAGE 201), BAKED IN THREE (8-INCH) ROUND CAKE PANS
> 1 RECIPE ALMOND CREAM WHIPPED TOPPING (PAGE 207), MADE AT LEAST 4 HOURS AHEAD OR SOYATOO WHIPPABLE SOY TOPPING CREAM
> 2 CUPS POURED CUSTARD, FRESHLY MADE (PAGE 200)
> 3/4 CUP RASPBERRY JAM
> 9 TABLESPOONS DRY OR MEDIUM-DRY SHERRY
> 12 OUNCES FRESH OR THAWED FROZEN RASPBERRIES OR MIXED RASPBERRIES AND STRAWBERRIES
> 2 TABLESPOONS SUGAR
> 2 RIPE BANANAS, SLICED
> GARNISH:
> 1/2 CUP TOASTED SLIVERED ALMONDS

1. Before assembling the trifle, cut each of the baked cake layers into 8 wedges. Set aside.

2. Make the almond cream whipped topping ahead of time or beat the Soyatoo topping and refrigerate it before assembling the trifle. Have the custard freshly-made and still warm.

3. To assemble, fit the wedges from one cake layer into the bottom of a 2-quart glass bowl or casserole. Spread the cake wedges with 1/2 cup of the raspberry jam. Sprinkle the cake with 3 tablespoons of sherry.

4. Top with the wedges from the second cake layer. Mix the berries and their juices with the sugar. Spread the berries evenly over this layer of cake and top with the sliced bananas. Sprinkle with another 3 tablespoons of the sherry.

5. Pour the warm custard over the berries, poking a table knife between the cake wedges and along the sides of the bowl to allow some of the custard to run down. Top the custard with the remaining cake wedges. Sprinkle the cake with the remaining 3 tablespoons of sherry and spread the remaining jam over the cake wedges. Refrigerate, covered, until serving time.

6. Just before serving, spread the chilled whipped topping of your choice evenly over the trifle, making decorative swirls with the spoon. Sprinkle the top with the toasted almonds.

Almond-Mango Trifle with Indian Spices

INDIA/U.K.

Serves 12

Rich almond, luscious mango, fragrant lemon, and cardamom evoke tropical delights, even in the form of a British trifle, and that's exactly what I had in mind for this company dessert. Six of us consumed about two-thirds of it in one sitting! The tangy filling is an Indian pudding (usually made with drained full-fat dairy yogurt) instead of British custard. But it is a lighter, vegan version that utilizes creamy silken tofu and lemon juice for a smooth and tangy, spice-laden treat.

In this trifle, it is positively decadent! Many of the components can be made – in fact, should be made – several days ahead of time: the cake, the whipped topping, the almond macaroon crumbs, and toasted almonds. Make them at least the day before serving. However, make the pudding just before assembling the trifle. Assemble the trifle the morning of the day it is to be served.

Pudding:
2 (12.3-OUNCE) BOX EXTRA-FIRM SILKEN TOFU
2/3 CUP SUGAR
1/4 CUP PLUS 2 TEASPOONS FRESH LEMON JUICE
1/4 TEASPOON SALT
1/4 TEASPOON PURE ALMOND EXTRACT
1/4 TEASPOON GRATED FRESH NUTMEG, PLUS MORE FOR
    GARNISH
1/4 TEASPOON GROUND CARDAMOM

To Assemble:
LEMON-ALMOND-CARDAMOM CAKE (PAGE 200)
1 CUP APRICOT OR PEACH JAM
1/2 CUP MEDIUM-DRY SHERRY (OR USE PEACH, APRICOT OR
    MANGO JUICE INSTEAD)
1 1/2 CUPS "ALMOND MACAROON" CRUMBS (BELOW)
2 TO 3 CUPS SLICED FRESH PEELED, PITTED MANGOES
ALMOND CREAM WHIPPED TOPPING (PAGE 207), MADE AT
    LEAST 4 HOURS AHEAD, OR SOYATOO WHIPPABLE SOY
    TOPPING CREAM
1/2 CUP LIGHTLY TOASTED SLIVERED ALMONDS

1. **Pudding:** In a food processor, combine the tofu, sugar, lemon juice, salt, almond extract, nutmeg, and cardamom. Blend until very smooth. Set aside.

2. **To assemble:** On the morning of the day you are serving it, cut the cooled cake layers in quarters. Cut each quarter in half horizontally. Spread the jam thickly on the bottom half of each quarter and top with the other half, like a sandwich. You will have eight "jam sandwich" cake wedges. Fit four of the "jam sandwiches" into the bottom of a 2-quart glass bowl. Reserve the other four.

3. Sprinkle the cake in the bottom of the bowl evenly with 1/4 cup of the sherry (or juice). Sprinkle 1/2 cup of the macaroon crumbs on top and then layer on half of the sliced mangoes. Smooth one half of the reserved pudding evenly over the mangoes. Place the reserved 4 "jam sandwich" cake wedges over the pudding layer. (If the bowl is wider at that point, leave a little more space in between the cake wedges).

4. Sprinkle the cake wedges with the remaining 1/4 cup of sherry (or juice), 1/2 cup of the maca-

Poured Custard

Serves 6   GF, SFO

This is a rich-tasting custard made using Bird's custard powder, which is vegan. If unavailable, you can use 4 3/4 tablespoons cornstarch plus a pinch of Spanish saffron instead. You can serve it chilled in dessert dishes, topped with fruit, or in a trifle or use it as a hot sauce poured over bread pudding or cake.

6 OUNCES (1/2 BOX; 3/4 CUP) EXTRA-FIRM SILKEN TOFU
2 CUPS WATER
4 3/4 TABLESPOONS PLAIN BIRD'S CUSTARD POWDER
1/2 CUP SUGAR
1/4 TEASPOON SALT
1 TEASPOON PURE VANILLA EXTRACT

Mix all of the ingredients except the vanilla in a blender and process until smooth. Pour the mixture into a medium saucepan and stir constantly over high heat until thickened. Whisk in the vanilla.

Microwave Option: Place the blended mixture in a 3 to 4-quart microwave-safe bowl and cook at 100% power (default setting) for 3 minutes. Whisk well. Cook at 100% power for 2 minutes more. Whisk well. Whisk in the vanilla.

If you plan to serve this cold, pour it into 6 custard dishes, cover with plastic wrap and chill.

Soy-Free Option: Rice and grain milks on their own do not always work well in custards and puddings. To make the recipe soy-free, use your favorite nondairy milk instead of the water, using 2 cups plus 6 tablespoons, omit the tofu and process it in a blender with 1/4 cup plus 2 tablespoons of raw cashews until smooth.

roon crumbs over that and layer the remaining mango slices over them. Smooth the remaining pudding evenly over the mangoes. Sprinkle the pudding with the remaining macaroon crumbs. Cover and refrigerate until serving time.

5. Just before serving, spread the chilled whipped topping evenly over the trifle, making decorative swirls with the spoon. Sprinkle the top with the toasted almonds and a little grated nutmeg.

Tip: The recipe can be halved and served in a 1-quart bowl.

"Almond Macaroon" Crumbs

Makes 2 2/3 cups   SF, GFO, <30

Since macaroons and Italian amaretti are made with eggs, we can't use the packaged cookies for the crumbs in this recipe. These fragrant crumbs have the same toasty, chewy, sweet texture and flavor and can be used in Italian desserts or sprinkled on fruit. They will keep for months in the freezer and you'll find many uses for them. For a gluten-free version, use gluten-free breadcrumbs.

1 CUP GROUND BLANCHED RAW ALMONDS
1 CUP DRY VEGAN WHITE OR SWEET BREAD CRUMBS
1/2 CUP MAPLE SYRUP, BROWN RICE SYRUP, OR AGAVE NECTAR
1 TEASPOON PURE ALMOND EXTRACT

Preheat the oven to 300°F. Combine all the ingredients in a medium bowl and mix well. Spread the mixture on two 10 x 15-inch baking sheets, nonstick or lined with baking parchment cut to fit, and transfer to the oven. Bake for about 15 minutes or until it has dried out a bit, but is still slightly chewy. Cool the pans on a rack and they are ready for use. Freeze any leftovers in zipper-lock freezer bags or in a rigid plastic container.

Tip: You can grind almonds easily and quickly in a small (clean, dry) electric spice or coffee grinder or a mini-chopper.

Lemon-Almond Cardamom Cake

Makes two 9-inch layers   SFO

You can easily and quickly grind the almonds for this cake in a small (clean, dry) electric spice or coffee grinder or a mini-chopper.
Note: *If using this recipe to make a trifle that calls for three 8-inch layers, divide the batter into three 8-inch round cake pans (prepared as in the recipe text) and bake for only 20 minutes or until they test done with a cake tester or toothpick.*

Dry Ingredients:
3/4 CUP WHITE WHOLE-WHEAT PASTRY FLOUR
1 CUP PLUS 6 TABLESPOONS WHITE UNBLEACHED CAKE OR
    PASTRY FLOUR
1/2 CUP GROUND LIGHTLY-TOASTED BLANCHED ALMONDS
1 1/2 CUPS SUGAR
4 TEASPOONS BAKING POWDER
1 TEASPOON GROUND CARDAMOM
3/4 TEASPOON SALT
Wet Ingredients:
1/4 CUP PLUS 2 TABLESPOONS VEGAN MARGARINE, CUT
    INTO PIECES
1 CUP WATER
3/4 CUP NONDAIRY MILK
2 TABLESPOONS FRESH LEMON JUICE
1/2 TABLESPOON VANILLA EXTRACT
GRATED ZEST OF 1 MEDIUM ORGANIC LEMON

1. Preheat the oven to 350°F. Spray the inside of two 9-inch round cake pans with baking spray or brush with Generic Pan Coating (page 184), or grease well with margarine and then flour them, tapping the bottom of the pans to remove any excess flour. Line the bottoms with baking parchment cut to fit.

2. Whisk the dry ingredients together in a large mixing bowl. Add the margarine and the water and beat with a hand-held electric mixer for 1 minute. Add the remaining wet ingredients and beat 1 more minute. (This batter is quite runny.) Divide the batter equally between the two prepared cake pans. Bake for 25 minutes or until

the cake layers test done. Cool on racks for 5 minutes, then loosen the edges of the cakes with a table knife and remove from the pans to the rack to finish cooling. Remove the parchment.

VARIATIONS

- **Plain Cake:** For a plain cake that can be used in much the same manner as a genoise or a plain white cake (in traditional trifle, for instance), omit the cardamom and grated lemon rind.
- **Lemon Cake:** Omit the cardamom.

New Vegan Tiramísu

ITALY

Serves 6 to 8   SFO

Who doesn't love tiramísu (which means "pick me up" in Italian) and, indeed, what's not to love? Creamy whipped cream and mascarpone cheese, light spongy cake soaked with liquor and espresso, a little chocolate on top – mmm! Unfortunately, the chances of encountering a vegan version in most restaurants are slim, so why not make your own? It's easy and every bit as scrumptiously, creamily decadent but without all that saturated fat. Tiramísu is a sort of Italian trifle and, like most trifles, it is best assembled and refrigerated the morning of the day you will be serving it. There are various components, but many of them can be easily made several days, even weeks, beforehand. It's fun to put it together, and you will be profusely thanked and complimented!

Vegan Cake Base:
1/2 RECIPE VEGAN SPONGE CAKE (PAGE 177)
Espresso/Liqueur Mixture:
1/3 CUP FRESHLY BREWED ESPRESSO OR ESPRESSO MADE
    FROM 1/3 CUP BOILING WATER AND 1 TABLESPOON
    INSTANT ESPRESSO POWDER
3 TABLESPOONS RUM, BRANDY, AMARETTO, KAHLUA, OR OTH-
    ER LIQUEUR, OR FLAVORED ITALIAN SYRUP (PAGE 171)
Vegan Mascarpone Filling:
2 CUPS VEGAN CREAM CHEESE; VEGAN MASCARPONE (PAGE 202)
OR SOY-FREE CREAM CHEESE-MASCARPONE (BELOW)

1/2 CUP SUGAR

2 TABLESPOONS RUM, BRANDY, AMARETTO, KAHLUA, OR OTH-
ER LIQUEUR, OR FLAVORED ITALIAN SYRUP (PAGE 171)

1 TEASPOON PURE VANILLA EXTRACT

Chocolate/Sugar Sprinkle:

1/3 CUP UNSWEETENED COCOA POWDER OR FINELY GRATED
VEGAN DARK CHOCOLATE

3 TABLESPOONS BROWN SUGAR

Vegan Whipped Topping:

ALMOND CREAM WHIPPED TOPPING (PAGE 207), MADE AT
LEAST 4 HOURS AHEAD; OR SOYATOO WHIPPABLE SOY
TOPPING CREAM; OR MIMICCREME (FOR SOY-FREE)

1. **Vegan Cake Base:** Bake the cake ahead of time in a 9-inch layer cake pan. Cool completely, then cut in half horizontally.

2. **Espresso/Liqueur Mixture:** Whisk the espresso and liqueur together in a small bowl. Set aside.

3. **Vegan Mascarpone Filling:** Combine the ingredients in a food processor and process until smooth. Refrigerate until ready to use.

4. **Chocolate/Sugar Sprinkle:** Combine the cocoa and sugar in a dry blender and blend until well mixed. Transfer to a small bowl and set aside.

5. **To assemble:** Fit one half of one horizontally-sliced cake layer into the bottom of a shallow 8 to 9-inch glass baking dish. Sprinkle the cake with half of the espresso-liqueur mixture. Spread the cake with half of the mascarpone filling, smoothing it over evenly. Sprinkle one-third of the chocolate/sugar sprinkle evenly over the filling.

6. Arrange the remaining cake layer slice on top of the mascarpone filling. Sprinkle the remaining espresso/liquor mix over the cake. Top the cake evenly with the remaining mascarpone filling and then sprinkle one-third of the chocolate/sugar sprinkle over that. Swirl the whipped topping decoratively over the layers and dust with the remaining chocolate/sugar sprinkle. Cover the bowl carefully with plastic wrap and refrigerate for at least 4 hours before serving. Cut into wedges to serve. Use within three days.

Vegan Mascarpone

Makes 2 cups

1/2 CUP PLUS 2 TABLESPOONS RAW CASHEWS

1 (12.3-OUNCE) BOX EXTRA-FIRM SILKEN TOFU

2 TABLESPOONS FRESH LEMON JUICE

1 PINCH SALT

Place the cashews in a dry food processor and process until ground almost to a paste. Loosen the cashew "paste" from the bottom and sides of the processor with a spatula. Add the remaining ingredients and process for several minutes until very smooth. You may have to stop the machine a couple of times and scrape the sides. Process the mixture until as smooth as possible. Refrigerate in a covered container if not using immediately.

Soy-Free Cream Cheese-Mascarpone

Makes 1 cup   SF, GF <30

1 CUP NONDAIRY MILK

1/4 CUP RAW CASHEW PIECES

4 TEASPOON FRESH LEMON JUICE

2 TABLESPOONS CORNSTARCH (OR 3 TABLESPOONS WHITE
RICE FLOUR)

2 TABLESPOONS VEGETABLE OIL

1/4 TEASPOON SALT

1. Place the milk and cashews in the blender and blend until very smooth—there should be no graininess at all. Add the remaining ingredients and blend well. Transfer the mixture to a small heavy-bottomed saucepan and stir constantly over medium-high heat until it thickens and boils. Reduce the heat to medium and cook 1 minute, stirring.

Microwave Option: Pour the mixture into a medium microwave-safe bowl and microwave on 100% power (default setting) for 2 minutes. Whisk well.

2. Scrape the mixture into a container and let cool to room temperature, then whisk or beat with an electric beater until smooth. Cover and refrigerate. Before using, beat it again with a whisk or electric beater. If it's too thick, thin with a little nondairy milk. Refrigerate in a covered container.

Lemon-Strawberry Tiramísu

ITALY/NORTH AMERICA

Serves 8 to10   SFO

Rich with almonds, fragrant with lemon zest, tangy, and sweet, this larger tiramísu is alcohol-free, topped with fresh strawberries, and contains more cake than the traditional recipe. It is a gorgeous spring or summer dessert! Like traditional tiramísu and trifle, this beauty is best assembled and refrigerated the morning of the day you will be serving it. There are various components, but many of them can be easily made several days, even weeks, beforehand.

Vegan Cake Base:
1 RECIPE VEGAN SPONGE CAKE (PAGE 177) OR VEGAN PLAIN
    CAKE VARIATION OF LEMON-ALMOND-CARDAMOM CAKE
    (PAGE 201)
Lemon Syrup:
1/2 CUP LEMON JUICE
1/2 CUP SUGAR
GRATED ZEST OF 1 LARGE ORGANIC LEMON
1 TO 2 TABLESPOONS LEMON LIQUEUR OR LEMON-FLA-
    VORED ITALIAN SYRUP (PAGE 171), OPTIONAL
Lemony Mascarpone Filling:
2 CUPS VEGAN CREAM CHEESE OR VEGAN OR (SOY-FREE)
    CREAM CHEESE MASCARPONE (PAGE 202)
1/2 CUP SUGAR
GRATED ZEST OF 1 LARGE ORGANIC LEMON
1/4 TEASPOON PURE VANILLA EXTRACT
To Assemble:
1 CUP TOASTED SLIVERED ALMONDS
ALMOND CREAM WHIPPED TOPPING (PAGE 207), MADE AT
    LEAST 4 HOURS AHEAD OR SOYATOO WHIPPABLE SOY
    TOPPING CREAM
2 PINTS FRESH STRAWBERRIES

1. **Vegan Cake Base:** Bake the cake ahead of time in two 9-inch layer cake pans. Cool completely, then slice in half horizontally.

2. **Lemon Syrup:** Stir the ingredients together in a small saucepan over high heat until the sugar dissolves. Reduce the heat to low and simmer for 5 minutes. Remove from the heat. Add the optional liqueur, if using. Set aside.

3. **Lemony Mascarpone Filling:** Combine the ingredients in a food processor and process until smooth. Refrigerate until ready to use.

4. **To assemble:** Have ready a shallow 8 to 9-inch glass baking or serving dish. Fit one of the whole cake layers into the bottom of the dish. Sprinkle the cake with one half of the lemon syrup. Spread the cake with half of the lemon mascarpone filling, smoothing it evenly. Sprinkle 1/2 cup of the toasted almonds evenly over the mascarpone filling. Arrange the remaining whole cake layer on top of the mascarpone. Sprinkle the remaining syrup over the cake. Top the cake evenly with the remaining mascarpone and then sprinkle with the remaining 1/2 cup almonds. Swirl the whipped topping over the layers. Cover the bowl with plastic wrap and refrigerate for at least 4 hours before serving.

5. Just before serving, slice the strawberries and arrange them artistically on top of the whipped topping. The berries must be sliced and placed over the tiramísu just before serving so that they don't "weep" into the whipped topping. Cut into wedges to serve. Use within three days.

Ukrainian Cherry Dumplings

Cherry Varenyki

UKRAINE

Serves 8   SFO

These delicate Ukrainian dumplings with a tangy sour-cherry filling make a lovely, unusual dessert with very little sugar.

Tip: *If you don't want to make your own dough, you can use ready-made gyoza skins (the round dumpling wrappers without eggs, available in most supermarkets).*

Dough:
2 1/2 CUPS UNBLEACHED WHITE FLOUR
1/2 TEASPOON SALT
1 TABLESPOON MELTED VEGAN MARGARINE
1/2 CUP NONDAIRY MILK
1/2 CUP WARM WATER
Filling:
1 (19-OUNCE) JAR PITTED SOUR CHERRIES IN LIGHT SYRUP,
**   DRAINED, SYRUP RESERVED**
2/3 CUP STRAWBERRY OR CHERRY JAM
1/2 TEASPOON GROUND CINNAMON
OPTIONAL: 2 TABLESPOONS CHERRY, STRAWBERRY, OR
**   RASPBERRY LIQUEUR OR ITALIAN SYRUP (PAGE 171)**
Cherry Syrup:
RESERVED SYRUP FROM THE JAR OF CHERRIES
1/4 CUP SUGAR
1 TABLESPOON CORNSTARCH
OPTIONAL: 2 TABLESPOONS CHERRY, STRAWBERRY, OR
**   RASPBERRY LIQUEUR OR ITALIAN SYRUP**
Garnish:
TOFU SOUR CREAM OR CASHEW SOUR CREAM (PAGE 33) OR
**   STOREBOUGHT; OR PLAIN SOY OR COCONUT YOGURT**

1. **Dough:** Combine the flour and salt in a medium bowl and add the melted margarine, milk, and water. Knead the dough until a smooth, soft dough forms. Cover the bowl with plastic wrap and let the dough rest for about 30 minutes.

2. **Filling and Syrup:** Drain the cherries and set the syrup from the jar aside to use for the cherry syrup. Mix the cherries with the jam, cinnamon, and optional liqueur, if using. Set aside, covered.

3. To roll out the dough, divide the dough in half, keeping the half that you aren't working with in a plastic bag. On a well-floured work surface, roll the dough out 1/8-inch thick in a circle about 16 to17 inches in diameter. An easy way to do this is to roll the dough out into a 1/4-inch thick circle, then drape it evenly over a well-floured deep bowl turned upside-down on the work surface. Gently stretch the dough over the bowl to thin the dough out to 1/8-inch-thick without tearing it. Stretch gently, working your way around the bowl a little at a time. Return the dough circle to the floured work surface.

4. Run a flexible dough cutter under the dough to loosen it. Cut about twenty 3 1/2-inch circles out of the dough with a biscuit or cookie cutter. Keep the cut circles covered. Repeat with the second half of the dough. You can re-roll the scraps and cut them out, too, if you like, but use as little flour as possible.

5. To fill the dumplings, place 1 teaspoon of the filling (1 teaspoon = 2 cherries and a little of the coating) in the center of each little circle of dough. Brush the edges of the dough circle lightly with water and fold over the Filling, turn-over-style. Pinch the edges to seal. Set the filled dumplings on baking sheets (any size) lined with baking parchment cut to fit. If you aren't going to cook the varenyki for a few hours, transfer the filled dumplings to a freezer on parchment-lined baking sheets. Take them out 15 minutes or so before you cook them.

6. When ready to serve, mix the reserved cherry syrup with the other syrup ingredients and heat, stirring constantly, to dissolve the sugar. Set aside.

7. Put a large pot of water on to boil. When it is boiling, gently drop 12 to 15 dumplings into the pot. Do not crowd them. Stir them briefly to make sure they don't stick together and boil for 3 to 4 minutes only. Do not overcook! Remove the dumplings with a slotted spoon and transfer to a colander. Place about 5 dumplings

into each dessert bowl and top with some of the cherry syrup and a dollop of tofu or cashew sour cream or soy or coconut yogurt. Serve warm.

Variation: Pan-fry the varenyki in a little vegan margarine until golden and serve as above.

TIPS

- A gyoza press is very inexpensive and really makes the process of filling the dumplings fast and easy – it folds, pinches, and seals!
- For future use, freeze the dumplings solid on parchment-lined baking sheets, then transfer the frozen dumplings to zip-top freezer bags. Thaw them before cooking.

Pomegranate and Walnut Turkish Delight

TURKEY

36 pieces   GF, SF

I am not usually a candy maker, but one day I had pomegranates that needed using. I juiced them and decided to try making this treat. We had just seen the film The Chronicles of Narnia: The Lion, the Witch and the Wardrobe, *and my grandchildren kept mentioning Turkish Delight, so I thought they might like to try it. It was quite refreshing and very beautiful.*

1 CUP PLUS 3/4 CUP WATER, DIVIDED
2/3 CUP UNSWEETENED POMEGRANATE JUICE, BOTTLED OR
    FRESH (SEE PAGE 206)
2 CUPS SUGAR
1/2 CUP PLUS 2 TABLESPOONS CORNSTARCH, DIVIDED
1/2 TEASPOON CREAM OF TARTAR
1/2 CUP CHOPPED LIGHTLY TOASTED WALNUTS
1/2 CUP CONFECTIONERS' SUGAR

1. In a saucepan, combine 1 cup water with the pomegranate juice and set aside.

2. In another saucepan over medium-high heat, combine the sugar and the remaining 3/4 cup water and stir until the sugar is dissolved and the liquid starts to bubble. Allow the mixture to boil, without stirring, until it registers 260°F on a candy thermometer (this takes about 15 minutes).

3. While the sugar mixture is coming to temperature, sift the 1/2 cup cornstarch and cream of tartar together into the water/pomegranate juice mixture. Whisk it until all of the lumps are dissolved. Cook it over medium heat, whisking constantly, until it becomes very thick and clear looking. Reduce the heat to low and continue stirring with a wooden spoon.

4. As soon at the candy thermometer in the sugar/water mixture registers 260°F, remove the mixture from the stove. Pour the hot mixture slowly into the cornstarch mixture, whisking vigorously. When it is thoroughly combined and formed into a thick sticky paste, add the walnuts and continue cooking, stirring all the while with a wooden spoon, over low heat for 45 minutes longer. The paste will continue to thicken during this time and should be very thick.

5. **Microwave Option:** I get impatient with making candy, which is one reason why I seldom make it, so I only cooked the mixture on the stove for 10 minutes and then I scraped it into a 2 to 3-quart Pyrex mixing bowl (you need plenty of room for boil-ups!) and cooked it, uncovered, in the microwave at 50% power for 15 minutes, by which time it became a very thick paste. You can microwave it from the time you add the walnuts for approximately 20 minutes at 50% power.

6. Whichever way you cook it, when the paste is very thick, remove it from the heat and use a spatula to transfer the paste into a well-oiled 8-inch square baking pan. Press the mixture evenly into the pan. Place the pan in the refrigerator to cool for at least 2 hours. It should be quite firm when cool. Remove the pan from the refrigerator. The bottom of the pan should be cold. If it is still warm, chill longer.

7. Mix the remaining 2 tablespoons cornstarch with the confectioners' sugar. Spread 1/4 cup of

this mixture over a sheet of baking parchment on your work surface. You should be able to lift the Turkish Delight out of the pan with your hands. Place the square of Turkish Delight on top of the sugar/cornstarch mixture and spread more of it over the top of the square with your fingers. Once the square is covered on all sides with a layer of the sugar/cornstarch mixture, use a sharp knife to cut it into 36 squares. Toss the small squares with more of the sugar/cornstarch mixture to coat them on all sides. Store in an airtight container.

Chocolate Panforte

ITALY

40 small slices   SF

Panforte, which means "strong bread" in Italian, is classified as a "fruitcake," but it's really more like a candy. Everyone I served it to was unfamiliar with it, but really enjoyed it and went back for more. Agave nectar makes an excellent substitute for the traditional honey. There are many versions of this Italian sweet. I took the liberty of using dried cranberries instead of other dried fruit, because they are nutritious, pretty, and seem tailor-made for the winter holidays. See page 198 for how to skin and toast hazelnuts at the same time. **Tip:** *This must be made 1 day before serving.*

1 CUP SKINNED AND TOASTED HAZELNUTS (FILBERTS)

4 1/2 OUNCES GOOD-QUALITY VEGAN BITTERSWEET CHOCO-
     LATE, CHOPPED

1/2 CUP DRIED UNSWEETENED CRANBERRIES (OR OTHER
     DRIED FRUIT)

2 TABLESPOONS HAZELNUT LIQUEUR OR HAZELNUT-FLA-
     VORED ITALIAN SYRUP (PAGE 171)

1 CUP PLUS 1/2 TABLESPOON UNBLEACHED WHITE FLOUR,
     DIVIDED

1/2 TEASPOON PLUS 1 TEASPOON GROUND CINNAMON,
     DIVIDED

2/3 CUP AGAVE NECTAR

2/3 CUP LIGHT OR DARK BROWN SUGAR

1/2 TEASPOON UNSWEETENED COCOA POWDER
CONFECTIONERS' SUGAR

1. Preheat oven to 300°F. Oil a 9-inch round cake pan and line it with a piece of baking parchment cut to fit. In a large mixing bowl, combine the nuts, chocolate, fruit, and liqueur. In a small mixing bowl, sift together the 1 cup flour and the 1/2 teaspoon cinnamon.

2. In a small saucepan, combine the agave nectar and brown sugar. Bring to a boil, stirring occasionally with a wooden spoon. Simmer for 2 minutes and remove from the heat.

3. Pour the syrup mixture into the mixing bowl with the chocolate mixture. Stir well. Gently fold in the flour and cinnamon mixture, then pour into the prepared cake pan. Smooth the batter with wet fingers.

4. In a small bowl, stir together the 1/2 tablespoon flour, the 1 teaspoon cinnamon, and cocoa, then sift the mixture over the batter. Bake until set, about 30 to 45 minutes. Remove the pan to a rack and cool completely, then refrigerate for at least one day.

5. The next day, loosen the sides with a table knife and overturn the candy onto a plate. Peel off the parchment and transfer it to a serving plate. Sift a little confectioners' sugar over the top. Cut the panforte into thin wedges. The candy can be kept well-wrapped in the refrigerator for about 2 weeks.

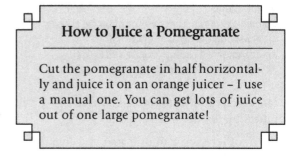

How to Juice a Pomegranate

Cut the pomegranate in half horizontally and juice it on an orange juicer – I use a manual one. You can get lots of juice out of one large pomegranate!

Italian Baked Fruit-Stuffed Peaches

ITALY

Serves 4   GF, SFO

This makes a great company dessert when peaches are in full season. The stuffing can also be used with pear halves.

- 1/2 CUP RAISINS
- 1/4 CUP DRY WHITE WINE
- 1/2 CUP CHOPPED TOASTED WALNUTS
- 2 TABLESPOONS PLUS 1 1/2 TABLESPOONS SUGAR, DIVIDED
- 4 RIPE FREESTONE PEACHES, HALVED AND PITTED
- 1/4 CUP MARSALA, MADEIRA, OR MEDIUM-DRY SHERRY
- 1 TABLESPOON VEGAN MARGARINE

1. Preheat the oven to 350 °F. Soak the raisins in the wine for about 30 minutes. Drain the raisins (reserving the wine) and chop finely. Mix the raisins in a medium bowl with the reserved wine, walnuts, and 2 tablespoons of the sugar. Scoop out a little of the peach flesh from the centers of the peach halves. Chop the peach flesh and add it to the reserved stuffing, stirring well. Fill the peach halves evenly with the stuffing and place the halves in a shallow oiled baking dish. Pour the Marsala over the peaches and sprinkle with the remaining 1 1/2 tablespoons sugar. Dot the tops with the margarine. Bake for 25 minutes and serve hot in dessert dishes.

2. **Serving Suggestion:** If you like, pass your favorite commercial soy creamer or homemade Nut Cream (page 197) or Rich Vegan Cream (page 194) for your guests to drizzle on their stuffed peaches.

Chocolate-Orange Sorbetto

ITALY

Makes 1 quart; serves 8   GF, SF, <30

This is a scrumptious treat any time of the year! It's very simple to make, too. Best of all, you don't need an expensive gelato maker to make it. An inexpensive electric or manual ice cream machine with the insert that you keep in the freezer works just fine!

- 3 CUPS WATER
- 3/4 CUP SUGAR
- 3/4 CUP ORGANIC CORN SYRUP, BROWN RICE SYRUP, OR AGAVE NECTAR
- 4.8 OUNCES VEGAN DARK CHOCOLATE, CUT INTO SMALL PIECES
- FINELY GRATED ZEST OF 1 ORGANIC ORANGE
- 1/2 CUP UNSWEETENED COCOA POWDER, SIFTED

Bring water, sugar and syrup to a boil in a large saucepan. Remove it from the heat and add the chocolate and orange zest. Let it stand 2 minutes and then whisk it until it is very smooth. Transfer the sifted cocoa into a large bowl and whisk in the hot chocolate mixture until smooth. Strain the mixture into a 1-quart Pyrex measuring pitcher. Chill the mixture thoroughly and then freeze according to the directions for your ice cream machine.

Almond Cream Whipped Topping

Makes about 2 cups   GF

This is my all-purpose whipped topping – rich, creamy, and light, with a lovely, subtle almond flavor. It can be the perfect shortcake topping when made with a little less agar powder (1/2 teaspoon), because traditionally, the cream for shortcakes is not whipped to stiff peaks but left soft. For best results, make the topping at least 4 to 6 hours before serving, or even several days ahead. The recipe is easily doubled for a crowd.

1 CUP BLANCHED, SLIVERED RAW ALMONDS

2 CUPS HOT WATER

2 TABLESPOONS SUGAR

2 TABLESPOONS CORNSTARCH OR 3 TABLESPOONS WHITE
    RICE FLOUR

3/4 TEASPOON AGAR POWDER (USE 1/2 TEASPOON FOR A
    SOFTER CREAM)

1/4 CUP FIRM SILKEN TOFU

1/2 TABLESPOON FRESH LEMON JUICE

1 PINCH SALT

1/2 TEASPOON PURE VANILLA EXTRACT

1/4 TEASPOON PURE ALMOND EXTRACT, OPTIONAL

1. In a blender, combine the almonds and hot water and blend until very smooth. Be patient and let it run for several minutes. Strain the resulting almond milk through a cheesecloth-lined colander over a clean pot, measuring pitcher or bowl. Use 2 layers of fine cheesecloth from a fabric store. Gather the cheesecloth up to make a "bag" and twist and squeeze the "bag" to squeeze out as much of the almond milk as possible. You can use the almond meal for a facial scrub.

2. In a small saucepan, mix 1/2 cup plus 2 tablespoons of the almond milk with the sugar, agar and cornstarch. Stir the mixture over medium heat until thickened and translucent.

3. Microwave Option: Mix in a 2-quart microwave-safe bowl (with room for the mixture to rise up) and cook 30 seconds on 100% power (default setting), whisk and repeat 3 more times or until thickened and translucent.

4. In the blender, combine 1 cup more of the almond milk, the silken tofu, salt, lemon juice, vanilla, and almond extract, if using. Scrape the cooked mixture into the blender. Blend until smooth. Transfer to a bowl and refrigerate for about 1 hour, then beat the mixture briefly so that it is creamy. Chill again for at least 3 hours.

Chocolate Soufflé with Crème Anglaise

FRANCE

Serves 4

Can there be anything more decadent than the dark, moist, extravagance of a chocolate soufflé? This vegan version is every bit as decadent as the original (though it doesn't rise quite as much). Like the original, it's a little fussy, but that adds to the specialness of the dessert. If you have the recipe components measured out ahead of time, the beater set up, ramekins prepared, etc., you will only have to visit the kitchen twice before removing these dark beauties from the oven and serving them with a flourish. The soufflés need to be served immediately after baking. For best results, make the Crème Anglaise earlier in the day.

Vegan Crème Anglaise (Vanilla Sauce):

2/3 CUP SOY OR ALMOND MILK

1 1/2 TABLESPOONS SUGAR

1/2 TABLESPOON BIRD'S PLAIN CUSTARD POWDER (OR
    CORNSTARCH WITH A PINCH OF SPANISH SAFFRON)

1 PINCH SALT

3/4 TEASPOON PURE VANILLA EXTRACT

1 TEASPOON VEGAN MARGARINE

Beaten "Egg Whites":

3 TABLESPOONS WATER PLUS

1 TABLESPOON LIQUEUR OF CHOICE OR FLAVORED ITALIAN
    SYRUP (PAGE 171)

2 TABLESPOONS ENER-G EGG REPLACER OR ORGRAN "NO
    EGG" (THESE ARE THE ONLY BRANDS THAT WHIP UP
    STIFFLY ENOUGH FOR THIS RECIPE) (SEE PAGE 15)

Chocolate Batter:

1/2 CUP MEDIUM-FIRM TOFU OR EXTRA-FIRM SILKEN TOFU

1/2 CUP SUGAR

2 OUNCES VEGAN SEMISWEET OR BITTERSWEET CHOCO-
    LATE, MELTED (SEE PAGE 210)

1/4 CUP NONDAIRY MILK

1/4 CUP UNBLEACHED WHITE FLOUR

2 TABLESPOONS UNSWEETENED COCOA POWDER

1/2 TEASPOON BAKING POWDER

1/4 TEASPOON PURE VANILLA EXTRACT

1/4 TEASPOON SALT

1. **Crème Anglaise:** Mix the milk, sugar, salt, and custard powder (or cornstarch and saffron) with a whisk in a small saucepan and stir over medium heat with a whisk or wooden spoon until it has thickened. Or, to use a microwave, mix the milk, sugar, salt and custard powder (or cornstarch and saffron) with a whisk in a medium microwave-safe bowl or 1-quart Pyrex measuring pitcher. Cook on 100% power (default setting) for 1 minute, then whisk the mixture vigorously. Repeat in 1 minute increments until the sauce has thickened.

2. Once the sauce has thickened, stir in the vanilla and margarine. Refrigerate, covered with plastic wrap, until serving time. To serve, heat the sauce gently in a double boiler over simmering water. When it is hot, transfer it to a small serving pitcher and keep it warm by placing it in a small pot of very hot water, but not on the heat.

3. Preheat the oven to 400°F. Lightly spray four 3-inch straight-sided ramekins with baking spray or brush with Generic Pan Coating (page 184). (Or grease the ramekins well with margarine and flour them, tapping the bottoms to remove any excess flour.) The first thing you want to do is get the "egg whites" beating because it takes at least 6 minutes to get it to the right fluffy consistency and you should have it beating while you make the batter.

4. **"Egg Whites":** Beat the water, liqueur, and egg replacer until a soft peak forms and remains, which takes about 6 to 10 minutes. You can use the smallest bowl with your stand mixer and the whipping attachment. You can also use the "egg whip" attachment with a modern food processor. **Important:** If you have only a hand-held electric mixer, mix the batter ingredients (with the exception of the melted chocolate!) before starting the "egg whites." When the "egg whites" are almost beaten enough, quickly melt the chocolate and add it to the batter in the food processor, then proceed. Important: Do not use an immersion/stick blender to beat the egg re-

placer. This failed for me, even with the whipping attachment.

5. **Chocolate Batter:** Combine all of the chocolate batter ingredients in a food processor or a blender and processing until smooth. I find it necessary to stop the processor after a few seconds, lift the blade and scrape any ingredients that have accumulated under it, replace the blade, then scrape the bowl, and blend again.

6. Scrape the batter into a medium bowl. Scoop the beaten "egg whites" over the batter and fold it into the batter with a spatula, using an over-and-under movement rather than a stirring motion. Mix only until you cannot discern one mixture from another and the batter looks foamy. The batter should actually start to foam up a bit.

7. Divide the batter quickly and evenly among the 4 prepared ramekins. Place them on a baking sheet, transfer to the preheated oven and bake them for 25 minutes. The soufflés should have risen and should be crusty on top after 25 minutes of baking. Remove them from the oven and serve hot with the warm Crème Anglaise.

Tip: White ceramic straight-sided ramekins are inexpensive and widely available wherever kitchenware is sold.

Creamy Cappuccino Pudding

Italy/North America

Serves 4   GF

This layered pudding is definitely good enough for company! It's a perfect light dessert to finish an Italian meal. I prefer to serve these puddings in glass coffee cups, so that guests can see the layers. Freshly made espresso is preferable, but you can also make it with instant espresso powder (use decaf, if you prefer).

1/2 CUP NONDAIRY MILK
1/2 CUP EXTRA-FIRM SILKEN TOFU
1 CUP STRONG ESPRESSO COFFEE (UNSWEETENED)

1/3 CUP SUGAR

2 TABLESPOONS CORNSTARCH

1 PINCH SALT

1 TEASPOON PURE VANILLA EXTRACT

1 TABLESPOON ALMOND, HAZELNUT, OR COFFEE LIQUEUR
OR ITALIAN SYRUP (PAGE 171), OPTIONAL

1/2 CUP ALMOND CREAM WHIPPED TOPPING (PAGE 207), OR
SOYATOO WHIPPABLE SOY TOPPING CREAM, CHILLED
FOR AT LEAST 3 HOURS

GARNISH: GRATED DARK CHOCOLATE, GROUND CINNAMON,
CINNAMON-SUGAR, OR UNSWEETENED COCOA POWDER

1. Using a blender or an immersion/stick blender in a deep 1-quart pitcher or container, whip the milk and tofu together to make a smooth cream.

```
┌─────────────────────────────────┐
       How to Melt Chocolate
  ───────────────────────────────

  Melting chocolate requires gentle heat.
  Overheated chocolate may scorch, lose
  flavor, and turn coarse and grainy. Stir
  melting chocolate only after it has begun
  to liquefy. Vegans have an advantage in
  this, because dark chocolate needs only to
  be stirred frequently during melting and
  not constantly, as with milk chocolate.
  Here are two good methods for melting
  chocolate so that it is smooth and glossy.

  • Microwave Method: Place coarsely chopped
    chocolate in a microwave-safe container
    and microwave at 50% power for 1 1/2 to 4
    minutes (depending on the power of your
    microwave), until the chocolate turns
    shiny. Remove the container from the
    microwave and stir the chocolate until
    it is completely melted.

  • Double Boiler Method: Place coarsely
    chopped chocolate in the top of a dou-
    ble boiler over hot, not simmering, wa-
    ter. Melt the chocolate, stirring after it
    begins to melt and stirring off and on
    until it is smooth. Remove the top part
    of the double boiler from the bottom.
└─────────────────────────────────┘
```

Add the espresso, sugar, cornstarch, and salt.

2. Transfer the mixture into a microwave-safe 11/2 or 2-quart bowl and microwave at full power for 1 minute. Whisk and cook 1 more minute or until thickened and translucent. Alternatively, you can cook the pudding, stirring constantly, in a 1-quart saucepan over medium-high heat until thickened and translucent. Whisk in the vanilla and liqueur, if using.

3. Pour the pudding into 4 small glass coffee mugs, glasses or glass dishes (no more than 1 cup capacity). Cover the puddings and chill for at least 4 hours.

4. Before serving, smooth 2 tablespoons of the whipped topping over the top of each serving of pudding. Sprinkle each with a little grated dark chocolate, cinnamon, cinnamon-sugar, or cocoa powder. Serve immediately or refrigerate for several more hours or even days, each cup covered with plastic wrap. Serve cold.

Chai Cappuccino Pudding

INDIA/NORTH AMERICA

Serves 4   GF

This spicy and unusual pudding would make a nice light dessert to follow a rich Indian meal. It is very pretty served in one-cup glasses, glass coffee cups or glass dishes, so that the layers can be seen.

1/2 CUP NONDAIRY MILK

1/2 CUP EXTRA-FIRM SILKEN TOFU

1 CUP STRONG CHAI TEA (UNSWEETENED) (SEE NEXT PAGE)

1/2 CUP LIGHT OR DARK BROWN SUGAR

2 TABLESPOONS CORNSTARCH

PINCH SALT

1/2 TEASPOON PURE VANILLA EXTRACT

1/2 CUP ALMOND CREAM WHIPPED TOPPING (PAGE 207) OR
SOYATOO WHIPPABLE SOY TOPPING CREAM, CHILLED
FOR AT LEAST 3 HOURS

CINNAMON-SUGAR AND CINNAMON STICKS

1. Using a blender or an immersion/stick blender (in a deep 1-quart container), whip the milk and tofu together to make a smooth cream. Add the chai, brown sugar, cornstarch, and salt.

2. Transfer the mixture into a microwave-safe 11/2 or 2-quart bowl or pitcher and microwave at full power for 1 minute. Whisk and cook 1 more minute or until thickened and translucent. Alternatively, you can cook the pudding, stirring constantly, in a 1-quart saucepan over medium-high heat until thickened and translucent.

3. Whisk in the vanilla. Pour the pudding into 4 small glass coffee mugs, glasses, or glass dishes (no more than 1 cup capacity). Cover and chill for at least 4 hours.

4. Before serving, smooth 2 tablespoons of the whipped topping onto each serving. Sprinkle with cinnamon-sugar and insert a cinnamon stick into the edge of each pudding. Serve immediately or refrigerate for several hours, each cup covered with plastic wrap. Serve cold.

Chai for Pudding

It's easy to make your own Chai tea blend. The cardamom is a must, but you can vary the other spices. Some possibilities are fennel, nutmeg, white peppercorns, star anise, allspice, coriander seeds, and vanilla. Here is the formula that I like, but feel free to experiment! Tea has far less caffeine than coffee, but if you want to avoid caffeine, use rooibos tea. Rooibos ("red bush" in Afrikaans, pronounced roy-bush) is made from the bark of a South African bush. It has a slightly malty flavor and can be enjoyed with milk and sugar. It reputedly has a high mineral and antioxidant content.

To Toast Nuts, Seeds, and Coconut

There are four easy ways to toast nuts, seeds, and coconut. The oven method is the best way if you are toasting a large quantity. If you have any leftovers, cool them completely, then store them in the freezer in zip-top freezer bags.

- **Dry Skillet Method:** In a dry skillet, such as cast iron, spread the nuts, seeds or coconut in an even layer and heat the pan over medium heat, shaking it often or stirring the contents with a wooden spoon – don't overcrowd. Keep stirring or shaking for about 5 minutes or until contents smell toasty and are as brown as you like them. Watch them like a hawk! Different nuts will toast at different rates, so don't mix types while you toast them.

- **Skillet Method with Fat:** This method results in a more uniformly browned look than when you use a dry skillet. Add a teaspoon of oil or vegan margarine to the skillet and proceed as above.

- **Oven Method**: Preheat the oven to 350° to 425°F. Place your nuts, seeds, or coconut on an appropriately-sized baking sheet and bake for a few minutes, watching them carefully and shaking or stirring occasionally. When they are golden and fragrant, which will take about 5 to 10 minutes, remove them from the oven. Oven-toasting nuts takes a bit longer than the skillet method, but they will be more uniformly browned without using fat.

- **Microwave Method:** This is a quick method, if you need only a small amount. Spread the nuts, seeds, or coconut on a microwave-safe plate and microwave on 100% power (default setting) for 3 to 5 minutes. Watch them carefully and remove them when slightly less browned than you want because they will continue to brown for a moment after.

1 1/2 CUPS WATER

2 WHOLE CLOVES

1/2 TEASPOON CARDAMOM SEEDS

2 BLACK PEPPERCORNS

1 (2-INCH) STICK CINNAMON

1 THIN SLICE FRESH GINGER

1/8 TEASPOON ANISE SEED

1 TABLESPOON LOOSE BLACK TEA OF ANY KIND (OR ROOI-
BUS TEA) OR 1 TEA BAG

Bring the water to a boil and add the spices. Cover and simmer gently for 10 to15 minutes. Turn off the heat and add the tea leaves (or bag). Cover and steep for about 10 minutes. Strain the tea through a fine tea strainer.

International Bread Sampler

As with every chapter in this book, I had some difficulty choosing only a few recipes from my repertoire, developed over forty-four years of baking bread (twenty-two of those years as a vegan). So, this collection is not representative of the entire international world of bread. Rather, it's a very personal collection of some old favorites as well as current favorites. I hope they'll inspire you to branch out with your own baking. Some of the recipes are just crying out for improvisation and variations.

The first three recipes in the chapter (not counting the vegan biscuit mix) are the only "quick breads" (non-yeasted), but they are likely not recipes you'll encounter in the average cookbook. The remaining recipes are yeast breads, which have been a passion of mine since I was eighteen years old. There are five sweet bread recipes (no butter, milk, or eggs, of course), which I hope will inspire you to devise your own vegan holiday breads or to veganize the holiday breads from your family or cultural heritage.

For instance, my father, Alejandro Jaime Urbina, a Peruvian of Spanish and Italian descent, fondly recalled the panetón (the Peruvian version of the Italian panettone) that his Tia Maria baked in a brick oven in the central courtyard of his boyhood home in Lima. Because of his memories, I began making panettone for Christmas many years ago, and my oldest daughter, Bethany, now continues this tradition. (Panettone is a rich yeast bread, slightly sweet, and flavored with citrus zest, dried fruit, anise, and almonds.) I later discovered that my father's Italian family, who immigrated to Peru from the Italian Riviera in the 1800s, may have been making "Panettone Genovese," rather than the "Panettone di Milano," which most Italians simply call panettone. The Genovese version is not as rich as the Milanese version and is flavored more exotically. It's the inspiration for my own version of vegan panetón.

International Bread Sampler

South African Mielie Bread

SOUTH AFRICA

Serves 6   SFO

This tender, slightly sweet bread is a vegan version of a traditional South African bread. It's very simple to make and very hard to stop eating! "Mielie" is the South African word for corn. This recipe calls for a can of cream-style corn, which is a vegan product.

1 CUP PLUS 1 1/2 TABLESPOONS NONDAIRY MILK

3/4 TABLESPOON ENER-G EGG REPLACER POWDER OR
     ORGRAN "NO EGG" NATURAL EGG REPLACER (SEE
     PAGE 15)

3 CUPS VEGAN BAKING MIX (PAGE 217)

1 1/2 TABLESPOONS SUGAR

1 (14-OUNCE) CAN CREAM-STYLE CORN (1 1/2 CUPS)

1/4 TO 1/3 CUP MELTED VEGAN MARGARINE

1. Preheat the oven to 400°F. Brush a shallow 2-quart round casserole or 9 x 3-inch cake pan with margarine.

2. In a small, deep bowl or measuring pitcher beat the milk and egg replacer together with an immersion/stick blender, electric mixer, or a whisk until frothy.

3. In a large bowl whisk the vegan baking mix and sugar together. Pour in the corn and the nondairy milk beaten with the egg replacer. Stir briefly – the batter will be lumpy. Pour the batter into the prepared casserole. Pour the melted margarine evenly over the batter. Bake for 25 minutes or until the bread is golden on top and shrinks away from the sides of the pan a bit. Serve hot.

South Indian Steamed Corn Bread

Makai Ka Dhokla

SOUTH INDIA

Serves 9   SF, GF

This steamed treat is similar to a savory cornbread. It's very tender when it is warm. I recommend eating it hot with Gujarati-Style Stewed Tomatoes (page 155) Together, they are absolutely scrumptious and visually stunning. Dhoklas are made from a variety of grain and legume flours – this one is great for people with wheat allergies because it is entirely made of corn.

1/2 CUP SOY MILK, NUT MILK, OR HEMP MILK

1/2 TABLESPOON FRESH LEMON JUICE OR CIDER VINEGAR

1 CUP CORN FLOUR (SEE PAGE 174)

1/2 CUP WATER

2 TEASPOONS SUGAR

1/4 TEASPOON GROUND GINGER

1/4 TEASPOON GARLIC POWDER

1/4 TEASPOON SALT, OPTIONAL

3/4 CUP THAWED, DRAINED FROZEN SWEET CORN

2 TEASPOONS OLIVE OIL, LIGHT SESAME OIL, OR COLD-
     PRESSED PEANUT OIL

1 TEASPOON LOUISIANA HOT SAUCE OR SRIRACHA SAUCE

1 TEASPOON FRESH LEMON JUICE

1 TEASPOON BAKING SODA

Topping:

1 TABLESPOON OLIVE OIL, LIGHT SESAME OIL, OR COLD-
     PRESSED PEANUT OIL

1 TEASPOON MUSTARD SEEDS

1 TEASPOON SESAME SEEDS

Garnish:

CHOPPED PARSLEY, CILANTRO, OR BASIL

1. In a medium bowl, combine the nondairy milk with the lemon juice or vinegar. Stir in the corn flour and water and continue stirring until smooth. Set aside. Oil an 8-inch square baking pan and set aside.

2. Prepare a steamer by using any pot, stir-fry pan or wok (with a tight lid) that can accommodate the baking pan. You can balance the pan on a flat steaming tray, 3 wads of bunched up aluminum foil or, in case of a stir-fry pan or wok, 2 chopsticks lying across the bottom. I like to use an electric wok or electric skillet for steaming. Have several inches of water simmering in the bottom of the pan.

3. Mix the other ingredients (except the baking soda) into the batter and mix it in well. Sift the baking soda over the batter and fold it in gen-

tly. Pour the batter evenly into the prepared pan and place the pan on your steamer arrangement. Cover the pot and steam over simmering (not boiling) water for 15 minutes or until a cake tester comes out clean.

4. While the dhokla is steaming, prepare the topping. Heat the oil in a small skillet. Add the seeds and fry until the seeds start to pop and crackle. Quickly remove from the heat.

5. Pour the topping over the hot dhokla. Sprinkle with parsley. Cut into squares and serve hot.

Flour for Non-Yeast Breads

Important – Please Read Before You Start Baking!

I prefer to use only moderate amounts of fat in my baking if at all possible. For this reason, I use pastry flour (white or whole wheat) in much of my non-yeast baking. In more traditional baking, the fat in the recipe coats the gluten (the wheat protein) and makes the gluten more tender, but using at least some pastry flour, made from soft wheat (which has a lower gluten content than either all-purpose flour or bread flour), means that you can get away with less fat in a recipe and still have a tender product.

In the non-yeast breads in this first section of the bread chapter, when I call for "unbleached white flour" or "whole-wheat flour," I am referring to "all-purpose flour." But, if I call for "pastry flour" (either white or whole-wheat), please be sure that pastry flour (or "cake flour" or "cake and pastry flour") is what you use, or the recipe may not turn out as you expect. In the U.K., "cake and pastry flour" is pretty much the same as North American, but in Australia, just use "plain flour" (which is their "all-purpose flour") because the gluten content is more similar to our pastry flour. (Read your labels!)

Tip: Don't use self-rising flour in these recipes – it already contains salt and leavenings!

To measure flour correctly, you need calibrated measuring cups made for measuring dry ingredients. Do not use a coffee cup or drinking glass. Lightly spoon the flour directly into the measuring cup from the container or bag and level it off with a table knife. Do not shake the cup. Do not pack the flour down.

If you need pastry flour right away and have none, you can make a fair substitute. For each cup of pastry flour you need, mix together 7/8 cup (14 tablespoons) all-purpose flour and 2 tablespoons cornstarch (some people use 13 tablespoons all-purpose flour and 3 tablespoons of cornstarch).

Irish Potato Biscuits

Spud Scones

IRELAND

Makes 12 biscuits   SFO

It may be hard to believe that such mundane ingredients can produce something so tasty, but these traditionally fat-free griddle scones are really delicious. (Griddle scones, by the way, are cooked on top of a stove instead of in an oven.) Try them with your next afternoon tea. Serve these homey biscuits hot, splitting them with a fork (like an English muffin), with preserves, jam, marmalade, vegan margarine, and tea, of course!

1 POUND RUSSET POTATOES, PEELED AND CUT INTO 1-INCH CUBES
3/4 TEASPOON SALT
1/4 CUP NONDAIRY MILK
1 CUP SIFTED UNBLEACHED WHITE FLOUR OR WHITE WHOLE-WHEAT FLOUR
1 TEASPOON BAKING POWDER

1. About 20 minutes before you are ready to make the biscuits, boil or steam the potato cubes in a saucepan until tender or microwave the potato cubes in a covered 2-quart microwave-safe bowl, with 3 tablespoons of water, on 100% power (default setting) for about 8 minutes or until tender. Drain the potatoes in a colander.

2. If you boiled the potatoes, transfer the potatoes back into the saucepan they were cooked in, cover, and place over low heat, or the residual heat of an electric burner which has just been turned off, for a few minutes to dry the potatoes out a bit. (Don't burn them!)

3. Mash the potatoes in a medium bowl or press them into the bowl through a potato ricer. Mash in the salt and milk. In a small bowl, whisk together the flour and baking powder and mix into the potatoes. Knead the dough lightly and roll it out on a lightly-floured work surface to

Vegan Baking Mix

Makes about 12 cups SFO, <30

This versatile mix is best made with pastry flour because it contains less fat than most biscuit mix recipes. We found the taste of vegan margarine to be far superior to that of vegetable shortening. The mix must be refrigerated. Use a good-tasting nondairy milk powder such as Better Than Milk beverage mix. I don't bother adding nondairy milk powder to the mix. I simply use liquid nondairy milk in the recipes. But if you are using the mix for camping and want to use only water, then add 1/2 cup plus 2 tablespoons nondairy milk powder. You can use this in recipes that call for commercial biscuit mix. Also, if you unable to refrigerate, use non-hydrogenated shortening instead of vegan margarine. This mixture will last about one month. You can cut this recipe in half, if you wish.

5 CUPS WHOLE-WHEAT PASTRY FLOUR OR WHITE WHOLE-WHEAT PASTRY FLOUR
5 CUPS WHITE PASTRY FLOUR
1/4 CUP BAKING POWDER
1/4 CUP SUGAR
1 1/2 TABLESPOONS SALT
1 TEASPOON CREAM OF TARTAR
1 1/3 CUPS COLD VEGAN MARGARINE, CUT UP IN PIECES (OR NON-HYDROGENATED SHORTENING)

Mix all of the ingredients in a large bowl, cutting the margarine in with your fingers until it is like crumbs. Store the mix in an airtight container.

For rolled biscuits, use about 3 tablespoons of nondairy milk per cup of mix. For drop biscuits, use 1/4 cup. Bake at 400°F for about 8 minutes.

Tip: Stir the mix well before you use it.

3/8-inch thick (you can cover your surface with a sheet of baking parchment, if you like. Cut the dough into twelve 2-inch rounds.

4. Heat a large, dry cast iron or nonstick griddle or skillet over high heat until drops of cold water dance on the top, then turn the heat down to medium. Alternatively, use an electric skillet or griddle at the same temperature you would set it for pancakes.

5. Bake the biscuits on one side for 5 minutes, then turn over and bake 5 minutes on the other side. They should be golden brown on both sides. Don't cook them too fast or the insides won't be thoroughly cooked.

VARIATIONS:

- **Northern Irish Potato Cake or "Fadge":** Omit the baking powder; roll each half of the dough into a 1/4-inch thick circle and cut each circle into "farls" (4 wedges). Cook as above. I was almost afraid to try this because it was unleavened, but it is quite delicious.
- **Oaten Farls:** Add two small handfuls of quick oats to the original "spud scone" dough. Roll each half of the dough into a 1/4-inch thick circle and cut each circle into "farls" (4 wedges), using quick oats to sprinkle on the rolling surface instead of flour. Cook as above.

Yeast Breads

Apulian Focaccia

Focaccia Pugliese

ITALY

Serves 6 to 8   SF

I can never make enough of this for family or company. This tasty potato-based dough from the Italian region of Apulia (Puglia) is light and springy, but still nice and chewy (not like the thick, bready stuff that passes for focaccia in many restaurants). I add bran and flax seed for more fiber and nutrition. When added to the unbleached white flour, it doesn't make the dough heavy at all. This makes a wonderful accompaniment to soups, salads, and pasta dishes.
Tip: *To save time, instead of potatoes, use 2 cups instant mashed potato flakes mixed with 1 1/3 cups boiling water. Do not add salt, margarine, or milk of any kind.*

8 OUNCES RUSSET POTATOES, PEELED AND CUT INTO 1-INCH
    CUBES
1 1/2 TEASPOONS DRY ACTIVE YEAST OR 1 TEASPOON
    INSTANT YEAST

1 CUP PLUS 2 TABLESPOONS WARM WATER (105° – 115°F)
1 TABLESPOON OLIVE OIL
3 1/2 CUPS UNBLEACHED WHITE FLOUR
1/4 CUP GROUND FLAX SEED
1/4 CUP WHEAT BRAN
2 TEASPOONS SALT
2 TABLESPOONS OLIVE OIL AND A SPRINKLING OF COARSE
    OR KOSHER SALT
2 TABLESPOONS CHOPPED FRESH ROSEMARY OR OTHER HERBS

1. About 20 minutes before you are ready to make the dough, boil or steam the potato cubes in a saucepan until tender or microwave the potato cubes in a covered 2-quart microwave-safe bowl, with 3 tablespoons of water, on 100% power (default setting) for about 8 minutes or until tender. Drain the potatoes in a colander. If you boiled the potatoes, transfer the potatoes back into the saucepan they were cooked in, cover, and place over low heat, or the residual heat of an electric burner which has just been turned off, for a few minutes to dry the potatoes out a bit. (Don't burn them!)

2. Mash the potatoes in a medium bowl or press them into the bowl through a potato ricer.

3. Use the potatoes in the dough while they are still warm but not so hot as to kill the yeast; they should be about the same temperature as the water for the yeast.

4. Stir the yeast into the warm water in a large mixing bowl or the bowl of a stand mixer. Let sit for 5 minutes. Add the oil and mashed potato.

5. In a medium bowl, combine the flour, flax seed, bran, and salt and mix well, then add to the liquid mixture in two additions – mix until the dough comes together. Knead the dough using one of the options on page 221.

6. **First Rise:** Transfer the dough to a large lightly-oiled bowl (unless you are using a bread machine), turn it over to oil the top, cover the bowl tightly with plastic wrap and leave it to rise in a moderately warm place until it has doubled in size, about 1 1/2 hours. (See also the Refrigerator Rise Option on page 220.)

7. **Shaping and Second Rise:** Punch down the dough. Oil a 10 x 15-inch dark baking sheet (a dark sheet browns foods better) with olive oil and sprinkle with flour, cornmeal, or semolina flour. Roll and pat the dough into a rectangle to fit the baking sheet. Pat and stretch the dough toward the edges to cover the whole sheet. Cover the sheet with a damp towel or place the whole thing inside of a large food-safe plastic bag, let it sit for 10 minutes and then stretch the dough a bit farther to the edges (the dough tends to shrink back a bit). Cover the sheet again and let it rise in a moderately warm spot until it has doubled in size, about 45 to 60 minutes.

8. If you prefer to bake the focaccia on a baking stone or unglazed tiles instead of on a pan, follow the directions for baking pizza on a stone or tiles in instruction #3 on page 223. This also covers using a baking peel or alternative.

9. While the dough rises, preheat the oven to 425°F. Just before you are ready to bake the focaccia, dimple the dough with your fingertips. Brush it or drizzle it with the olive oil and sprinkle the salt and rosemary over the dough. Bake for 20 to 25 minutes or until golden. Re-

Flour for Yeast Breads

If you live in the U.S.A., you can use the unbleached white or whole-wheat flour (which are classified as "all-purpose" flours) called for in the recipes in this chapter, or you might prefer to use bread flour instead. Bread flour, made from hard wheat, has a higher gluten (wheat protein) content than all-purpose flour, which is a plus when making yeast breads. (Gluten traps gases released by yeast in bread dough by forming cell walls around the gas. This gives bread its light texture and makes it rise well.)

Canadian all-purpose flour legally must contain 13 percent protein, which is in the range of U.S. "bread flour" (12 to 14 percent), so if you live in Canada, you don't even need to consider "bread flour" for these recipes.

In the U.K., "strong plain flour" or "strong bread flour" is what you need for yeast breads. Australian "plain flour" (their "all-purpose") is only in the range of 7 to 10 percent, so you would need the higher protein Australian flour, called "bread flour" or "baker's flour," which ranges from 11.5 to 13.5 percent for bread baking. Check the label for protein content and check the chart of flour types in Resources.

Tip: Don't use self-rising flour in these recipes – it contains salt and leavenings and is meant for quick breads.

move from the baking sheet, cut into squares, and serve warm.

Toppings: Other toppings can include plain tomato sauce with a drizzle of olive oil or sliced fresh tomatoes and herbs with salt and olive oil.

VARIATIONS

Grape Focaccia

Schiacciata All' Uva

Serves 6 to 8   SF

This variation of focaccia is one of my absolute favorites. It is perfect for breakfast or a snack – chewy, tart, and a little sticky and sweet. You can make this with either the potato focaccia dough or the artisanal bread dough. This is the most divine treat – so simple and fresh – you have to try it.

1/2 RECIPE APULIAN FOCACCIA DOUGH (PAGE 218), MIXED AND RISEN ONCE; OR
1/4 RECIPE NO-KNEAD CRUSTY ARTISANAL BREAD DOUGH (PAGE 227), USING THE RISEN, REFRIGERATED DOUGH.

Shape the dough into a focaccia as instructed in the recipe for the dough. Preheat the oven to 475°F. For the grape topping, use several small bunches of purple grapes – wine grapes are fine. I slice the grapes in half, remove the seeds, and push them gently into the patted-out dough, cut-side down, to release the juices. Be generous with the grapes! Sprinkle the grapes generously with coarse sugar, let it rise for 20 minutes and bake it at 475°F for about 20 minutes or until golden and crusty on the bottom. Serve warm.

Plum Foccacia

Schiacciata All' Prugna

Use sliced, pitted Italian prune plums instead of the grapes.

Potato Fougasse

FRANCE

Serves 8 to 10   SF

Fougasse (pronounced foo-gahs) is a French flatbread related to Italian focaccia and shaped to resemble a ladder or "tree-of-life" design. It's very easy to make, but impressive.

1 RECIPE APULIAN FOCACCIA DOUGH (PAGE 218), MIXED AND RISEN
TOPPING:
2 TABLESPOONS OLIVE OIL
1/2 TO 1 TEASPOON COARSE OR KOSHER SALT
2 TABLESPOONS FRESH CHOPPED ROSEMARY, OPTIONAL

1. Shaping and Second Rise: Punch down the dough and divide it in half. Roll or pat half of

Refrigerator Rise Option for Dough

Make the dough at least 10 hours before you are going to use it. Oil the kneaded, once-risen and punched-down dough all over with olive oil and place it in a plastic bag or in a bowl with room to double. A large zip-top bag works well – pat the dough into a thick disc before bagging it. If using a bowl, make sure that the dough is well-oiled and well-covered or it will dry out. Refrigerate overnight or for 8 hours. Note: Refrigerated dough needs 2 hours to come to room temperature before baking, so plan accordingly. A slow rise is actually a good thing – it increases the flavor and texture by allowing the growth of enzymes, called "ripening" the dough.

the dough out into a rectangle with rounded corners or it can be slightly narrower on the top. Pat it out with your hands to fit into 10 x 15-inch dark baking sheet (it won't go all the way to the sides), well oiled with olive oil and sprinkled with cornmeal. (A dark sheet browns foods better.) Cut a slit down the center of the rectangle, leaving 3 or 4 inches uncut at the top and bottom. Make several (4 or 5) diagonal slits, about an inch apart, in the dough on either side of the middle cut. You may want to cut a small slit in the center at the top and bottom, too. Do not cut through the outer edge of the dough. Gently pull the slits open (they will fill in a little as the dough expands during baking). Everyone has a slightly different design, so you don't have to follow my directions exactly. If you prefer to bake the fougasse on a baking stone or unglazed tiles instead of on a pan, follow the directions for baking pizza on a stone or tiles on page 223.

2. Repeat with the second half of the dough, or if you like, make a small focaccia with it as instructed in the main recipe or you can pat the dough out into a thick disc, wrap it in plastic wrap, bag it in a zip-top freezer bag and freeze it for the next time.

3. Sprinkle the top of the shaped bread with a little flour and leave it at room temperature until it has doubled in size, about 1 hour. Cover the bread with damp kitchen towels or place the baking sheet inside of a loose food-safe plastic bag while it rises.

4. Preheat the oven to 475°F. Just before you are ready to bake, brush liberally with olive oil and sprinkle coarse salt lightly over the dough. Sprinkle with rosemary, if using. Bake for 20 to 25 minutes or until golden brown and crispy. Remove the fougasse from the baking sheet to a cooling rack and serve it warm or at room temperature. You can simply tear pieces off rather than cutting it with a knife.

Kneading Options

To knead the dough in these recipes, choose one of the following kneading options:

Automatic Bread Machine: Use instant yeast and room temperature ingredients, including the water. Place the ingredients in the bread machine container in the order that is instructed in your machine's manual. Select the Dough (or Dough/Pasta) Cycle, which does not include baking the dough, and let it go to through the entire cycle. Remove the dough and proceed with the recipe as instructed below.

Stand Mixer: Knead the dough for 10 minutes with the dough hook of a stand mixer.

Food Processor: Mix the flour mixture ingredients together in the processor bowl. While the machine is running, add the mixture of the yeast dissolved in warm water, oil and mashed potato through the feed tube until the dough forms a ball on top of the blade. If it's too dry to come to a ball, add water, using just a few drops at a time, until it does. Process the dough for 30 seconds after it forms a ball.

By Hand: Knead the dough for 8 to 10 minutes on a sheet of baking parchment and oil your hands while you knead. It's best not to add more flour to this dough.

Neapolitan-Style Pizza

ITALY

Serves 4   SF

Since Naples is the original home of pizza and purportedly the absolute best place for it, I have researched what makes it so good. The pizza should be thin-crusted, toasty, and charred a little, and have high, soft, and blistered edges. The filling should not overpower the crust, but should be juicy and taste fresh. Each diner should have his or her own personal 9 to 10-inch pizza, hand-shaped (I have also given directions for two 14-inch pizzas). Everything should be done to approximate baking in a brick oven at very high heat. Here is my humble offering for home bakers.

Neapolitan Pizza Dough

Italian flour is softer (has a lower gluten content) than North American flour, so that's why I made the addition of pastry flour. Neapolitan pizza dough does not contain fat or sugar, by the way.

1 1/4 CUPS WARM WATER (BETWEEN 105 AND 115°F)
1 TEASPOON DRY ACTIVE BAKING YEAST OR 3/4 TEASPOON
   INSTANT YEAST
2 1/2 CUPS UNBLEACHED WHITE FLOUR
1 CUP WHOLE-WHEAT PASTRY FLOUR
2 TEASPOONS SALT

1. In a medium bowl or the bowl of a stand mixer, mix together the warm water and yeast. Let sit for 5 minutes. In another bowl, mix together the two flours and the salt, and add to the yeast mixture. Knead the dough using one of the four options listed on page 221.

2. Transfer the dough to a large lightly-oiled bowl (unless you are using a bread machine), turn it over to oil the top, cover the bowl tightly with plastic wrap and leave it to rise in a moderately warm place until it has doubled in size, about 1 1/2 hours. (See also the Refrigerator Rise Option on page 220.)

3. **To Bake:** 30 to 60 minutes before baking, heat your oven to 500 or 550°F, using a pizza stone

---

White Whole-Wheat Flour

White whole-wheat flour is whole grain wheat flour that has been milled using "white" or albino wheat rather than the traditional red wheat. White whole-wheat flour retains many more nutrients than traditional white flour, which has the bran and germ removed, because it is "whole" – nothing removed. White whole-wheat flour not only has a lighter color, but some bakers perceive a sweeter flavor than darker whole-wheat flours, which also tend to naturally retain a darker color during baking.

You may have read that white whole-wheat flour can be utilized in any recipe that calls for white flour. I wish that were true! But, remember that it still contains wheat and bran, which affects the performance of the flour (the resulting product may be heavier and coarser, and the bran can cut the gluten a bit, possibly affecting the rising power in a yeast bread).

In addition, hard white whole-wheat, which seems to be more readily available, is a high protein wheat, so you must make sure that's what you want for your recipe. Hard white whole-wheat contains 15 to 16 percent protein, which makes really excellent bread flour, but for non-yeast baking, soft white whole-wheat flour is what you should use. It is in the range of American all-purpose flour and pastry flour, between 9 and 11 percent. It's similar in gluten content to "Southern-style flour," which is the choice for Southern biscuits, pie crusts and quick breads. I have used it successfully as a pastry flour.

or unglazed quarry tiles on the bottom rack, if you can, leaving at least a 1-inch gap around the border. If you do not have a pizza stone or tiles, you can bake the pizza on a 10 x 15-inch baking sheet or 14-inch pizza pan on the very bottom of the oven. You can use convection, if you have it.

Important Tip: Do not start shaping the pizzas and topping them until you have preheated the oven. Pizza dough should not rise again before you put it in the oven! You want the dough to cook fast, but not dry out and you want the topping to be juicy. Be aware that toppings, sauce and oil that may drip on the clay may be difficult to remove. Just clean the stone or tiles as best you can – after they have thoroughly cooled – and the stains will not affect performance in the next baking.

4. Punch down the dough. Divide the dough into two or four balls.

5. **Shaping the Pizza:** You can use a rolling pin to shape the pizza, but Neapolitans argue that rolling the dough makes a flatter, less chewy crust. The easiest way to roll it out is on lightly-floured baking parchment.

To shape pizza without a rolling pin:
Method 1: On a lightly-floured sheet of baking parchment covering your work surface, holding your fingers flat, press the ball of dough out into a circle. Drape the circle over your closed fists. Keeping your thumbs out of the way, move your fists up and down, gently and evenly stretching the dough to make a 9-inch circle (more or less). For the final stretching, hold the edge of the pizza and keep moving the edge of the dough around through your fingers, letting the weight of the dough stretch it a little more, to 10-inch maximum across for the smaller ball of dough or a 14-inch maximum for the larger.
Method 2: On a lightly-floured sheet of baking parchment covering your work surface, holding your fingers flat, press the ball of dough out into a circle. Roll or pat the circle out to about 7 inch-

es across for the small ball of dough or about 10 to 11 inches for the larger ball. Drape the circle over a large over-turned round-bottomed bowl and gently stretch it around the edges until it is 10 inches for the small pizza or 14 inches for the larger, again using the weight of the dough to stretch it.

6. With either method, work slowly so that you don't tear the dough. If it does tear, you can patch it and seal it again. The pizza does not have to be absolutely round!

7. If you are baking the pizza on a baking stone or on unglazed quarry tiles, place the pizza dough rounds on well-floured sheets of baking parchment sprinkled with cornmeal or semolina. Top them as desired (page 225).

8. If you do not have a baking peel (paddle) to slide the pizza onto the stone or tiles, you can use a piece of stiff cardboard of the right size or an upside-down 14-inch pizza pan or 10 x 15-inch baking sheet. You will be able to pull or slide the parchment with the filled pizza on it right onto the peel, cardboard, or the flat side of the pan or sheet. Cut excess parchment from around the edge of the pizzas.

9. To top your pizzas, add desired toppings (see page 225) and drizzle each pizza with 1 to 1 1/2 tablespoons olive oil. Please do not omit this step! Eat fat-free all day if you have to, but the oil really makes the pizza indescribably wonderful. You are already cutting out so much fat by using no fatty meat and little or no vegan cheese.

10. To transfer the pizza to the hot stone or tile-lined oven rack, slide the pizza off the pan, cardboard, or peel by lining up the edge of it with the back edge of the stone or tiles, tilt the end nearest you upwards and jerk it gently to get the back edge of the pizza (still on the parchment) onto the stone. Then carefully pull back until the pizza (and parchment) is on the stone or tiles. Bake one pizza at a time, unless you have two baking stones or an entire oven rack (in a 30-inch stove) covered with tiles.

11. If you are baking the pizzas without stones or tiles, on pizza pans or baking sheets, place the dough on the oiled pans or sheets sprinkled with a little cornmeal or semolina. Top them as desired and then immediately place the pizza pan(s) or baking sheet(s) right on the floor of the oven.

12. At 500°F, a pizza will cook in about 8 minutes. The bottom of the crust should be crispy and golden, with a few scorched spots and the top should be bubbly and slightly browned, with a nice puffy edge. The crust should be chewy. Cut the pizza into wedges with a sharp knife, a pizza cutter or a pair of kitchen shears (my favorite). Serve immediately. Neapolitan pizza should be fresh, fresh, fresh!

TIPS

- Dark baking sheets or pizza pans brown the crust better.
- A Neapolitan pizza is not a receptacle for whatever leftovers are lurking in your refrigerator. Choose a few excellent ingredients and don't overdo it.

Pizza Sauce

Polpa di Pomodoro

Makes 4 cups   GF, SF, <30

Even when made with canned tomatoes (a good quality such as Italian San Marzano tomatoes are preferable), this sauce has a fresh concentrated tomato flavor. The combination of crushed tomatoes (quite thick) and pureed plum tomatoes makes the consistency of sauce that I like. It's easy as well as delicious, so don't bother buying over-salted commercial pizza sauce made with stale herbs anymore! This recipe makes a lot – freeze the leftovers for your next pizza night!

1/4 CUP OLIVE OIL
8 CLOVES GARLIC, MINCED
1 (28-OUNCE) CAN PLUM TOMATOES, WITH JUICE, PUREED
COARSELY IN A FOOD PROCESSOR
1 (28-OUNCE) CAN CRUSHED TOMATOES
1/2 TEASPOON SALT
FRESHLY GROUND BLACK PEPPER

Heat the olive oil in a heavy 2-quart saucepan over medium heat. Add the garlic and stir-fry for just a minute, then add both kinds of tomatoes. Add the salt and pepper to taste. Cook over medium heat, stirring now and then, uncovered, for about 10 minutes or until it has cooked down to the consistency you prefer. Taste for salt and pepper.

Tip: Herbs and sautéed onions should be added to the pizza toppings, rather than to the sauce.

PIZZA TOPPING SUGGESTIONS

Vegan Cheese: Cheese (mozzarella) is not supposed to smother the other toppings. For a vegan pizza, you can leave out the cheese altogether if you wish, but many of us miss the cheese. Fortunately, vegan mozzarella-style cheeses have vastly improved in recent times! See page 14 for vegan cheese recommendations. One ounce of vegan mozzarella per serving is plenty! Even the new vegan cheeses that melt well tend to get dry on the top. For this reason, it's best to put the

Leftover Pizza?

Pizza is meant to be eaten very hot, straight from the oven. Italians don't keep leftover pizza and reheat it. I must admit that I do when we have some leftover – but I reheat it briefly in a toaster oven. Pizza gets distressingly soggy and tough when reheated in a microwave, no matter how you do it!

cheese on top of the pizza sauce and then cover it with the vegetables and other toppings and then the olive oil drizzle last of all.

Use about 1/2 cup of Pizza Sauce on a 9 to10-inch pizza or about 3/4 cup on a 14-inch pizza. See page 224 for my recipe or use your favorite or a good-quality canned one. perhaps Lucini Italia or a good organic spaghetti sauce – such as the roasted garlic variety – which are generally better than prepared pizza sauce. Sliced really ripe, vine-ripened, summer tomatoes or slow-roasted tomatoes can be used instead of sauce.

Two Traditional Neapolitan Pizza Toppings:

These will give you an idea of the simplicity of Neapolitan pizza, but you can create your own special combinations with favorite ingredients.

- **Pizza alla Marinara:** Pizza Sauce; 2 sliced cloves of garlic; freshly-ground black pepper; a scattering of chopped fresh oregano; extra-virgin olive oil.

- **Pizza Margherita:** Italian canned crushed to-matoes or pizza sauce; vegan mozzarella-style cheese; fresh basil; extra-virgin olive oil.

Indian Flat Bread

Naan

INDIA

Makes 6   SFO

No need to buy this popular Indian bread or wait to go to a restaurant to enjoy it – it's actually easy to make and easy to make vegan. If you plan on serving the naan in the evening, make the dough the same morning.

    1 1/2 CUPS WARM WATER (BETWEEN 105 AND 115ºF)
    1 TEASPOON DRY ACTIVE YEAST (OR 3/4 TEASPOON INSTANT
        YEAST)
    1/4 CUP VEGETABLE OIL
    1 TEASPOON FRESH LEMON JUICE
    1/4 CUP PLUS 2 TEASPOONS SOY, HEMP, OR NUT MILK
    3 1/2 CUPS UNBLEACHED WHITE FLOUR

    1/2 CUP WHOLE-WHEAT FLOUR
    2 TEASPOONS SUGAR
    2 TEASPOONS SALT
    1/4 TEASPOON BAKING SODA
    1 TABLESPOON MELTED VEGAN MARGARINE
    1 TABLESPOON SESAME SEEDS (PREFERABLY BLACK) OR
        KALONJI (NIGELLA) SEEDS

1. Pour the lukewarm water into a medium bowl. Add the yeast and let it sit for 5 minutes or until it dissolves. Add the oil, lemon juice, and nondairy milk.

2. In a large bowl or the bowl of a stand mixer, whisk together both flours, the sugar, salt, and baking soda. Stir in the yeast mixture and mix until it forms a soft dough. Knead the dough using one of four kneading options on page 221.

3. Transfer the dough to a large lightly-oiled bowl (unless you are using a bread machine), turn it over to oil the top, cover the bowl tightly with plastic wrap and leave it to rise in a cool place for 8 hours or even overnight.

4. To shape the naan, transfer the dough to a lightly floured sheet of baking parchment. Cut the dough into six equal pieces. Shape each piece into a ball by rolling the dough on the counter or by using both hands to roll it into a smooth ball. Place the balls on the floured counter, cover with plastic wrap and let rest for 20 minutes.

5. After 20 minutes, transfer one ball of dough at a time to a lightly floured sheet of baking parchment on your work surface, flatten it slightly with the palm of your hand and push the dough out with your fingertips to a make a 7 to 8-inch round. Set aside, cover with plastic wrap, and repeat with the other dough balls. Don't turn the shaped dough over. You want to avoid creating a floury surface on the bread, so only flour the pieces well before you start shaping and keep the parchment only lightly floured. If the dough sticks, detach it with a dough scraper or spatula. Make sure you line the shaped breads up in such a way that you can remember the order in which

you shaped them, first to last.

6. About 45 minutes before you bake the naan, set an oven rack in the upper-middle rung. If you are using a baking stone or unglazed quarry tiles, place the stone or tiles on the oven rack, leaving at least a 1-inch gap around the border. Heat the oven to 500°F.

7. To finish the shaping: In order to make sure that the dough has had time to relax since the first shaping, do the second shaping in the same order that you did the first one. Take the first piece and push it out with your fingers to approximately a 9 x 7-inch oval. You can stretch it by draping it over the backs of your hands and pulling gently over your knuckles or a well-floured upside-down mixing bowl, the same as for stretching pizza dough. (For directions, see "To shape pizza without a rolling pin" on page 223.)

8. Place each shaped naan on a sheet of baking parchment dusted with flour, cornmeal or semolina and cut away most of the excess parchment around the bread. Pull on the front edge of the each one to make a bit of a point. Brush each with melted margarine and sprinkle on the sesame seeds. Cover the shaped naan if they are not going to be baked immediately.

9. Bake the naan without any further rising, one or two at a time, depending upon your oven capacity or whether you are using one baking stone, tiles covering the whole oven rack, or one or two baking sheets. Do the second shaping and topping of one or two naan, transfer them to the oven, and shape and top the next one or two while they bake, and so on, until all of the naan are baked. I make one at a time– they bake very quickly, so it goes fast!

10. If you are going to bake the naan on a hot baking stone or tiles, follow the directions for baking pizza on a stone on page 223. This covers using a baking peel, too. If you are baking the naan without a stone or tiles, on 14-inch pizza pans or 10 x 15-inch baking sheets, place the shaped naan on the oiled pans or sheets, sprinkled with a little cornmeal or semolina. Immediately place the pan(s) or baking sheet(s) right on the floor of the oven. Bake the naan until the tops have light golden spots and the bottoms are golden, 5 to 6 minutes. Remove them from the stone or tiles with a peel or long-handled spatula or remove the pans from the oven, and transfer the naan to a rack to cool for about 5 minutes, and brush with more melted margarine, if you like. Wrap them in a clean kitchen towel or place them inside an open paper bag until serving time (this is my preference).

Tip: If you have leftover baked naan, once they're completely cool, wrap them tightly in plastic wrap and store them for a day or so at room temperature or freeze them in zip-top bags for longer storage. To refresh them, wrap the naan (thawed, if frozen) in aluminum foil and heat in a 250°F oven until warm.

No-Knead Crusty Artisanal Bread

ITALY/FRANCE

Makes 4 loaves   SF

This recipe has changed my baking forever (and I have to add that my busy working-mother daughters love it too!). Your family and friends will think you've been slaving away all day while they devour your crunchy golden loaves. And yet, those loaves required only a few minutes of effort, giving you flexible timing, dough ready at a moment's notice, and results that rival the best of an artisan bakery – am I dreaming? No, it's for real! Real artisan loaves with robust flavor and a moist crumb with big holes, but so simple! (And you can use the same dough for focaccia, pizza, crusty buns, and flatbreads!) Plus, this bread is not completely "white," as I use whole-wheat flour for slightly over 1/3 of the flour. Amounts for halving the recipe (2 loaves) at end.

6 1/2 CUPS WARM WATER (BETWEEN 105 AND 115ºF)

**1 TABLESPOON DRY ACTIVE BAKING YEAST OR 3/4 TABLE-
SPOON INSTANT YEAST**

**1 1/2 TABLESPOONS SALT (OR SMALL CRYSTAL KOSHER
SALT)**

1/4 CUP OLIVE OIL

8 CUPS UNBLEACHED WHITE FLOUR, PLUS MORE FOR DUSTING

**5 CUPS WHOLE-WHEAT FLOUR OR WHITE WHOLE-WHEAT
FLOUR**

CORNMEAL AND FLOUR, FOR DUSTING

Important: To bake this bread in a covered pot or casserole, which acts as a "mini brick oven" and helps you achieve a wonderful crunchy, crackly crust, see the sidebar on page 229 for information on suitable containers.

1. Mix the yeast into the warm water in a large bowl, at least 8-quart capacity. Let it sit about 5 minutes. Add the salt and oil. Using a sturdy wooden spoon or a Danish dough whisk (see page 231), stir in the flours, mixing until there are no dry patches. The dough will be quite loose and messy-looking. Either place the bowl inside of a clean food-safe plastic bag and twist-tie it closed, leaving room for the dough to rise; or cover the bowl with its own snap-on lid, if it has one (don't snap it down all the way – the gas needs an escape hatch!) or cover with plastic wrap. Let dough rise at room temperature for 2 hours (or up to 18 hours).

2. You can prepare to bake all or some of the dough at this point or you can refrigerate all or some of it. (I think the bread is superior when made with refrigerated dough.) If you are going to store all of the dough in the refrigerator, oil the insides of two 4 to 6-quart food-safe containers, bowls or dough buckets ("dough doublers") with lids. Scoop half of the risen dough into one container and the rest into the 2nd container. Cover with the lids. Store in the refrigerator for up to 2 weeks (it will get slightly sourdough-y in flavor by then). In my opinion, using two smaller containers is preferable to 1

large one because the smaller ones are easier to stash in a crowded refrigerator! It is best not to use air-tight lids or the gasses in the dough may accumulate and pop off the lids. The dough is much easier to work with if you refrigerate it for at least 3 hours before shaping.

3. When ready to bake, don't punch the dough down. Cloak the dough with flour and cut off 1/4 of the dough with a serrated knife or bench knife (also called a dough cutter), for each loaf. Refrigerate any dough that you won't be baking at this time.

4. Cover your work surface with a sheet of baking parchment and flour it well. Place the dough on it, sprinkle it with a little more flour and stretch the dough and fold it over on itself once or twice. The dough will be quite sticky– keep your hands and the parchment floured and use a bench knife to handle the dough whenever possible.

5. Using just enough flour to keep the dough from sticking to the work surface or to your fingers, quickly shape the dough into a ball or an oval shape, depending on the shape of the pot you are going to bake it in. Do this by folding the dough under itself. Repeat with the other loaf/loaves you will be baking at this time.

6. Line a basket, bowl, pan, or oval casserole (with room for the loaf to double) with baking parchment (the shape and size depending upon the vessel in which you will be baking the bread). Use one for each loaf you will be baking. Sprinkle the parchment with flour, cornmeal, semolina, or bran.

7. Place the shaped dough seam-side-down on the parchment and dust it lightly with flour, semolina, bran, or cornmeal. Place each loaf inside of a food-safe plastic bag and twist-tie it closed, leaving plenty of room for the dough to rise. If the dough has been refrigerated, let it rise in a warm spot for about 2 hours; if it is not cold, rise at room temperature for about 1 hour.

8. Place the pot(s) and lids you'll use to bake the bread in the oven. Heat the oven to 475°F for at least 30 minutes. See information about baking vessels page 229.

9. **Baking the Bread:** Transfer the risen dough to the pot(s), using the parchment under the dough as a "lifter" and set the dough (parchment and all) into your hot pot, pan or casserole. (Don't worry – it won't stick or burn!) Cover with the lid(s) and bake for 30 minutes, then remove the lid(s) and bake another 15 minutes or until the bread is beautifully browned. Remove the bread from the pan immediately and cool on a rack.

Tip: Read pages 230-232 for information about the science behind this method and how I arrived at my particular version.

To make half the recipe (2 loaves) use:

- 3 1/4 CUPS WARM WATER (BETWEEN 105 AND 115°F)
- 1 TABLESPOON DRY ACTIVE BAKING YEAST OR 3/4 TABLESPOON INSTANT YEAST (THAT'S RIGHT – YOU DON'T HALVE THE YEAST!)
- 3/4 TABLESPOON SALT (OR SMALL CRYSTAL KOSHER SALT)
- 2 TABLESPOONS OLIVE OIL
- 4 CUPS UNBLEACHED WHITE FLOUR PLUS MORE FOR DUSTING
- 2 1/2 CUPS WHOLE-WHEAT FLOUR OR WHITE WHOLE-WHEAT FLOUR (PAGE 222)

Mrs. Darling's Alberta "Bun Pherogy"

UKRAINE/CANADA

Serves 8   SFO

Also spelled pierogi, these tiny golden pillows of soft yeast dough are baked in creamy almond milk and topped with buttery sautéed onions and dill – heaven on a plate! This is a vegan version of a Ukrainian-Canadian recipe given to me by a neighbor from Alberta, Mrs. Darling, who had learned from her Ukrainian-Canadian friends. It is hearty winter fare and an inexpensive main dish. I craved this for years until I finally veganized it, and I'm happy to share it with you. Leftovers can be frozen.

- 1/2 POUND MEDIUM-FIRM TOFU, DRAINED AND CRUMBLED
- 1 TABLESPOON TOFU SOUR CREAM (PAGE 33)
- 1 TEASPOON FRESH LEMON JUICE
- 1/4 TEASPOON SALT
- 1/3 CUP FINELY MINCED ONION
- 1/3 RECIPE RICH, FLUFFY VEGAN BREAD DOUGH (PAGE 232), RISEN ONCE
- 1 CUP ALMOND MILK (APPROXIMATELY)
- *Topping:*
- 1 TABLESPOON VEGAN MARGARINE
- 1 MEDIUM ONION, CHOPPED
- 1 TABLESPOON FRESH CHOPPED DILL WEED OR 1 TEASPOON DRIED
- TOFU SOUR CREAM OR CASHEW SOUR CREAM (PAGE 33) OR STOREBOUGHT

1. In a medium bowl, mash the tofu and sour cream with the lemon juice, salt, and onion. Mix well and set aside.

2. Roll out the dough to 1/4-inch thick on a lightly floured sheet of baking parchment. Cut the dough into 2-inch squares. Don't worry if the dough shrinks – you can quickly flatten it before filling.

3. Place about 1/2 teaspoon of the filling in the center of each dough square. (You will quickly find out how much you can use – you should be able to seal the little "loaves" with no leakage.) Bring two sides of the square up over the filling and pinch to seal. Pinch the ends to seal. It should look like a tiny loaf of bread.

4. As you fill them, place the little buns seam-side-down close together in a shallow 8 x 12-inch baking pan or gratin dish sprayed or brushed lightly with oil. When all the bun pheemogy are filled and nestled in the pan, cover the pan with a clean kitchen towel and let rise in a warm spot until doubled in size, about 40 minutes. Preheat the oven to 350°F.

5. **First Baking:** Bake until golden brown, about 20 minutes. At this point you can set them aside to finish baking just before eating or freeze them to finish and eat at a later date. Before freezing, allow them to thoroughly cool, then freeze them in zipper-lock freezer bags.

6. **Topping:** Before the second baking, melt the margarine in a medium nonstick skillet over high heat. Add the onion and sauté until soft and slightly browned, adding a few drops of water as necessary to keep from sticking. Set aside.

7. **Second Baking:** Preheat the oven to 350 F. Twenty minutes before serving, pour the almond milk into the pan of half-baked pheemogy, until it is about half-way up the sides of the little buns. Spray the tops lightly with oil from a pump sprayer. Sprinkle the sautéed onions and the dill over the top. Bake for 10 to 20 minutes or until the almond milk is partially absorbed

What Is a Danish Dough Whisk?

This is an inexpensive utensil that you'll wonder how you ever did without! It has a wooden handle and a round, swirled heavy wire head on it. It's perfect for mixing thick batters and wet doughs, such as these no-knead doughs, scones, muffins, soda bread, sourdough starter, etc. It costs under $10 and is available online.

and bubbly. The pheemogy should absorb some of the milk and the rest becomes almost a sauce. Serve hot with sour cream.

Tip: These can be partially baked ahead of time – even frozen for a time before the final baking.

Soy-Free Option: Instead of the tofu, sour cream, lemon juice, and salt, use 1 recipe Almond Ricotta (page 40), made without the citrus flavoring.

Ukranian Beet Leaf Holuptsi

Ukraine/Canada

Serves 6   SFO

An unusual Ukrainian-style recipe from Winnipeg, Manitoba, these are sometimes simply called "beet rolls," and the Ukrainian spelling can be holopchi or holubtsi. If you can't find fresh, intact beet leaves you can use Ruby or Swiss chard and cut away the tough stem down the middle. This recipe sounds odd, but it's quite delicious – it was a hit at the Denman Island Ukrainian Christmas celebration!

24 YOUNG, SOFT BEET LEAVES OR 12 LARGE OR 24 SMALL CHARD LEAVES, TOUGH STEMS REMOVED
1/3 RECIPE RICH, FLUFFY VEGAN BREAD DOUGH (PAGE 232), RISEN ONCE
1 TABLESPOON VEGAN MARGARINE

6 GREEN ONIONS, CHOPPED

4 CLOVES GARLIC, CRUSHED

1/4 CUP CHOPPED FRESH DILL WEED OR 1 TABLESPOON DRIED

2 CUPS BESCIAMELLA SAUCE (PAGE 37)

1. Wash, stem and pat dry the beet leaves. (If you use chard leaves, cut the large leaves in half.) Cut the bread dough into 24 more-or-less equal chunks and roll each chunk between the palms of your hands into an elongated log shape. Loosely roll each leaf around a "log" of dough. Place the leaf-wrapped "logs" side-by-side in a well-oiled 13 x 9-inch baking pan or roaster. Cover the pan with plastic wrap and let the rolls rise in a warm place for about 1 hour or until they have doubled in size.

2. In a medium nonstick skillet, heat in the margarine over medium heat. Add the green onions and garlic and cook until softened, about 2 minutes. In a saucepan, combine the green onion mixture and dill with the besciamella sauce, simmer for 2 to 3 minutes to blend the flavors. Set aside.

3. Preheat the oven to 350°F. Spray the tops of the rolls lightly with oil from a pump sprayer. Bake the rolls for 25 to 30 minutes. Heat the reserved sauce gently until warm. Serve immediately with the sauce drizzled over each serving of holuptsi.

Tip: If you are not serving them right away, remove from pan when they are cool and transfer them to zip-top bags to refrigerate or freeze.

Rich and Fluffy Vegan Bread
Makes 2 loaves   SFO

I have been making this dough for special breads for about thirty years. Even though it's made with almost half whole-wheat flour, it is light, fluffy, and rich-tasting. Potato is added to the dough because the starch in potato flour attracts and holds water, resulting in a soft, moist dough. This dough is the basis for two recipes in this chapter – Bun Pherogy

(page 231) and Beet Leaf Holuptsi (above), but I'm sure you'll find many uses for it. You only need 1/3 of this recipe for the aforementioned recipes, but the rest of the dough can be used for dinner rolls, Parker House rolls, 1 large or 2 small bread loaves, or to make sweet rolls and buns. Or, you can divide the remaining dough in half and freeze the dough in 2 freezer-lock bags for making more of these Ukrainian recipes at another time. Tip: To save time, instead of potatoes, use 1/2 cup instant mashed potato flakes mixed with 1/3 cup boiling water. Do not add salt, margarine or milk of any kind.

1 TABLESPOON SUGAR

3/4 CUP WARM WATER (BETWEEN 105 AND 115°F)

1 TABLESPOON DRY ACTIVE BAKING YEAST OR 3/4 TABLE-SPOON INSTANT YEAST

1 2/3 CUPS WARM RICH, FULL-FAT SOY MILK, NUT MILK, OR HEMP MILK

2 OUNCES RUSSET POTATOES, PEELED AND CUT INTO 1-INCH CUBES

1/2 CUP VEGETABLE OIL

1 TABLESPOON SALT

3 CUPS WHOLE-WHEAT FLOUR OR WHITE WHOLE-WHEAT FLOUR (PAGE 222)

3 1/2 CUPS UNBLEACHED WHITE FLOUR, DIVIDED

1. About 20 minutes before you are ready to make the dough, boil or steam the potato cubes in a saucepan until tender or microwave the potato cubes in a small covered microwave-safe bowl, with 1/2 tablespoon of water, on 100% power (default setting) for about 1 1/2 minutes or until tender. Drain the potatoes in a sieve or colander.

2. If you boiled the potatoes, transfer the potatoes back into the pot they were cooked in, cover, and place over low heat for a few minutes to dry the potatoes out a bit. (Don't burn them!)

3. Mash the potatoes in a small bowl or press them into the bowl through a potato ricer.

4. Use the potatoes in the dough while they are still warm but not so hot as to kill the yeast; they should be about the same temperature as the water for the yeast. Stir the yeast into the warm water in a large

mixing bowl or the bowl of your stand mixer. Let this sit for about 5 minutes. Add the milk, mashed potato, salt, oil, and whole-wheat flour.

5. Beat the mixture for 2 minutes with an electric mixer or 200 strokes by hand. Add 1 cup of the unbleached white flour and beat 2 more minutes or 200 more strokes. This is the "sponge." Let this sponge rise in a warm place, covered, until it has doubled in size. If you plan to knead the dough in an automatic bread machine, make the sponge by mixing all of the ingredients, except the remaining unbleached white flour, in the bread machine container. Select the dough cycle and let the "sponge" mix for 5 to 10 minutes, then unplug the machine and let it rise until it doubles.

6. After the sponge has doubled, mix in the unbleached white flour. If the dough is too sticky, add flour a little at a time, but aim for a moist dough. The amount of flour sometimes depends on the weather or the flour itself. Knead the dough using one of the kneading options on page 221.

7. Transfer the dough to a large lightly-oiled bowl (unless you are using a bread machine), turn it over to oil the top, cover the bowl tightly with plastic wrap and leave it to rise in a moderately warm place until it has doubled in size, about 1 1/2 hours. (See also the Refrigerator Rise Option on page 220.) Punch the dough down and use in your recipe.

8. To make two loaves of bread, shape into two loaves and place in greased 8 or 8 1/2 x 4 1/2-inch loaf pans. Preheat the oven to 350°F. Cover the loaves and let them rise for about 30 to 45 minutes or until they are well-rounded over the tops of the pans. Bake the loaves for about 30 minutes or until the loaves are golden brown. Cool them on racks for 10 minutes before removing them from the pans and transferring to a rack to finish cooling.

Hamantaschen

EASTERN EUROPEAN JEWISH

Makes about 36   SFO

There are many traditional goodies associated with the Jewish holiday of Purim, but by far the most popular is Hamantaschen (Haman's Hats), which is sometimes made with a cookie dough. The dough is folded in a triangular fashion around a sweet filling, to resemble Haman's hat. (Haman is the villain of the piece!) I prefer using this relatively rich vegan yeast dough, which is less fat-laden than cookie dough, but you'd never know it. Don't wait for a holiday to enjoy these.

1 CUP RICH, FULL-FAT SOY MILK, NUT MILK, OR HEMP MILK, PLUS MORE FOR BRUSHING PASTRIES
1/4 CUP VEGAN MARGARINE
1/4 CUP SUGAR
1/2 TEASPOON SALT
2 1/2 TEASPOONS (1 PACKET) DRY ACTIVE BAKING YEAST OR 2 TEASPOONS INSTANT YEAST
1/4 CUP WARM WATER (BETWEEN 105 AND 115ºF)
3 CUPS UNBLEACHED WHITE FLOUR (OR 1 1/2 CUPS UNBLEACHED WHITE FLOUR AND 1 1/2 CUPS WHITE WHOLE-WHEAT FLOUR, PAGE 222)
1 TEASPOON GRATED ORGANIC LEMON ZEST
1/2 TEASPOON PURE ALMOND EXTRACT
POPPY SEED FILLING, PRUNE FILLING, OR APRICOT FILLING (OR SOME OF EACH – FOLLOWS)
CINNAMON SUGAR OR CONFECTIONERS' SUGAR, OPTIONAL

1. In a small saucepan, scald the milk (heat to just before boiling). Remove the pan from the heat. Add the margarine, sugar, and salt. Stir until the margarine melts, then pour it into a medium bowl or the bowl of a stand mixer. Let it cool until is warm (between 105° and 115°F).

2. When the milk is warm, dissolve the yeast in the warm water for 5 minutes. Add it to the milk/margarine mixture, along with the almond extract and lemon zest. Stir in 1 1/2 cups of the flour and beat the mixture well. Gradually add 1 more cup flour to make a soft dough. Knead the dough us-
(continued on page 234)

The World of No-Knead Bread Baking

Vessels for Baking No-Knead Artisan Loaves

Be sure to heat the pot(s) in the oven as it preheats, so they are sizzling hot when you place the bread in them! You have a number of options for suitable baking pots. I have tried all of the following options, and they all work.

- **A cast iron or enameled cast iron pot** or **Dutch oven** with a lid. The dimensions should be about: 8 1/2 inches across the bottom, 12 inches across the top, and 5 inches deep.

- A glazed **ceramic casserole** measuring about 9 x 6 x 3 inches and almost straight-sided rather than sloping out.

- **A flower pot "cloche":** an inexpensive unglazed flower pot with a dish that 9 inches across the bottom, 11 inches across the top, and 2 inches deep; the pot itself is 7 inches across the bottom, 10 inches across the top, and 4 1/3 inches deep. Place the risen bread in the dish (with the baking parchment it rose on) and turn the flower pot upside down over it. Plug the hole in the flower pot with a wad of aluminum foil.

- Another option is a **clay baker/Romertopf.** I didn't think this would work at first, but as long as you soak it in cold water for 15 minutes before placing it in a cold oven to preheat, it works fine! I have several of them, bought cheaply at thrift stores. All of my clay bakers hold 2 or 2 1/2 quarts.

- You can also use smaller pots. If the pot is wide and shallow, your bread will spread out more. If it is deeper and narrower, it will be taller. It doesn't matter – it will be crusty! Some people use a deep cast iron skillet with a raised lid or Pyrex bowl over the top.

You're sure to find something suitable in your house or at a garage sale. I often bake 4 loaves at once, all in different pots, bakers, and casseroles!

No-Knead Bread Dough: Baking Outside the Pot

You don't have to bake the artisan no-knead dough in a preheated heavy pot or casserole. Here are some other ways to bake it:

- **Free-Form:** If you aren't aiming for an extra-crunchy crust, you can, instead, bake the bread as freeform hearth loaves on a baking stone, or in loaf pans. If using a loaf pan, bake the bread at 375°F.

- **Focaccia:** Take 1/4 of the dough and gently stretch it to fit a 10 x 15-inch baking sheet which has been brushed with olive oil and dusted with cornmeal. Place the sheet inside of a food-safe plastic bag while it rises, at room temperature or in a warm spot if the dough has been refrigerated, for 40 minutes. If you prefer to bake the focaccia on a baking stone instead of a pan, follow the directions for baking pizza on a stone on page 223.

  While the dough rises, heat the oven to 475°F, using convection, if you have it. When the dough is ready to bake, "dimple" the dough all over with your finger tips and brush generously with olive oil (or, alternatively, spread it with a simple tomato sauce). Sprinkle with fresh herbs and/or coarse salt, if you like. Bake for 20 minutes or until golden.

- **Pizza:** Use 1/4 of the dough for three thin-crust 12-inch pizzas or for two 14-inch pizzas. Do not raise the dough again before baking once it's on the pan – just top the pizza and bake at 500°F for 8 to 10 minutes. You can bake it right on a stone (see the directions for baking pizza on a baking stone in the pizza recipe on page 223) or on a dark pizza pan (dark pans brown the crust better). This wet dough is sticky, so I recommend patting it out on baking parchment and baking it on the parchment, too. This way, it will slide off your baking peel onto a stone easily, without sticking to the peel. Follow the directions in the pizza recipe on page 223.

- **Flatbreads:** Take fist-sized pieces of dough and roll them with a rolling pin into circles or ovals about 1/8-inch thick on well-floured baking parchment. Keep the balls of dough covered when you aren't working with them. For maximum "puff," try to avoid stretching the dough. Roll out from the center toward the outer edges, turn the dough a quarter-turn and repeat, doing this until it is the right size and an even thickness.

  Transfer the rolled-out flatbreads to trays or baking sheets (any size) lined with baking parchment and dusted with flour. Cover with clean kitchen towels and let them rise for 30 minutes. Cook the flatbreads quickly on both sides in a large preheated dry cast iron or anodized aluminum skillet over medium to medium-high heat. They should make "pockets."

The Science Behind the
No-Knead Method

Thanks to Harold McGee (On Food and Cooking: The Science and Lore of the Kitchen, Scribner, 2004) for explaining why the no-knead method works! He writes: "The long, slow rise does over hours what intensive kneading does in minutes: it brings the gluten molecules into side-by-side alignment to maximize their opportunity to bind to each other and produce a strong, elastic network. The wetness of the dough is an important piece of this because the gluten molecules are more mobile in a high proportion of water and so can move into alignment easier and faster than if the dough were stiff." In addition, the long rise produces umami flavor compounds that give the bread outstanding flavor.

ing one of the kneading options on page 221.

3. Transfer the dough to a large lightly-oiled bowl (unless you are using a bread machine), turn it over to oil the top, cover the bowl tightly with plastic wrap and leave it to rise in a moderately warm place until it has doubled in size, about 1 1/2 hours. (See also the Refrigerator Rise Option on page 220.)

4. Punch the dough down. Roll the dough out on a floured sheet of baking parchment about 1/8- inch thick. Cut into 3 to 4-inch rounds. Place 1 to 2 tablespoons filling of choice in the center of each round. Lift the edges at three equidistant points and pinch them together at the seams, leaving a little of the filling showing in the center. Place the filled pastries on 2 or 3 baking sheets (any size) lined with baking parchment cut to fit and let rise, covered loosely with plastic wrap, in a warm place for 1 hour. (They may not seem to rise very much.)

5. Preheat the oven to 350°F. If any "seams" have come apart during rising, pinch them closed again. Brush the pastries with milk. Dust the tops with cinnamon sugar, if using. Bake them for 15 to 20 minutes or until golden. Cool for at least 10 minutes on racks, but serve the pastries warm. Sprinkle the tops with confectioners' sugar before serving, if using.

6. **Fillings:**

Poppy Seed Filling: In a medium bowl mix together 1/2 cup plus 2 tablespoons poppy seeds, 1 1/2 cups raisins, 1/4 cup maple syrup or agave nectar, 1/4 cup melted vegan margarine, and 1 tablespoon lemon zest or 1 teaspoon lemon extract.

Prune (Dried Plum) Filling: In a medium saucepan, combine 1 cup pitted prunes (dried plums) and 1 cup water. Bring to a boil, then reduce to a simmer and cook, uncovered, until the prunes are soft and plump. Drain and add 1 tablespoon maple syrup or agave nectar, 1/2 teaspoon cinnamon, a pinch of ground cloves, and 1/2 tablespoon grated lem-

---

South American-Style Hot Chocolate

Serves 2   SFO, GF, <30

Frothy, rich, intensely chocolate, and only slightly sweet, this hot chocolate is perfect with the Peruvian-Italian holiday bread, panetón.

2 CUPS ALMOND OR FULL-FAT SOY MILK
2 OUNCES BITTERSWEET DARK EATING CHOCOLATE, ABOUT 70% COCOA SOLIDS, CHOPPED
1 TABLESPOON SUGAR
1 TEASPOON PURE VANILLA EXTRACT
1 TABLESPOON (OR MORE) FAVORITE LIQUEUR OR LIQUOR (RUM, BRANDY, PERUVIAN PISCO), OPTIONAL

Heat the milk until almost boiling, in a medium saucepan on the stove or in the microwave in a 1-quart microwave-safe measuring pitcher at 100% power (default setting) for 1 to 1 1/2 minutes. Stir in the chopped chocolate, stirring until it melts. Stir in the sugar and vanilla.

Froth the chocolate using a traditional molinillo, which you roll between your hands; or use a whisk, a plunger-type cappuccino frother, or a hand-held immersion blender. Another option is to whiz the mixture in the blender for a few minutes, but be sure to leave the cap off the middle hole in the blender top and cover it with a folded towel, so that the steam doesn't explode the hot chocolate all over you! You can microwave the chocolate for about 30 seconds at 100% power (default setting), if you like – the froth rises up in the microwave! Add the liqueur, if using. Serve hot.

on or orange zest (or 1/2 teaspoon lemon or orange extract). Stir and mash the mixture until it is the the the consistency of thick jam.

Apricot Filling: Exactly as for the Prune Filling, but use dried apricots instead of prunes. Or, you can use half dried apricots and half prunes (dried plums).

Tip: You can freeze the pastries (after thorough cooling) in zip-top freezer bags. When you want to serve them, thaw them thoroughly and reheat them in a 300°F oven for 10 minutes.

Panetón

Genovese-Style Peruvian Sweet Christmas Bread

ITALY/PERU

Makes 1 large loaf   SFO

In Peru, the traditional rich, aromatic, fruited yeast bread panetón is traditionally eaten with thick Peru-vian hot chocolate (page 237) during the Christmas season. It is a version of Italian panettone, flavored with citrus zest, dried fruit, anise and almonds, but many Peruvians are unaware of its Italian origins. My sugar-free version is based on "panettone Genovese," since my Peruvian-Italian family (and a large proportion of Italian immigrants to Peru in the 1800s) originated in the Genoa area of Italy. This recipe includes a bread machine variation, which is quite good (and I say this despite the fact that I'm normally not a huge fan of breads baked in a bread machine, though it's great for kneading and raising small batches of dough).

1/2 CUP WARM WATER (BETWEEN 105° AND 115°F)
2 TEASPOONS DRY ACTIVE BAKING YEAST OR 1 1/2 TEASPOONS INSTANT YEAST
1/4 TEASPOON SPANISH SAFFRON
1 TEASPOON FENNEL SEEDS
1/2 CUP RICH, FULL-FAT SOY MILK, NUT MILK, OR HEMP MILK
3 TABLESPOONS VEGAN MARGARINE
GRATED ZEST OF 1 MEDIUM ORGANIC ORANGE
4 TEASPOONS ORANGE FLOWER WATER, OPTIONAL (PAGE 196)

To Bake the Panetón in a Bread Machine

This recipe was developed so that it doesn't result in a typical bread machine über-fluffy loaf. The bread should be light, but not like "wonder" bread. Place the ingredients in the bread container in the order instructed for your machine. Do not add the fruit/nut mixture at the beginning of kneading. If your machine has a sweet bread cycle, it will beep when it's time to add these ingredients. Otherwise, you'll have to pay attention and add them toward the end of the kneading cycle, so that they don't get pulverized.

Use the sweet bread cycle or use the white bread cycle set for a "regular" crust. Check your machine's manual for the stages of the sweet bread cycle and set a timer for just before the beginning of the second rise. At that point make sure that the ball of dough is positioned evenly, so that you don't end up with a lopsided loaf. Then set the timer for 5 minutes before the bread will begin to bake. At that time, slash the top of the dough in a cross pattern with a sharp razor blade.

Tip: If your machine has a glass "window" above the bread, cover it with foil (on the outside). This results in a nice golden-brown top on the panetón. Remove it from the container immediately to cool on a rack.

3/4 TEASPOON SALT
1/2 TEASPOON GROUND CORIANDER
2 3/4 CUPS UNBLEACHED WHITE FLOUR
1/4 CUP WHEAT GERM (RAW OR TOASTED)
Fruit/Nut Mixture:
1/3 CUP GOLDEN RAISINS
1/3 CUP CHOPPED DRIED APRICOTS
1/3 CUP DRIED CURRANTS
1/3 CUP CHOPPED TOASTED PINE NUTS OR SLIVERED
    BLANCHED ALMONDS

1. Add the yeast and saffron to the warm water in a cup and let sit 5 minutes. Place the fennel seeds on a square of baking parchment and fold part of it over to cover the seeds. Crush the seeds with a heavy rolling pin. Alternatively, crush them (but don't grind them to a powder) in a coffee/spice grinder.

2. In a small saucepan heat the milk over medium heat just until it is hot, with bubbles around the edges. Or, heat in small microwave-safe bowl on 100% power (default setting) in the microwave for 30 seconds. Add the margarine and stir to dissolve. When the milk has cooled to between 105° and 115°F, add the dissolved yeast and water. Transfer to a large mixing bowl or the bowl of a stand mixer.

3. Add the orange zest, orange flower water (if using), crushed fennel seeds, coriander, and salt to the bowl. Stir in the wheat germ and 1 cup of the flour. Beat well for a minute or two, and gradually add the remaining flour. Knead the dough using one of the kneading options on page 221. Do not add the fruit/nut mixture to a machine, if using. Instead, knead them in by hand after the first rising as instructed below in the recipe.

4. Transfer the dough to a large lightly-oiled bowl (unless you are using a bread machine), turn it over to oil the top, cover the bowl tightly with plastic wrap and let it rise in a moderately warm place until it doubles in size, about 1 1/2 hours. (See also the Refrigerator Rise Option on page 220.)

5. **Adding the Fruit/Nut Mixture:** Transfer the risen dough to a lightly-floured sheet of baking parchment, and pat it into a flat rectangle. Sprinkle the surface with the fruit/nut mixture. Roll up the dough jelly-roll-style and fold up the ends toward the center. Knead the dough gently by folding and rolling until fruit/nut mixture is well-distributed throughout the dough.

6. Traditionally, this bread is baked in a special deep pan, but I usually make a round loaf. To shape it, pull the dough under itself to form a ball. Place the ball on a 10 x 15-inch baking sheet or 14-inch pizza pan. Cover and let rise in a moderately warm place until it has doubled in size, 1 to 2 hours. Preheat the oven to 350°F. Immediately before you place the bread in the oven cut a cross in the top of the dough about 1/2-inch deep with a sharp razor blade. Bake for 30 minutes in the center or upper half of the oven or just until the loaf is a deep golden brown and sounds hollow when tapped on the bottom. Cool thoroughly on a rack before slicing.

Velvety Sweet Yeast Bread

EASTERN EUROPE

Makes 2 loaves or 32 small rolls   SFO

I have always made special yeast breads to celebrate holidays. The sight of a golden round, rolled, or braided bread, glazed white with icing and wafting sweet aromas, greeted my family on holiday mornings and put me in the spirit! Making these breads gave me a connection, not only to my own female ancestors, but to women all over the globe. With this light, moist, low-fat, slightly sweet dough, I was able to veganize many traditional sweet yeast breads, rolls and holiday specialties, including the Italian and Peruvian varieties from my father's background.

I have included recipes for Scandinavian Christmas Bread (page 238) and a Hungarian sweet bread (page 239) using this dough, but do experiment by adapting your own favorite or family sweet breads using this dough as a starting point. I have also used this dough to make vegan challah and spiral raisin challah, vasilopita, Greek Easter bread, Italian Easter bread, julekage, hot cross buns, and cinnamon buns.

Tip: *to save time, instead of potatoes, use 3/4 cup instant mashed potato flakes mixed with 2/3 cup boiling water. Do not add salt, margarine, or milk of any kind.*

6 OUNCES RUSSET POTATOES, PEELED AND CUT INTO 1-INCH CUBES

2 1/2 TEASPOONS (1 PACKET) DRY ACTIVE BAKING YEAST OR 2 TEASPOONS INSTANT YEAST

2 CUPS WARM WATER (BETWEEN 105 AND 115°F)

1/4 CUP VEGAN MARGARINE OR OIL

1/2 CUP WHEAT GERM (RAW OR TOASTED)

1/4 CUP SOY FLOUR, CHICKPEA FLOUR (BESAN), OR SOY MILK POWDER

1/4 CUP MAPLE SYRUP, BROWN RICE SYRUP OR AGAVE NECTAR

1/4 CUP SUGAR

1 TABLESPOON FRESH LEMON JUICE

2 TEASPOONS SALT

1/4 TEASPOON TURMERIC

5 TO 6 CUPS UNBLEACHED WHITE FLOUR (OR 2 1/2 TO 3 CUPS UNBLEACHED WHITE FLOUR AND 2 1/2 TO 3 CUPS WHITE WHOLE-WHEAT FLOUR, PAGE 222)

1. Boil or steam the potato cubes until tender or microwave the potato cubes in a covered 1-quart microwave-safe casserole or bowl, with 1 1/2 tablespoons of water, on 100% power (default setting) for 4 minutes or until tender. Drain the potatoes in a colander. **Note:** If you boiled the potatoes, transfer the potatoes back into the covered pot they were cooked in and place it over low heat for a few minutes to dry the potatoes out a bit. (Don't burn them!) Mash the potatoes in a small bowl or press them into the bowl through a potato ricer. Use the potatoes in the dough while they are still warm but not so hot as to kill the yeast; they should be about the same temperature as the water for the yeast.

2. In a large mixing bowl or the bowl of a stand mixer, combine the water and yeast. Set aside for 5 minutes. When the yeast has dissolved, add the mashed potatoes, margarine, wheat germ, soy flour, maple syrup, sugar, lemon juice, salt, and turmeric. Mix in the white flour. Knead well for 5 to 10 minutes, using as little flour as possible. Knead the dough using one of the kneading options on page 221.

3. Transfer the dough to a large lightly oiled bowl (unless you are using a bread machine), turn it over to oil the top, cover the bowl tightly with plastic wrap and let rise overnight or for 8 to12 hours in the refrigerator (this dough is very sticky and handles best when cold).

4. Several hours before serving, shape the dough into two loaves, 16 large buns or 32 small rolls, according to the type of bread you are making. Line your pans with baking parchment to prevent burning. Cover the bread loosely with plastic wrap and a clean kitchen towel and let it rise in a warm place until it has doubled in size. This may take 2 or 3 hours. Bake at 350°F for 20 to 45 minutes, depending upon the size and shape, or until golden brown. (Solid round or pan loaves may take as long as 45 minutes; long, braided or ring loaves about 30 minutes; small rolls 20 minutes.) Cool on racks and decorate as you please.

Scandinavian Christmas Bread
Julekage/Yule Bread

SCANDINAVIA

Makes 2 loaves   SFO

This special holiday bread has a glistening sugar glaze and is filled with dried fruit, golden raisins, and fragrant cardamom. Julekage (pronounced yoo-ley-key-yeh) is served at Christmas in Sweden, Norway, and Denmark, where Christmas is taken very seriously! It is often served as a round loaf, but I prefer it as a braided loaf or wreath bread.

1 RECIPE VELVETY SWEET YEAST BREAD DOUGH (PAGE 237), RISEN

2 TEASPOONS GROUND CARDAMOM

1 TEASPOON ALMOND EXTRACT

1 CUP GOLDEN OR SULTANA RAISINS

1/2 CUP CHOPPED MIXED DRIED FRUIT
SWEET BREAD GLAZE (SEE SIDEBAR, NEXT PAGE)
SIMPLE POWDERED SUGAR ICING (SEE SIDEBAR, NEXT PAGE)
1/2 CUP LIGHTLY TOASTED SLICED ALMOND

1. Prepare the bread dough and let it rise in the refrigerator as directed on page 220. When you are ready to shape the bread, take the dough out of the refrigerator. Line 2 12 x 17-inch baking sheets with baking parchment cut to fit.

2. Divide the risen dough into two equal pieces, and cut each part into 3 equal pieces. Roll each piece into a 24-inch-long "rope." With a sharp knife, make 2 long cuts in one of the ropes, evenly spaced, leaving the dough attached at the top, with 3 strips of dough extending. Braid the 3 strips together, starting at the top – not too loose and not too tight. Tuck the bottom ends under the dough. Fold the very top part of the dough under and then poke it up through the hole at the top of the braid, just to fill the gap. Repeat with the second piece of dough. Place one braid on each parchment-lined baking sheet. The braids may look a bit messy, but they will look fine when they are baked. Leave the loaves in the long braided shape, or for a yule wreath bread, form the braids into rings and tuck the ends together so that they look neat and tidy.

3. Cover the bread loosely with plastic wrap and clean kitchen towels and let it rise in a warm place until it has doubled in size. This may take 2 or 3 hours. Bake at 350°F for 30 minutes, or until golden brown. After baking as directed, transfer the pans to racks, brush the loaves with glaze and cool thoroughly. Decorate with the icing and sprinkle with the sliced almonds.

Giant Hungarian Poppy Seed Spiral Bread

Beigli

HUNGARY

Makes 1 large or 2 medium loaves   SFO

This magnificent and beloved traditional Hungarian sweet bread is often prepared for holidays, such as Easter and Christmas. Sometimes Beigli (pronounced bay-glee) is made with a thin strudel dough, and sometimes with a soft sweet bread dough, as in the recipe. You often have the choice of a poppy seed or a walnut filling, but I have chosen to combine the two in a fruity lemon-scented filling, spiced with cinnamon.

Tip: *If you prefer, you can fashion this into 2 smaller breads, but the giant one is very impressive.*

1 RECIPE VELVETY SWEET YEAST BREAD DOUGH (PAGE 232)
FILLING:
1 1/2 CUPS POPPY SEEDS
1 1/2 CUPS LIGHTLY-TOASTED WALNUT HALVES
1 CUP CHOPPED PITTED PRUNES (DRIED PLUMS)
3/4 CUP SUGAR
1/2 CUP NONDAIRY MILK
1/3 CUP VEGAN MARGARINE
GRATED ZEST OF 2 MEDIUM ORGANIC LEMONS
1 TEASPOON GROUND CINNAMON
LEMON POWDERED SUGAR ICING (SIMPLE POWDERED
     SUGAR ICING (SIDEBAR) MADE WITH LEMON JUICE

1. Prepare the bread dough and let it rise in the refrigerator as directed in the recipe on page 220. When you are ready to shape the bread, take the dough out of the refrigerator. **Tip:** You can bake the bread the day before you serve it, or a even week ahead, in which case freeze it, double-bagged. To make the day before, start the dough 24 hours before you want to serve the bread. Let the dough rise in the refrigerator all day, as directed in the dough recipe (this dough does not handle well unless it is cold).

2. Mix the filling ingredients in a heavy saucepan

Bread Glazes

Starch Glaze

This simple glaze is used in place of egg white to help toppings adhere to the tops of loaves or for a shiny crust.

1/2 CUP COLD WATER
1 TEASPOON CORNSTARCH OR ARROWROOT

Mix the water and starch together in a small saucepan. Stir constantly over high heat until thickened and clear. Refrigerate in a jar until using.

Sweet Bread Glaze

Brushed on hot baked breads, this makes a sweet, shiny glaze. Heat equal parts of nondairy milk and maple syrup together in a small saucepan over medium heat. Do not boil or it will curdle!

Simple Powdered Sugar Icing

1 CUP CONFECTIONERS' SUGAR
1 1/2 TABLESPOONS NONDAIRY MILK, WATER, JUICE, OR LIQUEUR

Sift the confectioners' sugar through a sieve, then stir in the liquid until smooth. Spread on the warm bread loaf.

and bring to a boil. Cook the mixture, stirring often, over medium-low heat for about 10 minutes. The liquid will be absorbed. Set aside to cool.

3. When you are ready to shape the bread, take the dough out of the refrigerator. For one giant loaf, roll all of the dough into a rectangle 28 x 14 inches on a sheet of baking parchment sprinkled with flour. Spread with the filling to within 1 inch of all the edges. Roll the rectangle lengthwise in jelly-roll fashion and pinch the edge of the dough to the body of the roll to seal. On a piece of baking parchment cut to fit your pan, form the roll into a spiral (the pinched side on the bottom), starting from the center and tucking the end neatly underneath the dough. Use a 14-inch pizza pan or a 12-inch round cake pan for this loaf. Spray the loaf with oil from a pump sprayer.

4. For two medium loaves, divide the dough exactly in half and keep second half covered with plastic wrap while you work with the first. Roll each half of the dough into a rectangle about 8 inches wide and 24 inches long. Spread each rectangle with 1/2 of the Filling to within 1 inch of all the edges. Roll each rectangle lengthwise jelly-roll fashion and pinch the edge of the dough to the body of the roll to seal. On pieces of baking parchment cut to fit your pans, form each roll into a spiral (the pinched sides on the bottom), starting from the center and tucking the end neatly underneath the dough. Use 14-inch pizza pans, 10 x 15-inch baking sheets or 10-inch layer cake pans for these loaves. Spray the loaves with oil from a pump sprayer.

5. Cover the loaves loosely with plastic wrap and clean kitchen towels and let rise in a warm place until puffy, about 1 to 1 1/2 hours. Preheat the oven to 350°F. Bake the giant spiral loaf for 45 minutes and the smaller loaves for 30 minutes, or until golden. Transfer the pan(s) to racks and cool the loaves thoroughly before slicing with a serrated knife. They can then be frozen, if you wish. Decorate with the icing before serving.

Index to Countries and Regions in *World Vegan Feast*

World Vegan Feast contains more than 200 recipes from over 50 countries, as well as numerous provinces, regions, republics, and cultures. Many of these recipes are naturally vegan and authentic to that country, while others are veganized versions. The following is a list of the countries and regions represented in the book with corresponding recipe page numbers.

Resources
Retail and Online Sources

North America – U.S.A.

These online outlets carry vegan foods and a wide range of other vegan items. Most of these companies will ship to Canada, though the shipping may be a bit high. If you order from Canada, make sure they ship it by U.S. Postal Service, not UPS or FedEx, which can add considerable shipping and customs costs. (Personal experience, here.)

Cosmo's Vegan Shoppe

200 North Cobb Parkway, Bldg 100 Ste. 126, Marietta, GA 30062
Website: www.cosmosveganshoppe.com
800-260-9968

Food Fight Grocery

1217 SE Stark Street, Portland, OR 97214
Website: www.foodfightgrocery.com
502-233-3910

Mail Order Catalog for Healthy Eating

Website: www.healthy-eating.com
800-695-2241

Pangea

2381 Lewis Ave., Rockville, MD 20851
Website: www.veganstore.com
800-340-1200

Vegan Essentials

Website: www.veganessentials.com/
1-866-88-VEGAN or 262-574-7761

North America – Canada

Viva Granola Vegan Store
4148 St-Laurent, Montreal, QC Canada
Website: http://vivagranolaveganstore.com
514-903-VGAN (8426)

Karmavore Vegan Shop
610 Columbia Street, New Westminster, BC, V3M 1A5 Canada

Website: http://www.karmavore.ca/shop_new.php
604-527-4212

Vegan Essentials
Website: http://www.veganessentials.com
(a U.S. store, but you can buy in Canadian dollars and shipping is reasonable)
1-866-88-VEGAN or 262-574-7761

Outside of North America

United Kingdom

http://www.veganstore.co.uk
http://www.veganvillage.co.uk/shops.htm
http://www.shopvegan.co.uk

Australia

http://crueltyfreeshop.com.au
http://www.veganperfection.com.au/index.php

For other countries

Search the International Vegetarian Union database for vegan shopping at: http://www.ivu.org.

To Find Particular Ingredients

Sources for Beans and Grains

Your local natural foods store is the first place to look for beans and grains. If you can't obtain a good selection locally, here are some online sources:

U.S.A.

http://www.bobsredmill.com
http://purcellmountainfarms.com (heirloom beans)
http://www.kalustyans.com
http://www.bulkfoods.com

http://www.ranchogordo.com (heirloom beans; ships to Canada)

http://www.amazon.com (ships to Canada)

Canada:

http://www.websterfarms.ca (heirloom beans)

http://gallowaysfoods.com

Pure Gluten Powder (Vital Wheat Gluten)

U.S.A.

Reliable sources of pure gluten powder (Vital Wheat Gluten) are: Bob's Red Mill and Arrowhead Mills. Online vendors include: amazon.com, pleasanthillgrain.com, canning-pantry.com, kingarthurflour.com, healthy-eating.com (they call it "instant gluten flour"), and bulkfoods.com.

Canada

http://vivagranola.com/ (They call it "gluten flour," but it's the right product.)

Textured Soy Protein

Bob's Red Mill: organic and/or solvent-free textured soy protein (they call it "TSP", the granulated version only: http://www.bob-sredmill.com

Frontier Co-op: has unflavored organic textured soy protein in 2 different sizes: 1/4-inch pieces (similar to granules) and 1/2-inch pieces (small chunk): http://www.frontiercoop.com

Le-Sanctuaire.com sells a food-grade vegan, kosher jel powder (Genutine®) that is less expensive than small packets of kosher gel. http://www.le-sanctuaire.com

The Mail-Order Catalog: carries a granulated version and a chunk version:
http://www.healthy-eating.com
Kosher Jel or Genutine®
Amazon.com sells Diet Kojel, Unflavored ("diet" just means no sugar)

Pangea carries Unflavored Vegan Jel by Natural Desserts. http://www.veganstore.com

Vegan Essentials sells Lieber's Unflavored Jel http://store.veganessentials.com

Vegan Cheese

Daiya (http://www.daiyafoods.com
Dr. Cow (http://www.dr-cow.com
Galaxy Vegan (http://www.galaxyfoods.com/Products/SoyCheese/Vegan/)
Sheese (http://www.buteisland.com/)
Vegan Gourmet (http://imearthkind.com/)

Fair Trade and Organic Foods

When at all possible, I recommend purchasing fair trade organic coffee, cocoa, chocolate, sugar, and bananas.

Why? Please know that I'm not trying to guilt-trip anyone. I know that it is not always possible to buy organic food in every category. Sometimes, if you are on a budget, it is just too expensive. Other times, it just isn't available, especially in locations with few choices. We can all hope, however, that as organic foods increasingly enter the "mainstream," prices will become more affordable and availability will be addressed, but that's going to take political will and community action.

Firstly, I believe that it is particularly important to try as best we can to use organic fair trade brands of the products mentioned because of the fact that they are luxuries. By that, I mean that we can live without them. We wouldn't like to, but we can. Secondly, because it is not only our own health that is at stake, but also the health and well-being of those who toil to produce this food for us. The above mentioned products, in particular, are problematic in that they are often produced by underpaid workers (even children) who work extremely hard in unsafe and unfair conditions, frequently exposed to toxic pesticides and fungicides.

Find out more by reading the Fair Trade Q & A at http://www.globalexchange.org.

For Further Reading on Umami

I encourage you to learn more about umami as possible, as knowing its secrets can turn your cooking from average to great! I used these resources to write the section on umami in this book, but there are plenty more if you look.

"Mushrooms, the Umami Experience," (http://www.mushroomcouncil.org/Food-service_Sales_Tools/umami/index.html)
"My heart belongs to umami," by Heston Blumenthal *(The Guardian,* July 13, 2002. http://www.guardian.co.uk/lifeand-style/2002/jul/13/fish.foodanddrink)
"Umami or savoriness is difficult to explain but easy to enjoy," by Hsiao-Ching Chou *(Seattle Post-Intelligencer,* July 26, 2000)
"Umami: Taste Receptor, Tactile Sensation and Flavor Intensifier" by Matthew Citriglia (http://www.winegeeks.com/articles/115)

Emsley, John and Peter Fell. *Was it Something You Ate?* New York, NY: Oxford University Press, 2002.)
Kasabian, David and Anna Kasabian. *The Fifth Taste: Cooking with Umami.* New York, NY: Rizzoli, 2005.

Recipe Nutritional Data

For those who are interested in the nutritional analysis data for the recipes in *World Vegan Feast,* it can be found on my blog listed in chapter order at this link: http://veganfeastkitchen.blogspot.com/p/world-vegan-feast-recipe-nutritional.html (or look for the tab "World Vegan Feast Recipe Nutritional Analyses.")

U.S. to Metric Weight Conversion

If you cannot find the number you want, multiply your ounces by 28.35 to get the weight in grams, or multiply your grams by 0.0353 to get the weight in ounces.

1 ounce = 28.35g	8.8 ounces = 250g
1.8 ounces = 50g	9 ounces = 255g
2 ounces = 57g	10 ounces = 284g
3 ounces = 85g	10.6 ounces = 300g
3.53 ounces =100g	11 ounces = 312g
4 ounces = 113g	12 ounces = 340g
5 ounces = 142g	12.4 ounces = 350g
5.3 ounces = 150g	14.2 ounces = 400g
6 ounces = 170g	15.9 ounces = 450g
7 ounces = 198g	16 ounces = 454g
7.1 ounces = 200g	17.7 ounces = 500g
8 ounces = 227g	

Flour Terms and Equivalents

Terms:

U.S./Canadian term = U.K. English term
Cake and pastry flour = soft flour
All-purpose flour = plain flour
Bread flour = strong flour, hard flour
Self-rising flour = self-raising flour
Whole-wheat flour = wholemeal flour

Weight Equivalents:

U.S. to Metric

1 ounce flour = 3 tablespoons (30g)
1/4 cup all-purpose or plain flour, unsifted = 4 tablespoons = 1 1/4 ounces (35g)
1 cup all-purpose or plain flour, unsifted = 5 ounces (140g)
1 1/2 cups all-purpose or plain flour flour, unsifted = 8 ounces (225g)
2 1/4 cups all-purpose or plain flour flour, unsifted = 12 ounces (350g)
1 cup cake or pastry flour, sifted = 4 ounces (115g)
1 pound all-purpose or plain flour = 3 1/2 cups unsifted = 4 cups sifted (450g)
1 pound cake or pastry flour = 4 1/2 cups (450g)
1 pound whole-wheat flour = 3 1/2 cups (450g)

Metric to U.S.:

25g flour = 3 scant tablespoons
100g all-purpose or plain flour, unsifted = 3 1/2 ounces = 2/3 cup flour
275g all-purpose or plain flour, unsifted = 10 ounces = 2 cups
500g all-purpose or plain flour, unsifted = 17 1/2 ounces = 3 1/3 cup flour

Index

Vegan Heritage Press
Paperback, 232 pages,
ISBN: 978-0-9800131-1-5
$18.95, 7½" x 9"

American Vegan Kitchen

Delicious Comfort Food from Blue Plate Specials to Homestyle Favorites

Tamasin Noyes

Do you ever crave the delicious comfort foods served at your local diner, deli, or neighborhood cafe? This cookbook shows you how to make vegan versions of your favorite dishes in your own home kitchen.

These 200+ recipes will satisfy vegans and non-vegans alike with deli sandwiches, burgers and fries, mac and cheese, pasta, pizza, omelets, pancakes, soups and salads, casseroles, and desserts. Enjoy truly great American flavors from tempting ethnic dishes to the homestyle comfort foods of the heartland.

From coast-to-coast and cover-to-cover, *American Vegan Kitchen* helps you serve up great homestyle vegan recipes for breakfast, lunch, dinner, and desserts. The book contains eight pages of full-color photos and helpful icons to bring American comfort food home to your table.

See Tami's blog at: www.veganappetite.com.

Vegan Heritage Press
Paperback, 216 pages,
ISBN: 978-0-9800131-2-2
$14.95, 7½" x 7½"

Vegan Unplugged

A Pantry Cuisine Cookbook and Survival Guide

Jon Robertson with recipes by Robin Robertson

Vegan Unplugged is your go-to source for gourmet pantry cooking in a variety of worst-case scenarios. Make tasty meals whenever the power goes out from storms, hurricanes, and blackouts. These recipes are quick and easy, and can be made in fifteen minutes or less. This makes the book ideal for camping, boating, or anytime you just don't feel like cooking.

Vegan Unplugged provides easy, practical tips on how to shop for, store, and quickly prepare nonperishable pantry foods. Make great dishes such as Almost-Instant Black Bean Chili, Pantry Pasta Salad, Fire-Roasted Blueberry Cobbler, and more. This book is a "must have" for anyone who wants to be ready for anything with great-tasting, nutritious pantry cuisine.

See Jon's blog: http://veganunplugged.blogspot.com.

About the Author

The author of eight vegan cookbooks, **Bryanna Clark Grogan** has devoted over forty years to tasty, healthful cooking. She has been a contributor and reviewer for *Vegetarian Times* and has conducted cooking workshops and classes at numerous vegetarian gatherings in North America, including the NAVS Summerfest; EarthSave's Taste of Health in Vancouver, B.C.; the Seattle, Washington and Portland, Oregon VegFests; the International Scientific Conference on Chinese Plant-Based Nutrition and Cuisine in Philadelphia; and the McDougall Celebrity Chef Weekend in Santa Rosa, CA. Bryanna's recipes appear in *No More Bull!* by Howard Lyman, the *The Veg-Feasting Cookbook, Cooking with PETA*, and on Dr. Andrew Weil's websites. Bryanna also developed the recipes for the groundbreaking book, *Dr. Neal Barnard's Program for Reversing Diabetes.* Bryanna's blog can be found at **http://veganfeastkitchen.blogspot. com**. A vegan for more than twenty years, Bryanna lives, cooks, and writes on beautiful Denman Island, British Columbia.